A Nation Unraveled

CIVIL WAR AMERICA

Caroline E. Janney and Aaron Sheehan-Dean, *editors*

This landmark series interprets broadly the history and culture of the Civil War era through the long nineteenth century and beyond. Drawing on diverse approaches and methods, the series publishes historical works that explore all aspects of the war, biographies of leading commanders, and tactical and campaign studies, along with select editions of primary sources. Together, these books shed new light on an era that remains central to our understanding of American and world history.

A complete list of books published in Civil War America is available at https://uncpress.org/series/civil-war-america.

SARAH JONES WEICKSEL

A Nation Unraveled

Clothing, Culture, and Violence in the American Civil War Era

The University of North Carolina Press *Chapel Hill*

Set in Arno Pro by Westchester Publishing Services
Manufactured in the United States of America

Library of Congress Cataloging-in-Publication Data
Names: Weicksel, Sarah Jones, author.
Title: A nation unraveled : clothing, culture, and violence in the American Civil War era / Sarah Jones Weicksel.
Other titles: Clothing, culture, and violence in the American Civil War era | Civil War America (Series)
Description: Chapel Hill : The University of North Carolina Press, [2026] | Series: Civil War America | Includes bibliographical references and index.
Identifiers: LCCN 2025022650 | ISBN 9781469689135 (cloth ; alk. paper) | ISBN 9781469689142 (pbk. alk. paper) | ISBN 9781469689159 (epub) | ISBN 9781469689166 (pdf)
Subjects: LCSH: Clothing and dress—Political aspects—United States—History—19th century. | Clothing and dress—Social aspects. | Clothing and dress—Economic aspects. | Women and war—United States—History—19th century. | Clothing trade—United States—History—19th century. | Military uniforms—Social aspects—United States—History—19th century. | United States—History—Civil War, 1861–1865—Social aspects. | BISAC: HISTORY / United States / Civil War Period (1850–1877) | SOCIAL SCIENCE / Ethnic Studies / American / General
Classification: LCC GT610 .W48 2026 | DDC 973.7/1—dc23/eng/20250615
LC record available at https://lccn.loc.gov/2025022650

Cover art: Sample of plantation-made cloth, c. 1861–65.
Photograph courtesy of the American Civil War Museum, Richmond, VA.

For product safety concerns under the European Union's General Product Safety Regulation (EU GPSR), please contact gpsr@mare-nostrum.co.uk or write to the University of North Carolina Press and Mare Nostrum Group B.V., Mauritskade 21D, 1091 GC Amsterdam, The Netherlands.

For

Ava & Keith

In Memory of

Al & Tillie

Contents

Illustrations

Acknowledgments

In the course of researching and writing this book, I relied upon the generosity of many colleagues, friends, and institutions, making it an impossible task to thank all of those who have played a role in this project. I shall try, nevertheless.

This book contains many people's stories—stories that are told through objects, images, and texts that are held in museums, archives, libraries, and other collections across several states. I am grateful to the staff of each of these institutions, who thoughtfully guided me in navigating their collections. I would particularly like to thank the staff at the American Antiquarian Society; the American Civil War Museum, especially Robert Hancock; the William Clements Library; the Historical Society of Pennsylvania; the Library Company of Philadelphia; the National Archives and Records Administration; the Newberry Library; the Smithsonian Institution; and the Virginia Museum of History and Culture.

Funding support from an Andrew W. Mellon Postdoctoral Fellowship at the University of Pennsylvania's Wolf Humanities Center was critical to this book's preparation. So, too, was the generous support of several research fellowships. A Committee on Institutional Cooperation–Smithsonian Institution Fellowship provided a year of research and writing at the National Museum of American History and the National Museum of African American History and Culture. Residential fellowships at the American Antiquarian Society, the Library Company of Philadelphia, the Historical Society of Pennsylvania, and the William Clements Library at the University of Michigan, Ann Arbor, allowed for extensive use of their collections. My year as a graduate scholar-in-residence at the Newberry Library provided me with a collegial space to research and write.

At various stages of this project, colleagues and fellow conference panelists have read portions of this and related work. Special thanks are due to Joshua Brown, Dana Byrd, Peter S. Carmichael, Joan Cashin, Christopher Dingwall, Laura F. Edwards, Judith Giesberg, Daniel Greene, Earl Hess, Kathleen Hilliard, Sara Hume, Katherine Lennard, Brian Luskey, John McCormack, Stephanie McCurry, Jennifer Mittelstadt, Megan Kate Nelson, Dael Norwood, Emily Remus, Seth Rockman, Martha Sandweiss, Kathryn Schumaker, Susan

Gaunt Stearns, Jenny Tone-Pah-Hote, Katherine Turk, Mark Wilson, and Tara Zahra. Thanks are also due to the members of the Wolf Humanities Center's 2018–19 Forum on "Stuff" and the US History, Material Culture, and Gender and Sexuality Studies Workshops at the University of Chicago.

My colleagues at the National Museum of American History engaged me in long conversations about objects. I would especially like to thank Ellen Feingold, Amanda Moniz, Nancy Bercaw, Nancy Davis, Mary Elliott, Jennifer Gloede, Jon Grinspan, Bart Hacker, Katherine Ott, Fath Davis Ruffins, Madelyn Shaw, and Margaret Vining.

This book could have no better home than with the University of North Carolina Press. I am deeply grateful to Mark Simpson-Vos for his guidance throughout the process, beginning with our very early conversations that helped me determine my narrative path forward. As series co-editor, Aaron Sheehan-Dean provided deep reading, probing clarifications, and support for my object-based approach to the Civil War. I thank Zara Anishanslin and Jason Phillips for their careful peer review. Their insights and questions, have made this a better book. My thanks also to the wonderful staff of UNC Press for sharing their expertise that enabled this book to become a physical object, especially Thomas Bedenbaugh and Tara Jordan. To all, I am grateful for their willingness to work with so many images, which serve as visual footnotes in support of this book's argument.

History and material culture have been at the center of my intellectual life since I was an undergraduate at Yale University. Edward S. Cooke Jr. is due special thanks for his many years of continued mentorship and enthusiasm for the work I have pursued. John Mack Faragher, David Blight, Caitlin Crowell, John Demos, and Rebecca Tannenbaum were instrumental in my development as a historian and encouraged me to chart my own path to study history with material culture.

I continued to develop my approach to working with objects in the Winterthur Program in American Material Culture at the University of Delaware. There, I was fortunate to have the guidance of scholars of material culture who introduced me to the many ways of walking around an object, especially Wendy Bellion, Linda Eaton, Ritchie Garrison, and Brock Jobe. Katherine C. Grier helped me learn how to be a historian who works with material culture—I hope she can see her marks within. I am indebted, too, to the teachers and mentors with whom I had the privilege to work at the University of Chicago, including Mark Bradley, Matthew Briones, Bill Brown, Jane Dailey, Shannon Lee Dawdy, Adam Green, Thomas C. Holt, Amy Lippert, Julie Saville, Eric Slauter, James Sparrow, and Amy Dru Stanley.

I owe a large debt of gratitude to historians who engaged this book from its origins. Thavolia Glymph helped me to think through complex problems, to seek creative solutions to research questions, and to tell people's stories as they lived them. Jim Grossman asked me probing questions that helped me to refine my arguments and approach. Christine Stansell pushed me to remain true to my method and pursue difficult questions.

I am especially grateful for the many years spent closely working with Kathleen Neils Conzen and Leora Auslander. I have spent countless hours with Kathy in wide-ranging conversations, from our respective family histories to teaching methods to current research projects. Those conversations not only taught me how to ask good historical questions but were also instrumental in shaping my approach to both researching and teaching history. I am a better historian because of her support and persistent questioning.

Leora Auslander played a pivotal role in refining my approach to studying history through things. Over the years, she has helped me work through many snags and difficult writing, offered opportunities to collaborate, and buoyed my spirits. She has unconditionally supported me through every turn of my education and career. No amount of thanks does justice to her influence on me as a scholar, as a teacher, and as a person.

My colleagues at the American Historical Association have provided me with my current intellectual home. Jim Grossman pressed me to "get the book done" and encouraged me throughout the process. It is actually finally done because of the support of the entire townhouse, and especially Dana Schaffer, Brendan Gillis, Alexandra Levy, and the always-encouraging, ever-reliable research and publications team with whom it has been my great privilege to work: Laura Ansley, Lauren Brand, Lizzy Meggyesy, Sarah Muncy, and Alana Venable.

Over the years, friends have given me encouragement in many forms, from places to stay on research trips, to welcome breaks and conversations. Elisa Jones, Emily Romeo, and I supported one another through graduate school and beyond. Amanda Moniz and I have curated together and continue to engage one another in our research and writing pursuits. Katie Knowles has pieced together the history of many a puzzling garment with me. Jennifer Lynn Barnes helped me strategize, while Neha Mahajan Hertzog has been my confidante and planned out our families' joint vacations. Alexandra Levy and Laura Ansley have been constant friends—and have endured hearing far too many an object story. Devon Allen has been a steadfast companion in navigating the ins and outs of working-parent life. Ellen Feingold has been both an intellectual collaborator and an unwavering source of support in all aspects of life. Meghan Titzer and I first met in the dorm room randomly assigned to us as college freshmen. Since then, she has been my constant friend, travel companion, and my daughter's Aunt Meg.

Chris and Joe Weicksel have treated me as their daughter since I entered their lives. Chris has been my sounding board and a never-ending source of encouragement. Joe has not only read every page of every article I've written but also immersed himself in Civil War historiography, marking references to clothes along the way. My aunt, Jeanne, has indulged me as a historian on our tours through many cities and beyond.

My parents fostered my love of history as we traveled to historic sites and national parks in my home state. I was the first of our family to leave farming since the 1890s and they worked tirelessly to make it possible for me to go to college. They have accompanied me into many an antique shop and listened to many a history story. Most importantly, they have supported me with their love from 3,000 miles away.

My maternal grandparents, Al and Tillie, have long since passed away. I wish they could have seen this book, but their years of unconditional love, pride, and support have been more than enough to last my lifetime. This book is in memory of them.

Keith has been my partner in life for nearly twenty years. I have relied upon him for his patience, love, wry sense of humor, and the encouragement to take the time to finish writing on Chincoteague Island. Our daughter, Ava, has become my museum sidekick, my fellow investigator of what she calls "mysteries of the olden times," and the most joyful part of my life. Ava and Keith have listened to war stories of many kinds over the years. This one is for them.

A Nation Unraveled

Introduction

On a morning in June 1865, Susan Bradford and her sister, two well-to-do white women, drove their carriage into Tallahassee, Florida. It was three months after Robert E. Lee's surrender at Appomattox Court House and the fall of Richmond; the final fighting of the American Civil War was over, and Confederate soldiers were slowly coming home. Bradford recalled her shock as she encountered some of the men walking down the street: a sight that made her "blood boil." First there was a young man in a gray Confederate coat—but "every button had been cut from his uniform and replaced by large orange thorns skewered through the button holes to keep the coat closed." Then she saw her cousin—one who had received a "splendid new uniform" just months before. Its appearance was now marred by thin black crepe fabric sewn over the gold stars on his collar and the chevrons on his sleeves. The gilt brass buttons, too, "were wearing mourning," covered in the same black fabric. The sight, Bradford recounted, brought her "perilously close to tears."[1]

These buttons and braids, collars and sleeves, had not been draped willingly to mourn the loss of the Confederacy. Bradford's cousin and his fellow soldiers had taken off or obscured their uniforms' insignia to comply with a federal order conditioning their return home. With war at an end, the defeated were no longer to wear material signs of their role in the fight.

Bradford angrily surveyed the changes, further outraged by the sight of a lieutenant whose gold lace had been ripped from his sleeves and his collar. Requiring men to remove their insignia was the equivalent of "striking a man when he was down," Bradford declared, and she found the order "despicable in my mind." She also conveyed the limit of that order's effect, as the coat's wool fabric defied the mandate. "Where the braid had been removed," Bradford observed, "the unfaded gray shows his rank as plainly as ever." Though Bradford's blood boiled at the defacement of the uniform's symbolism, she took a hint of pleasure in the wool's subtle declaration of Southern protest.[2]

Bradford's diary reveals how she grappled with Confederate defeat on an ideological and political level, but the loss also had implications for her material experience of the everyday world. The war's personal, intimate impact was evident in her visceral reactions to that material world. And she was certainly not alone. At the heart of Civil War Americans' experiences of the conflict were the daily objects they saw and touched. The meaning of the Civil War was present even in the clothing that people wore upon their backs. For Bradford, her cousin, and countless others, clothing was its own battlefront.

A Nation Unraveled is a history of clothing as a ground on which the Civil War was fought and as a tool for living through the conflict. It offers a new way to tackle questions of how Americans learned to wage a civil war in a democratic nation and how they confronted anxieties produced during—and by—that war. Indeed, the Civil War occurred at a particular moment of confluence in the histories of politics, gender, selfhood, and clothing manufacture and use. In this moment, Union and Confederate identities were created not only in Washington or Richmond, but also at the ground level. Maintaining identities fell not only to politicians, generals, and prominent writers but also to a public tasked with maintaining support—both material and ideological—for brutal, deadly fighting. In the mid-nineteenth century, women, who would play a critical role in supporting the war, were finding an increasingly prominent political voice and presence in public life. At the same time, questions about meanings of selfhood and the individual's place in society were circulating in American thought. Clothing proved central to all these dynamics.

In 1860, most Americans owned very little clothing, but its provision and maintenance frequently occupied their thoughts and their time. Clothing production was on the verge of industrialization, and its expressive and transformative qualities were becoming increasingly apparent as the availability of fabrics and garments expanded to ever-wider segments of American society. But for most Americans, North and South, the everyday experience of making and mending clothing remained entirely familiar. In its ubiquity, it was profoundly layered with meaning.

Clothing, then, was one of the answers to how Americans waged war against one another across a range of practical, political, emotional, economic, and cultural battlefronts. It had both "offensive" and "defensive" dimensions; it was a way to create positive associations, but also a means through which people experienced war's costs. From the outset, clothing provided a means—if not always successful—to assuage the anxieties created by this war. How could patriotic fervor be instilled in a populace that needed to rally to fight a war that many did not understand or fully support? How could social hierarchies be maintained as slavery stood at the precipice of collapse? How would formerly enslaved people be incorporated into a free society? How might a woman survive changes in her family's economic support? Clothing grounded these abstract questions and ideas in the material world.

In the pages that follow, we will see how Civil War Americans employed clothing and the practices of dress to shore up and resist political identities, to give material form to competing conceptions of freedom, to challenge and reinforce gender roles, and to confront the government's role in civil society in the process. In turn, clothing was a central means by which people experienced how war was waged against them—something they felt intimately, that penetrated their identities, and that had far-reaching consequences for their outlook on the postwar era. By restoring the material world's pervasive role in how people engaged in this war, *A Nation Unraveled* provides a deeper way of seeing war.

Clothing bore such significance because nineteenth-century Americans did not simply regard choices of attire as a reflection of a person's identity.[3] They also believed that clothing could transform—that it could shape an individual's morality, civility, gender, and piety, among other characteristics. Clothing could literally make the man or woman. That transformative power inhered both in the physical garments themselves and in how people treated others according to the signals sent by their wearing—signals regarding social status, personal dignity, work habits, and more. This belief in clothing as transformative was tied to a larger understanding of the material world's ability to create order (and disorder) in society through the manipulation of both people's bodies and how they lived out their daily lives. From the planning of cities and the design of penitentiaries to the provision of aid to indigent people and the "Americanization" of Native peoples and their cultures, those who lived in this era saw material worlds as having a powerful influence on life's experience. Nineteenth-century Americans' testimonies make clear they understood clothing to exert such an influence.[4]

Civil War historians, however, have only recently begun to explore the influences of material culture on Americans' experiences during the era. Some have taken up the influence of the natural environment in the conduct and outcome of the war. Others have considered the competition over scarce resources—food, fodder, ammunition—or the meaning invested in wartime relics.[5] *A Nation Unraveled* is part of this recent "material turn" in Civil War historiography, but it differs in that it is an object-based project—one whose research is grounded in the physical things themselves. In broad strokes, the stories that follow allow us to understand the depth of how war penetrated daily life by focusing on the intimate, visceral, material experiences that shaped how people moved through the world. I do not propose to argue that clothing altered the Civil War's battles or its outcomes. Clothing did, however, affect people's ways of living out—and with—this war and its aftermath.

The Civil War was, in many ways, about fabric: about the right to enslave humans to produce cotton that would ultimately be carded, spun, and woven into textiles. One of the first commodities to be industrialized, cotton, and the lucrative nature of its production, dashed antislavery advocates' earlier hopes that slavery would eventually die out. The expansion of slavery and of states' rights to control the institution lay at the core of the political and social divisions that led to secession and war. These divisions unraveled the nation, not only throwing into question the future of the United States, but also posing a crisis in cultivating identities and national loyalties. In the end, the Union prevailed, and the postwar nation was faced with the hard task of not only reuniting the states, but also incorporating a new group of free people into the nation.

Cultivating shared identities grounded in patriotism was particularly critical in a civil war—a conflict between people with shared language, backgrounds, cultures, and government; a conflict in which families and friends abruptly found themselves on opposing sides. In this context, the cultivation and maintenance of strong social and cultural identities were key elements in waging war. Yet, in 1860, as political tensions were rising to a fever pitch, neither the federal United States government nor the soon-to-be-minted Confederate States of America (CSA) possessed strong central governing capabilities. In the absence of the robust state machines that played key roles in later wars, the hard task of fighting this war and establishing and maintaining the shared identities necessary for victory largely fell upon the populace. On both sides, clothing was a key instrument by which civilians, soldiers, and the government could wage war—not only as a critical element of wartime supply, but also as a means of fostering loyalties, shaping identities, and making people into citizens. Clothing, at times, proved better at initially arousing than fully maintaining patriotic fervor; better at cultivating resentment than loyalty; more effective at communicating resistance and division than solidarity; and more effective at giving the appearance of racial integration than establishing acceptance.

The Civil War was not the first war to require the mobilization of resources to clothe and supply soldiers, nor the first in which making and wearing cockades or homespun cloth were political statements. In prior American wars, people wore specific clothing and symbols on their bodies to identify their allegiances, and military uniforms identifying opposing armies were standard on the battlefield.[6] Punishment for military transgressions involving the stripping of a uniform spanned the American Revolution and the Civil War. The theft of possessions from homes and the stripping of clothes from the battlefield dead, too, are historically common to war. Civil War Americans commented frequently upon the resonance between sartorial practices in the American Revolution and the war in which they themselves were fighting and living through. Clothing, in other words, had long been important to wartime conduct and experience.

But the Civil War was also different. From its outset, the future of the ability to own and regard human beings as possessions—as "things" that could be bought and sold—was hanging in the balance. Emancipation and the dismantling of the institution of American slavery transformed human property from things into people. In a war in which not only definitions of property, but also individual and collective identity, were at stake, those things most closely associated with people's identity—the clothes they wore on their bodies—were imbued with great power to shape the world.

Rethinking the intimate, material experiences of war requires breaking down the artificial boundaries scholars have constructed between North and South.[7] To do so, *A Nation Unraveled* moves back and forth between Northern and Southern experiences, though largely on Southern ground. This is not to suggest an equivalency but, rather, to highlight commonalities of certain experiences and to explore in all of its complexity just what clothing meant for this war. This is not to imply that sectional distinctions did not matter. To the contrary, those distinctions mattered a great deal, particularly in regard to enslaved labor in the South. Yet it is by examining both North and South within the same framework that we gain greater clarity on why clothing could be such a powerful tool by which to wage war and to experience it.

Understanding the power of clothing also requires breaking down the boundaries between battlefront and home front that have often characterized histories of the war. Clothing often quite literally crossed those boundaries. Moreover, changes on the battlefield spurred changes on the home front, and what was occurring on the home front had important implications for soldiers in the field; together, they shaped the cultural and material circumstances and consequences of war.[8]

By war's end, the federal government loomed larger in people's everyday lives than this generation of Americans had ever experienced. But it was not inevitable that a federal government with more expansive powers would emerge from this conflict, nor was the shape or reach of that government predetermined. Rather than focus solely on actions and responses to the United States government in an effort to understand the consolidation of federal power, a focus on clothing helps twist the kaleidoscope to bring into view people's engagement with the military and the Confederate and state governments.[9] Mobilization for war, accompanied by the sudden need to clothe—and keep clothed—tens of thousands of men, prompted the individual state, federal, and Confederate governments to adopt new policies, enforce new taxes, collaborate (although not always effectively) with volunteer organizations, manage uniform production and distribution, and negotiate the provision of garments as a form of public welfare, among other actions. During and immediately following the Civil War, then, people living throughout the United States experienced on an unprecedented scale the government's intervention in their everyday dress practices.

Such everyday dress practices had long been a means of distinguishing social hierarchies and demarcating gender.[10] Prior to the Civil War, that social order shakily rested on fault lines of class, gender, race, and region. The enslavement of nearly 4 million people whose labor made up the backbone of the Southern economy meant that the bulk of Southern social and political power rested with elite enslavers and those whose fortunes were made possible by the slave system, a system that denied enslaved people even the basic human right to be in possession of one's own body. Small planters, yeoman farmers, free Blacks, and poor whites, too, navigated this economic, political, social, and cultural world defined by race-based slavery. Much of Northern society felt at a physical and social remove from slavery, but many Northern fortunes and laborers, too, had ties to slavery, from manufacturing companies to shipping businesses. Indeed, one Massachusetts minister described slavery as a serpent whose hiss was "audible in the whirl of every spindle, and the vibration of every loom, in the muttering of every waterwheel, and in the whistle of every engine."[11] Elite Northern families retained social and political power over the middling classes, whose numbers were increasing and to which many working-class men and women, immigrant and native born, aspired.

Gender roles in nineteenth-century America were never starkly defined, though white ideals predominated, and men were more closely associated with public spaces and women with the domestic realm. Elite and middle-class women were always pushing at the boundaries of white gender norms, whether by seeking employment, volunteering with benevolent organizations, or involving themselves in reform efforts like abolitionism. Nor was there a single understanding of manhood but, rather, different ideas and models of manly behavior from which men pieced together the component parts of their own sense and enactment of manhood.[12] How men and women lived out their lives was influenced by racial and class distinctions. "Poor, working-class, and enslaved women," Thavolia Glymph explains, "could see more clearly where American life had provided room for some women to maneuver and enjoy rights and privileges denied to them, and the payoff." No matter their class, women could not claim the same rights or freedoms as their brothers, husbands, sons, or fathers.[13]

These Americans were all part of an Atlantic economy of fabric and fashion, clothing themselves in both imported luxury and American-made textiles and ready-made goods.[14] In 1861, while clothing itself was not fully mass produced, its making and care were part of a vibrant consumer culture of accessories, dry goods stores, and a wide range of remedies and time savers, all of which were situated on the precipice of ready-made. War hastened the standardization of clothing production. Transformations in the circulation of information and the ability to reproduce images using lithographic and photographic technology also meant that Americans were increasingly aware of *la mode*—much of which emanated from France and Britain.[15] Finished dress goods, including fabric and trimmings, were available for purchase in dry goods, fancy goods, and, by the late 1850s, emerging department stores in Eastern cities. These goods were also increasingly made available in smaller communities and in Western states and territories by way of an expanding transportation network of roads and railroads.[16] The primary mode of foreign style transmission, however, was the reprinting of foreign fashion plates in American periodicals like *Godey's Lady's Book*.[17] American women did not, however, generally adopt wholesale the elaborate styles depicted in these illustrations. Most white middle-class Americans wore simplified versions of the European styles they read about in ladies' magazines—skirts were often narrower, trimmings less elaborate, and the fabric not quite as fine as that recommended by fashion editors. American women's clothing styles of the late 1850s included wide skirts, flowing sleeves, and the extensive use of trimmings, while men's clothing was becoming increasingly standardized in the form of the plain, somber three-piece suit composed of a coat, vest, and trousers.[18] Of course, not all Americans favored women's fashions of the 1850s and 1860s. The wide crinoline, more commonly known as a hoop skirt, of this period prompted the scrutiny of dress reformers who sought to simplify women's costume, whether as a statement of women's rights or in conjunction with health reforms.[19]

Photography played an increasingly important role in circulating fashions between various locales, constructing individual identity, and conveying a sense of one's style through dress. This was especially true after 1854, with the production of affordable cartes de visite, small albumen prints mounted on thick cards. Measuring 2⅛ by 3½ inches and mounted on 2½ by 4 inch cards, these photographs were easily exchanged, or slipped into the folds of a letter and mailed to friends and family.[20] As Oliver Wendell Holmes noted in 1862, "Card portraits as everybody knows have become the social currency, the green-backs of civilization."[21] But people did not simply allow these photographs to speak for themselves—they often narrated the experience of having their picture made and critiqued the clothing they had chosen to wear.

The democratization of dress had significant symbolic power in relation to the Revolutionary legacy of homespun and Americans' elevation of simplicity to a national value. Defined in opposition to European ostentation, the "simple dress of an American citizen" became a political slogan in the 1850s.[22] As Michael Zakim has argued, the mass-produced male suit "emerged as the badge of a uniquely virtuous American polity, the only place in the civilized world where citizens could not be classed by their appearance, as contemporaries never tired of insisting."[23] Although this was overstated, for American dress did indeed convey social and economic status (consider, for instance, the enslaved South), clothing was frequently cited as a visual marker of the more democratic nature of American society. European immigrants, whose reference point was a more hierarchically structured fashion system, frequently remarked upon this distinction.

In addition to changes in fashion, nineteenth-century Americans, like others in the Western world, experienced widespread innovations in the processing of raw materials and the production of clothing that made those fashions possible, ranging from the adoption of the cotton gin to carding machines and the sewing machine. While the cotton gin separated cotton fibers from the seeds, carding machines mechanically disentangled cotton or woolen fibers, smoothing them for the spinning process. In both cases, machines were rapidly replacing the laborious process of removing seeds by hand, or disentangling fibers with handheld combs or "cards." Although weaving spun yarn into cloth continued, on a small scale, to be done by hand, mechanized looms were also in operation throughout the United States.[24]

Research and experimentation with various chemical compounds, metallic and nonmetallic substances, vegetables, and insects expanded the range of dyes, mordants (which helped set dye), and processes for dyeing and finishing cloth.[25] These innovations, combined with changes in labor organization and greater access to cotton, gave rise to a ready-to-wear clothing industry. But this industry did not expand so rapidly that it fully displaced earlier modes of production.[26] Many Americans wore clothing that was sewn exclusively at home. However, those who had more money to spend often pieced together wardrobes with home-sewn garments, clothing sewn by tailors and expert seamstresses (who were often called upon to fit and sew the most difficult pieces of a garment), and ready-made items purchased from retail stores. Tailors, dressmakers, seamstresses, and milliners, who made and sold hats, remained important community figures. In the South, enslaved women and men played critical roles in both the production of cloth and clothes; many were skilled seamstresses and tailors, while others were mantua makers who created elaborate gowns for the elite.[27]

Sewing was performed through a combination of hand and machine work. While the sewing machine appeared for consumer purchase in the late 1840s, the machine's capabilities were limited. As a result, sewing machines were primarily used for sewing straight seams, such as those on the inseam of a pair of pants; areas with curvatures (neckbands and cuffs, for instance), decorative stitching, and areas requiring sewing within a confined area (such as buttonholes) all continued to be handsewn. Sewing machines were more widely available in the North, but many Southerners purchased them as well.[28]

Clothing was not the disposable, ephemeral item that it is today. As Laura F. Edwards shows, clothes and textiles more generally were not merely consumer goods but "economic instruments, backed by law." Textiles and clothing had social and economic value and legal principles associated with them.[29] With the exception of the upper echelons of American society, most people owned no more than a few changes of clothing for each season.[30] Even with decreases in prices, clothes remained, by and large, expensive. These were material objects in which people stored value. A winter coat, for example, could be pawned for ready cash in the summer and redeemed before temperatures began to drop in the autumn. Dresses, pants, shirts, and other garments could also be sold and purchased on a secondhand clothing market, where one person's worn-out calico could become another's best dress.[31] Furthermore, bankruptcy laws allowed for clothing beyond a certain value to be counted among the assets to be sold and converted into cash to pay a bankrupt person's debts.[32]

Caring for clothing was a major component of household work, in terms of laundering, starching, and ironing, which were together a weekly, daylong chore.[33] In the mid-nineteenth century, clothing was infrequently laundered. While undergarments might be washed after several uses, clothing made from fabrics difficult to launder might be washed only when it became visibly soiled. To thoroughly clean a silk dress, it needed to "be entirely taken to pieces," with the skirt and sleeves detached from the bodice. Even then, some housekeeping manuals advised, "unless the silk is of very good quality, it will not be worth while to take the trouble of cleaning it."[34] As cotton fabric began to replace linen and wool in popularity, the frequency of laundering increased, because cotton could be washed with greater ease and less fear of irreparably damaging the fabric.[35] Enslaved Black women performed the arduous tasks of laundering and ironing their enslavers' clothing as well as their own.[36] In the North, paid servants performed these tasks in elite households. In Northern and Southern cities, women took in other people's washing as a source of income. Throughout the nation, many women of the middling and lower classes performed this work for their households.

Clothing repair, too, was tasked to enslaved women or hired seamstresses or tailors, or it was performed within the household. Ripped hems, a hole in a bodice, or a dull appearance were not necessarily reasons to cast off a piece of clothing—garments were often mended and dyed several times before being discarded. Ladies' magazines and sewing manuals advised women on repurposing faded or damaged clothing, whether by adding trimming to cover holes, "reviving" the fabric's color with solutions, or disassembling adult garments to refashion them into children's clothing. Clothing that might no longer be worn could be cut up into quilting blocks and at times used for batting to pad a quilt. Even when soiled, torn, and beyond repair, clothing retained at least a modicum of value such that it was worthwhile for "ragpickers" to gather and sell discarded garments to paper manufacturers or businesses devoted to finding, sorting, buying, and selling rags and other old materials.[37]

Clothing, and objects more generally, do not simply reflect something about a culture but, rather, play an active role in the creation of meaning and orient people to, and enable them to act in, the social, political, and physical worlds they inhabit.[38] People value their belongings for their ability to constitute their personal identities and for their emotional value.[39] Clothing can function both as a mode of social and cultural communication and as a mediator between the human body and the environment. It communicates status, gender, nationality, aesthetics, occupation, sense of propriety, attitude, trends in thought, and a person's knowledge of fashion, among other meanings.[40] Because of both its proximity to the body and its reflection of a moment in time, clothing is an important vessel that stores and cues memories and is often saved as a reminder of a past time or person. Garments also discipline the body, permitting and restricting movement. Simultaneously a luxury and a necessity, clothing—understood in its broadest definition to be all that is worn on the body—is consumed across all cultures and all levels of society; it is a critical element of daily life irrespective of time and space.[41] But clothing's role in shaping experience, the meanings it conveys, its appearance, and its modes of production and consumption are historically contingent.

The materiality of clothing and other objects—their style, construction, materials, and tactile qualities—is critical to understanding both their roles in people's lives and their historical significance. So, too, are the discursive aspects of those objects—the social, cultural, and political meanings that are embedded within and created by their production and use. Objects have effects in the world—communicative, emotive, expressive, performative, and, at times, violent effects.[42] And their meanings shift as people make, buy, use, and transform them.[43] The theoretical underpinnings of the history that follows are situated within the context of the "life cycle" of objects—the trajectory of an object's existence from its conception through design and production, to its purchase or acquisition, and to its use, redistribution, repurposing, transformation, and, finally, abandonment, destruction, or preservation. The stages in the life cycle of a piece of clothing are interdependent, but the meanings it assumes and creates differ according to people's relationships to the object at a particular moment in that object's life cycle.[44] The same uniform coat, for instance, could be a source of income for a government-employed seamstress, while it shaped a soldier's experiences of battle and, for his descendants, might serve as a memento that stores memory of the wearer and the war.

Interweaving material, textual, and visual sources, this project deploys a form of interdisciplinary inquiry that chips away at the long-standing methodological boundaries that have led historians to rely predominately on texts in their study of the past, while it still maintains a rigorous focus on historical context and analysis. These sources, drawn from more than thirty archives and museums, include armor, civilian and military clothing, fabric scraps, and various accoutrements related to dress and clothing production; personal correspondence, diaries, and memoirs; newspapers, tailors' guides, advertisements, etiquette books, and fashion magazines; scientific, medical, and trade journals; organizational, governmental, and military records and publications; and photographs, drawings, cartoons, and sheet music.[45]

The chapters that follow are divided into four parts according to the life cycle of clothing and are roughly chronological, beginning with the adoption and production of army uniforms and ending with the preservation of clothing as relics of war. The life cycle of clothing progresses from design, adoption, and production; to purchase, consumption, use, and maintenance; and, finally, to deterioration, destruction, and preservation. Clothing was continuously created, worn, destroyed, and preserved during the war, but there was also something of a life cycle to the different dimensions of clothing's importance. At the beginning of the war, design, production, and acquisition took precedence; at war's end, the preservation of garments was paramount. Both Northern and Southern experiences appear in the same chapters.

Such an organizational structure may feel unfamiliar to some readers. Indeed, the chapters that follow proceed less like a standard historiographic recounting of the Civil War and more like the progression through an exhibition gallery's space, moving back and forth through time and space to explore the making, wearing, destroying, and saving of clothes and clothing culture.

This story begins with "Making," a section that focuses on how making clothing and dress culture were central to making war. It begins with the widespread adoption of military styles and design and the creation of a wartime clothing culture tied to military uniforms, before turning to the physical production of those uniforms and the conflicts that arose in the process. Brass and braid were the material embodiments of a manhood defined by patriotic allegiance, virility, and social rank. Understanding the creation of and society's buy-in to this uniform culture—this "brass manhood"—is necessary to understand the importance of women's work in producing the clothing that made up that uniform culture. At the same time, as soldiers grew accustomed to the challenges of war, a "battlefront style" of undergarments and shirts made at home emerged among soldiers, linking manhood not to a public culture of brass, but to familial ties—both emotional and economic. As national, state, and local governments worked to meet the demands of clothing armies, clothing took on a central role in making war. Political implications were reinforced and expanded as elite and middling women embraced the opportunity to see their sewing contributions elevated to and praised on the national stage. As working-class women worked to sew the uniforms that were critical to both wartime supply and shoring up shared identities, they became embroiled in another kind of "warfare" that centered on women's roles and relationships to the government.

"Wearing" shifts the vantage point to consider how civilians confronted and felt the effects of war and emancipation through the clothes they wore. Clothing—as well as the lack of it—shaped people's bodies and daily lives, offering us access to how war affected civilians on a material level in ways that conditioned their approach to interpersonal relationships, involvement with the government, and the politics of daily life. For many, predominantly white, relief workers, clothing was a means of attempting to mitigate the presumed effects of slavery and prepare people for freedom; for many Black refugees, however, it was also a means of resistance.

The use of clothing to create, shore up, and resist social, cultural, racial, and gendered identities made it a potent object by which to wage both physical and emotional warfare. "Destroying" addresses how war was waged and felt through acts of clothing destruction and defilement, and through the disintegration of dress practices. Violence, violation, and destruction involving clothing included the stripping of bodies on the battlefield, the looting of clothing from Southern houses, and the use of stolen clothing to craft narratives during wartime. Off the battlefield, Southerners experienced war and its effects on social hierarchies through the unraveling of their dress practices. Although less physically violent, such changes were not just about surface-level appearance—they shook people to their core and waged emotional war within them. Compounding such changes was the entanglement of the state and dress culture. At war's end, a ban on Confederate uniforms and regalia—and, as a result, participation in "brass manhood"—both laid the groundwork for Lost Cause ideology and set the stage for violent racial conflicts in the postwar era.

The final section, "Saving," explores the broader phenomenon of people keeping and preserving clothing—whether stolen or their own—to narrate, remember, and come to terms with war. People on both sides began collecting, stealing, and saving clothing as wartime relics at the very beginning of the war. Those acts of clothing preservation shaped memories and legacies of the Civil War that continue to reverberate through American society today.

The language of cloth and clothing provides a ready source of metaphors for talking about national union and dissolution. Before a cotton or woolen textile can be made, the raw materials must first be cultivated, harvested, and processed. The burrs and snags must be picked out and the fibers carded and aligned before being spun into yarn. Only then can the yarn be woven into fabric: fabric that can be plain, intricately patterned, or dyed with vibrant colors before it is cut, pieced together, and sewn into clothing. A map of the United States looked in 1861 (and continues to look today) like a patchwork quilt, its seams haphazardly sewn along mountain ridges, waterways, and invisible lines on the landscape. Like burrs, dirt, and seeds that prevent poorly processed cotton fibers from being spun into the smoothest of yarns, class tensions, racial and gender inequalities, and competing economic, social, religious, and cultural interests prevented the creation of a tightly woven nation. Those fibers could be carded—through compromises and mutual interests—such that the yarn might be spun and the cloth woven, but from its beginning the Union was never an easy one, pieced together from states that were cut from competing economic and political interests, and differing views on freedom, enslavement, and expansion. Slavery, like the single thread that is picked and pulled until the fabric comes apart at the seams, was ultimately what caused the nation to come unraveled.

The history that follows has frayed edges and unfinished seams. A study of clothing and culture does not lend itself to a tightly woven narrative, because the meanings surrounding clothes are fluid and multilayered, taking on new dimensions and significance for each individual and according to different circumstances. This book is meant to unsettle the way we think about the Civil War, to recapture the visceral nature by which people experienced it. Those experiences did not often occur in the same narrative arc by which we have typically related the war's stories—with a beginning, climax, and resolution. Rather, people experienced horrific violence followed by long periods of mundane daily life, only to be thrust back into the midst of death and dying or the threat of looting. So, too, will the reader traverse an uneven landscape of ordinary life punctuated by violent flashpoints.

The chapters that follow focus on various moments—remarkable and mundane—that capture the complexity of clothing's ability to shape and mediate the contours of historical experience and change. That Susan Bradford's postwar ire centered on clothing was no coincidence. Amid the conflicts and transformations that accompanied the American Civil War era, making, wearing, destroying, and saving clothing were central to the ways in which people waged war and how they experienced its effects. But clothing also offered ordinary people a path forward in this devastating war that was felt with an immediacy—an intimacy—by soldiers and civilians across the nation.

Part I
Making

Shirt made by Nellie Palmer for her brother, Kennedy Palmer, c. 1862.
Courtesy of the American Civil War Museum, Richmond, VA.

Watching from a distance as a man walked between rows of the Thirteenth Virginia's encampment, one would have thought a Confederate artillery soldier was approaching, given away by his telltale bright red collar and cuffs and the brass sleeve and breast buttons glinting in the sun. But on closer inspection, nothing about his clothing was quite right, beginning with the fact that he was wearing not a coat, but an ordinary shirt. Now stained on the breast, its fabric pocked by small holes, this shirt was then a crisp light blue flannel. Its wool collar and sleeve cuffs still maintain their vibrant color and the gilt brass buttons still maintain much of their luster. But those buttons are stamped not with military insignia but, rather, a stylized leaf pattern. Still, the bright red cuffs and collar clearly identify the shirt as belonging to an artilleryman. Except, it didn't.

This shirt was made for and worn by Kennedy Palmer, a private in the infantry, the army division whose soldiers engaged in direct combat. So what was Palmer doing with a shirt that not only misidentified him, but was not even an actual artillery coat?

When Palmer marched into the first Battle of Bull Run in July 1861, it was as he is in this photograph, wearing the typical clothing of a private, including a sack coat, pants tucked into his boots, and a gray forage cap. Palmer, who enlisted in support of the secessionist cause seven days after the bombardment of Fort Sumter, was a printer by trade, his occupation likely predestined, given that he was the son of the *Winchester Virginian*'s editor.[1] With a bedroll tied diagonally across his body and a canteen on his hip, his uniform both protected his body and marked him as a member of Company H of the Thirteenth Virginia Infantry. The brass insignia on his cap and brass buttons on his coat were part of the material means by which Palmer participated in a broader public culture that celebrated military uniforms as evidence of virile manhood—a brass manhood. His forage cap provided a physical link to his home and his aunt, who, like so many women, had made it herself in the effort to outfit Palmer for war.[2]

But those clothes wore out as Palmer navigated the mud and muck of camp life, three months of imprisonment at Fort Delaware, and thousands of miles of marching from Manassas to Port Republic to Richmond to Antietam to the Wilderness until he was wounded at Harper's Ferry in July 1864. At some point, his sister, Nellie, made Palmer this distinctive shirt from light blue wool flannel, using red wool flannel on the collar and cuffs in imitation of an artillery soldier's uniform coat. She clearly prized the material trappings of brass manhood; in contrast to the typical use of three or four bone or ceramic buttons, she sewed eight brass buttons to the front of her brother's shirt.

Carte de visite of Kennedy Palmer, 1861. Courtesy of the American Civil War Museum, Richmond, VA.

But in making this shirt, Nellie Palmer also contributed to her brother's participation in a more individualized style—a battlefront style—that emerged during the war.

Bound up in Kennedy Palmer's shirt are multiple stories of making. Creating patriotic support through a wartime culture. Producing clothing. Making war. These are histories about the central role played by clothing in Americans' ability to wage war against one another.

CHAPTER ONE

Six Feet of Soldier with Brass Buttons

Dressing Men for War

In July 1863, William Willoughby, a Union soldier stationed along the North Carolina coast, wrote a letter home to his wife, Nancy, in New Haven, Connecticut. The Battle of Gettysburg had ended a few days prior, but Willoughby was not writing about battle, nor much of anything related to military movements. Instead, he asked her to make "two more shirts yes four more if you will—like those two plaid wool shirts" she had previously made. The sizes, he noted, should be "two of one size and two of the other."[1]

This was just one in a series of clothing requests made by Willoughby going back several months, including shirts and caps of different sizes. He was also keenly interested in an accounting of the money Nancy spent on materials and of her labor. Over time, Willoughby's instructions became increasingly detailed: "Select buttons as will not be likely to pull out from the eye. *Boardman* wants you to make two button holes on the sleaves of his two shirts instead of buttons and buttonholes and then send two buttons so he can link them together and have sleeve buttons *I mean two buttons for each sleeve* . . . and mark each mans shirts make them well and strong and of as good material as the last."[2] The garments were not for William himself. The Willoughbys were running their own informal, possibly clandestine, clothing business and his comrades were their customers. William Willoughby was clearly committed to supplying a quality product to his customers. The Willoughbys had a lively market for home-sewn shirts among William's Union comrades in North Carolina, for whom the details of their clothing mattered. The pages that follow explain why those soldiers considered it worthwhile to have clothing shipped several hundred miles from Connecticut, rather than draw it from a quartermaster, and just why Boardman was so concerned about his buttons.

Civil War soldiers' uniforms are generally understood within the broader context of disputed government contracts and manufacturers who were responsible for establishing a standard commercial sizing system for men—a system that thrust the already-burgeoning ready-made clothing industry into the modern era of mass production.[3] Certainly this was a development of no small matter—the widespread acceptance of a sizing system shaped the modern garment industry. However, the ways in which soldiers and their families experienced the sudden large-scale demand for uniforms was far more complex. That is a story about mud and mire, ill-fitting boots, chafing pants, and stolen knapsacks. It is a history of people grappling with available technologies and production methods, remedying governmental failures, and working out the problems of fitting clothes to the conditions of battle and camp life.

Uniforms were critical in waging war, performing not only the practical purpose of clothing men's bodies, but also the work of shoring up the collective identities and community support necessary for successfully deploying and supporting armies. Uniforms were central to creating shared identities that centered on soldiers' manhood; the donning of a uniform signaled a man's transition from civilian to soldier and defined a relationship to the government. Supply shortages and quality problems meant that uniforms were often more effective at initially arousing patriotic fervor than maintaining it.

Within the complex relationship between the home front and battlefront developed both a public culture of manhood and private and public struggles to maintain soldiers' comfort, health, and appearance. Soldiers' garments helped people parse the blurred boundaries between manhood, duty, and incompatible gender norms for men within the context of war. People understood many of these garments as possessing transformative qualities: Brass elevated a soldier's status; a fitted uniform replaced the rags worn by a "slumped slave," transforming him into a "battle-ready" man; body armor purportedly "steeled" a soldier's body and mind for battle. Clothing, the process of provisioning, and the circumstances of war intertwined to define gender, and in the process shaped people's everyday experiences of, and attitudes toward, an expanding federal government.

Competing and complementary understandings of manhood were expressed through multiple material forms that evolved during the war, including body armor and a "battlefront style" of brightly colored shirts and body armor. But at the outbreak of war, white Americans across the United States and its territories turned to the same clothing culture as a public means of defining manhood. In the midst of sectional strife, both sides of the conflict adopted uniform culture not just as their military culture but as the dominant culture writ large. This was a culture that defined both manhood and womanhood in the context of war—it was, I argue, a national "brass manhood."

Brass Manhood

Military uniforms were not new to American society in 1861. Commanding officers in both the Union and Confederate armies had shared the same uniform at the United States Military Academy at West Point, worn the same uniform in the ranks of the regular army, and fought in the same uniform in Mexico just fifteen years prior.[4] Many men who were not part of the regular army were also engaged in a culture of specialized uniforms through participation in militias and fraternal societies.[5] What was new in 1861 was the *scale* of uniform use—this was unparalleled in American history. Whereas the number of uniformed men in the Mexican-American War of 1846–48 did not exceed 100,000, that number swelled to nearly 3,000,000 in four years during the 1860s—a thirtyfold increase. Furthermore, whereas militia uniforms were generally worn on special occasions, during wartime those uniforms became daily wear. In part because of the scale and frequency with which they were worn, uniforms were central to the wartime creation of a dominant vision of manhood among the broader public that was embodied by the soldier standing tall in a glinting, polished uniform. This brass manhood was codified not only in actions and ideals but also through its material enactment. It required a particular kind of clothing.

One might expect how men thought about their uniforms to be regionally specific. Such differences would make it seem more plausible—more rational—that Americans would find themselves engaged in a ruthless war against one another. But such emphasis on sectionalism can do us a disservice, causing us to seek out the differences and therefore miss the similarities that are clearly present. Certainly regional variations existed—the public nature of honor, especially in the South, for instance, lent itself to using clothing as a means of signaling and creating identity. But it is the similarities that made clothing such a powerful tool by which people waged and experienced war.

In the mid-nineteenth century it was by no means a foregone conclusion that the military uniform would become a dominant public definition of American manliness—in fact, in light of earlier attitudes toward the army, it was a rather surprising development. Just fifteen years earlier, in 1845, 30 percent of enlisted men were illiterate and many Americans looked down on soldiers as "shiftless individuals" who had enlisted because they "could not or would not engage in the industrious pursuits of normal society."[6] With the mass enlistment of men during the Civil War, however, soldiers were no longer perceived as "shiftless individuals" but, rather, as heroic, patriotic husbands, sons, and brothers. The success of this shift was tied to the public celebration of a culture of military uniforms.

Both the United States and Confederate governments attempted to establish uniformity in army dress. However, both governments' inability to supply volunteers meant that the collaborative efforts among states, communities, and families resulted in a wide variety of uniforms, among them, US Army and Confederate regulation uniforms, state regulation uniforms, privately purchased garments, state-purchased uniforms, and locally or family-designed clothing.[7] In both the US and Confederate armies, regiments were drawn from individual states and their companies were typically composed of soldiers from neighboring communities. With patriotic sentiments running high, soldiers' dress expressed both community and state identity.[8]

Requirements that both US and Confederate officers supply their own uniforms further complicated armies' appearance.[9] Although officers were expected to abide by army regulation, a variety of fabric colors appeared during the first year of the war. Both Confederate and US soldiers wore uniforms of varying colors resulting from both personal choice and inconsistencies in the availability and quality of fabric and dye. One Union soldier, for instance, began the war wearing his dark gray New York state militia uniform coat. What soldiers wore was critical to military success on several levels and so, over the course of time, the US Army worked to standardize what men wore in the field. As production, procurement, and supply lines were established, the mixed uniform coats and pants necessarily worn by so many volunteer soldiers at the start of the war were not only no longer necessary, but also deemed dangerous. In March 1862, the Department of the Missouri issued General Orders, declaring, "The attention of all officers is called to the Army Regulations and orders relating to uniforms. Officers wearing gray or mixed uniforms or overcoats in the field will be arrested and tried for disobedience of orders and neglect of duty."[10] At stake was the misidentification of soldiers during battle and an increasing identification of gray with the Confederacy and blue with the Union. Indeed, having clothing that distinguished one army from the other was deemed so critical that the 1863 Lieber Code, which set out rules of wartime conduct for the US Army, demanded that any enemy uniforms seized and worn by federal troops have "some striking mark or sign" on them to "distinguish the American soldier from the enemy."[11] But at the outset of the war, the stark division later drawn between Union blue and Confederate gray did not yet exist. Instead, both armies wore a motley, though often polished, mix of blues, grays, reds, greens, and browns.[12] However, the one thing that they all shared at the outset of war—with few exceptions—was insignia of rank and brass buttons.

Brass and braid were the material embodiments of a manhood defined by patriotic allegiance, virility, and social as well as military rank. Levels of adornment, down to the level of detail on buttons, tended to correspond to social class and also provided other signals of social affiliation. While the lowest-

Stamped brass uniform button, c. 1861–65. Object No. 2011.4.5. Collection of the Smithsonian National Museum of African American History and Culture.

ranking privates usually wore either flat brass buttons or those stamped with state seals, officers wore gilt brass buttons—brass overlaid with gold—sporting elaborate designs, or staff buttons marked with their branch of service. Some were marked with an eagle, or "CSA," while others were stamped with a "C" for cavalry, "I" for infantry, or "A" for artillery. Other symbols identified a soldier's state—Louisianans sported pelicans, while New Yorkers wore the state seal, and South Carolinians donned palmettos. Despite the variety in design, there was a simple rule by which to assess uniforms: The more brass buttons and gold braid a man wore, the higher his rank, making this an easy way for (often-clueless) new recruits and civilians to recognize an officer.

The speed at which a soldier might be promoted within the ranks changed dramatically during the war, and the ability to wear increasingly elaborate insignia and buttons changed as well.[13] Keeping up with the changes clearly mattered to soldiers as well as the women upon whom they relied for labor. But it could be confusing. As one Confederate woman expressed with exasperation, "I suppose I will learn all the different uniforms after awhile. The Infantry is gray, trimmed with blue, the buttons are of brass and the officers have gold lace on their sleeves, a chevron they call the design on the sleeves; a captain has three gold bars on his collar; the privates do not have any gold lace."[14] This woman's sentiment was reiterated frequently in the North as well: "Now-a-days," the *Wisconsin Daily Patriot* noted, "when uniformed

The gold braid and double row of gilt brass buttons identify this coat as that of a colonel. Confederate army frock coat worn by Colonel Robert Harper, c. 1861–65. Courtesy of the Division of Military History, National Museum of American History, Smithsonian Institution.

men are standing at all the corners, and are to be met on all the streets, it is pleasant to know just how to tell at a glance the rank of the wearer and the particular branch of the service with which he is connected."[15]

Newspapers, advertising manuals, and broadsides included textual descriptions and illustrations that helped the public decipher the insignia on men's uniforms. A colored broadside depicting "Our Union Defenders," for instance, provided a central block of illustrated portraits of the highest-ranking Union officers, bordered by depictions of chevrons, shoulder straps, swords, and soldiers standing in the position of drill commands. At a size of nearly three feet by three feet, this broadside was intended to be displayed on a wall. Notably, the guide to shoulder straps and sleeves was meticulously cut from one extant copy, perhaps to serve as a person's own reference guide in a more portable form.[16]

People of all classes received instruction in reading uniforms through media ranging from newspapers to playing cards. In the fall of 1861, for instance, newspapers across the North—from Massachusetts to Ohio and Wisconsin—

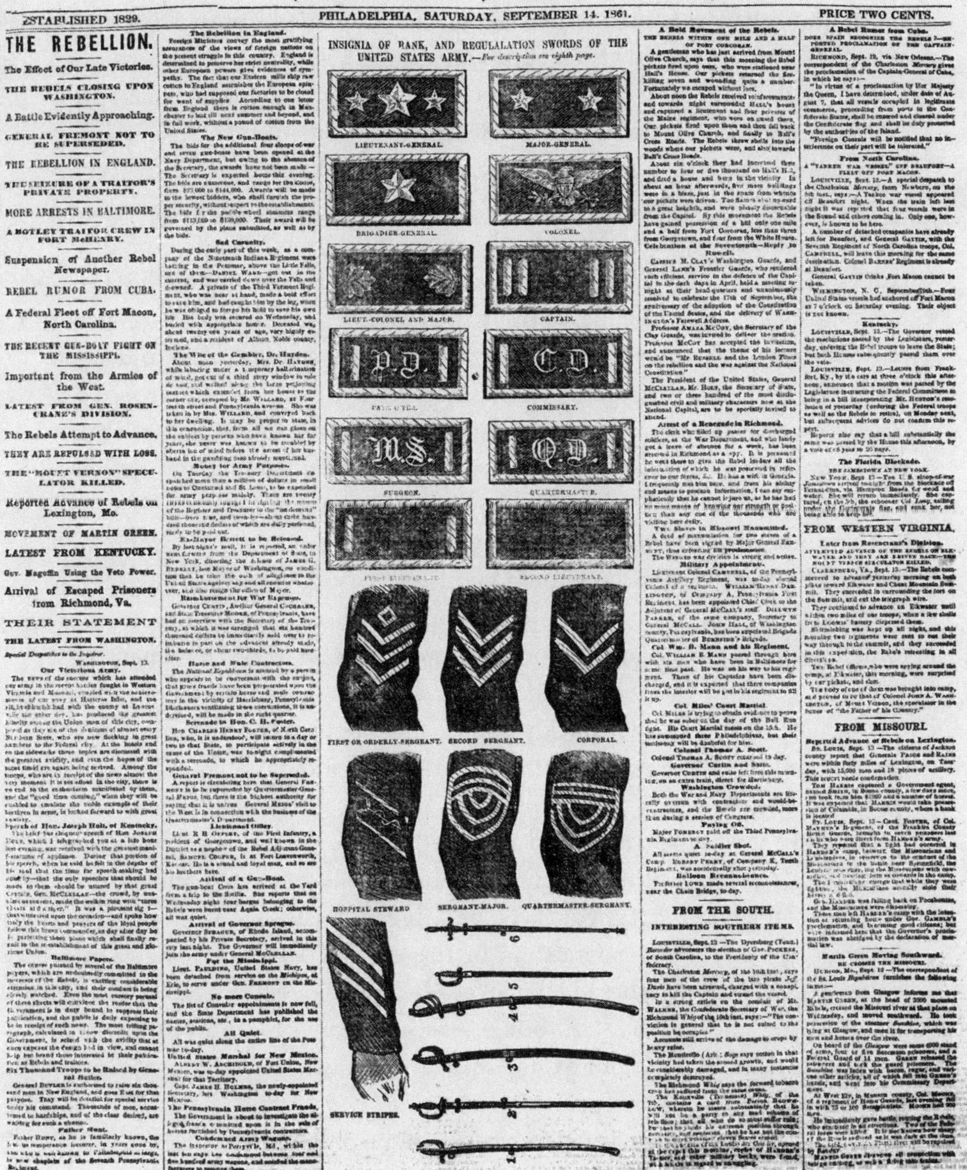

The Philadelphia Inquirer.

ESTABLISHED 1829. | PHILADELPHIA, SATURDAY, SEPTEMBER 14, 1861. | PRICE TWO CENTS.

THE REBELLION.

The Effect of Our Late Victories.

THE REBELS CLOSING UPON WASHINGTON.

A Battle Evidently Approaching.

GENERAL FREMONT NOT TO BE SUPERSEDED.

THE REBELLION IN ENGLAND.

THE SEIZURE OF A TRAITOR'S PRIVATE PROPERTY.

MORE ARRESTS IN BALTIMORE.

A MOTLEY TRAITOR CREW IN FORT McHENRY.

Suspension of Another Rebel Newspaper.

REBEL RUMOR FROM CUBA.

A Federal Fleet off Fort Macon, North Carolina.

THE RECENT GUN-BOAT FIGHT ON THE MISSISSIPPI.

Important from the Armies of the West.

LATEST FROM GEN. ROSENCRANZ'S DIVISION.

The Rebels Attempt to Advance.

THEY ARE REPULSED WITH LOSS.

THE "MOUNT VERNON" SPECULATOR KILLED.

Reported Advance of Rebels on Lexington, Mo.

MOVEMENT OF MARTIN GREEN.

LATEST FROM KENTUCKY.

Gov. Magoffin Using the Veto Power.

Arrival of Escaped Prisoners from Richmond, Va.

THEIR STATEMENT

THE LATEST FROM WASHINGTON.

Our Victorious Army.

The Rebellion in England.

The New Gun-Boats.

Sad Casualty.

INSIGNIA OF RANK, AND REGULALATION SWORDS OF THE UNITED STATES ARMY.—*For description see eighth page.*

A Bold Movement of the Rebels.

A Rebel Rumor from Cuba.

From North Carolina.

Kentucky.

The Florida Blockade.

FROM WESTERN VIRGINIA.

FROM MISSOURI.

Reported Advance of Rebels on Lexington.

Arrest of a Renegade in Richmond.

Military Appointments.

Col. Wm. B. Mann and his Regiment.

Col. Miles' Court Martial.

Colonel Thomas A. Scott.

Balloon Reconnoissance.

FROM THE SOUTH.

INTERESTING SOUTHERN ITEMS.

Martin Green Moving Southward.

The front page of a September 1861 issue of the *Philadelphia Inquirer* instructed readers on reading the stripes, stars, and chevrons on military uniforms. "Insignia of Rank, and Regulation Swords of the United States Army," *Philadelphia Inquirer*, September 14, 1861.

reprinted a *Philadelphia Inquirer* article detailing the specifics of insignia worn by soldiers. Accompanied by a front-page illustration of the various shoulder straps and sleeve badges worn by ranking officers, this article described the shapes, letters, stars, colors, and materials from which insignia were made, and provided explanations regarding the number of buttons worn on the front of a coat.[17] Soldiers, most of whom were volunteers with no prior military experience, were also offered instruction on identifying insignia. The *Automaton Regiment, or Infantry Soldiers' Practical Instructor,* for instance, offered soldiers the opportunity to join "theory to practice, by manoeuvering a mimic regiment in the quiet of his bivouac or quarters" using printed diagrams and small cards. Included in this set was a key to identifying the shoulder straps and sleeve insignia worn by men of different ranks.[18] By referring to publications like these, both soldiers and civilians could learn to decode and participate in the clothing culture surrounding them.

Some signals were easier to understand, such as the use of materials that were reminiscent of gold, a rich color that had long been associated with wealth, hierarchy, and royalty. The physical properties of those materials also had important implications for their wear. Brass—the material from which military buttons were made—could be plated, or gilded, with thin layers of bright yellow gold. However, unlike a pure gold button, brass was both affordable and durable. Furthermore, as opposed to an alternative metal like tin, brass could be easily polished.[19] This meant that even in the context of war, where cloth became quickly soiled and opportunities to thoroughly launder clothing were infrequent, the buttons on a coat could still be kept shiny and bright.

Similarly, gold-wrapped thread was used for the details of corps badges, shoulder straps, and other insignia.[20] Whereas silk or cotton thread typically lays flat against cloth, gold-wrapped thread is raised, giving it a three-dimensional, coiled appearance, as in the case of an eagle insignia that included gold-wrapped thread sewn over a bed of gold sequins, all set against a black velvet background.[21] Although over 150 years later most of the gold leaf has worn away, it did not oxidize and tarnish easily, ensuring that the insignia maintained its vibrant color in the 1860s.

Fashion is typically assumed to have been the prerogative of women, and soldiers are thought to have been concerned with their appearance no further than meeting inspection requirements at a dress parade.[22] But the soldiers—and their clothes—tell us otherwise. Photographs of soldiers visually attest to the fact that gold thread–embroidered insignia and brass buttons were highly prized and culturally significant. Buttons and shoulder

Gilt was applied to this tintype to emphasize the uniform's insignia and brass buttons. Tintype, unidentified Union soldier, c. 1861–65. Courtesy of the Liljenquist Family Collection of Civil War Photographs, Library of Congress Prints and Photographs Division, Washington, DC.

straps were frequently hand colored with gold hues, while red and blue highlighted the chevrons on men's sleeves, all of which offered a striking (if now faded) contrast to the gray- and sepia-toned likenesses of the men. Such pride was not reserved to officers. Each piece of brass worn by an unidentified US soldier in the tintype shown above, for instance, has been hand colored, including his belt buckle, breastplate, the button on his cap, and jacket and sleeve buttons. An album of soldiers in the Twenty-Fifth Regiment of the United States Colored Troops (USCT), whose ranks included both formerly enslaved and free Northern Black men, is a visual testament to the power of brass. The majority of the men's photographs, including that of John Walls, have been hand tinted, and gilt applied to their buttons and other insignia, although the luster of the gold has faded on some. By paying for hand-colored photographs, these soldiers, or their families, illustrated—quite literally—the importance of brass buttons and gold insignia to their identity as soldiers.

Men took great pride in the performative aspects of wearing brass buttons. As one soldier reflected on his promotion, "A year ago this time I was learning

John Walls was nineteen when he mustered into Company G of the Twenty-Fifth Regiment of the US Colored Infantry. The gilt applied to his tintype emphasizes the brass on his uniform. Tintype of John Walls, 1864–65. Object No. 2014.88h. Collection of the Smithsonian National Museum of African American History and Culture, Gift of Aneita Gates, on behalf of her son, Kameron Gates, and all the descendants of Captain William A. Prickitt.

guard-duty and squad-drill on foot; now I ride around on a big horse, have *two* rows of brass buttons on my coat (you should have seen the men look last night at parade, as I wore the new coat for the first time). [I] am generally just as big as I can swell."[23] It was not only other soldiers who created significance surrounding this performative culture of brass buttons. Some men considered it an honor to cut a button from their uniform to leave with a young woman when they departed for the war. One soldier described "the glory of finding ourselves the heroes of the hour, and reciprocated the crowd's interest, parting with many of our buttons to the prettiest girls."[24] Those buttons were also intended for the civilian public's visual consumption through both contact with actual soldiers and the frequent use of brass manhood imagery in print culture. In addition to their work manufacturing buttons and sewing uniforms, women were central to the production of brass manhood through the significance they constructed around those uniforms, in part by recognizing the sexual desirability of soldiers in uniform—what one woman described as a "surging, intoxicating stream of brass buttons, epaulettes, and sword-belted manhood."[25]

At times, public captivation with brass buttons verged on fetishization, especially in the context of women's relationships and infatuations with soldiers. Kate Stone, a young Louisianan, wrote of a "perfect love of a lieutenant in blue [Confederate] uniform and brass buttons galore. Six feet of soldier with brass buttons is irresistible, and all the girls capitulated at once."[26] Similarly, Floridian Susan Bradford noted, "They all look fine to me and I grow more patriotic all the time."[27] In a fictitious story published in a Northern periodical, young ladies "wriggled along delightedly through the streets because [of] a resplendent being, composed principally of brass buttons." An officer, the author continued, "would have been a very fascinating person without his brass belongings, but with them, he was perfectly irresistible."[28]

An explosion of popular print culture during wartime reiterated and expanded the importance of brass manhood to public culture more broadly. Ranging from illustrated stationery and envelopes to colorful sheet music covers and playing cards, and to large broadsides and prints intended for display in parlors, this popular culture brought soldiers and their uniforms into the household as part of the everyday experience. The American Card Company, for instance, printed playing cards that replaced the king with a colonel and the jack with a major, both of whom sport detailed buttons, shoulder straps, and epaulettes. The instructions explain that the emblems used, including the soldiers, eagles, shields, stars, and flags, were "as familiar as household words, everywhere among the American people."[29]

"An Eagle on His Button"

It was two years into the war before Black men were officially allowed to enlist in the US Army. By that point, the US government had established its provisioning system. Unlike their white counterparts, many of whom had experienced the uneven flurry of activity in community efforts to outfit companies, Black men immediately stepped into a system of quartermasters and depots. The cultural value attached to brass manhood as it was adopted amid public pomp and circumstance at the beginning of the war contributed to racially charged debates over the military enlistment of African American men. In his exhortation to Black men to join the US Army, Frederick Douglass explicitly linked African Americans' military participation with future claims to citizenship: "Once let the Black man get upon his person the brass letters US; let him get an eagle on his button, and a musket on his shoulder, and bullets in his pocket, and there is no power on the earth or under the earth which can deny that he has earned the right of citizenship in the United States."[30] Muskets on shoulders and bullets in pockets have taken precedence in historians' interpretation of Douglass's speech. And yet, for Douglass, the initial action in claiming the rights of citizenship through military service was to mark a man's body with the insignia of the United States—to put on the trappings of brass manhood.

Choosing a uniform for Black soldiers was the first step in shaping the path that Black men's future might take through military service to the nation. Douglass recalled a conversation with Abraham Lincoln in which "[Lincoln] said that he had difficulty in getting colored men into the United States uniform; that when the purpose was fixed to employ them as soldiers, several different uniforms were proposed for them, and that it was something gained when it was finally determined to clothe them like other soldiers."[31] Debates over how to clothe Black soldiers predated the official creation and mustering in of the United States Colored Troops (USCT) in 1863. US general David Hunter, who began the unauthorized recruitment of formerly enslaved South Carolinians in 1862, requested that Secretary of War Edwin Stanton send him 50,000 pairs of scarlet red pantaloons for Black soldiers.[32] Similarly, Adjutant General Lorenzo Thomas, who, in 1863, was placed in charge of African American recruitment in the Military Division of the Mississippi, suggested to Stanton that rather than issuing "the clothing of the army" to newly organized Black companies, "a distinctive dress of less cost would be better—something a little more gay."[33] Such requests were significant, given that the federal government was increasingly streamlining both the production and appearance of army clothing. To clothe already-segregated Black regiments in a strikingly different uniform would be an additional public, material admission of the government's complacence with—indeed, reinforcement of—inequality based on racial difference. There was, then, as Douglass recalled of his conversation with Lincoln, "something gained" when Black soldiers were issued regulation uniforms. However small a victory, wearing Union blue rather than scarlet red pantaloons was an important first step in Black soldiers' ability to claim the right to equality and citizenship in the American nation.[34]

At stake in the debate over uniforms was Black men's right to participate in a publicly celebrated form of manhood that tied them to the nation. Although both Northern free Black men and formerly enslaved men all fought in the USCT, public discourse and popular culture tended to associate Black soldiers with former enslavement.[35] In both textual and visual discourses, for a formerly enslaved man to become a soldier was no ordinary feat. The formerly enslaved were believed to require a "metamorphosis": The *chattel* needed to become a *man* before he could fight like a *soldier*. This transition from "contraband" to soldier was described and depicted as a ritualistic process.[36] Union colonel Robert Cowden wrote that after a new Black recruit passed a physical examination, his hair was shaved and then the soldiers proceeded "to strip him of his filthy rags and burn them, and scour him thoroughly with soap and water."[37] The new recruits were then outfitted with the remainder of their gear. As Jacob Bruner, a USCT officer, explained to his wife, "As fast as we get them we clothe them from head to foot in precisely the same uniform that 'our boys' wear, give them tents, rations, and Blankets and they are highly pleased and hardly know themselves."[38]

This process was portrayed as a metamorphosis that hinged on stripping off the material costume of the rags of slavery and donning a uniform. Many of these images are fictitious or posed, display clear artistic license, and draw on racial stereotypes to convey their message. Indeed, the conditions of formerly enslaved people entering army camps were, at times, exaggerated for political purposes, and the "ragged slave" became both a visual and literary trope. Such images and the rhetoric of transformation that accompanied them might have seemed rather deceptive from the perspective of the formerly enslaved men who became soldiers. Black male civilians had been wearing army clothing long before they were allowed to enlist. Many had been provided with *rejected* army clothing by government officials and army officers. It was clothing that was either poorly made or deemed too worn for use by white soldiers, but it was army clothing all the same. These visual narratives are nevertheless critical to understanding both how abolition-minded people depicted Black soldiers and the ways in which clothing was believed to shape and portray the inner self.[39]

A pair of photos of Hubbard Pryor, a Georgian who liberated himself and joined the Forty-Fourth US Colored Infantry, represents this form of visual storytelling.[40] Like many such photographs, Hubbard's was likely staged. In the first, meant to show Pryor before his enlistment, he sits slumped on a rickety chair. His shirt sleeves are rolled up, his ragged pants stuffed into his boots. He sits in an ungentlemanly manner with his legs spread apart and a foot rolling to the side. Tears and holes are apparent throughout his clothes and a worn slouch hat covers his head. In the second photograph, by contrast, Pryor stands straight and tall, his shoulders thrust back and his bare arms respectfully covered, sporting a clean uniform complete with a belt buckle, pants, hat, and brass buttons. With its close-fitting jacket and leather straps that bind the gear to the torso, the uniform disciplines both the body and the man through its very materiality. He appears ready for orders, standing at attention, disciplined, and a wholly changed person—his posture and neatness convey, by mid-nineteenth-century standards, a sense of self-worth and manliness. The distribution of photographs like that of Hubbard Pryor was partly intended to demonstrate to a racist Northern public (who feared the process of emancipation) that the

Private Hubbard Pryor before and after enlistment in the Forty-Fourth US Colored Infantry, October 10, 1864. Photographer: T. B. Bishop. RG 94: Records of the Adjutant General's Office, Series: Letters Received, 1863–88, National Archives and Records Administration, Washington, DC.

trappings of brass manhood could provide a path forward for formerly enslaved men.[41] The power of these images lies in the contrast of the clothing—an evolution from tattered rags to a clean, crisp, more fitted uniform.

Yet, Black men experienced their participation in the public culture of brass manhood differently from their white counterparts. While white men passed through towns, popping off buttons to bestow upon young ladies and showing off their shoulder straps, those same badges, buttons, and insignia placed a target on African American men who wore them. Black Union soldiers were to be treated by the same rules of war as white soldiers. However, as one veteran explained, this policy "did not change the opinion of the Southerners, who, notwithstanding the use which the Confederate Government was making of the negro, still regarded him, in the *United States* uniform, as a vicious brute, to be shot at sight."[42] Captured Black soldiers were often killed rather than taken as prisoners of war. In response to a request for instructions on how to treat "slaves taken in federal Uniform," the Confederate secretary of war responded, "They cannot be recognized in any way as soldiers subject to the rules of war and to trial by Military Courts . . . and to repress any spirit of insubordination, it is deemed essential that slaves in armed insurrection should meet condign punishment, summary execution must therefore be inflicted on those taken . . . under circumstances indicative beyond doubt of actual rebellion."[43] Death, he asserted, was the fitting punishment for a slave who dared to put on the Union uniform.

The experience of Samuel Johnson, a sergeant in the Second US Colored Cavalry, illustrates just how critical the clothing that a Black man wore was to his safety and the outcome of his capture. In a deposition documenting Confederate outrages against Black soldiers, Johnson reported that at the time Plymouth, North Carolina, was recaptured by Confederate forces, "all the negros found in blue uniform or with any outward marks of a Union soldier upon him was killed—I saw some taken into the woods and hung—Others I saw stripped of all their clothing, and they stood upon the bank of the river with their face riverwards and they were shot. Still others were killed by having their brains beaten out by the butt end of the muskets in the hands of the Rebels." Johnson survived the attack only because he "pulled off my uniform and found a suit of citizens clothes which I put on," an act that might have marked him as a deserter had he been discovered by his own forces, but ultimately saved his life.[44] The Confederate soldiers who captured Johnson believed he was a local slave, allowing him to survive the attack and eventually return to his regiment.

The brutality Johnson narrowly escaped happened on Southern soil, but Black soldiers' safety was far from guaranteed in Northern or Union-occupied areas. Black soldiers were rebuked, taunted, and physically attacked by white Northern civilians as they walked along the street or attempted to take public forms of transportation.[45] During a violent attack in Philadelphia, boys stoned a Black soldier, pummeled him with a billy club over the head, and ripped the chevrons from the sleeves of his uniform.[46] In addition to the physical beating this man endured, the boys made an explicit effort to tear the insignia of the man's army rank from his uniform, a symbolic act that stripped the man of his military identity. In a similar incident, a white teenager tore off the shoulder straps of a Black surgeon's uniform minutes after he boarded a train in Baltimore.[47]

White Union soldiers also proved a threat. USCT soldier Joseph T. Wilson remembered an incident in which "I attempted to pass Jackson Square in New Orleans one day in my uniform, when I was met by two white soldiers of the 24th Conn[ecticut]. They halted me and then ordered me to undress. I refused when they seized me and began to tear my coat off." Although he escaped with his clothes, it was, Wilson asserted, "nothing strange to see a Black soldier *a la Adam* come into the barracks out of the streets."[48] Because clothing functions not only as a form of bodily protection, but also conveys status and identity, to strip a man of his clothing was to commit more than physical assault—it also symbolically stripped a man of his public identity, humanity, and decency. Although the humiliation associated with forced, public nakedness applied to white and Black men alike, in the military, removing soldiers' uniforms or insignia was a method of military punishment.[49] That official stripping of insignia and uniforms was reserved for soldiers who had committed a crime illustrates that such acts against Black men were intended as more than humiliation—it was an effort to deny them the material ability to participate in brass manhood.

Maintaining Brass Manhood

While wearing a brass-buttoned uniform admitted men to a celebrated public form of manhood, experience in the field routinely dashed expectations of privilege. Keeping up the polish of a uniform depended on soldiers' navigation of government bureaucracy, families' ability to supply clothing, and the urgent demand for garments that offered durability and protection. For many men, army service was their first significant encounter with the workings of the national, rather than local, government in their daily lives. Indeed, soldiers frequently used the words "army" and "government" interchangeably. Rank-and-file soldiers expected to draw clothing from the quartermaster, as clothing allowances were included in the terms of their enlistment and pay. Some found encounters with the quartermaster contentious and even infuriating, in part due to problems resulting from insufficient supply, poor coordination of supply lines, the theft of knapsacks from transport wagons, and the distribution of goods made from shoddy, a recycled fabric. Not only Confederates, but Union soldiers, too, found themselves nearly barefoot, without overcoats, and in desperate need of a new pair of pants. The struggle to maintain the materials of brass manhood resulted in alternate, often family-based, supply lines and new opportunities and challenges for seamstresses and tailors as they worked to clothe absent bodies.[50]

Soldiers understood the donning of the uniform as a physical contract between themselves and the government. The army's failure to fulfill that contract provoked disillusionment among individual soldiers. Union soldier

John Babb's struggle to obtain appropriate clothing and shoes is instructive in the ways in which it colored his attitude not only toward the war but also toward the federal government itself. Babb wrote home to his parents in Maryland describing his need of several clothing items, including woolen shirts. With irritation he explained that he could not buy the shirts himself because he had not been paid for nearly five months. Babb also requested help procuring a pair of "long boots with thick soles," writing: "I am very near bare footed, and cannot get a pair of Government shoes to fit me."[51]

One month later, Babb wrote with even greater vitriol toward a government that had still not paid him or delivered fitting shoes. "I wish this war was at an end, for I am sick and tired of it," he lamented. "It really seems to me that we are not fighting for our *country* but for the freedom of the negroes." His letter reflects not only divisions among Union soldiers on emancipation but also the ways soldiers' political views could be colored by the army's inability to address their material needs.[52] His irritation must have increased when, a few weeks later, his company's knapsacks—which were transported from Washington, DC, to the soldiers' camp—were found to have "been rob[b]ed of everything they contained," except a solitary pair of stockings.[53] Once his new boots arrived, courtesy of his father—two and a half months after he requested them—and he found himself "in splendid quarters . . . to live in"—a seized brick house—Babb's perspective on army life seems to have improved.[54]

Men's experiences of drawing ill-fitting clothing from the quartermaster, the challenge of accessing clothing, and its cost shaped soldiers' frustration with the government and motivated them to request clothing from home, drawing family members into the role of providing what the government did not. The disruption of war, men's absence from their usual employment, and unreliable government pay systems introduced economic uncertainty into the homes of both Northern and Southern soldiers. As a result, soldiers and their families worked together to maximize their pay, choosing to draw some of their clothing from quartermaster stores and have other items sent from home. If a soldier did not use his entire clothing allowance, that money was instead paid to him in cash and could be sent home or used for other supplies or comforts. Confederate Theodore Livingston, for instance, had intended to buy his clothes himself, but then discovered that the price was exorbitant. Instead, he wrote, "I will send a pattern tomorrow for a coat and if mother can, I would like she would send me a coat & vest of the kind my last pants were—if not some pretty homespun that will not fade or linen."[55] The money saved could be used to purchase clothing that men found more suitable, of better quality, or simply less expensive.

Even with families at home who had the means and ability to secure clothing for them, Theodore Livingston and John Babb struggled to maintain the trappings of brass manhood. Those challenges were greater for formerly enslaved Black soldiers. While the Union uniform was considered an uplifting form of dress, it also reinforced a relationship of dependence between formerly enslaved Black soldiers and the federal government because that uniform was *required* by the army in order for a man to conform to regulations, and its distribution and cost were controlled by the government.[56] During weekly inspections, US officers were ordered to "minutely inspect the arms, accoutrements and dress of each soldier."[57] Failure to comply with dress requirements could result in reprimand. "If we don't have clean clothing," one white soldier wrote, the colonel "will punish us."[58] Like Babb and Livingston, many white soldiers relied upon their families to send them additional clothing, including shirts, socks, and drawers: clothing that was worn underneath their government-issued uniforms. This made it possible for them to forego drawing new clothing from the quartermaster so that they would instead receive its equivalent in pay.

Black soldiers, however, especially those who had recently freed themselves, did not have access to the same resources. Indeed, nearly all families of Black soldiers from the border states remained enslaved.[59] These men's families could rarely supply clothing of any kind, and what clothing formerly enslaved men had when they enlisted was generally worn out and very unlikely to pass inspection, and therefore they depended on the quartermaster for their clothing. Despite their disadvantage in regard to pay and their inability to supplement their garments with supplies from families, Black soldiers were no less exempt from army regulations regarding dress. As one military report noted, "The pay of these Colored Troops has proven but little more than sufficient to provide their necessary clothing."[60] The deduction of lost, replacement, and new clothing from monthly pay, then, had more significant implications for formerly enslaved men in the United States Colored Troops than for many white soldiers.

In both the North and South, white soldiers developed well-organized networks by which to obtain clothing from home and customize it to meet their own sense of comfort. Yet, shipping clothing from home required access to clothing or people with sewing skills, as well as cash to pay for its shipment or a connection to someone returning to the battlefront. Officers and privates from families with disposable income were thus more easily able to maintain and replenish the trappings of brass manhood.

Women, both relatives at home and strangers living in the vicinity of army encampments, as well as male tailors, played a critical role in facilitating men's access to new clothing and the repair of old clothing. In fact, soldiers often relied upon family members to contact, and contract with, local tailors on their behalf. This access both assisted men in maintaining their appearance within the context of brass manhood and provided them with individualized clothing. The advantage in having clothing sent from the home front included the ability to make special requests in terms of materials, construction, decoration, and fit—options unavailable to those purchasing mass-produced clothing issued according to a sizing system. And this is why Boardman's buttons mattered.

Bill and Jim McFall, two brothers from the small planter class who served in the South Carolina Palmetto Sharp Shooters, corresponded with their sisters about clothing throughout the war. To outfit himself comfortably and to his own standards, Jim orchestrated a series of connections from afar. He instructed his sister to consult with another man—likely a fellow soldier—on the "stile" of pants and coat he needed. Jim relied upon his sister to decide whether a sack or dress coat would "look & do best" for him but asked that she trim the coat collar and cuffs to reflect his rank. Gold cord, he suspected, could be purchased in nearby Columbia, South Carolina, but he directed her on where to find the additional uniform trimmings at their house. By the time the style was determined and the trimmings procured, at least four people were involved in supplying Jim McFall with his coat and pants. When his clothing arrived, he was very pleased that it fit "vry well."[61]

Getting a suit of clothing to fit "vry well" was important to the way in which some men presented themselves, particularly when it came to officers' uniforms. It was not merely the buttons and braid but also the fit of the coat that crafted brass manhood. This, however, was a challenge for men who were often encamped or on the march several hundred miles away from their homes. Although ready-made clothing was available, middling and elite customers still favored tailoring for men's coats and pants. A diagram in Genio Scott's 1859 *Cutter's Guide* details the number of measurements necessary for properly fitting a uniform frock coat—the back torso of the coat alone involved a series of seven measurements to achieve the correct proportions.[62]

The differences between a tailored coat and a ready-made coat cannot be thoroughly detailed when the bodies themselves are absent. However, the clothing itself provides clues. A jacket worn by Henry Gansevoort, for instance, was padded with horsehair to create an additional inch at its thickest point and then seamed to keep the horsehair confined to small pockets, preventing it from shifting within the lining and creating a lumpy appearance. Such a measure was likely taken to build up Gansevoort's chest, making it

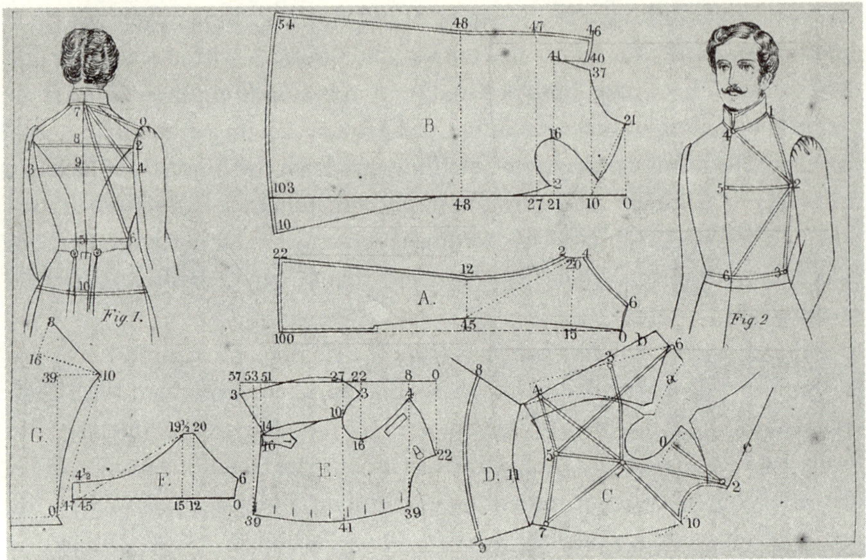

This plate instructed cutters on the various measurements required to properly fit a frock coat to an individual man's body. Genio C. Scott, *The Cutter's Guide: Being a Series of Systems for Cutting Every Kind of Modern Garment* (New York, 1859). Courtesy of the American Antiquarian Society, Worcester, MA.

appear rounder and more prominent.[63] With the expertise of a tailor, sleeves and pants could be cut to the actual length of a man's arms and legs; attention would be paid to the movement of the fabric so that a coat would have "spring" to its skirt; and padding could be inserted to fill out a man's chest and achieve a particular silhouette. As tailors' archetypes suggest, an inexperienced person could not easily take such measurements, much less understand which measurements needed to be applied exactly versus allowing for stretch and seams.[64]

Wartime, then, posed a problem for fitting clothing to men: Their absence often meant that the process of measuring and tailoring needed to be performed without a physical body. Preexisting relationships with tailors in their home communities proved valuable in the event that men wanted new, custom-fitted coats or pants. Indeed, the account book of Petersburg, Virginia, tailoring business Gruter and Gerecke recorded not only the items a man purchased, but also his measurements for pants, coats, and vests. These records allowed tailors to cut and sew orders like those recorded in the account book as simply "Pants by old measure."[65] But this, too, posed a problem: Many men found that their body shapes changed during the war as a result of physical exertion and new kinds of labor. One soldier noted, "I guess I have lost flesh doing so much marching."[66] Jim McFall confessed, "I am afraid I have grown so much since I had any [pants] made at home that my old measure will not do. However if you think you all can get them to fit me fix them up and send them." The tailor in town, he thought, might be able to "guess pretty well by the old measure."[67] He had attempted to have new measurements taken, but the local "Taylor I went to had lost his tape." Without a measuring tape in the vicinity, McFall thought his best option was to have his sister "make up my suit by guess and send it forward."[68]

Occasionally, men conveyed their measurements in letters or offered advice on how the clothing should be cut. Bill McFall directed, "If you have to have me a pair cut tell who ever cuts them not to cut the legs so looss, to cut them loose in the thigh and taper the leg down at the foot. It will save cloth and do better."[69] Many drafting techniques required only a few measurements be taken from the specific customer—the remaining measurements could be extrapolated using a patented set of scales or tables.[70] This was also helpful in remaking coats. One man offered his fellow officer his dress coat and was glad to find that Theodore (a tailor in Worcester, MA) had applied his "celestial" principle "under the arms," so that a Beaufort, South Carolina, tailor could "easily make an exact fit for the upper sphere."[71] As a result, the officer's friend was able to wear a well-fitting coat—one originally made in Massachusetts and remade in South Carolina. Others, however, were not so fortunate. When a Virginia soldier's coat arrived from home, he found that it was "an inche or two short in the skirts & the pocets were a little too high." Nevertheless, he found the coat comfortable and the pants that went with it "first rate."[72]

Tailors living in the vicinity of encamped soldiers were sought out for their expertise in cutting and fitting officers' pants and coats, but local women were also eagerly hired. While some were seamstresses by trade, others were compelled by wartime circumstances to sew and take in washing for pay. Soldiers' need and desire for clothing repair, alterations, and washing drew men and women into contractual relationships that, in many instances, defied the association of women's wartime sewing as patriotic. From the perspective of the Confederacy, local Southern women were sewing for the enemy when they took in Union soldiers' clothing. These women may have been Unionists, or, after two years of occupation, had grown used to the presence of Union soldiers. In Washington, North Carolina, in January 1864, George Bowen drew a new overcoat from the quartermaster. One month later, he took the coat to Sally Ann Huggins to have custom pockets sewn into it. The pockets, however, seem to have been not quite right—one week later, he had

Mrs. Rhodes fix the pockets that Huggins had sewn. Soon thereafter he bought a new shirt from a clothing store in town and drew a new pair of pants from the quartermaster. He then "went and got some red stripes 1½ inches wide and some silk cord" and "took them to Mrs. Mannings to have them sowed on," paying her twenty-five cents for her labor.[73] Bowen went to great lengths to outfit himself, supplementing clothing drawn from the quartermaster with that he purchased from a local store, relying upon three local white women to sew on his insignia of rank and to customize his clothing to fit his particular needs and desires.[74]

When soldiers had access to and could afford women's labor, they were often willing to rely upon local white and Black women to launder, mend, and sew their clothing. In the absence of those women, they relied upon their own skills. Robert Fairfax, for instance, asked that his mother send "enough red flannel or some woolen material to line my overcoat- which I can get done by a lady staying at Herbert's." But, he instructed, "she had better send with it some strong thread & needles, so that I can do it myself, if it should be necessary."[75] Mending clothing in the field was very common, as evidenced by both men's correspondence and the garments themselves, with multiple colors of thread used to repair split seams or tears. Men like Fairfax who mended their own clothing frequently did so with the help of a "housewife."

A sewing kit made from cloth, a housewife or *hussif*, was carried by many soldiers and served as an emotional connection to the home front. As their name implies, sewing was associated with the domestic chores of the household, but these sewing kits were also linked to individual women who frequently made or resupplied them. One kit, owned by a Union soldier, had a blue silk lining and red edging, as well as a small pincushion made from a striped fabric. Soldiers frequently requested that their mothers, sisters, and wives send them needles, thread, and other sewing implements. One soldier asked his wife to send him dark worsted fabric to patch his clothes.[76] By responding to such requests, women and families at home supported soldiers' efforts to maintain their uniforms and thereby their brass manhood.

Battlefront Style

Although US military policy moved toward greater regulation, governmental failures to provide adequate access to new clothing meant that not only individual men, but the government, too, needed families to keep men supplied. While the Confederacy continued to rely upon such family- and community-based support throughout the entire war, the US government had greater success in supplying not only uniform coats and pants, but also undergarments. The shortcomings of such supply during the first years of the war had, however, created a space in which many soldiers engaged their families in a "domestic supply line."[77] Once established, soldiers continued to rely upon that supply line for both physical and emotional support, which often took the form of garments supplied from home.

In this context, what I term a "battlefront style" of shirts and undergarments emerged among soldiers that met their needs on the battlefront and linked manhood not to a public culture of brass but to the more intimate realm of familial ties and cloth. This manhood, too, was defined within the context of war and in relationship to women, but it typically centered on reciprocal duties within the family that called upon men and women to provide support to one another, both economically and emotionally. This family-based manhood was not incompatible with brass manhood. In fact, the material culture through which it was created—the home-sewn shirts, drawers, and knitted socks—provided the base layers of clothing over which the outer garments of brass manhood—the uniform coats—were worn. A woman might contribute both to the creation and affirmation of brass manhood and to this more individualized battlefront style of undergarments.

The ability to customize a uniform varied greatly by rank. Officers also had more freedom to design their own uniforms, while privates could typically express their individuality only beneath their outer uniform coat. Technically, a man's outer garments—his coat and pants—were expected to adhere to army regulations in terms of color, cut, and style, but undergarments, including shirts and drawers, seem to have drawn little attention from officers who inconsistently enforced uniform regulations.

In the requests and instructions they sent to their loved ones, soldiers were shaping a material culture of manhood created through more intimate connections to home or through purchase from people on the home front. Soldiers possessed limited access to the burgeoning array of available fabric, yet they still had the desire to wear it. Battlefront style took many forms, but was generally characterized by colorful or patterned fabrics, including plaids, calico prints, and stripes, and/or incorporated a distinctive feature into its design or embellishments—something that would set a shirt apart from the plain shirts issued by the quartermaster. Colors, cuts, fabric, and fasteners were among the items soldiers sought to customize in their shirts. Recall that Confederate Theodore Livingston was specific in his preference for a new coat and vest made from the same fabrics as the last pair of pants his mother had sent him. If there was not enough material left, his next choice was a "pretty homespun" made with a good dye that would not quickly fade.[78] And this is where Boardman's buttons come into play.

William and Nancy Willoughby made their money by selling battlefront style to soldiers. William's requests typically included a variety of shirts, allowing him to supply fellow soldiers with more individualized clothing. He told Nancy that he wanted "2 calico shirts as soon as you can make them. I want them made of something fancy not so dark as those you made [before]."[79] He also requested at least three different fabric patterns, "some of them to be a large size plaid filled in with smaller plaids."[80]

As these requests suggest, both durability and aesthetics were of concern to soldiers, especially when unreliable quartermaster stores and long shipping times could delay the resupply of clothes. William was careful to select fabric that would simultaneously uphold the wear and tear of soldiering and appeal to his customers. He asked Nancy to make shirts from sturdy cloth "that will not fade by washing" in a variety of prints and fabrics, including woolen or cotton plaids. To aid his customers in avoiding a patched-up appearance when their clothes inevitably tore, William had Nancy "enclose 2 or 3 Small pieces of the cloth Say 3 or 4 inches Square suitable for mending or patching the elbows" from the same cloth as that from which the shirts were made.[81]

Shirts worn under the coat allowed soldiers to express their own sense of style, improve their comfort, and provide a material connection to their loved ones. Historian Joseph Beilein Jr. draws a distinction between guerrillas' shirts and the "conventional military uniform," which he defines as "clothing of the same color and cut worn by every man in the army, with only slight alterations denoting rank, unit, and branch of service."[82] While guerrillas' shirts did offer a striking contrast to a uniform coat and pants, soldiers who wore the "conventional military uniform" also personalized their own appearance through their shirts—shirts that were seen and worn on a daily basis in camp. Although not as elaborate as guerrillas' shirts and rarely elaborately embroidered, these shirts were nevertheless distinctive. Surgeon Edwin Booth's dark maroon wool flannel shirt, for instance, was printed with Confederate Second National flags—a brightly patterned contrast to a more basic, unbleached cotton shirt.[83]

Other shirts were less flamboyant, but nevertheless individualized. Luther Jerrel wore a cotton shirt printed with small purple flowers; William Terry, a brown cotton shirt with a distinctive white linear pattern.[84] M. Page Lapham wore a shirt with an elaborately pleated breast. Edward Crozier wore a white cotton shirt with printed pink stripes and dots and ruched material on the breast. Such a design not only made Crozier's shirt distinct; it also would

Edwin G. Booth's expression of his own battlefront style was a shirt made from maroon wool flannel fabric printed with the Confederate Second National Flag. This print was available in multiple colors of fabric. Shirt, c. 1861–65. Courtesy of the American Civil War Museum, Richmond, VA.

This cotton shirt worn by Edward W. Crozier has ruched material at the breast, which would have made his chest appear larger. Now yellowed with age, it was originally white with a pink stripe and dot pattern. Shirt, c. 1861–65. Courtesy of the American Civil War Museum, Richmond, VA.

have affected the appearance of his body, building out his chest in a manner similar to the padded coat worn by Henry Gansevoort.[85] Not all clothing was custom made in ways that were obvious to other men. Andrew Beam's light brown cotton shirt appears unremarkable, but it too was personalized by his wife, featuring an unusual breast pocket inside the shirt.[86]

It is easy to attribute the variation in fabrics to circumstances of irregular supply in the Confederacy. Coupled, however, with style variations in the shirts—interior pockets, ruched panels, decorative stitching—and comments in soldiers' letters, it is clear that desire for personalization accounts for many of these variations. Elaborate embroidered designs on guerrillas' shirts, for instance, "articulated the bond between a particular guerrilla and a female supporter."[87] Some women employed decorative stitching to personalize even shirts made from the coarsest quality of cloth. A dark blue wool shirt worn by a Confederate soldier, for instance, has decorative cream-colored stitching on the pocket, cuffs, collar, buttonholes, and breast—none of which was necessary for its construction.[88]

When soldiers in the conventional army wore individualized shirts beneath their brass-buttoned coats, their brass manhood was both literally and figuratively supported by their engagement in a more intimate manhood rooted in familial duty. Like using one's housewife kit to repair a garment, wearing a personalized shirt connected soldiers to the maker, serving as a material reminder of the inseparable connections between the war front and the home front. Yet those personalized shirts also played a role in the aesthetics of soldiers' style, as they found themselves living together in a hypermasculine environment where the clothes they wore were noticed and remarked upon by other soldiers. In camp and while on fatigue duty, soldiers often unbuttoned or took off their jackets, revealing the shirts they wore beneath. The opinions of other soldiers mattered. A Virginian shipped back home a cap his wife had just sent him because he feared other soldiers "would laugh at the color of it." He understood that his wife did not have a wide selection of materials from which to choose, and he assured her that while "this cap suits me very well about home," he refused to wear it in camp or on the battlefield.[89]

As soldiers attempted to work out the problems of life in the field in relation to their clothing, it became clear that the exigencies of war were creating a context in which some men began to rethink the primacy of brass manhood and placed more value in clothing that was suited for war. Not all soldiers bought into brass manhood, believing that practicality far outweighed concerns over appearance. In the eyes of New York Infantry captain J. Jones, dress coats were "well enough for soldiers in barracs," but they were impractical for soldiers "*in the field*." Jones wrote a letter to the quartermaster general in which he declared that every item used by the army that was "not directly connected with & essential to its complete appointment as an engine to put down the rebellion" should be "*expurgated*." He suggested that long frock coats should be replaced by shorter jackets, and that there should be "*no braid trimming*" on the sleeves. He offered a series of criticisms of dress coats—they were more expensive, more difficult to clean, and "the tails of the dress coat are always in the way on a campaign." The army dress coat, he concluded, was "one of the greatest monstrosities in the shape of clothing I ever saw."[90] Jones's attitude toward the "monstrosity" of gold braid does not seem to have been widely held. His general concern about the connection between clothing and soldiers' ability to put down the rebellion, on the other hand, was widely debated.

"Iron Clad" Men

Ideas about victory, manhood, and clothing collided on both the battlefront and the home front when it came to the production, marketing, and use of one particular kind of garment: the bulletproof vest.[91] The sale and purchase of such body armor were highly regionalized, with its use primarily, though not exclusively, limited to US soldiers, offering a window into debates over Northern conceptions of manhood. Through their rhetoric, armor advertisers crafted a particular vision of the war—one in which the relationship between the soldier and the state need not be one of martyrdom. Advertisements celebrated not the citizen-soldier whose duty it was to sacrifice his life, but the professional soldier who embraced the bravery, strength, and grit of the battlefield and whose duty it was to live to fight another day, end the war, and return to his home unscathed. As Gerald Linderman has shown, the overwhelming number of casualties and a shift toward the military expediency of fighting behind entrenchments eroded the culture of courage that was so prominent in 1861.[92] It was in this context that advertisers could simultaneously tug at the heartstrings of families and friends at home and appeal to the logic of military strategy. In this formulation, it was not only a man's patriotic duty but also his familial and manly duties to protect his life. "There were a good many men," John Billings recalled after the war, "who were anxious to be heroes, but they were particular. They preferred to be *live* heroes. They were willing to go to war and fight as never man fought before, if they could only be insured against bodily harm."[93]

"Iron tailors," as Billings referred to them, attempted to assuage the "situation and sufferings" of these men by manufacturing bulletproof garments. As one soldier wrote, "To be 'iron clad' when the bullets should fly as thick as hail! What more could a soldier ask?"[94] For many of these soldiers, their primary concern was the effectiveness of armored garments; others, however, needed to be assured both that armor was effective *and* that wearing a bulletproof garment did not undermine their claims to manhood and patriotism. Advertisers responded by actively working to simultaneously convince potential buyers that bulletproof technology was worthwhile, and to distance steel garments from the taint of cowardice by suggesting that wearing armor was, in fact, the more patriotic and manly decision—and that it could be worn secretly. Claims about the ability to hide the use of a vest and the manliness of wearing it seem antithetical. But given the emphasis nineteenth-century society placed on the outward appearance of clothing in judging character, the ability to hide its use from others is best understood as a marketing ploy used at a time of flux in cultural attitudes toward bodily protection in battle. During a war in which men were forced en masse to confront battlefield deaths, such marketing could appeal to soldiers who believed they should protect themselves with armor yet were conflicted over how others might view them.

One particularly extensive advertisement in the New Haven, Connecticut, *Columbian Register* for G. D. Cook and Company's bulletproof vest—an entire broadsheet column in length—captured the range of arguments advertisers used in marketing the use of body armor as manly and patriotic.[95] Attempting to preserve one's life, advertisers implied, was a sign of a man's true devotion to the nation, and would, therefore, enable a soldier to achieve greater valor in battle. In this view, armor-clad soldiers were more powerful and valuable to their country. The Cook and Company advertisement claimed that General Stoneman, a well-known cavalryman, had instructed the advertiser to tell soldiers that "I wear one, for if my life is worth giving to my country, it is worth preserving for my country and family."[96]

This appeal to the importance of the family, the protection and support of which factored into many men's understanding of manhood, extended to calls upon family members to return that protection. "Where is the wife who would not make almost any sacrifice to feel sure that her husband would be returned to her alive?" asked one advertisement.[97] Friends and family members did indeed purchase and gift armor to departing soldiers. The friends of Lieutenant Lyon, for instance, "bestowed on him a handsome sword, sash, belt, pistol, shoulder-straps, and *steel vest*": a sign, one of his comrades wrote, that those friends "have had an eye not only to his adornment and effectiveness, but to his safe return."[98] Another soldier's wife was prepared to purchase a vest for him, but he informed her that he wanted only "a military vest to keep me warm, without any steel in it. I am not afraid of the bullets."[99] At least a few benefactors outfitted entire regiments with protective armor, including one Massachusetts man who presented a bulletproof vest to each man in the Thirty-Seventh Massachusetts. Elisha Hunt Rhodes noted that the regiment was referred to as "the 'iron clads,' because when they arrived every man had a steel plate in his vest."[100]

Advertisers also attempted to convince soldiers that although bulletproof garments might seem a new and novel technology, the use of steel armor was more generally becoming part of everyday life. To protect oneself with a vest, one advertisement asserted, was no different than serving on an ironclad gunboat, or fighting from behind the walls of a fort—they were all simply good military tactics: "Does any one call Admiral Foote or Lieut. Worden cowards because they fought in iron-clad gunboats?"[101] The advertisers acknowledged outright that men would associate armor with cowardice. But to do so, they suggested, was simply evidence that a man was a new, inexperienced recruit. The advertisement claimed that, according to a Union general, only "men not accustomed to war will call it cowardly to wear a bullet proof vest."[102]

Some soldiers agreed with the rationalizations presented in advertisements, especially in regard to preserving their lives for the sake of their families. In late March 1862, for instance, Illinois officer John Cheney wrote home to his wife Mary about recent happenings in camp. "I think they are a good thing and may buy one," he relayed.[103] Likewise, drummer Thaddeus Reynolds declared, "When I get to Elmira I am going to buy me an army steel plated vest."[104] Many, however, were still anxious about the potential accusations of weakness and were defensive about their decision to purchase armor. Captain William Vermillion, for instance, told his wife of his purchase, explaining that "I intend to wear it, not through cowardice but because I consider it my duty to protect myself in every manner possible." An intense feeling of responsibility for preserving his life had led him to wear the vest, but, still, Vermillion instructed his wife, "Don't speak of it to anyone, Dollie. The boys here don't know it."[105] This desire to wear protective garments, yet hide their use from one's comrades, was an element seized by advertisers in their marketing ploys.

Soldiers with reservations about the potential association between armor and cowardice were assured that the garments had the "appearance precisely the same as the regular Military Vest" and that the metal plates were "entirely concealed."[106] Advertisers went so far as to refer to them as "Secret Steel Breast Plates" or "Secret Armor."[107] Indeed the illustration that accompanied the advertisement for the "Soldiers' Bullet Proof Vest" portrayed a typical military vest, complete with a collar, watch pockets, and brass buttons.[108] Vests surviving in museum collections confirm the assessment of one soldier, who described them as "nothing more than ordinary vests with metal plates between the lining and outside of the front of the vest."[109]

While a few proponents of bulletproof garments overtly confronted the question of cowardice, whether by promising that the vests would go undetected or by proclaiming the bravery of those men who chose to wear them, other advertisers approached this conundrum using tendentious, coded language, emphasizing the strength, power, value—and thereby, manliness—a soldier could gain from using a bulletproof vest. Body armor, advertisers claimed, had the ability to confer manliness upon a soldier—"the soldier protected" was "twice the man as the soldier exposed."[110] Furthermore, a soldier who wore a bulletproof vest would "return a wiser and stronger man."[111] By this estimation,

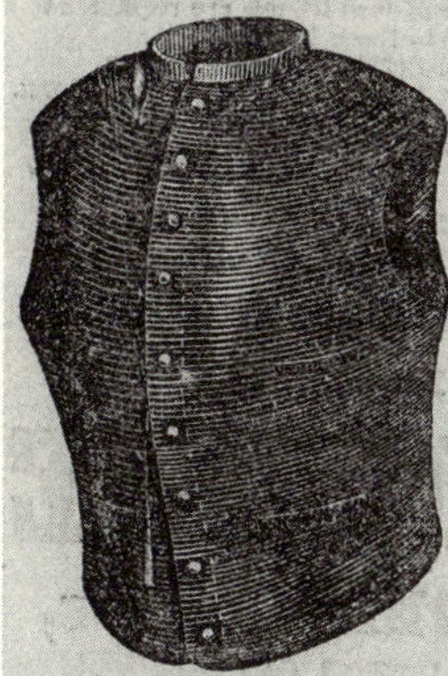

The Soldiers' Bullet Proof Vest

Has been repeatedly and thoroughly tested with Pistol Bullets at 10 paces, Rifle Bullets at 40 rods, by many Army Officers, and is approved and worn by them.

It is simple, light, and is a true economy of life — it will save thousands. It will also double the value and power of the soldier; and every man in an army is entitled to its protection. Nos. 1, 2, and 3 express the sizes of men, and No. 2 fits nearly all.

Price for Privates' Vest, $5. Officers' Vest, $7. They will be sent to any address, wholesale or retail.

Sold by MESSRS. ELLIOTT, No. 231 Broadway, New York, and by all Military Stores. Agents wanted.

Advertisement for "The Soldiers' Bullet Proof Vest," *Harper's Weekly,* March 15, 1862. Courtesy of the American Antiquarian Society, Worcester, MA.

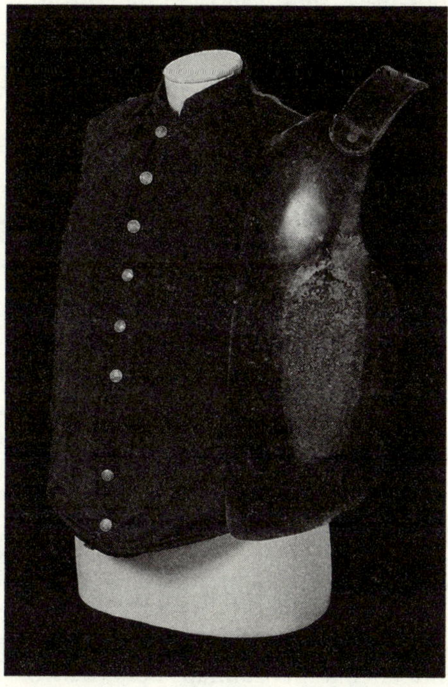

Bulletproof vest, manufactured by G. D. Cook and Company, New Haven, CT, and sold as the Soldiers' Bullet Proof Vest, c. 1861–65. Courtesy of the Pitt Rivers Museum, University of Oxford, Oxford, UK.

the garment had the power not only to improve a man's physical strength, posture, and physique, but also to strengthen his inner resolve. Garments possessed the ability to steel both a soldier's body *and* his mind against attacks from the enemy, thereby *emphasizing*—not undermining—his manliness and grit. "Let the soldier feel that he can defy bullet and bayonet," declared an advertisement in *Frank Leslie's Illustrated Newspaper*, "and he will carry everything before him."[112] It was precisely in these terms that an incident was relayed concerning the successful use of a bulletproof vest during the Battle of Oak Grove, Virginia. After one lieutenant who was wearing a "steel-plated" vest was struck by two bullets in the chest, "he frankly confesses that when he discovered the first ball did not hurt him, he 'was ten times as brave' as he had been."[113]

Importantly, the material object itself and the technology used to manufacture it conferred this strength and value upon a man by exacting a physical transformation on the body and manipulating his posture. Judgments about a person's character and station in life were made on the basis of their posture and the way in which they carried themselves. A tall, erect posture conveyed discipline, self-worth, and manliness.[114] Mid-century writers and illustrators frequently depicted failed men as stooped beggars, and images of slumped, shuffling slaves reflected developing theories in phrenology and physical anthropology that linked race, body shape, and upright posture to gender and intelligence.[115] According to advertisers, the bulletproof vest had an advantage over ordinary vests: It would keep "the wearer erect," adding "grace and dignity to his *form*."[116] This image of the soldier standing tall, both supported and empowered by his steel vest, directly countered that of the hunched soldier "skulking behind" his armor.

The material components of the vest provided the means of physical, and thereby inner, transformation. Rigid metal plates worn over the breast and secured by hooks or leather straps on the shoulders required a soldier to stand straight, lest the plates press uncomfortably into his abdomen or the straps become dislodged from his shoulders. Other styles of armor, with straps that bound the metal to the man's body, encased the body and had a similar effect on a man's ability to stand straight. Through his erect posture, advertisers claimed, the soldier exuded a new confidence to his comrades that he wore into battle.

In addition to asserting control over the body's movement, the materiality of bulletproof vests of Smith's design was also important to their concealment. The steel breastplates were said to be expertly made such that they could be "so neatly fitted inside of a military vest as not to be noticeable."[117] In actuality, when considering how the vest as a material object would have fit

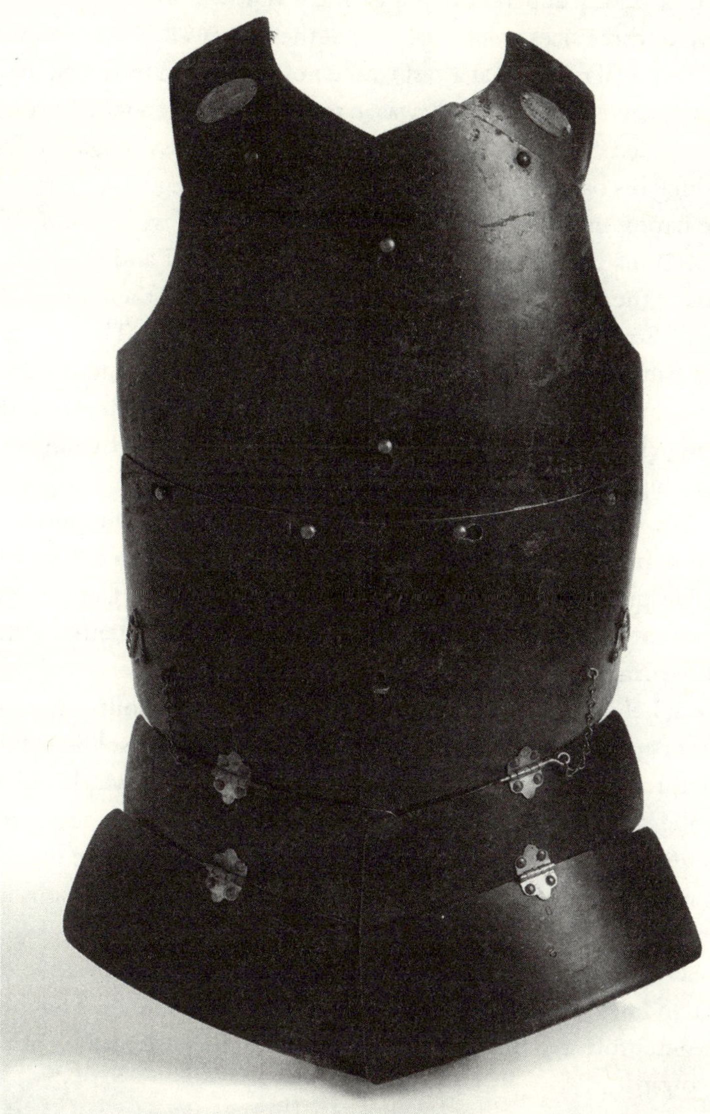

Manufactured by the Atwater Armor Company in New Haven, CT, this Adjustable Armor was made of four interlocking plates of japanned sheet iron, to which two optional sets of double-hinged panels could be attached to serve as hinges that permitted the legs to flex, while still protecting the pelvis. Straps and buckles attached to the sides of the armor allowed for it to be tightened, or "adjusted," around a man's torso. The armor could be disassembled into six single panels that could then be placed into a knapsack during a march. Body armor owned by Brigadier General William G. LeDuc, manufactured by Atwater Armor Company, New Haven, CT, c. 1862. Used with permission from the Minnesota Historical Society, Minneapolis, MN.

the body, it is readily apparent that a garment that was available in a maximum of two or three sizes would not have fit the body well. Furthermore, the rigidity of the metal meant that a vest would not move with the body, thereby belying its presence when the body was in motion. And even when a vest was entirely concealed, were a soldier to die, his "secret cuirass" could be found out, tarnishing his bravery and honor in battle, and placing his willingness to die for the nation into question. Soldiers wearing armor were found on numerous occasions having died from wounds to the head and other unprotected areas of the body, or because bullets had perforated their armor. After the Battle of South Mountain, for instance, troops of the Thirtieth Ohio walked the battleground, where they "found an officer of a South Carolina regiment in a breast plate of hardened steel, thick and heavy, after the fashion of old, fitting close up the neck and under the armpits, and reaching to the waist, with a bullet through his forehead."[118]

By late 1863, while they may have continued to be available for purchase in stores or from peddlers, protective garments seem to have faded from advertisements. Despite a shift away from frontal assaults in massed columns in the latter half of the war, the questionable effectiveness and potential physical danger of wearing body armor outweighed the increasing acceptability of fighting from behind protected entrenchments.[119] Indeed, contrary to *Scientific American*'s positive assessment of this technology, many soldiers did not find a bulletproof vest to be "very strong in proportion to its weight."[120] Hot, heavy, cumbersome objects that were only marginally effective, such protective garments did not fulfill advertisers' promises. Certainly some men were saved by the use of steel breastplates, but others suffered painful deaths when bullets tore through the metal encasing their chests. The rigid steel plates improved the erectness of a man's posture, but their awkward fit slowed soldiers' movement and made marching uncomfortable. While some men felt bolder in battle when protected by steel, most shrunk from its use for fear of being labeled a coward.

The account of Major Sidney Willard's death illustrates these conflicted cultural attitudes toward bulletproof vests. According to his eulogist, Cyrus A. Bartol, Willard was wearing armor when a minié ball struck his steel breastplate, "became flattened, glanced off, and entered the groin," causing him to fall off his horse and onto his face. Willard died of his bullet wound "calm and easy" in the field hospital—viewed as a sign of his soul's peace. Nevertheless, his eulogist found it necessary to assert that Willard wore the steel vest only because it was given to him "as a token from Col. Wild," an officer whom he greatly respected. Willard, the eulogist continued, "would not have worn [body armor] of his own accord," citing the fact that prior to this skirmish, he had "carried it on his saddle."[121] Indeed, by his own admission Willard "did not own or wear a steel vest" prior to receiving Wild's gift.[122] Willard wore the armor not out of fear, Bartol implied, but, rather, out of gratitude for the gift. This miscalculated decision, Bartol asserted, should not overshadow the fact that Willard was "a brave, noble man, and a good commander" who was "well prepared" to "lay down his life for his country!"[123] In doing so, the eulogist attempted to offer a resolution to the tension between Willard's use of armor and the bravery of his death.

Even in the failure of bulletproof technology, the discourses surrounding its manufacture, marketing, use, and abandonment reveal the blurred boundaries and definitions of manhood, duty, and cultural aspects of death. This was a culture astride two ages: a moment in which competing ideals of manhood and duty coexisted—one that demanded the bold sacrifice of life for the sake of the nation, and another emerging culture in which the protection of life was paramount. Such conflicting ideas of manhood are embodied by the contrasting images of the wartime martyr and the timid, skulking, armor-wearing soldier. Soldiers debated, rather than outright rejected, the use of body armor, suggesting that the culture of the Good Death that pervaded the antebellum era was not altogether entrenched.[124] To the contrary, it was beginning to be questioned early in the war and not merely after four years of bloodshed. Men desired to protect themselves yet feared the implications of dying in a "steel cuirass," which would call into question their preparedness to die and place into limbo their families' assumptions about the state of their soul. And yet, advertisers challenged the idea that patriotic duty required an unflinching willingness to die for one's country. These advertisers, in much the same way as did authors of popular wartime literature, helped to direct and shape readers' and consumers' responses to the war.[125]

By promoting bulletproof garments, advertisers created a context in which Americans began to imagine how using technology to preserve one's life could be considered a noble and manly act, one that increased the "value" of the soldier to both his country and his family. To confront the enemy was certainly brave and manly, but to protect oneself from the enemy conveyed an even stronger sense of the meaning of manhood and commitment to both nation and family. Some soldiers, in spite of the derision underlying taunts about wearing "iron stoves" or wearing armor on their backsides, bought into these advertisers' claims in the midst of suffering, death, and loss. And yet, their hesitancy to embrace bulletproof vests and attempts to hide the use of protective garments from comrades reveal cultural tensions over sacrifice.

This was a shifting, but not yet fully altered, culture in which death and manhood were intertwined. The rhetoric armor advertisers injected into the popular press contributed to a discourse in which it became possible to imagine, but not yet fully realize, the compatibility of patriotism and protecting a soldier's mortality using new forms of technology. Despite the manufacture of ordinary military vests with steel plates, armor and brass manhood remained incompatible for US soldiers.

Could brass manhood survive the war? At war's end, there were certainly ragged Confederate soldiers lacking shoes and wearing worn-out pants. Nevertheless, many Confederates were supplied throughout the war. In late 1864, for instance, Confederate Jim McFall continued to be concerned with both battlefront style and his participation in brass manhood, even in the final months of the war—a moment in which, according to the dominant historical narrative of Confederate scarcity, he should have been concerned with anything *but* the style and polish of his clothing. He instructed his sister that he would like decorative cord on his new uniform coat, writing, "If you can get some cord I would prefer it to cuffs & collar I expect Bob could get some in Columbia [SC] you will understand where I want the cord around the place where the cuffs would be."[126] New buttons, too, were needed. "I expect you had better get Bob to send to Columbia for some staff buttons," he wrote. If enough South Carolina "Palmetto buttons can be gathered up," he noted, "they will do." However, Jim wanted to be sure that gold lace would be affixed to the sleeves of the coat, denoting his promotion to the rank of first lieutenant, and instructed his sister on where she would find that lace at home. When his new uniform arrived one month later, shipped from South Carolina to Richmond, Jim declared that his new suit of clothes "fits vry well I am vry proud of it I put them all on this morning and I feel once more like a white man."[127]

The centrality of uniforms and brass buttons to gendering men and women in wartime culture was not limited to either the North or the South. This was a shared material culture of gender, patriotism, and military prowess that was recognized on all sides of this conflict. Because this brass manhood was so prominent throughout the North and South, it was, as we will see, also a potent material object by which to assert control over one's enemy. At the end of the war, the US government denied former Confederates the right to continue to participate in that brass manhood. In response, those former Confederates—men and women—would create an alternative definition of manhood that no longer relied on brass or the pomp and circumstance of war.

But in 1864, when Jim McFall declared that his new uniform, complete with gold lace, stripes, and brass buttons, made him look "like a white man," he sought to distinguish himself from the African American men to whom he considered himself superior. Yet the uniform as a mark of distinction reserved only for white men was challenged and overturned during the war. Black men's fight for their right to take part in the culture of brass manhood drew manhood, race, and the government into tension with one another in unprecedented ways, simultaneously complicating and heightening the cultural significance of brass buttons in the context of war.

Brass manhood remained the dominant public culture of manhood during the war, but it was one part of a larger story of changing and competing visions of masculinity during the war. Compatible and reinforcing, but also sometimes conflicting, visions of manhood existed among governments, soldiers, and civilian society. The brass manhood embraced by the Union and Confederacy at the beginning of the war was challenged by the difficulty of maintaining it on the battlefield, and another conception of manhood defined by the more intimate relationships among family members emerged alongside it. In the North, so, too, did a manhood emerge that valued not the bravado of the battlefield or the martyred, brass-buttoned officer, but, rather, the soldier's commitment to preserving his life for the sake of both family and nation. These visions of manhood were created and expressed through the garments men wore—through brass-buttoned coats, brightly colored shirts, and body armor.

None of this—from ruched shirts to government-issued drawers—was possible without the people and skills that produced cloth and clothing. As textiles became critical war matériel, their production became newly politicized and the women who worked at looms and with needles emerged as both patriotic supporters of the nation and enemies of the state.

CHAPTER TWO

To Make War upon Women

Producing Clothes for War

On July 6, 1864, US general William Sherman and his army reached the town of Roswell, Georgia, twenty miles north of Atlanta. There, along the hilly banks of Vickery Creek rose textile mills and factories flying British and French flags. Suspicious of this claim of neutrality, a US Army officer dismounted from his horse and stepped into the factory. Deafened by the din of whirling spindles and clanging machinery running at full capacity, the officer and his men walked through the rows of over 200 looms, where more than 400 white women and children were producing heavy cloth amid bits of wool, cotton, and dust filling the air, the tiny particles choking their lungs. As the millworkers cast furtive glances toward the soldiers, the officer reached out to one of the looms and lifted a piece of cloth—"a very little investigation showed that on each Webb, of piece, the cabalistic letters, C.S.A., were woven in the wool." At his order, the machines whirled to a stop.[1]

As the workers cleared the factory, US soldiers carried thousands of yards of finished cloth deemed suitable for US Army and hospital use from the building.[2] When they finished, the soldiers saturated raw cotton with oil and lit a spark. As flames licked at the sides of the building, soldiers followed Sherman's orders to "arrest the owners and employees and send them, under guard, charged with treason." Sherman was adamant that laborers with manufacturing skills were "as much prisoners as if armed." And, lest his instructions be misunderstood, he ordered the officers to "arrest all people, male and female, connected with those factories, no matter what the clamor." Soldiers loaded female factory workers and a few male supervisors onto railcars bound for the North. "The poor women will make a howl," Sherman cautioned. "Let them take along their children and clothing, provided they have a means of hauling or you can spare them."[3] The Roswell millworkers' crime was their work in making gray woolen cloth that would ultimately be sewn into uniforms or otherwise used by the Confederate army. These workers were complicit in supplying materials that maintained the Confederate army and civilians.

The hundreds of Roswell millworkers sent north were but one part of a much larger system of wartime clothing production that supplied the US and Confederate armies with the materials to make war. Civil War–era uniform supply has traditionally been situated in the context of the high-level provisioning of armies, government contracts, the celebrated efforts of women's patriotic sewing circles, and, to a lesser extent, families supplying clothing for their husbands, sons, and brothers.[4] Beginning with the level of the initial manufacture of cloth, to understand what exactly went into making the uniforms cut from it, twists the kaleidoscope, revealing a larger cast of historical actors involved in military clothing production. At the center of this work were interconnected networks of textile factory workers, spinners, weavers, tailors, cutters, quartermasters, government contractors, women's patriotic sewing societies, and seamstresses, including working-class and enslaved women and children.[5]

For some women, uniform production was the answer to the question of how to survive changes in their family's economic support. For others, it presented an opportunity to make further gains in civic spaces or claims upon the government. Tailors received no specific military service exemptions, and many served in the army; some who remained on the home front may have been older than the conscription age, while others worked directly for the government. These men reimagined their businesses to meet the needs of a citizen-soldier clientele, while longtime US Army seamstresses, like those at Philadelphia's Schuylkill Arsenal, found their jobs at risk when the work of uniform production was newly imbued with patriotic meaning and transformed into a form of public welfare for soldiers' wives. For the Roswell textile workers, the mill's 1861 pivot to supply the Confederate army with cloth held the promise of ensuring their families' economic stability during wartime, but, by war's end, it had prompted the dissolution of those families and the utter destruction of the world as they knew it.

In 1860 sewing was typically understood as a domestic chore whose work occurred within the confines of the household or was a respectable occupation for working women, but it took on complex political meaning in the context of governmental need to supply clothing to armies. Political implications were reenforced and expanded as elite and middling-class women embraced the opportunity to see their sewing contributions elevated to and praised on the national stage. But as working-class women labored to make cloth and sew uniforms that were critical to wartime supply, they became embroiled in another kind of warfare that centered on women's roles and relationships to one another and to the government. Throughout the United States, the production of military cloth and clothing was a flashpoint in the war's larger, gendered conflicts over labor, loyalty, treason, and belonging.

The gendered production of cloth and clothing—and the narratives crafted around this labor—also articulate the longer, more nuanced trajectory of both

Northern and Southern women's engagement in a range of capacities with the government and its officials. Through cooperation, clashes, and discourses surrounding clothing, relationships between the government and private citizens were tested and negotiated. Contact with the government ranged from dealing with individual officers and local clothing depot quartermasters and tailors, to contact with state governors and high-ranking officials in both the federal and Confederate governments. For these women, it was not only their relationships to male soldiers, or their own loyalty or sacrifice, but also their *skills* that drew them into interactions with the government. What mattered was their physical ability to card, spin, weave, sew, knit, and—while it typically went unacknowledged—compel enslaved women and command domestic servants to do those same tasks. Women encountered both conflict and violence in their interactions with the government; they also engaged in cooperative—even collaborative—relationships with it. Those relationships were defined by a culturally gendered set of skills centered on sewing. Patriotic sewing societies' work in solidifying the perceived relationship between loyalty and sewing also had consequences for working-class women in both the North and South whose jobs involved textile and clothing production. These various interactions and the importance the government placed on women's textile skills had important implications not only for women's wartime experiences but also for how their work was valued by society and remembered in popular culture. Evolving governmental attitudes toward women's work resulted in the public elevation of some women's experiences and the simultaneous erasure of others.

Prior to the Civil War, women communicated infrequently with government officials and, when they did, addressed a limited number of topics. War, however, increased the necessity and frequency of citizens' communications and encounters with the government.[6] In their efforts to disentangle Southern women's relationship to the government's increasing visibility in everyday life, scholars have tended to focus on experiences of Union occupation.[7] However, Southern women's conflicts with the US Army and government were situated within a much broader context of their expectations for, demands of, and quarrels with local and state governments as well as Confederate officials. If we lengthen our purview to encompass the 1860s and 1870s, women's conflicts with the government related to wartime clothing production appear less like anomalies of wartime occupation and, instead, as a sustained struggle punctuated by flashpoints over the state's shifting recognition of women's political personhood. In their work as seamstresses, millworkers, and sewing society members, women had an active, if not always overtly intentional, role in shaping the dimensions of the state's developing relationship to individual citizens.

Textile and clothing production was central to how many people—and especially women—lived out the American Civil War: a way through which they both tackled war's opportunities and acutely experienced war's costs.[8]

Making Cloth

The outbreak of war presented a monumental task: producing the coats, pants, shirts, drawers, socks, shoes, buttons, and other accoutrements that made up the military uniforms that were central both to shoring up allegiances and to clothing soldiers' bodies. The logistics of outfitting men with clothing proved complicated and difficult; the modern apparatus to efficiently provision large armies did not yet exist. The war economy and systems of supply in both the North and South were quite decentralized, evolved over the course of the war, and involved public and private enterprise on both sides of the conflict.[9] Indeed, not only the quartermaster general of the US Army, but also the quartermasters of each individual state, placed orders for thousands of uniforms in 1861.[10] Federal, state, community, and family-based efforts combined to support the Union and Confederate armies—neither of which was prepared to clothe the thousands of men who volunteered to fight for their respective causes. In April 1861 the US government was equipped to supply only the regular army—a force of 17,000 men. By June, quartermaster operations had increased twentyfold to outfit a rapidly expanding Union army of over 500,000 men. In 1865, the total strength of federal forces exceeded 1,000,000.[11] Supplying the amount of clothing required by these men during four years of war was an unprecedented undertaking. During the first year of the war alone, the US Quartermaster's Department purchased 1,281,522 greatcoats, 1,446,811 uniform coats, and 3,039,286 pairs of trousers, not to mention nearly 1.5 million blankets and 230,000 canvas tents.[12] In the South, too, manufacturers accelerated production. Arkansas textile manufacturer Henry Merrell, for instance, increased his mill's production of cotton and woolen goods and hired 100 women to weave and sew, enabling the daily production of 400 suits of clothing. During a six-month period in 1862–63, the Atlanta Depot produced 37,000 uniforms and 90,000 cotton shirts while three depots in Mississippi were producing 2,000 uniforms per week. All this was supplemented by packages of clothing sent to the battlefront by families and soldiers' aid societies.[13]

The production of such clothing depended, of course, on steady access to textiles. The complicated nature of textile and clothing manufacture transgressed Northern and Southern, Union and Confederate boundaries. Northern mills led the nation in industrial-scale textile manufacturing, and ready-made clothing manufactories were well established.[14] But Southern states, too, had an expanding network of textile manufactories that were well equipped to supply cloth for the war effort.

Woolens like those produced at Roswell were preferred over cotton goods for both outerwear and socks because of their durability, insulating qualities, and ability to wick moisture away from the body. Northern states had greater capacity to supply woolen goods due to a larger sheep population and ready trade with the British woolens industry, but Southern states, too, had significant wool-producing capacity. This was especially the case for communities located along the Appalachian mountain range in Georgia, Maryland, North Carolina, Tennessee, and Virginia—the geography of which made farming difficult but sheep-raising lucrative. Indeed, by 1860, several Appalachian counties alone were manufacturing textiles from 2,461,198 pounds of cotton and 1,126,277 pounds of wool—half of which was exported to regional and distant markets.[15]

Contrary to widely held beliefs about the rudimentary nature of Southern textile manufacturing, an expanding, vibrant system of textile mills produced cotton and woolen goods throughout the prewar South, especially in Georgia, North Carolina, South Carolina, Arkansas, Tennessee, and Virginia.[16] Indeed, textile production was the fourth most important category of Southern Appalachian industry, encompassing the manufacture of cloth, calico printing, wool carding, and the production of finished clothing goods.[17] In an 1864 survey, thirty-one mills located in Georgia, Alabama, and South Carolina confirmed producing more than 20 million yards of goods annually, including 1.5 million yards of woolen goods—the equivalent of 250,000 uniforms. Dozens of smaller mills were also in operation, but their output was not recorded in the survey.[18]

Expertise developed in New England textile mills played a critical role in the development, management, and labor force of many of these Southern textile mills. Numerous Southern mills adopted the Northern system of using white female labor, supplementing that labor force with enslaved workers. We tend to think of Northerners and Southerners as firmly rooted in a regional or political identity, but migration was common in the years leading up to the Civil War. With the outbreak of war, people from all social classes discovered themselves on one side or the other of a secessionist line. Many would have understood themselves as Unionists or Southern sympathizers, but for some people—especially those whose economic resources were tied to their current location—living in the South or the North was simply their reality. The war brought a decades-long circulation of people, goods, machinery, and textile manufacturing knowledge between North and South to a grinding halt.

Consider, for example, the Roswell Manufacturing Company, founded by Roswell King—a native New Englander—outside Atlanta, Georgia.[19] In 1860, Roswell Mills employed in key management positions several men who were originally from New England or the Mid-Atlantic region.[20] The mills' machinery was designed and produced by a Northern firm, Rogers, Ketchum, and Grosvenor.[21] In fact, King's own son spent two and a half years learning the manufacturing business at this Paterson, New Jersey, firm, returning to Roswell to build and operate a woolens factory.[22] Not only management, but also female employees, had Northern ties: Millworkers included native Southern women, but also immigrants who traveled to Georgia by way of the Northeast and Mid-Atlantic regions. These networks of knowledge translated into networks of transaction. Although located in rural Georgia, by 1860, the Roswell Manufacturing Company was drawing on personal connections and business networks to distribute goods to buyers in other Southern states, as well as Northern cities, including Baltimore, Philadelphia, and Newark.[23] Indeed, as late as February 22, 1861, four days after Georgia seceded from the Union, the mills' owner was corresponding about providing textiles to the Philadelphia market.[24] The start of the war disrupted not only trade in raw and finished goods, but also the movement of people and their knowledge.

War brought an immediate need for cloth throughout the South, and the King family found their "business matters very snug." At the beginning of the war the Roswell Manufacturing Company was the central employer around which the town of Roswell was organized and upon which its inhabitants relied. Four stories high, the mill facilitated all steps in cloth production: Picking and packing were performed on the fourth floor, which opened onto a village street. The cotton was carded on the third floor, spun on the second, and woven on the first. Local women working in the mills produced yarn, rope, and a range of fabrics, including tenting, flannel, and a cotton/wool blend known as Roswell Grey. "We are running the looms full time," Barrington King wrote in May 1861, "and make 4500 yds per day. Good demand this spring for all our cloth."[25] Demand far outpaced the mills' production capacity. The woolen mill, King noted, "cannot fill orders, had to decline one for 20,000 yds from Tennessee."[26] US brigadier general Kenner Garrard recorded Roswell Mill's production rates in July 1864, just before Sherman's advancing army burned the mills. "There were some fine factories here," he wrote. One woolen factory, capacity 30,000 yards a month, and has furnished up to within a few weeks 15,000 yards per month to the rebel Government. Capacity of cotton factory 216 looms, 191,086 yards per month and 51,666 pounds of thread, and 4,229 pounds of cotton rope. This was worked exclusively for the rebel Government.... There was six months' supply of cotton on hand." There was cloth, Garrard wrote, "that had been made since yesterday morning, which I will save for our hospital (several thousand yards of cotton cloth)."[27] Such a narrative runs counter to the accepted assumption that Southern cloth production was minimal before the war and that the Union army's hard war paralyzed supply. Indeed, with its supply and workers, Roswell Mills could have continued production well into 1865.

Making Clothes

As textile workers wove cotton and wool into bolts of cloth, seamstresses, tailors, and cutters throughout the North and South worked to measure, cut, and sew that cloth into army uniforms. In the process, sewing—once considered a household chore, enslaved women's work, or one of only a few occupations deemed by society to be acceptable for white women—became politicized. Some white women actively worked to politicize sewing, seizing the opportunity to increase their voice and presence in the civic sphere. Others combatted new barriers resulting from that politicization that impeded their ability to support themselves and their families. In both Northern and Southern postwar reminiscences, elite and middle-class women prided themselves on their "sacrifices" for their respective causes, highlighting their roles in the formation of soldiers' aid societies, sewing uniforms and battle flags, and picking lint for wound dressings. However, although they were memorialized in song and poetry, these efforts represented only one subset of the textile work in which women engaged. A diverse range of sewing women, along with male cutters (who specialized in cutting fabric) and tailors, were responsible for the implementation of large-scale uniform production in both the North and South.

Their motivations for sewing were numerous. Enslaved women were ordered to weave and sew for both the Confederate government and private use. Work that some white women considered a patriotic contribution, others relied upon for financial support. Seamstresses were paid by families to sew uniforms for their husbands, sons, and fathers. Women living near quartermaster depots took up piecework for the government, sewing together fabric cut out by male cutters. Wage-earning women in both the North and South were employed by privately owned clothing and textile manufacturing firms, as well as by state-run clothing bureaus and warehouses. Occasionally, impoverished soldiers' wives and widows were employed by soldiers' aid societies as a form of relief.[28] Some women sewed for the duration of the war, while others did so only periodically as necessity or opportunity dictated.

Soldiers' aid societies have garnered an outsized place in narratives about wartime clothing production. While some were quite essential in initially fitting up local companies, others wasted hundreds of hours sewing havelocks—neck coverings attached to hats—that were quickly discarded. In the course of the war, sewing reemerged as a mark of pride for elite women. This was not the intricate sewing associated with embroidery—that female art had retained its social power. Instead, it was a willingness to learn and engage in the practical tasks of marking patterns, cutting fabric, and plain sewing that became a mark of patriotic expression. Recounting the stories of aid societies risks reinforcing an inflated sense of these societies' material contributions to the war. In reality, the vast majority of soldiers' clothing was produced by army depots, manufacturers, and family members. However, understanding the attention afforded to these societies both during and following the war is critical to understanding the cultural significance of the wartime politicization of clothing manufacture and other flashpoints around sewing women's labor. It is an opportunity, too, to restore to this well-worn narrative the work of the enslaved women and the working-class and poor white women whose hands were responsible for much of the output of these societies—societies to which they themselves would never have gained admittance as full members.

As middle-class and elite women threw their support into the wartime provisioning of armies and formed soldiers' aid societies, they embraced patriotic rhetoric to describe their work. Recurring comparisons to the American Revolution in both Confederate and Union propaganda evidenced a shared national culture rooted in the memory of the Revolutionary experience that celebrated elite white women's relationship to wartime support—both in their material contributions and in sending men to war. Women were urged to "look to the example of their revolutionary foremothers, to make the family and domestic sacrifices that the country required."[29] In Georgia, Governor Joseph Brown called upon "the ladies, whose fervent patriotism, burning zeal, and energetic action in our glorious struggle, rekindle in our minds the memories of the immortal women of the Revolution of 1776."[30] Northerners rejoiced "always to hear that our friends are patriotic—how the blood of '76 still courses through their veins."

The patriotism of 1776 might have been rekindled, but women's ability to sew and knit varied extensively. Elite women throughout the nation tended to be well versed in needlework, but not the "plain sewing" skills required for garment construction. And so they suddenly found themselves learning to knit and sew, often struggling with the tasks. In contrast to women who stitched for a living or regularly repaired their family's clothing, young women attending the Lasell Seminary in Auburndale, Massachusetts, made "bungling mistakes" as they worked on soldiers' clothing.[31] One Philadelphia woman noted that her ladies' group had begun "talking about knitting" but acknowledged that "we will have to learn as none of us know how."[32] Another woman was very proud to be able to write, "I have learned to knit on purpose to knit socks for the soldiers. This is my fourth pair."[33]

In the South, enslaved women were compelled to sew for the Confederate army. Formerly enslaved people recounted these seamstresses' work. Nancy Johnson, for instance, remembered being "nearly frostbitten" because "my old Missus made me weave to make clothes for the soldiers till 12 o'clock at night."[34] Many years later, a Works Progress Administration interviewer recorded one man's recollection that his enslaver in Texas "had de women folks on de plantation to make up lots of clothes for de soldiers. I has seen several wagonloads of clothes hauled off from dar at one time."[35]

While many women were engaged in learning how to outfit men for war, elite Confederate women seem to have taken pride in crafting a narrative of helplessness when it came to the process of making clothing. Their narratives often begin with an admission of ignorance about sewing, knitting, weaving, or spinning, then express a willingness to accept the challenge, followed by failure at their first attempt to sew a shirt or knit a sock, and ultimately mastery of the ability to productively contribute to soldiers' provisioning. Floridian Susan Bradford, who was herself a member of a sewing society, wrote, "The women of the South had never known what it was to work with their own hands but now nothing, which could contribute to the welfare of the soldiers, was too hard for them to do. Dainty fingers sewed on uniforms and flannel shirts, and later on, when no cloth could be had from which to make these needed garments, they learned to spin and weave and knit and sew, that their loved ones might be clothed."[36] Such narratives are so common—in both wartime and postwar accounts—that they are a trope of Confederate women's writing.

It often required months of practice for many Confederate sewing society members to become efficient at plain sewing, yet textual evidence shows that elite women were immediately active in "fitting up" companies of soldiers. Certainly many white women were themselves sewing soldiers' shirts, pants, and coats. But "making" uniforms also meant supervising enslaved women as *they* did the sewing.[37] Specific sewing tasks are not frequently mentioned in white women's diaries—they usually note that they "sewed" with the society. However, we can extrapolate from those that *do* detail the work process. Louisianan Kate Stone gathered with a sewing society to cut out cloth, which was then given out to the members to be sewn. Those same sewing society members likely took cut fabric home for enslaved women to sew into uniforms. As a former enslaver recalled, "We had no sewing machines and the work was done by ourselves and our [enslaved] seamstresses. Mine made fourteen pairs of drawers in a week for that [patriotic sewing] association, and never seemed hurried."[38]

The reminiscences and diary excerpts of Susan Bradford help to piece together the relationships between the work of enslaved Black women and white women's sewing societies.[39] When war broke out, Bradford was fifteen or sixteen years old. She and her mother worked with their neighborhood sewing society in which they met "first at one house and then at another, and all of us sew steadily all day long. Mother cuts many of the garments and Mrs. Manning helps her." Two carpenters, Peter and Mack, who were enslaved by the Bradfords, facilitated the packing and transportation of soldiers' clothing by making "packing cases and it is astonishing how many garments go forward from the Bradford neighborhood."[40]

Bradford acknowledged her own lack of sewing skills at the beginning of the war: "I did not know much sewing at first; at the beginning I made Charley Hopkins two flannel shirts but I am ashamed to say Lulu did most of the sewing." Bradford credited herself, writing "I made" the shirts even though Lulu, an enslaved nurse, sewed them.[41] Watching Lulu sew the flannel shirts likely helped Bradford improve her own sewing skills. By April 1862 she claimed, "Now I can take any kind of a garment and make it entire, even the buttonholes, though Sister Mag says my button holes 'gape.' I mean to improve on them."[42] Bradford learned to sew. Nevertheless, how many other shirts that were described as "made" by female enslavers were actually sewn by the women they enslaved? It is impossible to know. But Bradford and other women's descriptions throw into question the attribution of the clothing donated by many elite Confederate sewing societies.

In 1861, a composite photograph was created of twenty-eight members of the Ladies Soldiers Friend Sewing Society, to which Bradford and her mother belonged. At the center of the photograph is a woman with a cotton card in her hand, flanked by two women seated at sewing machines with pieces of cloth. Surrounding the women is an image of neatly stacked piles of bound clothing or blankets flanked by an elegant chair and sewing machine table across which a piece of fabric is draped. From the cotton cards used to work

Photograph of Susan Bradford [Eppes], by Charles P. Walker, 1864, Tallahassee, FL. Courtesy of the State Archives of Florida, Florida Memory.

raw materials, to the sewing machines, to the finished piles of goods stretching into the distance, to the list of women's names, the collage visually asserts that these women were crucial to supplying soldiers. No evidence suggests that anyone other than these white women themselves performed the work of carding cotton, sewing clothes, or readying packages for shipment; the work performed by Mack, Peter, and Lulu has been erased.

In both the North and South, sewing societies claimed the work of white women who were not admitted, indeed would have been refused admission, to the societies' membership. Poor and working-class white women sewed clothing that was distributed by the societies, whose members praised themselves for their good deeds in providing a way for lower-class women to support themselves. Some of the women who sewed and knitted were domestic servants employed by Northern women, including three Irish American servants who knitted socks that their employer claimed as part of her own

Photocollage, Ladies Soldiers Friend Sewing Society, Tallahassee, FL, 1861. Courtesy of the State Archives of Florida, Florida Memory.

contribution.[43] In other instances, the US Sanitary Commission provided fabric and patterns to sewing societies, which distributed the materials to working-class women, paying them wages donated by local benefactors.[44] In South Carolina, Louisa McCord Smythe's sewing society paid poor white women, whom she referred to as "the poor sand-hill women," to sew so that they could earn money while their husbands were in the army. She recalled one woman who requested she be allowed to sew for the company in which her husband served. A "bundle of cut-out work was reached down from the shelf and handed to her. As she took it, there on the outside (each suit was labelled) was her husband's name. Poor thing, she took that bundle of coarse cloth in her arms and cried over it as though it were a part of him!"[45] While this woman had the opportunity to sew clothing for her husband that she would likely have been unable to purchase herself, the majority of women sewed for unnamed men. In the end, it likely made little difference for many of the sewing women, who were motivated more by the promise of income than by contributing to the war effort as an act of patriotism.

Lulu enabled Susan Bradford to participate in the Soldiers Friend Sewing Society and taught her enough plain sewing skills to be able to produce a shirt. But even women who were skilled knitters and seamstresses had much to learn about making clothing that met soldiers' particular needs. As the war ground on and casualties mounted, Northern relief societies soon recognized that soldiers' needs for clothing had changed shape; they required warm winter clothing and garments suitable for hospital use, in addition to the usual jackets, pants, shirts, socks, and drawers to replace those that had initially been provided. To facilitate women's production of warm woolen mittens and hospital slippers, patterns were printed and distributed by Northern soldiers' relief societies, as well as in periodicals, newspapers, and advertisements. When paging through the articles and illustrations of periodicals like *Godey's Lady's Book* and *Peterson's Magazine*, women encountered a series of patterns, recommendations, and illustrations to aid them in providing clothing and related articles to soldiers in the field. These patterns were printed in miniature, often in an arrangement that required a bit of imagination to parse out the various cuts and measures. Such patterns needed to be translated into a larger version, pinned or traced onto fabric, and then cut out. Women who possessed basic sewing skills but needed more information on how to transfer the patterns they found in periodicals could find such instruction in those same periodicals. *Peterson's* responded to the "many new subscribers" who had asked how to transfer patterns printed in the magazine by providing instructions on how to make one's own transfer paper and then trace the outline onto the material.[46]

Patterns advised women on the most useful items for soldiers at the same time as they provided instruction on how to sew and knit, something that would have been especially useful for those girls and women who were picking up knitting needles or making slippers for the first time. The distribution of patterns also helped to standardize particular items distributed to soldiers, especially mittens and hospital slippers, ensuring that women who followed the pattern would produce a useful, functional item. The conditions and needs of military life were not well known to many Americans—civilians or soldiers—particularly in the first year of the war. Efforts were made to inform the public as to what was useful—and useless—to soldiers, helping the public to meet the demands of life in the field. Simple details—like woolen, rather than cotton, socks—could make a drastic difference in a soldier's comfort and the longevity of their clothing.

Some items needed to be redesigned for soldiers' use. As one officer informed the public in a newspaper article, woolen mittens would be necessary to prevent frostbite during the cold winter months. While many women had previously knitted mittens, the typical design in which the thumb was separated from the other four fingers was impractical for soldiers in the field. Diagrams on how to knit "Army Mittens" depicted a separate forefinger and thumb, which would allow a soldier to pull a trigger while still wearing mittens. A New York City hosiery company provided knitting diagrams for such Army Mittens that were then distributed to soldiers through the Women's Central Relief Association.[47] A mitten forefinger could be knit just as easily as a thumb. The diagram's detailed descriptions on how to add and finish the forefinger helped women to knit practical mittens with just a bit more yarn and time.

As in the case of mittens, other patterns provided detailed instructions on how to make clothing suitable for soldiers in hospitals, whose numbers were rapidly increasing. A Philadelphia druggist, Henry C. Blair, printed up paper patterns to use in making hospital slippers for sick and wounded Union soldiers. In addition to the pattern outlines, the paper on which it was printed included a notice of the need for slippers, an advertisement, and written directions regarding materials, cutting, and sewing. The pattern was designed with economy of time and expenditure in mind. Citing a newspaper article, the pattern sheet claimed that the slippers could be made in one hour, which was "infinitely better than spending several days over a single pair," as "it enables each person to do so much more, and there is, and is likely to be, a large demand."[48] The slippers could be made by laying the paper pattern down on a piece of "Old Material of any color or pattern that will make a warm slipper"

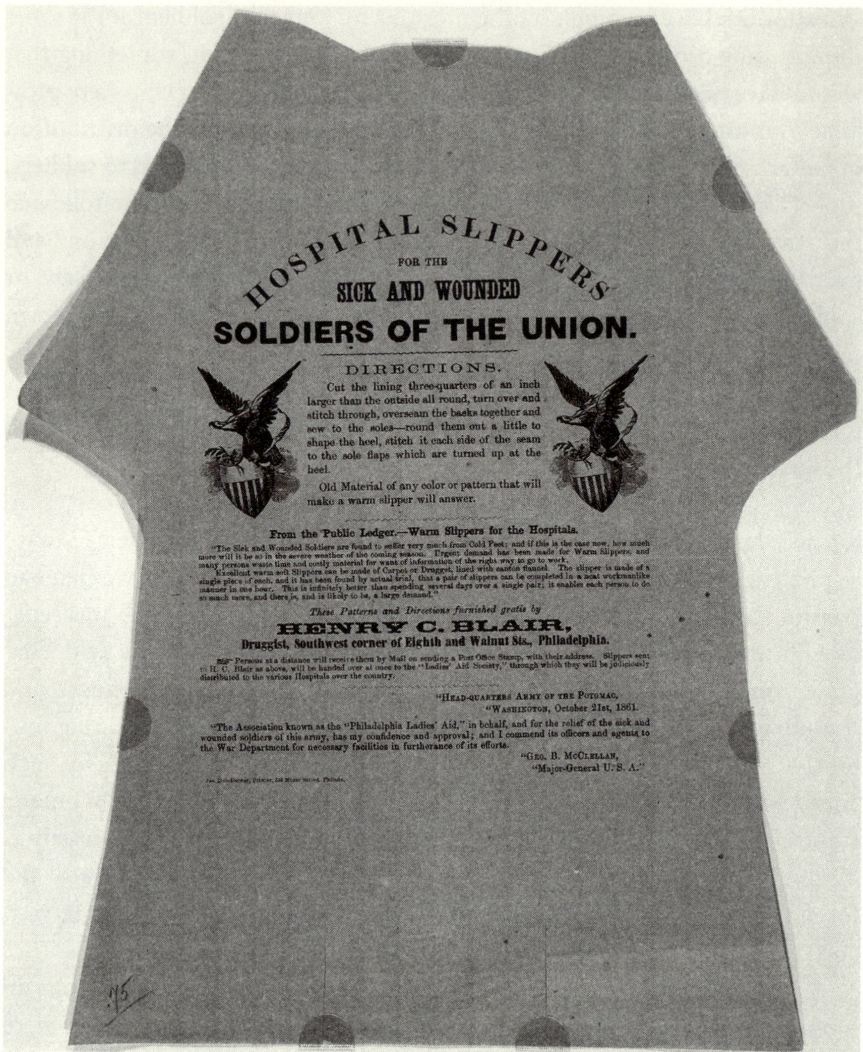

HOSPITAL SLIPPERS
FOR THE
SICK AND WOUNDED
SOLDIERS OF THE UNION.

DIRECTIONS.

Cut the lining three-quarters of an inch larger than the outside all round, turn over and stitch through, overseam the backs together and sew to the soles—round them out a little to shape the heel, stitch it each side of the seam to the sole flaps which are turned up at the heel.

Old Material of any color or pattern that will make a warm slipper will answer.

From the Public Ledger.—Warm Slippers for the Hospitals.

"The Sick and Wounded Soldiers are found to suffer very much from Cold Feet; and if this is the case now, how much more will it be so in the severe weather of the coming season. Urgent demand has been made for Warm Slippers, and many persons waste time and costly material for want of information of the right way to go to work.

Excellent warm soft Slippers can be made of Carpet or Drugget, lined with canton flannel. The slipper is made of a single piece of each, and it has been found by actual trial, that a pair of slippers can be completed in a neat workmanlike manner in one hour. This is infinitely better than spending several days over a single pair; it enables each person to do so much more, and there is, and is likely to be, a large demand."

These Patterns and Directions furnished gratis by

HENRY C. BLAIR,

Druggist, Southwest corner of Eighth and Walnut Sts., Philadelphia.

☞ Persons at a distance will receive them by Mail on sending a Post Office Stamp, with their address. Slippers sent to H. C. Blair as above, will be handed over at once to the "Ladies' Aid Society," through which they will be judiciously distributed to the various Hospitals over the country.

"Head-quarters Army of the Potomac,
"Washington, October 21st, 1861.

"The Association known as the "Philadelphia Ladies' Aid," in behalf, and for the relief of the sick and wounded soldiers of this army, has my confidence and approval; and I commend its officers and agents to the War Department for necessary facilities in furtherance of its efforts.

"Geo. B. McClellan,
"Major-General U. S. A."

Pattern, "Hospital Slippers for the Sick and Wounded Soldiers of the Union" (Philadelphia, 1861). Printed Ephemera Collection, Library of Congress, Washington, DC.

and tracing its outline. For the exterior of these slippers, women frequently cut up ingrain carpet, which was warm, flexible, and colorful, or drugget, a thick woolen fabric, and lined it with softer flannel.[49] A similar pattern published in *Peterson's Magazine* instructed women to "cut the carpet all in one piece exactly after the diagram."[50] Following the diagram, the slippers could be made by making ten straight and four slightly curved cuts in the fabric; making five folds; sewing the lining down along the edges; and then stitching up the toe, the heel, and the top of the foot. The most difficult parts were the curved cut and the hand pressure required to pass the needle through both the flannel and the drugget or carpet. True to the pattern makers' claims, the slippers could be simply made, provided one had the tools to cut carpet.

Blair's slipper pattern was not simply a set of directions. It was also an advertisement of the druggist's commitment to the Union cause and reified the patriotism of the Philadelphia Ladies' Aid Society, with whom Blair partnered in this endeavor. Two eagles clutching shields and olive branches visually mark the patriotic nature of the slipper pattern. All finished slippers, the pattern noted, would be "judiciously distributed to the various Hospitals over the country" by the Philadelphia Ladies' Aid Society. It also included a statement written by George McClellan, commander of the Army of the Potomac, bestowing his "confidence and approval" upon the Ladies' Aid Society for its work on behalf of sick and wounded soldiers.

The women who participated in patriotic sewing societies were not only praised for their work; they were also invited into more direct relationships with the government. The need for clothing necessitated communication between the government and those who could assist in supplying clothing, including both organizations and individuals. This frequently took the form of issuing circulars to aid societies that were reprinted in newspapers. In South Carolina, for instance, the quartermaster general explained that depots were being established in Charleston and Columbia to receive donations and distribute clothing. The department would "receive all donations of clothing, say frock coats and pantaloons, of heavy worsted goods, shirts and drawers of heavy homespun or flannel, wool, or heavy cotton socks, blankets, new or second hand, also heavy shoes."[51]

Wartime need for soldiers' clothing increased the frequency of women's contact with government officials throughout the Union and the Confederacy. However, circumstances of Confederate supply meant that Southern women found themselves in more frequent direct contact. As a circular issued by the governor of North Carolina explained, "The scarcity of material for sale in this state, and the uncertainty of procuring supplies from abroad, force us to rely on our domestic resources."[52] Similarly, in his effort to confront the cost of material, the quartermaster general of South Carolina issued a circular to the soldiers' aid societies on behalf of the governor, noting that "these laudable 'Associations' of ladies and gentlemen, are cordially welcome as coadjutors in this noble work" of supplying clothing.[53]

Georgia's governor Brown went further in his attempt to persuade women to participate in the outfitting of Georgia's soldiers. While public rhetoric often declared that women's work would be rewarded with eternal gratitude, Brown offered a more tangible form of acknowledgment in the state's records. Laying out a system through which donations would be received and recorded by the county clerks of the Superior Court, Brown promised that each donor would have her name and contribution entered into a book that would be sent to the Executive Office of the State of Georgia, where it would "be deposited among the permanent records of the State."[54] By donating uniforms and other supplies, women could receive state recognition as individuals, offering them an opportunity to have a relationship with the state—however tenuous—that was based on their own identities and contributions and entirely unrelated to those of their male relatives.

Brown's letter was published in newspapers throughout Georgia. Some of the women who read and responded to Brown's call viewed the letter as inviting them into a collaborative effort with the governor, writing directly to him to report their communities' efforts and to request assistance in procuring or paying for materials. Sarah Bugg, president of a soldiers' aid society, confirmed having "read with pleasure [Brown's] feeling and patriotic letter," and wrote to inform the governor that her society had "500 yards of Janes, which we propose to cut and make up for the Oglethorp Rifles now at Manassas." But Bugg was either unable or unwilling to donate the cloth, informing him that the society would proceed to cut and sew only if Brown purchased the fabric for them.[55] Women's expectations that the governor would work with them in their effort to aid soldiers continued. Julia Fisher, for instance, wrote to Brown in 1862 to "beg" his "kind assistance and co-operation in our plans for the relief" of Georgia soldiers fighting in Virginia.[56]

In many instances, sewing societies and individual women were willing to provide the labor but wanted the government or larger organizations to supply the material. The United States Sanitary Commission discovered, after a short trial of furnishing materials, that the plan was "working so badly for its own interest, that it has been compelled to abandon it." Nothing, the commission asserted, except for "the unbought, freely-given services of our people at home, both in furnishing *material and labor*, can avail to meet the vast demand for Hospital Clothing existing among our brave, suffering troops."[57] Similarly, in North Carolina, Governor Henry T. Clark attempted to engage people across all classes in the effort to supply winter clothing for troops in a circular, asserting that "every family can spare one or more blankets without personal inconvenience, or a pair of woolen socks and it is believed that for such a purpose a call would be responded to with alacrity." County sheriffs were instructed to "act as agents of the State," circulate the notice, and employ agents to solicit contributions and record the names of donors.[58] In Alabama, one woman wrote that she was "knitting socks for the volunteers; every lady in the state is requested by the Governor to knit one pair of socks."[59] Through such requests and instructions, Confederate state officials were drawing white women of all classes into a more direct relationship with the government and, by virtue of not providing material, elevating their work as a sacrifice to the nation.

The patriotic sock knitter was culturally significant for both the Union and Confederate causes. But whether a woman's knitting or sewing was categorized as patriotic was largely based on whether or not she was paid for her work. Sewing was a womanly sacrifice when one's time was donated to an aid society or the clothing was sent to a family member. The rhetoric of patriotism injected into soldiers' clothing supply had a political valence with far-reaching consequences for women who were seamstresses by trade or worked in the textile industry. The working-class women who labored in textile mills or with needle and thread over piecework obtained from clothing depots were given little credence in their patriotic intentions and were even looked upon with suspicion. Their sewing work was not a patriotic act, but a potential liability.

While the stitches were the same, the context in which seamstresses employed by quartermaster depots and arsenals worked looked very different from that of middle-class and elite ladies' sewing societies. This was in part due to the scale of work undertaken. Understanding working-class women's labor requires understanding the kinds of garments they were producing and the context of manufacture in which they worked. In theory, soldiers of the same rank wore the same uniform. But as shown by the challenge of maintaining brass manhood and the existence of a battlefront style, soldiers in both armies wore clothing that varied widely in color, cut, and style, especially during the first year of the war. While some companies chose distinctive uniforms to set themselves apart and promote a sense of camaraderie, others sought to replicate the uniforms worn by the US Army. Written directions regarding official uniforms for both the Union and Confederate armies existed, but even those descriptions could be misinterpreted. Still, both armies had official uniform regulations that outlined the amount and type of clothing issued to soldiers. In its effort to rapidly increase the production of uniforms that met these regulations, the US Quartermaster's Office worked to standardize the supply and appearance of all Union troops as men received new clothing allowances. In both armies, men's clothing allowance in the first year of service included two caps, one cover, two coats, three pairs of trousers,

The soldier on the left wears a frock coat, while the musician on the right wears a shorter shell jacket. Unidentified Union soldiers, c. 1861–65. Liljenquist Family Photograph Collection, Library of Congress, Washington, DC.

three flannel shirts, three pairs of drawers, a leather stock, four pairs of stockings, four pairs of bootees, and a greatcoat.[60]

Of these items, making coats and greatcoats required the greatest amount of time and skill on the part of seamstresses. This was true not only for officers' uniforms, which tended to have more complicated construction, but also for those worn by the lowest-ranking privates. As evidenced by tailors' and cutters' guides and surviving garments, a single coat worn by a private required several measurements, multiple pieces of fabric, pockets, and usually two or more types of cloth—one for the exterior, another for the lining, and, at times, a third for decoration—as well as several buttons. Although army regulations initially called for soldiers of all ranks to wear long frock coats, shell jackets quickly became the favored outer garment for most soldiers. These shorter jackets were not only more practical in the field, but also more economical to make in terms of both time and materials, requiring fewer measurements, fewer cuts, and less cloth. Shell jackets were not as warm as frock coats, as they covered less of the body, making overcoats highly desirable during the colder months of the year.

Developments in the emerging ready-made clothing industry facilitated the production of large quantities of clothing. In the 1840s and 1850s, tailors working at the US Office of Army Clothing and Equipage at Philadelphia's Schuylkill Arsenal developed a standardized sizing system for clothing based on their determination that men with a certain chest measurement were likely to have a corresponding waist size, shoulder width, and leg, arm, and torso lengths. The implementation of this sizing system meant that when war erupted in 1861, army clothing depots and private clothing manufacturers could work toward producing a range of common sizes.[61] Indeed, one tailoring manual noted, "Our diagrams are calculated for proportionate or common forms of any size."[62] This sizing system meant that most soldiers wore clothing that was not well fitted.

Male tailors and cutters provided the precision of professional pattern making, the skill of cutting cloth to reduce wasted remnants, and the maintenance of a sizing system. The number of seamstresses far outweighed the number of tailors and cutters. The Atlanta Depot, for instance, employed 3,000 seamstresses, but only twenty-seven male cutters.[63] The Schuylkill Arsenal employed fifty cutters and more than 5,000 seamstresses.[64] Women typically made uniforms worn by lower-ranking soldiers, along with undergarments, including drawers, shirts, and socks, worn by men in all ranks. This was a continuation of prewar practices, as women frequently sewed undergarments, choosing to spend money instead on tailored outer garments like pants, coats, and vests.[65]

Although women's sewing circles dominate postwar reminiscences, the vast majority of military garments were produced through an outwork system based out of army clothing depots that employed cutters, tailors, seamstresses, and inspectors. An unlined Union Zouave-style coat in the Smithsonian's collection offers an opportunity to observe the construction process. A tailor determined the dimensions of the various pieces of this coat, creating a pattern from which a coat in this particular size could be replicated many times. Cutters used shears to cut the woolen cloth for the exterior of the coat, as well as that for an interior lining, which was usually made of flannel or cotton, leaving only enough excess fabric as was required for the seams. All of the component parts, including pockets, for a single coat were then tied into a bundle for delivery to, or pickup by, a seamstress. The jacket would have been lined with another layer of fabric to offer greater durability and protection to the wearer. In the South, the majority of this work was performed through a putting-out system in which women took their work home and returned finished goods. In the North, where ready-made clothing manufactories were already well established, however, this work was divided between putting-out and factory work.

The clothing depot system was not a product of the Civil War, but the war *did* necessitate the expansion of that system to facilitate the manufacture of uniforms for both the Union and Confederate armies. At the same time, some Southern states also had independent procurement programs.[66] The expansion of these depot systems opened up opportunities for additional employment at both established depots and new locations, bringing work to more communities and drawing greater numbers of people into direct contact with the government. The depot system's rapid expansion exposed its shortcomings in production capacity, creating a context in which contracting with manufacturers became the norm. All of these depots were modeled after the Schuylkill Arsenal, also known as the Philadelphia Clothing Depot.[67] In addition to Philadelphia, major Union depots were located in St. Louis, Missouri; Cincinnati, Ohio; and New York City, while Confederate depots were located across the South, including Richmond, Virginia; Montgomery, Alabama; Houston, Texas; Shreveport, Louisiana; and Columbus, Athens, and Atlanta, Georgia.[68]

Depot locations were crucial—both to facilitate prompt provisioning for soldiers and to offer employment opportunities. Depots typically hired several male tailors and cutters and a much larger number of women as seamstresses. While some of these women had made their livelihood as seamstresses prior to the war, for others, sewing for pay was a wartime undertaking. Depending on their personal circumstances and the needs of the depots, some women worked continuously, while others sewed only occasionally. Indeed, some women continued to sew in the postwar era to support themselves and their families.[69]

Both Southern and Northern women found themselves in conflict with the government as a result of their work sewing uniforms. In some instances, they instigated that conflict themselves by making demands upon the government for work. Southern women, however, were in the unique position of being accused of aiding the enemy through their sewing work. Philadelphia and the greater Atlanta area offer opportunities to examine not only the relationships among clothing depots, surrounding communities, and the economy, but also the ways in which this work brought women into a more direct relationship, and at times conflicts, with the government. These conflicts centered on loyalty, treason, gender, and labor.

US government manufacturing became a form of public welfare during the war. This was, in part, due to depot-level army supply officers' efforts to shape military procurement, championing public enterprise over private contracting.[70] Historically, the Schuylkill Arsenal had employed women to produce uniforms, setting a precedent for the hire of women on a broader scale. Employment patterns in wartime manufactories, Judith Giesberg explains, fit comfortably with traditions of "working-class respectability that anticipated women moving in and out of the workforce at different stages in their lives."[71] But wartime also raised the question as to who was entitled to that work. This debate created tension not only between soldiers' wives and laboring women without relatives in the army, but also between immigrant and native-born laborers—male and female. Ability and access to sewing work became so firmly bound up with expressions of patriotism that Northern working-class seamstresses-by-trade found their jobs threatened by a growing opinion that army sewing should be reserved for those women who could prove their support for the Union—usually evidenced by having sent a male family member to war. In Philadelphia, the question as to who should be able to access these jobs created conflict both within the community and between seamstresses and the arsenal's commanding officers—a conflict that ultimately made its way to the White House and the desk of the secretary of war.

Uniform production managed by the Schuylkill Arsenal had provided Philadelphia seamstresses with employment since the first decades of the nineteenth century; wartime demands for increased production opened up additional opportunities. In April 1861, the number of employees jumped from a few hundred to around 2,700; just a few months later, that number exceeded 5,000. In 1864, Colonel Crosman, the commanding officer of the arsenal, noted that he was employing 5,127 "sewing women." At least an additional fifty male cutters cut and bundled cloth for those sewing women to pick up and take home to sew, returning it to the arsenal, where male packers and laborers prepared the clothing for distribution.[72] In the context of war, women who might have typically relied upon their husbands' income pursued opportunities to sew for pay, bringing them into direct competition with seamstresses-by-trade. Unlike during wars in the twentieth century, there was no shortage of labor to produce clothing.

In 1863, Mary Morris and Lizbeth Moore, wives of Union soldiers, wrote to Secretary of War Edwin Stanton, expressing their frustration and desperation resulting from the Schuylkill Arsenal's refusal to hire them: "My friend and me have gawn out to the arcnell fore imployment but we have not got it i think it is time now that thare whase somping done fore the sufing Solders wifes at home it is some time cince our husbent whare pade off and whe have not some times any thing to eat."[73] Morris and Moore demanded to know why they were refused employment, asking, "is it be cause whe re solders wifes"? They had witnessed other women enter the arsenal and receive work, only to be turned away themselves. They asserted that "I think the solders wifes arten to be the first to get the worke whe aur willing to live on a half a life wile our husbents is fiting fore the safety of our country." The government's failure to care for soldiers' wives and families, they suggested, prevented those soldiers' male friends and neighbors from enlisting themselves: "I think thare wod be more to go but they dont whant to see thare wifes sufer as them who have gone." Three weeks later, a reply was sent to the women: "The Secretary [of War] instructs me to transmit to you, the enclosed copy of a report received from the QuarterMaster General to whom your letter was referred ~~from which you will be satisfied that you have no reasonable cause of complaining~~."[74] Only the clerk's letter copy survives, so we cannot know for certain whether this crossed-out line was included in the reply to Morris, but the sentiment is nevertheless clear: Women were "complaining" where no complaint was to be made.

Later that year, Colonel Crosman discharged more than 100 women whose families were "opposed to the war" or who were unable to provide written evidence of their relationship to the US Army. This new order, *Fincher's Trades Review* reported, "resulted in the displacement of all but about one hundred and fifty of the old hands, and some nine hundred new and inexperienced seamstresses have taken their places."[75] *Fincher's*, an advocate for laborers, covered the developing conflict between Crosman, arsenal seamstresses, and the women who took their jobs, arguing that working women were in greater need of jobs than were soldiers' wives. "Sewing women" who did not have the support of soldiers' pay, *Fincher's* argued, were among the most in need of work—the claims of "poor sewing women were more urgent, as [female employees who had relatives in the army] received the pay and bounties of the soldiers." The sewing women, on the other hand, "had to depend on a small pittance, earned from week to week" through their piecework for the arsenal.[76]

The sewing women responded with a petition to Secretary Stanton demanding back their jobs, noting their relationship to the Union army and asserting their loyalty. They insisted upon being treated on equal terms with their male arsenal counterparts, decrying the double standard of this new policy as "oppressive and prejudicial" toward women because men who had "neither friends nor relatives in the service" retained their jobs, while women of similar standing had lost theirs. In response, women forged documents to verify their loyalty and colluded to maintain control over their share of government work.[77] Former employees and their supporters decried the "tyrannical decrees of Col. Crossman," who had "descended from the exalted position of a military hero, to make war upon women."[78]

Like members of soldiers' aid societies, the government attempted to link sewing and patriotism by making it a livelihood accessible through women's relationships to male soldiers. This approach to assigning sewing work as a form of public welfare was welcome relief to many soldiers' female relatives, but it was simultaneously how arsenal workers experienced war's suffering. Arsenal seamstresses-by-trade aired their grievances to the Schuylkill Arsenal's military officials and directly confronted the government, taking to Washington, DC, their objections to policies they considered discriminatory.[79] Their success was limited, as they struggled for the remainder of the war to regain access to jobs that had been lost.

Northern arsenal seamstresses were not the only working-class women who became embroiled in arguments over loyalty as it related to their jobs. Patriotic sewing societies' work in solidifying the perceived relationship between patriotism and clothing production also had consequences for Southern working-class women whose jobs involved textile and clothing production. While the Schuylkill Arsenal had long been a fixture of working-class women's employment, the clothing depot system in the rebellious states was established in the context of war. The wartime focus on supplying soldiers both disrupted local economies and created opportunities for white women's work.

These predominantly poor white and yeoman women were faced with wartime struggles and shortages that left them with little recourse and few opportunities to earn a living. Many women took advantage of their proximity to a quartermaster's depot. One woman recalled, "This pay work was given to the wives of poor soldiers many of whom would walk into town to get it long distances from the neighboring sandhills."[80] Poor soldiers' wives, widows, and seamstresses-by-trade picked up bundles of cloth cut by male cutters in the quartermaster's clothing warehouses, which they then sewed at home for pay. Regardless of whether they took part in this army outwork system, or their motivations for sewing uniforms, women's work sewing soldiers' clothing later affected their efforts to make claims of loyalty to the United States. Directly, or indirectly, they had supported the Confederacy. This had financial consequences in the postwar era.

Between 1871 and 1873, Southerners submitted paperwork to the Southern Claims Commission, a US federal government organization through which

Southerners filed claims for reimbursement of personal property losses resulting from the war.[81] Only Southerners who could provide evidence of their unflagging loyalty to the United States throughout the war were eligible for such reimbursement. The cultural association between women, sewing uniforms, and loyalty that pervaded both Northern and Southern discourses was critical to the success or rejection of women's claims. Female claimants were explicitly asked, "Did you ever belong to any sewing society organized to make clothing for Confederate soldiers or their families, or did you assist in making any such clothing, or making flags or other military equipments, or preparing or furnishing delicacies or supplies for Confederate hospitals or soldiers?"[82] Whereas Northern women's work sewing uniforms for soldiers was not only portrayed in patriotic terms, but also understood as a form of public welfare, the Southern claims commissioners, exercising a victor's justice, took a narrow view of women's work as seamstresses: if a woman had sewn clothing that ultimately ended up on the back of a Confederate soldier, her claims were rejected.

Sewing and semiskilled textile work were inherently problematic occupations for Southern women because federal officials interpreted their wage labor and piecework as evidence of complicity with and support for the Confederate cause. Women's motivations for engaging in wartime clothing production were immaterial to the claims commissioners. Some of these women had been seamstresses-by-trade before the war, while others took up sewing uniforms for private families or the quartermaster's office as a means of supporting themselves during wartime. While a number of these women were indeed Confederate soldiers' wives and widows, others were single women or had been widowed before the war and were attempting to eke out a living in a war-torn economy. They claimed that they did not support the Confederate cause; they needed to make a living.

Both Elizabeth Grubb and Lusana Muselwhite worked as seamstresses prior to the war. It was, after all, one of the most common occupations for wage-earning white women. In Savannah, Georgia, for instance, more than 40 percent of working white women and more than 50 percent of free Black women were employed in the clothing trade in 1860, the majority as seamstresses.[83] Grubb's and Muselwhite's prewar occupation made no difference for their postwar claims. Grubb's claims of property loss were officially denied because she "was employed at times in making clothing for the rebel Quartermaster's Dept," even though she "did very little of this."[84] Muselwhite, on the other hand, "sometimes made clothing for soldiers, but it was for private families & to make a living."[85] Although the commissioners viewed both

Grubb's and Muselwhite's sewing work as evidence of their support of the rebels, the women's motivations were likely more complicated. In 1860, Grubb was a thirty-six-year-old widow, living alone with her nine-year-old son in Atlanta, in a neighborhood where other Atlantans employed in the clothing trade also lived. Both she and Muselwhite sewed for a living, and in the context of the war and the redirection of resources to army supply, much of the work available to seamstresses was intended for army consumption.

Another woman's claims were rejected not only because her sons served in the Confederate army, but also because she provided clothing to them when they entered the army. Sarah Baldwin argued that she "furnished them with nothing except some clothing when they started to the war. I gave them no money or equipments, I had no money to give I never contributed to aid or support them while in the service." The commissioners of claims, however, found it "hard to believe that Mrs. Baldwin did not sympathize with the cause for which her sons were perilling their lives, especially as she furnished them with clothing when they entered the Confederate Army."[86]

One of the most illustrative examples of the ways in which sewing uniforms trumped all other evidence for claims of loyalty is the experience of Carrie Hambrick, who petitioned the US government for reimbursement of livestock and other property requisitioned by the US Army totaling $429.75. The final report rejecting her claim asserted that the "Claimant admits that she was employed in the Rebel Q.M. Department at Atlanta sewing on soldiers clothing." The significance of this employment was made clear: "This is voluntary aid and comfort to the Rebels for which Claimant received compensation, and for which she has no excuse. It was as much as a woman of her circumstances had opportunity to do for aid of the Rebellion."[87] The commissioners admitted, however, that Hambrick performed "a very commendable act of humanity towards a Union officer" who was shot and taken prisoner before he escaped and stumbled upon Hambrick's house in the woods outside Atlanta.[88]

That officer testified in front of the Southern Claims Commission in regard to not only Hambrick's role in saving his life—taking him into her home, nursing his wounds, and helping him escape back to Union lines—but also her loyalty to the United States. He asserted that he learned while living with her that Hambrick believed that "the south commenced the war against the government without just cause. That she had nothing to complain of against the government that it was good enough for her." The officer also relayed Hambrick's reflections on her husband's death, which left her a widow with two toddler-aged children: "She told me that her husband was 'conscripted' into the rebel army but died at the hospital . . . and that she was glad that she could say that her husband died before he had fired a gun against the flag of his country."[89] Despite the compelling testimony of this former US soldier, the claims commissioners rejected Hambrick's claims based on her answer to the question of whether she had ever been employed by the Confederacy: a question to which she truthfully replied that she "had nothing to do with the soldier part of the war," but "was employed by the rebel Quartermaster's Department at Atlanta Ga to sew on some clothing for the army" and "was thus employed for two months." Hambrick's two months of piecework outweighed any claims to support of the Union that were illustrated by her actions in nursing a Union officer.

Such rulings of the Southern Claims Commission were in part intended to limit the amount of restitution paid by the federal government, but the records also reveal the tension between women's patriotism with their textile and sewing skills and the very question of whether women could be considered traitors or commit treason against the federal government by performing such work. In its refusal to approve claims by women who had sewn for the CSA, the commission asserted that sewing was political work. These were the same tensions at stake in General William Sherman's decision to expel the Roswell millworkers from the South.

US blockades and embargoes targeted the provision of supplies to the Confederate army throughout the war.[90] However, Sherman escalated this approach in his 1864 campaign by employing a policy designed to deprive both the army and civilians of provisions in an effort to break the back of the Confederacy. While the Union army's march through Georgia was primarily focused on the destruction of raw materials and infrastructure—especially railroads—Sherman also ordered the destruction of manufactories, like Roswell Mills, to prevent them from further supplying the Confederate army.[91]

But Sherman faced a dilemma in Roswell: Would destruction of the mills' machinery be sufficient? Or was it also militarily expedient to remove the artisans and laborers who operated that machinery? What should be done with the female millworkers? The Lieber Code—Lincoln's 1863 General Order No. 100—explicitly stated that no distinction was to be made on "account of the difference of sexes" when it came to the treatment of war-traitors, war-rebels, and spies. However, the millworkers did not fit the definitions of traitors, rebels, or spies laid out in the code. Instead, their actions were best categorized as those of "disloyal citizens" giving "positive aid and comfort to the rebellious enemy without being bodily forced thereto." The code granted army commanders the authority to "expel, transfer, imprison, or fine" disloyal citizens. However, such treatment was specifically reserved for those who refused to "pledge themselves anew as citizens obedient to the law and loyal to the government."[92]

Sherman loosely interpreted these instructions. As one news correspondent traveling with Sherman's army told the Washington, DC, *Daily National Intelligencer*, "Red tape was about to become involved in a hopeless entanglement with crinoline, tent cloth, and cartels, when Gen. Sherman interposed and solved the knotty question by loading [the millworkers] into one hundred and ten wagons and sending them to Marietta to be sent north of the Ohio and set at liberty."[93] Fearing that, upon release, the female millworkers would return to textile production, Sherman not only imprisoned them on grounds of treason, but also forcibly relocated the women north. As outlined in the Lieber Code, technically only people who refused to "pledge themselves anew as citizens" would be expelled. Yet surviving evidence offers no indication that the millworkers were ever asked to take such a pledge of allegiance to the United States. Rather, Sherman focused on the threat these workers' skills posed for the US government. But this in itself posed a conundrum: Were the millworkers willing participants in supporting the Confederate cause? And if their work was compulsory, should they still be classified as "disloyal citizens" who were providing aid to the enemy?

The Washington, DC, *Daily National Intelligencer* argued the women had been compelled to labor at the mills, writing, "Giving 'aid and comfort to the enemy' they most assuredly were, and much valuable tent cloth; but in the case of many of them it was an involuntary service, since they had been confined and compelled to labor there without cessation from the breaking out of the rebellion."[94] There is no evidence to suggest that the millworkers were forced to work in the mills by anyone or anything besides economic necessity—the mills had long been the main source of income for many Roswell-area families. Numerous workers were immigrants who had made their way to Georgia via New England and the Mid-Atlantic. The opportunity to work there would have been all the more desirable after war broke out and many men joined or were conscripted into the army. Indeed there was some degree of recognition among Union soldiers that the women's primary impetus for working at the mills was not patriotism—although their potential patriotism should not be discounted—but necessity; many of these women relied on millwork for their livelihood both before and after the war. One soldier remembered that, as the mills were set on fire, "it was feeling to witness how they wept, as this, their only means of support, was consigned to destruction."[95] This distinction between subsistence and patriotism, however, had little bearing on the millworkers' treatment. Sherman simultaneously declared the mills "tainted with treason" and dismissed the women as "simply laborers"—it was not their devotion to the Confederacy but, rather, their ability to aid it that was a threat to the federal government.[96] Women's usefulness to the Confederate cause—not their patriotic loyalty—made them dangerous. These women were military actors.

Sherman made it clear that it was the women's skills—*their knowledge of the machinery used in cloth production*—that made them a threat to the United States. This decision to imprison the millworkers was part of the broader expulsion of civilians from Atlanta—a city, as one soldier noted, that was "said to have furnished the most supplies of different kinds towards sustaining the rebellion of any city in the south."[97] But the *Richmond Examiner* offered another explanation that hinged on the threat Southern textile production posed to the "Yankee empire." Sherman, the paper asserted, "feels that the girls in Georgia have no business with the spinning and weaving of cotton; sow cotton they may, hoe it, pick it and gin it; but the weaving and spinning thereof is done at Lowell and Lawrence, in Massachusetts." The women needed to be evicted and relocated, the *Examiner* suggested, "because that factory, or some other, might be erected in that neighborhood, and those same hands might begin seditiously spinning and weaving the cotton fiber again—to the manifest detriment of industrious mill-owners in Massachusetts."[98]

Sherman instructed commanding officers to "send all the owners, agents, and employees to Indiana to get rid of them there."[99] There, he believed, the women could be "turned loose to earn a living where they won't do us any harm . . . the women were simply laborers that must be removed from this district."[100] He further asserted that the army would "retain them until they can reach a country where they can live in peace and security."[101] Loaded into wagons, the women were transported along a path from Roswell to Marietta, Georgia, where they were then sent to Chattanooga, Tennessee, before moving on to Nashville and then Louisville, Kentucky. Despite Sherman's assertion, the prospects for the women to successfully find employment in Indiana after being "turned loose to earn a living" were tenuous at best. Although the women were skilled laborers, textile manufacturing jobs along the Ohio River were not readily available, as the mills located along the Ohio River had laid off workers or closed due to cotton shortages resulting from the war. Some ultimately made their way to New Albany, Evansville, and Jeffersonville, Indiana, where their presence strained local resources.[102]

Although Sherman asserted that the women's textile skills posed the greatest threat to the US government, others disagreed. Some of those who opposed Sherman's actions believed the introduction of more "secesh" women—and their rhetoric—along the Ohio River, and especially in the border states of Kentucky and Tennessee, to be more dangerous. Andrew Johnson, then military governor of Tennessee, feared their presence would "add to the rebel or Copperhead sentiment and increase opposition to the Government." Sending Southern civilians north was, more generally, he wrote, a poor military decision, for it simultaneously resulted in the depletion of Union resources and alleviated conditions in the South.[103]

The forced relocation of the women, combined with the inconsistency with which news—and rumors—traveled, led to speculation about Sherman's intentions in both Southern and Northern newspapers. While some articles reported that the women were to be sent north, others informed readers that the women were "to be sent out of the limits of the United States" or "shipped to Canada and left to perish without money or friends."[104] The question as to what should have become of the millworkers was contentious. "What had they done to call down such a judgment?" the *Richmond Daily Advertiser* demanded. "They were the daughters of the poorer white people who abound in the hill country of Georgia, and had found a safe and honest employment in the cotton factory, not under such loathsome conditions as English factory girls, but under good care for their health and morals, and at sufficient wages, whereby they were enabled to assist in the maintenance of many a family, while their brothers were away, perhaps in Lee's army." Sherman's actions proved, the *Macon Daily Telegraph* asserted, that "the Federal government is running a race with Russia, in cruelty to female 'rebels,'" a reference to the 1863 January uprising in Poland.[105]

The incident prompted outrage from both Southerners and Union supporters who believed that women and children should be shielded from the violence of war. Numerous papers published articles on the incident with headlines that included "The War upon Women" and "More War upon Women." The *New York Commercial Advertiser* published an article (reprinted in Southern newspapers) declaring Sherman's actions a "frightful disgrace." The *Advertiser* noted that "it is hardly conceivable that an officer, wearing a United States commission of Major-General, should have so far forgotten the commonest dictates of decency and humanity, (Christianity apart) as to drive four hundred penniless girls hundreds of miles away from their homes and friends, to seek their livelihood amid a strange and hostile people."[106] The newspaper editors hoped that the story would "prove to be unfounded," for the sake of both Sherman's reputation and "our national good name."

While these women likely sought security, the presence of this particular group of federal soldiers offered them little. Not only was any opportunity for financial security destroyed with the burning of the mills, but the security of their own bodies was also threatened and in some cases violated. The occupying Union soldiers offered their opinions of the women's bodies, their behavior, and their prospects of sexual encounters—whether consensual or forced. "We captured a large factory afire and the operatives eight hundred females almost for one apiece.... some were very gay, silks, laces &c and were perfectly willing to play the agreeable to the wretched Yankees, others were as cold and rigid as iceburgs ... threatening us with all the judgments of Heaven and Southern Confederacy for sins in burning the factory, warehouses and government property thereby stopping the manufacture of 5,000 yards of cloth per day. Awful was'ent it."[107] Private Henry Orendorff wrote, "I just wish they would issue them [the women] to us soldiers."[108] While these men may have limited their assessment of these women as sexual objects to their diaries and letters, others did not.

The Refugee Aid Commission in Louisville, Kentucky, struggled to assist the Roswell women and other Southern refugees who had made their way to the city. Two hundred refugees were living at the Refugee House—a female hospital prison—while an additional one hundred were located several blocks away at another female prison located in a house seized for that purpose. Still others were "scattered in the woods around New Albany, Jeffersonville, and our own city." Looking ahead to the approaching winter months, the commission was concerned that "the winter will find most of them poorly protected from its storms and snows, and they will all flock instinctively in to the city for help."[109] The commission had reason to worry. In December, the New Albany, Indiana, *Daily Ledger* reported, "Two refugees, a man and his little daughter, were found dead on Tuesday, in a miserable hovel, near the river between this city and Jeffersonville. Their names were unknown, and it is supposed they either starved or froze to death."[110]

The experiences of the Roswell millworkers and the concern over their roles in textile manufacturing demonstrate just how critical women's skills were in a war that demanded large quantities of cloth for the support, and thereby success, of the armies. Southern textile millworkers possessed the ability to aid the Confederacy, simultaneously making them a powerful threat to the Union army and a vulnerable population when in the presence of that army. Tensions existed among the various threats posed by these women. On the one hand, the women were viewed as economic competition, because textile production was considered the prerogative of the Northeast. On the other, removing those women and their textile skills to the North created a burden on the local economy, drawing in more mouths to feed and bodies to clothe, as well as introducing an ideological threat through secessionist allegiances they might have embraced. At the beginning of the war, these women were in possession of a critical wartime resource—skill in textile production. That knowledge shaped both how they lived through the war and ultimately how they experienced its violence through direct conflict with an arm of the federal government.

Women's wartime and postwar experiences in testing government responsibility and authority were part of a working out of the dimensions of gender and political personhood. This occurred at a moment in which women were presumed to be far removed from the workings of the government. At the start of the war, women's ties to the nation were expressed in terms of patriotic duty and the support of men, who were considered legitimate political and military actors. But in these instances of conflict over clothing production, women engaged the government on their own terms—whether by making demands for employment at Philadelphia's Schuylkill Arsenal or through the act of submitting applications to the Southern Claims Commission. In doing so, they made claims to a legitimate relationship to the government—a government that they believed had a responsibility to them as individuals and not only as the wives or daughters of men. Although women were considered noncombatants, their actions had lasting implications that shaped the limits of the kinds of protection and support the government was willing to afford them. Women's loyalty was assessed not only according to their rhetoric, but also by the skills they possessed.

Part II
Wearing

Cotton apron in US flag motif, made and worn by Mary Himes Fox, New Bethlehem, Pennsylvania, 1862. Gettysburg National Military Park, Museum Collection, GETT # 41560. Courtesy National Park Service.

Thirty-four stars. Thirteen stripes. With its bold red and pale blue, this apron would have clashed with nearly every garment over which it might have been worn—whether made of ginghams, calicos, plaids, or figured silks—and that was precisely the point. The apron was meant to be loud, flashy, and noticed by all. Far from the variety of apron intended to protect one's dress from splatters of food and grease in the kitchen, this type of apron was a common decorative garment worn over a woman's dress, pinned to the bodice, and tied around the waist. Easily removed and thereby more easily cleaned than a dress, decorative aprons simultaneously served utilitarian purposes and enhanced the appearance of a dress.

But this apron was not mere decoration. When Mary Himes, a young woman in her early twenties, sewed the apron in 1862, she laid out the design with intention. The symbolism was clear: Thirteen stripes from the United States flag representing the thirteen original colonies. And thirty-four stars to represent *all* thirty-four states in the Union and not just those that remained loyal. This apron was intended to deliver a political message: The objective of this war was to preserve the union of all the states. To include stars representing only the loyal states would have been to admit that those in rebellion had successfully seceded from that union. The cause of the war, whether Himes recognized it or not, was woven into the very fabric of her apron. At the heart of the war was the production of the cotton from which the apron was made, having likely been planted, grown, and harvested by enslaved laborers, before being spun and woven in a textile manufactory.

Mary Himes was the daughter of a cabinetmaker in the western Pennsylvania town of New Bethlehem, its population just 380 in 1860.[1] In her eagerness to connect herself to the events unfolding around her, she was like many young women living in small towns throughout the United States whose communities sent men to war. In wearing her apron, Himes joined thousands of civilians—US and Confederate—who wore patriotic symbols and colors, some of whom opted for flag aprons like that sewn by Himes. "The bib" of Union aprons, one newspaper described, "is studded by stars and the skirt is streaked with stripes, and warm, true, brave hearts beating under all."[2]

To rally support for the war and identify their allegiances, these women—either in the North or South—didn't need to be seen wearing their star and stripe-emblazoned aprons while walking among throngs of people in New York City or New Orleans. One could wear their patriotism on their sleeve—or over their skirt—wherever they lived. And both the US and Confederate governments needed those civilians to embrace and materially display that patriotism if they were to sustain a violent, bloody, and drawn-out war.

CHAPTER THREE

They Call It Patriotism; I Call It Indigo Dye

Dressing Civilians for War

The Civil War opened another chapter in Americans' long and storied history of using cloth and clothing as political statements. As manufactories shifted to wartime production, arsenals increased uniform orders, and communities banded into military companies, a new consumer landscape was emerging. Americans sought to display their sentiments, and merchants and advertisers marketed commercialized versions of Union and Confederate identity to appeal to customers' patriotic zeal.[1] Stores and advertisers marketed items ranging from war-themed playing cards, games, and toys to patriotic stationery and newfangled body armor. In cities, store windows enticed passersby with bunting and ribbons in patriotic colors, while bookshops stocked volumes on military drill and tactics. Fabric, dresses, bonnets, jewelry, cockades, and more were imbued with patriotic meaning. From the outset, clothing was an important, material way in which to answer the pressing question of how patriotic fervor could be instilled in a populace that needed to rally to fight a war that many did not yet understand.

Far from superficial decoration, civilians' cockades, ribbons, and other patriotic accoutrements played a crucial role in shoring up political identities as the nation was tearing at its seams. As they navigated the changing landscape of clothing consumption, Northerners and Southerners placed an emphasis on both the outward appearance of their clothing and the inward knowledge of where it originated. Fueled by efforts to celebrate regional economies and the desire to avoid lending economic support to their enemies, they initiated, as in previous decades, efforts to support home manufacture and self-sufficiency. Cockades, military-inspired fashion, and patriotic colors appeared in the wardrobes of men, women, and children across the North and South. But as with the pomp and circumstance of brass manhood, civilian dress, too, often proved more successful at initiating than sustaining patriotic enthusiasm for war, especially as clothing emerged as a central site by which some civilians experienced war's costs.

People have historically looked to clothing as a means of identifying and assessing people; it was a critical part of "figuring out," as Kate Haulman puts it, "how to read people socially."[2] But war brought with it an urgent challenge of being able to distinguish people's allegiances. The US and Confederate governments answered this problem by adopting official uniform colors. But civilians wore no such uniforms. Instead, throughout the early 1860s, apparel appeared ranging from dresses, shirts, aprons, and wrappers to collars, cravats, jewelry, and hats, expressing patriotic sentiments through colors, printed fabrics, designs, military-inspired fashions, and a range of state and national motifs and symbols. Precisely how such civilian clothing could be used to instill patriotism was not fixed but, rather, a process of trial and error that included not only donning symbols and colors that referenced the nation and individual states, but also consideration of international trade and local economies.

Worn for centuries to signify military or political allegiance, the cockade—a rosette or knot of ribbons—was reinvigorated prior to the Civil War by South Carolina's Minute Men. This paramilitary disunionist group wore blue cockades to associate themselves with the Nullifiers of 1832, who had, in turn, borrowed the style from the British oppositionist tradition.[3] Writing home from the University of Virginia in November 1860, one man reported that "a great many are wearing the *blue cockades*, thus showing that their sentiments are disunion & civil cominnations."[4] By the winter of 1860, cockades were pinned to the hats and coats of fire-eaters in other Southern and border states, sporting design and color variations and stamped gilt buttons declaring state allegiances. Supporters of the Union also adopted cockades into their dress, often in the form of red, white, and blue ribbons held together by a gilt button stamped with an eagle surrounded by stars.[5] Women and children, too, pinned these badges to their hats, dresses, and coats.

Numerous designs and materials were used to craft cockades and badges, including palmetto fronds and straw woven into the shapes of palmetto trees, stars, rosettes, and circles, and occasionally painted. Ribbons made of silk, velvet, and other fabrics were pleated or looped into similar shapes. In the South, cockades were often state oriented and some designs were popular enough to merit mention in newspapers. According to an article detailing styles of Southern cockades, many South Carolinians wore "three layers of very dark blue cloth, notched at the edges and fastened together by a gilt button" with a palmetto and the phrase "'Animis opibusque parati'—'Ready with our minds and means.'" Marylanders, too, wore a blue double rosette, but with blue pendants and the Maryland state arms.[6] In other instances, black-and-white rosettes were adopted in a nod to a color combination made fashionable during the Revolutionary War. Many secession cockades were made at home and often incorporated state uniform buttons or symbols. One woman's cockade was made of looped red velvet by her mother, while another, made in North Carolina, had three small pinecones attached.[7]

Supporters of the Union were also donning cockades. In New York City, observed *Harper's New Monthly Magazine*, "The passengers in the streets wear badges, rosettes, and cockades of the trinity of patriotic colors."[8] As in the South, many Northerners made their own cockades, but others were purchased from local merchants. For twenty-five cents, one could buy "The Washington Union Cockade," which included "a beautiful Melainotype Likeness of Washington surrounded by a Rosette in red, white, and blue, with red, white and blue streamers."[9] By purchasing this cockade, one could, as an advertisement declared, "SHOW YOUR COLORS!!!" Another design incorporated streamer ribbons printed with "Constitution" and "Union." In January 1861, a Portland, Maine, shopkeeper received a supply of Union cockades that were "got up very tastily, and if any one wishes to signify by outward signs his loyalty to the Union, a good opportunity is offered."[10]

By design, these cockades were precisely that: outward signs of one's allegiances. These were not the equivalent of modern "I Voted" stickers, nor even campaign buttons, that typically lay relatively flat against one's clothing or hat. Rather, cockades' three-dimensional nature meant that they projected from the body with streamers that moved in the wind or as a person shifted their body, making them very visible. A now-faded red silk rosette-shaped badge, for instance, was built up from six layers of pleated silk and two streamer ribbons, all held together by a North Carolina state uniform sleeve button. A star-shaped cockade woven from palmetto, with a crescent moon and star button at its center, would likewise have stood out to passersby. Regardless of their color or the allegiance they signaled, cockades shared one thing in common: they were meant to be noticed.

And in the first few months of 1861, local newspapers reported on the incidents that resulted precisely from people taking notice—notice of traitorous male disunionists' appearances in town with cockades on their hats or pinned to their coats. In Centralia, Illinois, people took a secession cockade from a man's hat, "threw it into some not over nice place, and escorted the wearer to the train which was about to leave."[11] In April, just days before shots were fired on Fort Sumter, a man wearing a large secession cockade in Baltimore was chased by a mob and "was only protected from violence by the interference of the police."[12] Accusations were thrown fast and loose, with men's hats and lapels scrutinized for cockades, as people attempted to distinguish friend from foe, particularly in areas where loyalties were mixed.

Made from six layers of pleated pink silk, this cockade measures 5 inches long and 2.5 inches in diameter. At its center is a North Carolina state uniform sleeve button. Cockade, 1860, North Carolina. Courtesy of the American Civil War Museum, Richmond, VA.

Woven from palmetto, this star-shaped cockade includes a brass sleeve button stamped with a crescent moon and star. Measuring 2.25 by 2.25 inches, it would have been very visible on the wearer's clothing. Secession cockade, c. 1861–65. Courtesy of the American Civil War Museum, Richmond, VA.

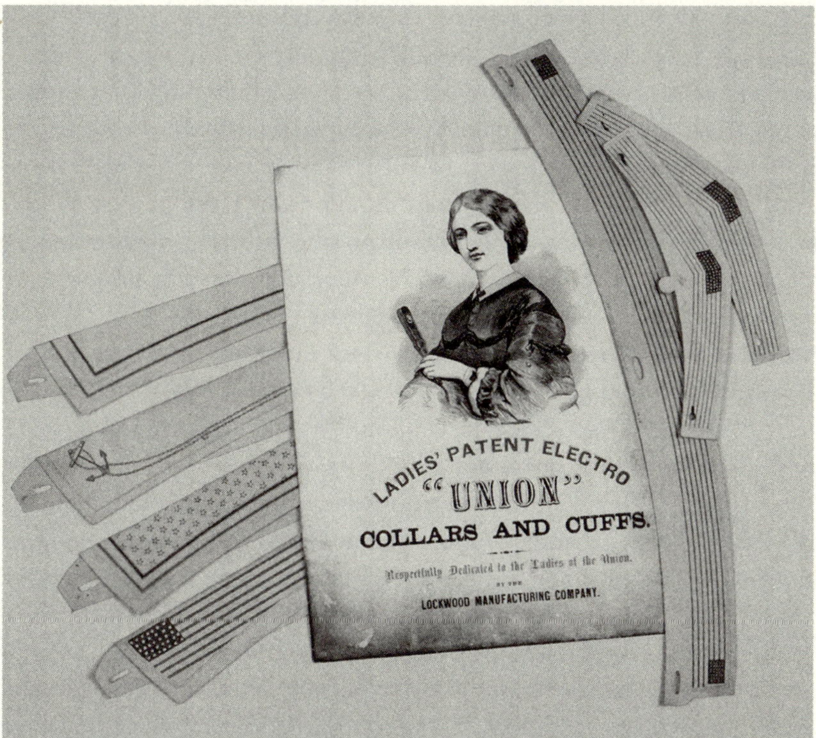

These disposable paper collars and cuffs could be worn to protect dress fabric. They were printed with a variety of patriotic symbols. Ladies' patent collars and cuffs, Lockwood Manufacturing Company, c. 1863. Courtesy of the Library Company of Philadelphia.

The red, white, and blue tricolor of Union cockades was repeated, *Harper's New Monthly Magazine* observed, "in shawls, in cravats, in ribbons" on the streets of New York City.[13] In similar ways to the New York public, civilian men, women, and children throughout the nation marked through clothing their allegiances to the Union, to the Confederacy, and, particularly in the South, to their home states. Manufacturers and merchants were eager to supply and profit from this surge in patriotic display. As with cockades, many types of overtly patriotic dress took the form of items that were worn on or over a person's clothing, such as an apron, collar, or cravat. In Philadelphia, the Lockwood Manufacturing Company produced "Ladies' Patent Electro 'Union' Collars and Cuffs"—paper collars and sleeve cuffs printed with stars and the American flag. Many women's dress styles required the use of detachable fabric collars and cuffs that allowed for easier cleaning of these parts of the dress that were easily soiled by sweat. In lieu of fabric or lace, a woman could affix the disposable Union collars or cuffs to the neck and sleeves of her dress to simultaneously protect the fabric and show support for the Union cause.[14] While paper collars were subtle, Union aprons like that made by Mary Himes were loud, flashy, and remarked upon in newspapers from Iowa to Kentucky to Pennsylvania. "We all have views now, men, women, and little boys," wrote New Yorker Jane Stuart Woolsey, "from the modestly patriotic citizen who wears a postage stamp on his hat to the woman who walks in Broadway in that fearful object of contemplation, a 'Union bonnet,' composed of alternate layers of red, white, and blue, with streaming ribbons 'of the first.'"[15]

In areas where loyalties were mixed or when enemy soldiers were passing through, such clothing was used to taunt one's enemies. One Confederate soldier recounted his experience in Grafton, Virginia (later West Virginia), where he found himself "surrounded by those who have no sympathy for Southern rights." When Confederate troops arrived in town in 1861, "a number of little girls with Union aprons, Union Flags, and wearing bonnets trimmed with Union Ribbon, walked the streets, waving their flags at every soldier they saw." The girls protested the Confederates' arrival, but the troops, the soldier claimed, took no notice of the girls' patriotic garb and the girls were "permitted to return home without the satisfaction of being noticed or insulted in any way whatever."[16] Similarly, a *Harper's Weekly* image of "A Female Rebel in Baltimore—An Everyday Scene" depicts a woman dressed in a voluminous skirt with hoops, and an apron of Confederate colors pinned over the bodice and skirt.[17] While the narrators of both of these incidents say that soldiers were amused by or "took no notice" of women and children's clothing, these acts were nevertheless subversive.

Such displays of allegiance continued throughout the war and took on added meaning in the context of occupation. In Union-occupied Winchester, Virginia, women wore badges of mourning following the death of Stonewall Jackson in 1862. One woman wore a black crepe rosette with a brass Virginia button, even when she learned that women would be arrested for wearing such badges and that rosettes had been torn from other women's dresses by Union soldiers.[18] As these black mourning rosettes suggest, not all symbols of patriotism were declared in bold colors, but they were nevertheless recognized as such. Winchester women wore calico and gingham sunbonnets as secession bonnets, as well as white muslin aprons, all of which drew the ire of occupying soldiers who viewed them as disrespectful. "They were adopted," one woman claimed, "for their cheapness and for their defense against staring soldiers, but they resent it and say they are intended as an insult by intimating that we do

HARPER'S WEEKLY.

A JOURNAL OF CIVILIZATION

NEW YORK, SATURDAY, SEPTEMBER 7, 1861.

"A Female Rebel in Baltimore—An Everyday Scene," *Harper's Weekly*, September 7, 1861. Courtesy of the Library of Congress, Washington, DC.

not care how we dress while they are here!"[19] In occupied Memphis, Tennessee, Confederate women abandoned hoops, having "agreed among themselves not to wear them. It is their secret sign—their badge—their rebel flag."[20]

British and European textile manufacturers continued to supply both Northern and Southern markets during the war. Silk firms crafted patriotic handkerchiefs. London-based firm Foster, Porter & Co., Ltd. printed a silk handkerchief depicting a US flag behind a smoking cannon surrounded by a border of wavy red stripes and blue-and-white stars, and the declaration "The Union, Constitution, and the Flag Must and Shall be Upheld."[21] Meanwhile, a competitor printed Confederate leaders' portraits on silk handkerchiefs in a range of colors as the company explored possibilities for a Confederate market.

A young boy in Edgar County, Illinois, wore an infant dress made from printed cotton fabric with this design. Flag- and cannon-printed cotton fabric, c. 1860–65. Courtesy of the Library Company of Philadelphia.

Confederate captain John M. Johnson purchased one for his wife in Richmond, lending success to the company that copyrighted the design, which was "Registered by W. H. Tucker Kayess, London for 1863. 1864. 1865."[22]

Textile manufacturers also printed Confederate symbols on bolts of cloth that slipped through the blockade, including a cotton wool flannel fabric available in at least three colors that was printed with the Second National Flag of the Confederacy. Suppliers to Northern markets offered cotton fabrics in a range of designs, including stars, American flags, George Washington's portrait, and motifs with text that read "Union, Our Country, Union for Ever, or The CONSTITUTION must be PRESERVED."[23]

Swatches of these printed fabrics were used in quilts and to make pin cushions, and scraps were saved as mementos, but the fabrics were also used to make adults' and children's clothing. Recall, for instance, Edwin Booth's Second National Confederate Flag shirt—his own expression of battlefront style.[24] Some parents also dressed their children in similarly politicized clothing that was specially made for them. In a small town in Edgar County, Illinois, a store clerk and his wife dressed their son, born in 1862, in an infant dress made from cotton fabric printed with an alternating American flag and cannon motif.[25] More than novelty was at play in dressing these young children in flag prints. A child wearing a US flag print in the Union state of Illinois could seem unremarkable, but it was a contentious and potentially risky political statement in Edgar County, where Copperhead sentiments ran high and multiple deadly clashes occurred between Illinois infantry regiments and this radical faction of Northern Democrats who opposed the war and supported a peace settlement with the Confederacy.[26]

Military uniforms were made for and worn by the young sons of both Abraham Lincoln and Jefferson Davis—uniforms that conformed to the standards of brass manhood. The Confederate artillery uniform of Jefferson Davis Jr. (1859–1864) included a gray shell jacket with red piping, cuffs, and collar, as well as gilt brass buttons and gold braid on the sleeves. Tad Lincoln (1853–1871), on the other hand, was photographed in a dark blue Union uniform complete with shoulder straps, a gold sash, gilt brass buttons, and a Union kepi with US insignia. It was given to him as part of a courtesy commission granted by Secretary of War Edwin Stanton.[27] Entirely symbolic and a novelty for the boys themselves, as neither child actually served in an army, these uniforms nevertheless referenced what was at stake in the war—the future of a nation and the youth who would inherit it.

One need not have been the child of a political leader to find themself clothed in their family's patriotic sentiments. A young South Carolina girl wore a dress made from a First National Confederate, or Stars and Bars, flag. Cut into pieces, the short-waisted dress has a white bodice with red vertical stripes, red stripes at the shoulders, and a full skirt made of three tiers of alternating red and white fabric, with a vertical dark blue stripe that includes the stars. While this dress referenced a Confederate nation, the dress worn by the girl's brother was South Carolina through and through. Made of a deep cobalt blue, the dress is readily identifiable as the South Carolina state flag, with a gold palmetto tree on the skirt and a Zouave-style jacket trimmed in gold with a gold quarter moon on the breast.[28] This use of bright colors and printed fabrics was a marked departure from typical clothing intended for small children, which was often white cotton or linen that could be easily bleached clean. Clothing children in patriotism was, in fact, quite inconvenient.

Women and children overtly adopted military-inspired styles into their wardrobes. While Zouave-style jackets were inspired by French Zouave uniforms in the Crimean War, the style took on new meaning with the raising of US and Confederate units who adopted these Zouave-style uniforms, with

Confederate artillery uniform made by Varina Davis for Jefferson Davis Jr., 1864. Courtesy of the American Civil War Museum, Richmond, VA.

Thomas "Tad" Lincoln, portrait by Mathew Brady, 1864. Mathew Brady Photographs of Civil War–Era Personalities and Scenes, RG 111, National Archives and Records Administration, Washington, DC.

their baggy pants and open, cropped jackets. Variations on this style were quickly adopted in women's and children's fashions. "For children of both sexes," wrote *Godey's Lady's Book*, "these Zouaves are all the rage; they are made of all kinds of materials, thick and thin, but the white pique suit with broad, gay ribbon sash and the little turban hat with plume, makes a very pretty and stylish costume."[29] With bold embroidery, colorful trim, and an open jacket, civilians' Zouave fashions created direct connections to the uniforms worn by highly celebrated military units, like the New York Fire Zouaves.[30]

Such uniform-inspired fashion and brass buttons were particularly important to how Northern and Southern women of the middling and upper classes constructed their own gendered identities during wartime, even going so far as to use military buttons on their own clothing. As one woman wrote, "We wore our homespun dresses, made en train, trimmed in [South Carolina] palmetto buttons on the shoulders and on the sleeves, à la militaire."[31] Wearing brass buttons was a material way in which women expressed patriotism and physically marked their connection to soldiers, thereby tying their sense of womanhood to that of brass manhood. As one Union woman wrote, "A lot of us girls went down . . . as the soldiers were passing through and they cut buttons from their coats and gave them to us as souvenirs. . . . We wear . . . earrings made of the buttons the soldiers gave us."[32] The earrings this woman wore likely resembled a pair made from Confederate Navy buttons in which an ear wire was attached to the button back. With no additional embellishment, the earrings preserved the appearance of the buttons as buttons, rather than incorporating them into a larger piece of jewelry. Simple designs such as these made quite clear the connection between a woman's jewelry and a soldier's uniform.

Women's appropriation and feminization of these symbols of manhood seems to have been unproblematic in terms of the association between brass and manhood. Such usage may have been considered a tribute because women's fashions generally did not copy, but rather were inspired by, military insignia and employed otherwise-feminine elements of fashion, including hoops, bustles, and brightly colored silks. One red dress incorporated details that are reminiscent of the stripes and epaulets of military coats, and although the buttons on the dress are not made of brass, they give the illusion of it. Another cream-colored dress incorporated dark blue sleeve stripes, a collar, and horizontal stripes across the front closure, all of which were outlined in gold, as well as buttons with gold-colored stars and shoulder decoration resembling epaulets. These military-esque decorations were deliberately feminized; the fringe on the shoulders is made from mother-of-pearl spangles in place of bullion—an ornamental trimming made with twists of gold thread that was

These buttons were taken in 1866 to Webb's Jewelry Store in Baltimore, Maryland, to be made into earrings and a matching set of pins. Given the date of their creation, these earrings were likely intended as a memento or worn as an intentional slight against Union victory. The design itself, however, would have also been used during wartime. Pair of earrings made from Confederate Navy buttons, 1866. Courtesy of the American Civil War Museum, Richmond, VA.

typically used on officers' epaulets. Wearing such dresses expressed patriotic sentiment and knowledge of current fashion, but it was also a means by which women defined their own appearance in relation to brass manhood.

That a culturally acceptable female military role existed in conjunction with, if not officially part of, the military, and incorporated uniform style may also have contributed to the acceptability of women's adoptions and feminizations of select pieces of male attire into their wardrobes. The recognized and celebrated role of the vivandière was associated with a feminized version of a military uniform. Vivandières—who sold food to soldiers and occasionally provided medical care—modeled their clothing after the bloomer costume, including a shortened dress and baggy pantaloons.[33] A garment in the Smithsonian's collection, for instance, has three rows of brass buttons and red facings on a dark blue coat, giving it the appearance of a military coat. A photograph of vivandière Mary Tepe, on the other hand, shows her wearing a Zouave-style jacket.

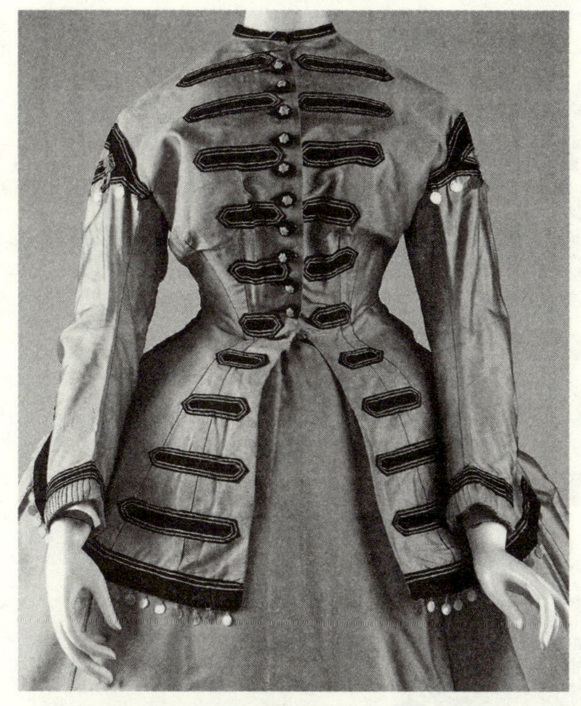

The dark blue sleeve stripes, collar, and horizontal stripes across the bodice of this dress resemble a military coat like that worn by cadets at the US Military Academy at West Point in 1860. The fringe on the shoulders is made from mother-of-pearl spangles that are reminiscent of military officers' shoulder epaulets. Afternoon dress, c. 1860–65, American. The Metropolitan Museum of Art, New York, Gift of Mary Pierrepont Beckwith.

The stripes and shoulder decoration on this dress are reminiscent of military style, while the buttons, with gold stars, give the illusion of brass. Afternoon dress, c. 1865, American. Brooklyn Museum Costume Collection at the Metropolitan Museum of Art, New York, Gift of Dr. and Mrs. Edward N. Goldstein, 1983.

Mary Tepe, a vivandière, poses for a photograph wearing bloomer-style clothing and a Zouave jacket. Photograph of Mary Tippee (Tepe), c. 1863. National Archives and Records Administration, Washington, DC.

Clothing—whether a loud, colorful Union apron or the more delicate flag pattern of a child's jacket—allowed people to wear their patriotism on their sleeve. But it could also be used seditiously—and people occasionally worried that those around them might lie about their political allegiances to gain access and entry into spaces for traitorous purposes. And some people did. More frequently, however, the clothing and accoutrements worn by civilians served to shore up political identities as the nation was unraveling along secessionist lines. To send men to fight was difficult, and to maintain support for war as men died was even more challenging. But as in other wars, steeled nerves and patriotic motivation could be mustered in a material landscape of support found in colorful bunting, flying flags, and civilians bedecked in patriotic prints and colors. That clothing meant something. And when soldiers encountered people in clothing that declared their allegiance to the other side, it could be unnerving—no matter the bravado with which they dashed it aside. That clothing served as material reminders that Union and Confederate sympathizers were in their midst, and posed the lurking question, If women and children would flaunt enemy colors in public spaces, what might they or their family members do in private?

While the use of flamboyant, patriotic symbols was common, especially in the early months of the war, people's day-to-day clothing—that over which many of those colorful accoutrements were worn—remained remarkably unchanged. Children continued to wear holes into clothing that needed mending, babies soiled dresses of white linen or cotton, and men and women wanted to update their wardrobes with the latest fashions. As they worked to maintain their sartorial practices during wartime, people faced increasingly urgent questions: Where exactly would the fabric and supplies come from? From whom would they purchase it? How would governmental intervention affect them? And what were a civilian's responsibilities in a war that was, at its heart, all about the raw material from which many of their clothes were made?

Cotton was, indeed, the common denominator in many aspects of clothing's relationship to this war. The states in rebellion possessed the raw material, while the loyal states controlled the majority of textile manufacturing. As Union blockades expanded, getting Southern cotton out to markets and finished products back in grew increasingly difficult, cost prohibitive, and, in some cases, impossible. As Union occupation of the Mississippi Delta expanded, the North regained more steady access to cotton as the federal government took over plantations, enslaved laborers, and the crops they produced. But throughout it all, both sides looked—Unionists with suspicion and Confederates with eagerness—to Britain, the textile powerhouse of the nineteenth century, and France, a primary source of exquisite silks and fine fabrics. Throughout the country, civilians began to worry about where their money was being spent and the importance of supporting the local economy.

In the South, the ability to profitably raise cotton using slave labor was at the heart of the war. Celebrating the Southern manufacture of raw cotton into clothing, then, was a natural extension of support for economic and political independence from the North. Expressing allegiance to the Confederacy through clothing did not require bright cockades or flag-print fabric. Drab browns and Southern-produced calicos worked, too. The Confederacy, Joanna Cohen explains, "framed nonconsumption as the best kind of civic virtue."[34] Government propaganda and persuasive rhetoric crafted a glorified public image of patriotic sacrifice that coexisted and clashed with women's more private avoidance, or even revulsion toward, homespun. Certainly some Confederate women embraced making and wearing homespun cloth as a political symbol and badge of sacrifice. However, many others—like Dolly Burge—wore it only as a last resort when clothing wore out, garments could not be borrowed, or new materials could not be purchased. What exactly, then, was Confederate "homespun" and why were Southern women so conflicted about wearing it?

The term "homespun" conjures up an image of coarse, scratchy, stiff brown cloth spun and hand woven by women in low-lit homes. However, as Laurel Thatcher Ulrich has extensively documented, it was the late nineteenth-century preoccupation with colonial American self-sufficiency that gave birth to the conception of homespun as a quintessential American fabric.[35] Historians of the Civil War have generally subscribed to the definition of homespun as a "homemade fabric made of cotton, linen, or wool" that "became a symbol of Confederate nationalism during the Civil War."[36] However, women and men living in the 1860s would have taken issue with this emphasis on "homemade" cloth because of our modern association of "homemade" with the domestic setting. When Confederates spoke of homespun they referred to cloth made "at home" in the sense that it was produced locally or regionally—and not necessarily in a domestic dwelling. Furthermore, they referenced cloth that exhibited far greater variety in color, texture, and even fiber than has been assumed.

Technically defined as a coarse woolen cloth, homespun was a term that more broadly referred to any coarse or loosely woven material resembling "a coarse woollen cloth formerly made by weavers using hand looms."[37] Homespun was simultaneously employed by Confederates to refer to cloth made on industrial-sized looms at local textile manufactories, to that woven on hand looms by enslaved women on plantations, and to that woven by white women who had access to spinning wheels and looms. In an article titled "Homespun" in the *Augusta Chronicle*, for instance, two of the "most beautiful and accomplished ladies" in Huntsville, Alabama, were praised for walking on the street while "dressed in frocks made at the Bell Factory."[38] Furthermore, contrary to romanticized images of preindustrial life, homespun did not need to be purchased directly from its maker or the manufactory. It was also sold unceremoniously in dry goods stores. Macon, Georgia–based John H. Kein & Company, for instance, advertised not only a "magnificent assortment of silk and dress goods," but also "Homespuns."[39]

Participation in Confederate homespun campaigns was heavily gendered and considered an important form of women's political expression. Newspapers and public officials frequently praised the public appearances of women dressed in homespun. "Hurra for Southern women and Southern manufactures!" declared one newspaper, while another asserted, "This may be called true devotion to the South—patronising Southern industry."[40] As Lisa Tendrich Frank notes, "Southern politicians, newspaper editors, and civic leaders urged women to replace ornamental pursuits with the patriotic tasks of spinning and weaving cloth."[41] Colonel Donald, of Leake, Mississippi, for instance, sent out tickets to a party requiring each woman to "come dressed in Mississippi manufactured apparel, in the manufacture of which she must, in some way, assist."[42] Donald required young men only to *dress* in Mississippi manufactured cloth, not to be involved in its manufacture. Elite young women had an overwhelmingly positive response to such homespun campaigns, readily adopting it into their wardrobes and chastising those who refused to follow the trend.[43] And, indeed, nearly 100 people—male and female—attended Colonel Donald's party, attired as requested.[44]

There are strong echoes between Confederate valorization of homespun and the Revolutionary moment nearly a century earlier. Homespun balls, elites' adoption of homespun clothing, and the association of homespun with national identity characterized both the Confederate and Revolutionary impetus for adopting homespun. In fact, the motivations behind Confederate homespun propaganda were actually quite similar to those of colonial elites. As Leora Auslander has shown, the Revolutionary and Early National periods "were characterized by the forming of an evolving American aesthetic that was not simply a renunciation or a return to a fantasized simpler life, but rather an effort to shape a particular republican and particular national self."[45] In the 1860s, as in the late eighteenth century, the significance was not that homespun was being produced but, rather, that elites were choosing to wear it.[46] Confederate men and women were actively engaged in crafting an identity apart from Northern fashion.

Supporting homespun manufacture was considered material evidence of "what Southern girls for Southern rights will do." As the Augusta, Georgia, *Daily Constitutionalist* punned, homespun "may be coarse, but after all, is it not the best course to patronise our own home production?"[47] In the words of Carrie Belle Sinclair's popular 1862 song (sung to the tune of "Dixie," "with spirit"), "The Southern Girl; or The Homespun Dress":

> We envy not the Northern girl, her robes of beauty rare,
> Though diamonds grace her snowy neck, and pearls bedeck her hair
> Chorus: Hurrah! Hurrah! For the sunny South so dear;
> Three cheers for the homespun dress the Southern ladies wear!
>
> . . . .
>
> Now, Northern goods are out of date; and since Old Abe's blockade,
> We Southern girls can be content with goods that's Southern made.

We scorn to wear a bit of silk, a bit of Northern Lace
But make our homespun dresses up, and wear them with a grace.

This sentiment was not only conveyed in song. Sallie Clayton recalled her and her friends' embrace of homespun in fall 1860: "To show our patriotism at this critical time, we were all clad in homespun dresses made by our own hands." She declared themselves "a proud set, and confident of being the first to appear in Georgia cotton; so in our simply made blue and white and brown checks, with all eyes upon us walked proudly from the Union Depot out to the grounds on Fair Street near the cemetery."[48] Kate Cumming noted that one daughter of a wealthy planter was, "like many of the rest of our ladies . . . determined to be independent of foreign manufacture. She has three pretty homespun dresses of different colors, which she manufactured herself, out of the raw cotton."[49] By foreign, she referenced not only Britain and France, but the US North as well.

Cumming claimed that her acquaintance had "manufactured herself, out of the raw cotton," three different colors of homespun fabric that was then sewn into dresses. But, as the daughter of a wealthy planter, did she, like so many of the elite white women involved in outfitting soldiers, consider the direction of enslaved workers to be part of her own work in manufacturing? Certainly, by their own account, many Southern women of the planter and small planter classes engaged in manual labor producing cloth and clothing. Yet Colonel Donald's demand that women attending his Mississippi ball wear clothing "in the manufacture of which she must, in some way, assist" allowed for a great deal of slippage in what it meant to "assist" in making cloth or dresses.[50] Indeed, enslaved women were responsible for much of the textile and garment production on Southern plantations before and during the war. These scraps of fabric, for instance, have a history of having been made during the war by people enslaved by J. J. McIver in Darlington, South Carolina. Who, among the thirty-four women and girls he enslaved, produced this cloth remains unknown. Their skill, however, is preserved in the distinct patterns of checked, plaid, and plain cloth that they wove from four colors of yarn.[51]

Black and white women sewed coarser cloth purchased from merchants, and prepared raw materials to produce the cloth in their own homes. Handling raw materials was a particularly disconcerting physical experience for elite Southern women. "Cotton cards," one woman explained, "were handled by hands that had known no heavier toll than to thrum the strings of the guitar, harp and other musical instruments. Home-woven garments were made by fingers never accus-

These swatches of plantation-made cloth have a history of having been made by people enslaved in Darlington, South Carolina, by J. J. McIver. Fragments of homespun Southern cloth, c. 1861–65. Courtesy of the American Civil War Museum, Richmond, VA.

tomed to heavier work than that of silken embroidery."[52] They emphasized the experience of their "smooth, dainty fingers" becoming accustomed to the practice of sewing quickly, rather than as a pleasant, social pastime.[53]

The materials themselves lend credence to women's emphasis on the physicality of processing cotton and wool, as well as the difference between sewing everyday clothing and uniforms and embroidering or even mending their own clothing.[54] Processing wool, for instance, required washing, carding, combing, and spinning before yarn could be woven or knitted. Carding wool by hand was a very physical process—the wool was drawn between two wire-toothed paddles until the tangles and bits of sticks or burrs were removed and the fibers aligned in one direction. The wool itself had an odor and was greasy to the touch because of the lanolin secreted by sheep's sebaceous glands. The sensory experience—the smells, touch, and physical motions—associated with carding wool was far removed from that of not only embroidering silk, but also sewing finished cloth. Some of this fabric would have felt very different in their hands, especially as coarser fabrics became the norm—a sensory reminder of their changing circumstances.

The coarseness of many homespun fabrics dyed with alternative sources did not automatically lend itself to durability. Some women complained that

These cotton cards are made of wood and wire bristles. They were used to disentangle cotton fibers in preparation for spinning. These cards are believed to have been used by the Gunter family of Fayetteville, Arkansas, during the Civil War. Cotton cards, c. 1860. Courtesy of the American Civil War Museum, Richmond, VA.

"Confederate dye" did not stand up to washing.[55] The process by which yarn was dyed at home was markedly different than the increasingly scientific processes of the art of imparting colors to cloth so that it would resist washing and wear.[56] Indeed, James Napier's 396-page *Manual of the Art of Dyeing* was also published under the title *Chemistry Applied to Dyeing*; it discussed not only the effects of heat and light on colors and fabrics, but also metallic and nonmetallic substances, mordants, and both vegetable and animal matters used in dyeing.[57] Rich, brilliant, lasting colors were achieved through an understanding of the interactions of heat, fiber, mordants, and other substances, as well as knowledge of the complex procedure of processing raw materials into dye, preparation of yarn or cloth to receive dye, methods of dyeing, and the process of finishing to set the dyes. Indeed, in order to achieve "Turkey Red," one manual recommended no fewer than seventeen separate steps.[58] Calico, cotton fabric that was dyed through a "printing" process using plates or rollers, was subjected to a series of finishing operations to remove excess dye before being "glazed," a heated pressing process that required specialized equipment and made "the surface of the cloth smooth, compact, and uniform."[59] It is no wonder, then, that Confederate women found that dresses made from home-dyed fabric did "not wash as well as calico."[60] As a result, while homespun could be purchased at a lesser price, some women believed the more expensive calicos to be a better bargain because they stood up to wear and thereby lasted longer. Calicos, however, were for many women "a rare treat."[61]

The problems of home-dyed cloth could have socially disastrous—if humorous—results. Elizabeth Lyle Saxon recalled an incident involving four girls from a wealthy Alabama planter family whom she visited frequently. The girls were among those who had gone "wild with the 'non-consumption' craze, going back to homespun jeans, lye soap, etc., long before necessity was upon us." With the approach of a Confederate ball in 1861, the girls sewed themselves homespun dresses, "making them with long trains, low neck and short sleeves," and trimming them with lace "suitable for the dress of a duchess at a court ball." Saxon considered the dresses "vile-smelling, common checked goods," such as were used for slaves, but, nevertheless, noted that when the girls appeared at the ball, they "looked as lovely as when in satin and lace, for the dresses fitted their perfect figures to a charm." But their odor was repellent. One of the young men in attendance inquired of Saxon:

> "Miss Lizzie, what in heaven's name is it that smells so awfully about those girls?"
> "Why, it is a new perfume they are using," I said. "They call it patriotism; I call it indigo dye."
> "Oh," he said, "it is the dresses; why didn't they wash them? It is a horrid smell."

To make matters worse, the fabric was improperly dyed and finished, likely due to the lack of an appropriate mordant to set the dye. When the girls returned from the ball, "they were a beautiful blue all about their necks," where the dye had rubbed off. The girls, Saxon reminisced, "hardly allowed the word homespun ever to be uttered to them until we really had to make it at home and wear it."[62]

Women's complaints about homespun clothing should not be discounted. As we will see in chapter 6, through this language of deprivation and loss, women were beginning to create the foundations for what would eventually become a well-articulated Lost Cause ideology. Indeed, the possibility of home dyeing gone awry did not dissuade women from attempting to produce aesthetically pleasing garments—and many were quite successful. Alice Thomas, for instance, obtained Saxony wool from her uncle's sheep, carded it by hand, and spun it into thread. Not content with an earthy brown color for her dress, she used cochineal—a crimson pigment derived from a parasitic Central American insect—to dye part of the yarn pink, and cedar boughs to dye the remainder gray, ultimately weaving the yarn into a pleasing pink-and-gray-striped pattern.[63] Similarly, Kate Cumming remarked on a friend's "very pretty homespun dresses. The material was grown, spun, and woven on her own plantation. The colors were very pretty, dyed from the bark of trees and wild roots."[64]

The colors may have been pretty and the patriotism strong, but there was also a counternarrative to this Confederate propaganda. When choosing homespun over silk at a dry goods store was a choice, elite women could take pride in scorning silk or Northern lace. But when it was no longer a choice, but the only option, their enthusiasm for wearing homespun quickly faded. For many women, their enthusiasm for homespun never outweighed their desire for imported calicos, linens, and silks, and they readily purchased such goods. Yet they soon found their spending thwarted by government regulations. Early in the war, both the central Confederate government and Southern state legislatures enacted policies to govern civilians' and soldiers' access to goods, among them, cloth and clothing. Of course, the start of the war did not immediately affect many of the goods that were available for purchase, because businesses either had large stocks on hand or were able to keep trade connections open. In August 1861, the Depot of Wheeler & Wilson's Sewing Machines in New Orleans, for instance, advertised "a full supply of Machines, Needles and Fixings, Silk, Linen and Cotton Thread, of all colors and sizes."[65] That changed with the expansion of Union blockades and occupation, along with speculation and Confederate redirection of textile production toward army supply, all of which further disrupted and restricted Southerners' access to textiles, clothing, and accoutrements.[66] As Northern supplies were cut off and imports became increasingly difficult to obtain, cloth, yarn, thread, buttons, needles, and other supplies necessary for making clothing were available only at a premium, and sometimes not at all.[67] This not only contributed to a gradual muddling of the materiality of Southern social hierarchies, but also created a context in which Southerners—elite, poor, and enslaved—felt in a very material way the government's intervention in their sartorial practices, an experience that shaped their understanding and expectations of, and direct involvement with, government authority.

Previous scholarship addressing wartime Southern textiles has highlighted the effects of the Union blockade, the scarcity of raw material, the paralyzing effects of reliance on Northern and British imports, and, more generally, the South's lack of manufacturing infrastructure.[68] However, while these factors certainly contributed to problems in the regional economy, the lack of raw materials and the dire state of Southern production capabilities have been overstated. There were, in fact, a significant number of mills producing hundreds of thousands of yards of cotton and woolen goods—particularly in Georgia and North Carolina—for much of the duration of the war. Indeed, as Bess Beatty has noted of North Carolina, many mills in that state operated both day and night to meet wartime demands for both cotton and woolen cloth.[69] That cloth, however, was intended for army use, and Confederate laws incentivized, and at times required, textile mills to devote their labor and resources to military production. In an 1863 report on Atlanta's markets, for instance, the *Augusta Chronicle* relayed, "No cotton goods are coming in. The foolish legislation has thrown all the factories into contracts for the [Confederate] Government."[70] Julia Fisher lamented, "There is no cloth to be had and no thread, no yarn—nor anything to do with."[71] From the civilian perspective, then, the scarcity of textiles available for consumption was not as simple as the Union blockade. Rather, it was directly tied to a more general Confederate government policy that "cannibalized" the regional economy.[72] White Southerners recognized that, when it came to accessing domestic goods, many of their problems stemmed from their own policies and not simply from Union blockades.

Domestic textile production was only one aspect of the broader governmental regulation of Southerners' access to clothing. As early as May 1861, just one month after the attack on Fort Sumter, the Confederate Congress began instituting new regulations on imports in an effort to "provide revenue from commodities imported from foreign countries" to fund the war. Establishing a series of tax schedules ranging from 5 to 20 percent according to the value of the import, the act applied to a broad range of goods, from liquor to furnishings to textiles. Clothing, objects of personal adornment, and the materials from which they were made figured prominently in the act, including jewelry, precious stones, and imitations; trimmings; articles of clothing intended for men, women, and children; and manufactures made from a wide range of fibers, furs, and hair, including Delaines, silk, wool, worsted, cotton, flax, fur, hemp, leather, velvet, angora, and mohair. Furthermore, needles of all kinds, for sewing, darning, and knitting, were subject to tax, as were particular dyes, including indigo, which produced a deep blue, and dragon's blood, a bright red plant-based resin.[73]

To be sure, there were vocal Southerners who fervently supported the purchase only of Southern-made goods. In 1860, women in Lowndes, Alabama, for instance, called for a boycott of Northern goods.[74] Store owners, too, attempted to appeal to such sentiments. As Lawrence Glickman explains, "Just as American manufacturers turned the non importation movement of the

American revolution into a business opportunity, many Southern entrepreneurs seized on the spirit of non intercourse to attract shoppers." One business declared that "Southern and Northern Clothing could not agree together on the same shelves, therefore, we would say that the Northern Clothing must and shall quit the Store."[75]

While the taxes imposed on goods affected the importation, availability, and cost of new dress goods, these items were not altogether banned. Those who could afford to, or had connections to do so, continued to purchase imported goods. Dry goods stores still had stock purchased prior to the war and continued to offer imports, as well as Northern- and Southern-made goods. That all changed with the Confederate Congressional Act passed in February 1864 prohibiting "the importation of luxuries, or of articles not necessaries or of common use," a decision that Jefferson Davis later defended by asserting that the use of the prohibited merchandise was "only for the indulgence of luxurious habits." Davis further singled out "all the finer fabrics of cotton, flax, wool, or silk" as objects of indulgence.[76] The consequences of being caught importing such luxuries could be financially devastating for the owner of the goods, who would be forced to forfeit everything on the ship and required to pay a hefty fine of double the value of the prohibited articles. This act also extended the reach of the government into the homes of potential purchasers, for it clothed collectors, naval officers, surveyors, and customs officers with the authority to enter not only ships and vessels entering Confederate ports, but also dwelling houses, stores, and any other building, with the intention to search for and seize these goods.[77] Such taxes and prohibitions against imports, limited access to cloth, and inflated prices created very real problems for Southern civilians. The government's role in this was not lost upon those experiencing these problems.

Northerners, too, experienced government-imposed changes to imported goods, but whereas the Confederacy first taxed and then prohibited the importation of luxury goods in 1864, Northern citizens experienced only an increase in their taxation. In the previous decade, the ability to purchase consumer goods, including clothing, was marketed as a symbol of Northern superiority and its free-labor political economy.[78] In the context of war, "advertisers and shopkeepers took advantage of new commercial opportunities and conflated shopping for new goods with a struggle on behalf of the Union's cause."[79] Yet the US government implemented tariffs and taxes to both encourage people to purchase US-made goods and to pay for the war using tax revenue. In 1861, Congress passed, and Lincoln signed into law, the Morrill Tariff Act, which was designed to protect US manufacturing. This measure had been under consideration prior to the war and was thwarted by Southern senators, but it took on new expediency following Southern secession. Revenue from the tariff paled in comparison to the steep price of funding a multifront war, however. The Internal Revenue Act of 1862 expanded domestic taxes to help fund the federal government.[80] In both instances, clothing and textiles were affected. The Morrill Tariff included a wide range of textiles, from woolen and worsted yarns and thread to plaid flannels, Delaines, linens, hollands, damasks, and silks, among others. Ready-made clothing for men, women, and children was also taxed, ranging from shawls, hats, shirts, stockings, and drawers to silk ribbons, laces, buttons, and other trimmings.[81] While the Morrill Tariff affected imports, the 1862 act both increased duties on foreign imports and directly taxed a broad array of domestic manufactures, including "cloth and all textile or knitted or felted fabrics of cotton, wool, or other materials," among them silk, worsted, flax, hemp, and jute.[82] All consumers of cloth and clothing were thus required to support the government through such measures.

Despite increases in the cost of imported textile goods, Northerners continued to purchase them. As Joanna Cohen notes, "While northern consumers were asked to pay an additional price for the privilege, the Civil War detached the consumption of imported luxury goods from the moralizing restrictions proposed by protectionists."[83] Still, some Northerners expressed concern over the origins of those goods. The knowledge that foreign textile firms were supplying both Northern and Southern markets, and the very real possibility that Britain—with its manufacturers so tied to US cotton supply—could throw its financial and political support to the Confederacy, led supporters of the Union to revisit an American tradition of nonimportation.

In 1864, moneyed women in Washington, DC, and New York City organized societies to discourage the purchase of imported luxury goods, with a particular emphasis on wearing apparel. This was not a call to produce cloth and clothing within a domestic setting but, rather, an effort to lend support to local manufacturers and decrease American spending overseas. Spurred by anxiety about the millions of dollars being spent in foreign markets, the aims of these societies had historical precedents in both the nonimportation movement of the 1760s, which was a boycott of British imports in protest of taxes, and the free produce movement's boycott of goods produced using raw materials that relied on slave labor during the 1830s and 1840s.[84]

By waging war against their households' unnecessary expenditures toward foreign goods, Union women could keep more gold within the country and be assured that they were aiding the US government in waging war against the Confederacy. This was not an argument for across-the-board nonimportation.

However, the societies did "aim at reducing our imports until they are at least even with our exports, thus raising the standard of our own depreciated currency, and, by keeping the gold in the country, enabling us to meet the expenses of the present war with greater ease."[85] In Washington, DC, the Ladies' National Covenant's objective was specifically to purchase "no imported articles of Apparel where American can possibly be substituted, during the continuance of the war."[86] The list of apparel ranged from foreign silks to satins and laces.

Members disagreed over the language used in the articles of incorporation, with one woman pointing out "the folly" of a society against "foreign gewgaws, which permitted every woman to judge for herself whether she could get along without them."[87] And indeed, without a strict requirement that women wear American-made fabric, the recommendation that domestic fabrics be used "whenever they can be substituted for those of foreign make" would have had limited results. The bulk of silks, velvets, and worsted wool fabrics worn by American women were made in England and France, while American manufacturers focused on cotton kerseys, twill, and broadcloth.[88]

The long-standing tension resulting from organizations being run and populated by women, yet given social and political credence through male benefactors, reared its ugly head yet again with the founding of these nonimportation societies. At the inaugural public meeting of the Women's Patriotic Association held at the Cooper Union in New York City, 2,500 women were in the audience, as well as the all-female executive committee, yet only men lectured or made remarks.[89] Maria Daly, president of the society, referred to the male speakers as "elderly men called in to give advice" who "prosed fearfully." Columbia University president Charles King, she said, "addressed us as females, a word suggesting, as Mrs. Delafield said, a cat with kittens." In his address, King assured women—on behalf of all men—that "they would be still more lovely and still more honored" if they abstained "as far as possible from all indulgence in articles of luxury in dress and adorn themselves with fabrics that we ourselves produce."[90] Daly interpreted his remarks as suggesting that women dressed to please men. She refuted the idea and found the speeches patronizing, writing, "They patted us on the back and said they were sure we would be good little dears and give up our laces, French bonnets, and sugar plums, if we knew how well the gentlemen would think of us."[91]

While men speechified, women set to work compiling a list of "retail dealers in American fabrics" and descriptions of the goods sold by them.[92] Maria Daly was soon frustrated by her efforts to work with US-based manufacturers, declaring them "very little worthy of our patriotic assistance." She was discouraged by their tendency to raise prices "to as high a mark as will enable them to undersell the foreign article." They took "no pride in making a good article," she claimed, and made it "as flimsy as possible."[93] For Daly, there was a line to be drawn between patriotism and profit.

How were others to know of your support for US-made goods? Members of the Washington committee adopted a way to declare one's commitment to domestic goods: a "black bee, with wings enameled according to nature, worn with a tri-colored ribbon, a little in front of the left shoulder."[94] The black bee and its red, white, and blue ribbon was a new version of a cockade. But rather than declaring one's political allegiance, it instead visually confirmed that, while, yes, this dress was made from a luxury fabric, it was a US-made luxury fabric. Despite these efforts and the intentions of the leaders of the Northern nonimportation societies to establish similar covenants in each of the loyal states, this movement was short-lived. The elevation of homespun to the level of a political statement remained primarily a Confederate phenomenon that accompanied the initial fervor of war.

That such political statements were made through dress signaled the emergence of a public politics that, in the absence of war, would have been unnecessary. Here we see at work a shifting, gendered space in which women's allegiances—and not only those of their male family members—were essential. The colors, cockades, and patriotic symbols incorporated into civilians' dress played important roles in rallying people's support for the war. Seeing women and children on porches, in windows, and along roadsides wearing cockades and waving flags was noted by many soldiers as they marched off to war. They helped to contribute to a celebration of brass manhood in their adoption of military-inspired style and brass-button jewelry. But the realities of war also brought into question the expediency of civilians continuing to import and wear prewar fashions and fabrics, especially when they might be purchased from a foreign power that might throw its support to the enemy. Women's choice of fabrics and other clothing items had important political and economic valences so much so that they were not only judged in the court of public opinion, but also restricted by governmental policies. At the same time as women navigated the changing landscape of wartime clothing consumption, the effects of war were becoming more evident, particularly in the South, where those changes included emancipation. As Black men, women, and children freed themselves, some of the same civilians who had once pinned a cockade to their breast or bonnet found themselves confronting a new clothing challenge: What role would clothing play in the process of freedom?

CHAPTER FOUR

Confronting Emancipation

Clothing and Transformation

Daylight had just broken onto an October 1865 morning as women, men, and children gathered outside of a former plantation carriage house now used to store clothing. They were not originally from Wadmalaw Island; they had traveled to South Carolina's Sea Islands along the path of destruction of Sherman's troops as they marched to the sea early that year. They, like thousands of other people, were starting over, having emancipated themselves and come together to forge free lives in new communities. The war was over, but resources were hard to come by—they needed shelter, food, and clothing, having brought with them only what they could carry. They waited patiently for newly arrived relief workers from the North to open the doors of the carriage house to distribute clothing. And they needed everything from basic undergarments to outerwear. Dresses, shirts, pants, chemises, drawers, socks, and shoes. Coats, shawls, and hats. They needed them in every size. Gowns for babies; pantaloons and short frocks for children; long skirts, bodices, pants, and shirts for adults.

"Imagine a small room piled on all sides with clothing of every description, size, shape, pattern and material," wrote Martha Schofield, a white Quaker from Pennsylvania, as she attempted to describe her first experience distributing clothing to these formerly enslaved people on Wadmalaw Island as part of the Pennsylvania Freedmen's Relief Association. In that storeroom, with clothing towering around them, Schofield and four other relief workers sorted through thirty boxes of clothing sent from the North.[1] As they sorted, the hundreds of Black men, women, and children waited outside in vain, for it was not until the following day that the process of distributing clothing would begin. Schofield and her fellow relief workers took one family at a time, recording their names and providing each person with an outfit. The individuals were not given an opportunity to look through the clothing themselves; not given a choice of patterns, silhouettes, or materials that might appeal to them and their own sense of style. Rather, Schofield noted, they were provided with "what our judgment saw fit to give." In three days, more than 500 people were "suited." "It was very tiresome dressing men, women, children, and babies," Schofield wrote. And then, the clothing ran out. "There are many that must go away unclothed," she confided. "It seemed hard but we could not help it." It was nearly two months before she noted that more clothing had arrived to be sorted.[2] But this time, it was not thirty boxes, but three.

In these boxes and barrels of secondhand clothing, relief workers like Martha Schofield saw not only the means to carry out their charitable work but also an opportunity—one that would allow them to shape what freedom looked like in the material world. And that is precisely what was at stake in the process of providing clothing to recently emancipated people: what freedom—and free people—looked like. Relief workers had their own ideas as to what that freedom should look like, but so, too, did formerly enslaved people. Although supportive of emancipation, many relief workers—white and Black—still harbored biases toward formerly enslaved people and worried about the challenges posed by the upending of a social order that was predicated on enslavement. They worried about the social and economic implications of emancipation—about social hierarchies, literacy, labor, and people's souls. But they also worried about the material world in which they lived. What *should* a postemancipation society—and the people who lived in it—look like? How could material goods shape new definitions of freedom? And how might clothing be employed in limiting the bounds of that freedom?

In the wake of slavery's collapse across the South, hundreds of thousands of men, women, and children actively sought to make sense of the possibilities and uncertainties freedom brought—men, women, and children, as Leon Litwack has described, "for whom enslavement composed their entire memory."[3] As they sought to reorder their lives, hundreds of thousands of Black refugees found their way to Union lines, were placed on abandoned and confiscated lands by federal officials, and came together to form their own communities. In the process of emancipation, formerly enslaved people were determining their own hard-won pathways forward. But relief workers assumed they knew better, and they employed the wearing and making of clothing as important tools in answering these pressing questions. White Northerners saw clothing as a solution to the challenges of emancipation because they lived in a world in which the physical environment was believed to affect the inward condition of a person. In the eyes of many relief workers, the transformations in habits and worldviews effected by wearing appropriate clothing, combined with lessons learned through its production and maintenance, would lay the necessary groundwork upon which formerly enslaved people might then receive a broader education—about labor contracts, property ownership, religion, and other concerns—considered necessary for successful navigation of the possibilities and challenges posed by freedom.

That belief was rooted in a longer history of approaches to reform. For many relief workers, a new set of clothes was the necessary first step in erasing the "marks of bondage."[4]

But they made a significant miscalculation. Relief workers' approach to clothing formerly enslaved people was based on the assumption that clothing worn in slavery was unsuitable for free people, in part because it had been worn within the confines of a system that relief workers understood to allow no freedom of choice. But Black refugees brought with them a host of experiences with and attitudes toward self-fashioning. These were people who, as Stephanie Camp argues, had long "claimed, animated, politicized, and enjoyed their bodies—flesh that was regarded by much of American society as no more than biddable property."[5] While enslaved people's expressiveness, as Katie Knowles has shown, was contained within the power dynamics of the slave system, they nevertheless expressed themselves through clothing choices.[6] Formerly enslaved people drew on these experiences as they actively built their own material culture in freedom—a material culture that was far more varied than relief workers' writings would lead us to believe and one that was based on their own aspirations and prior experiences. It is no wonder, then, that everyday conflicts erupted as freedom began to take shape in the material world.

Agglomerations of Rags

To be sure, there were strictures on enslaved people's ability to clothe themselves as they desired. Enslavers were the primary providers of clothing, and they engaged in the extensive trade of "plantation goods" produced by Northern manufacturers specifically for consumption by enslaved people. "Negro cloth," Seth Rockman explains, "was a woefully unspecific descriptor" for "dozens of fabrics intended to outfit slaves" sold to Southern plantation owners.[7] Ranging from "Fine Double Kersey" to "Plain Cotton Osnaburg," these fabrics were generally plain, and made as cheaply as possible without sacrificing their sturdiness. Enslaved people embellished the limited clothing provided as their yearly allowance. They also made their own purchases, bartered for calicos and buttons, and repurposed and reworked clothing that had been discarded by their enslavers.[8] Some people altered clothing gifted to them, such as the "gay" yet "cheap calico" that one enslaver ordered, noting she had "always given a dress of such to every woman after having a young child."[9] Many enslaved women dressed themselves in clothing they made from fabric they had dyed and woven themselves. Some were skilled seamstresses and expert dyers who could work with pokeberries, indigo, poison ivy, bay leaves, tree barks, and other natural dyes to produce vibrant colors that they set using vinegar, saline, alum, urine, and water as mordants.[10] They wove the cloth into a variety of patterns, from stripes to plaid to flowers. As Stephanie Camp shows, "Women, whose bodies were subject to sexual exploitation, dangerous and potentially heartbreaking reproductive labor, and physically demanding agricultural labor, worked hard to bring personal expression and delight into their lives."[11] One way in which they achieved such delight was through the color, pattern, silhouette, and decoration of their clothing.

Few examples of clothing worn in slavery survive, but we can glimpse the vibrance of some of those garments through the words enslaved people and white observers recorded in textual and oral history accounts. One woman wore "a white muslin dress, flounced up with blue and a blue hair ribbon on my curls."[12] Another woman's winter dress was dyed with pokeberries, while her summer dress was dyed with yellow mustard seed.[13] Another chose a yellow dye for her dress and painted her shoes yellow to match. Men, too, acquired fancy clothes, including one man who wore "a magnificent black satin waistcoat." In 1860, Manuel was described as "well-dressed," while Henderson Sears had on "a hickory shirt, black Cas. Pants, and black round coat."[14] Isabella "wore ear rings, and was quite tidy in her dress."[15] Frills, flounces, sashes, beads, "chinzes with sprawling patterns," bright handkerchiefs, fancy aprons, and clothing "every color in the rainbow" were all noted as being worn by enslaved women on their way to church.[16] Men wore coats in a wide range of styles, and women starched their skirts to make them fuller, added flounces, and combined various textures and colors of fabric and embellishment. Some made their own hoops or used those that had been discarded by white women.[17] Such clothing was often worn away from the eyes of enslavers, with the drabber, yet functional, linsey-woolsey, osnaburg, and cotton dresses, shirts, and pants making up people's workaday attire.

Through such clothing practices, enslaved people had for decades resisted the strictures of enslavement. And then came the war. As with white Southerners, the degree to which wartime affected enslaved people varied across time and geographical location. The same policies governing goods and blockaded ports affected enslaved people alongside their enslavers, who also decreased their expenditures on slave goods, including clothing. To be sure, enslaved women continued to card, spin, weave, and sew, but enslavers' attention to work and resources was often heightened. Clothing wore out and wasn't replaced. Dr. James P. Greves, superintendent and physician on a plantation on Port Royal Island, related, "They are generally destitute of clothing of all kinds. Their masters issued to them their last supply in December, 1860; consequently they suffer from want of necessary clothing."[18] According to one soldier in Virginia in 1861, an enslaved man confirmed similar circumstances, noting he had been clothed "pretty well, till dis year. Massa hab no money to spend dis year. Don't get many clothes dis year."[19] One woman recalled receiving "no clothing for 3 years except one cotton dress, one yarn Dress, Shoes & stocking" during the war.[20]

As a result, relief workers encountered not the vibrancy of the enslaved clothing culture of prior years, but people in desperate need of new clothing. Many formerly enslaved persons had only the clothing they wore on their backs, although some had packed parcels that included their enslavers' clothing when they left. Hard treks through rain, mud, dirt roads, and tangled thickets further damaged their clothing, some of which was just barely serviceable. "They were dressed," one observer wrote, "no, not dressed, nor clothed, but partly covered by every conceivable thing which could be put on the back of a biped."[21] And it was this image of destitution that many relief workers believed was the material results not just of war, but of decades of enslavement. They considered it material confirmation of the image of slavery portrayed by abolitionists, as Thomas C. Holt describes, as "an inhuman travesty that left slaves themselves looking something less than human."[22]

The needs resulting from the neglect of enslaved people's bodies were overwhelming, and, along with food, the provision of clothing was one of the highest priorities for relief workers. Members of relief organizations, Union soldiers, travelers, and formerly enslaved people themselves frequently described conditions of "extreme destitution" and individuals "having but a single garment."[23] Teacher Harriet Buss "saw them all the day after their arrival in Beaufort and such a sight I never saw before. You can scarcely imagine what a medley array of clothing, or rather rags in place of clothing, they presented. They were almost wild with the idea of being free. Had they been brought from heathendom, they could scarcely have looked much worse."[24]

Relief workers expressed immediate concern for the well-being of refugees' bodies and the clothing that covered them. This was not merely a practical concern about protection from the elements, however. Driving relief workers' efforts was the belief that the interior effects of bondage were evidenced by the material appearance of former slaves. Many observers saw the degenerating effects of slavery manifested in, and reproduced by, the "astounding agglomerations of rags" worn by people who resembled "an extraordinary collection of scarecrows," dressed, as they were, in ill-fitting, unstructured garments made from a wide range of fabrics, carpeting, and sacks.[25] The poor condition, inferior quality, style, and perceived disarray of clothing worn by formerly enslaved people was believed to reflect and reproduce disorder, poor habits, lack of self-respect, laziness, and degraded morals, among a host of other social ills. Images of enslaved people in tattered clothing circulated as cartes de visite and in the popular press, reinforcing this perception. These undisciplined, unruly bodies, immodestly clad in ragged, mismatched articles, were viewed as unsuitable and ill prepared for life in a society that associated sartorial practices, bodily discipline, cleanliness, and good taste with morality, piety, self-respect, civility, and gender roles. And so relief workers and army officials immediately set to work finding new or better clothing for them.

Clothing recently emancipated people presented a logistical challenge for both military officers and relief workers, a problem compounded by the prospects of mass slave emancipation: Who would provide the clothing? How would it be distributed? Some assumed this responsibility fell to the federal government. In the interim period between Lincoln's announcement of his intentions for emancipation in September 1862 and its implementation in January 1863, New York general W. K. Strong urged Secretary of War Edwin Stanton to act quickly in order to limit the government's incurred expenses in clothing Black refugees. Strong noted that "the only clothing at the disposal of the government consists of army clothing." Clothing freedpeople using the same-quality material as that used for the army for suits, jackets, and pants would cost between eight and ten dollars apiece—a hefty sum. The solution, he asserted, was to instead purchase "negro goods designed for the southern market" that sat in Northern warehouses, unable to be sold since the start of the war. That clothing, he advised, could be purchased for as little as one quarter of the price of army-quality clothing, at $2.50 to $3.00 apiece, resulting in a savings of hundreds of thousands of dollars for the government. Strong urged Stanton to take action immediately, so as to secure the materials and clothing at a low cost before the Emancipation Proclamation took effect, at which time manufacturers would likely realize they could charge a higher price for the same goods.[26] It is unclear whether Stanton acted on Strong's recommendations, but, regardless, his plans had a significant flaw. Strong was concerned only with clothing male army laborers; there was no provision for clothing women and children. This was instead a problem for civilian relief workers to solve.

Surrounded by thirty boxes of clothing on Wadmalaw Island, Martha Schofield experienced an outpouring of donations, the majority of it secondhand. Many people were eager to donate, from schoolchildren who raised small sums of money to associations like the Western Freedmen's Aid Commission, which organized clothing collection across fourteen states and distributed it to nineteen refugee camps.[27] Others had no desire to assist freedpeople. Writing from Beaufort, South Carolina, one doctor feared that asking for assistance from certain organizations could prove harmful. "I will not ask of the Soldiers Aid Society for anything for the blacks," he wrote. "It might lessen the zeal of some of the sisters, and I should be sorry to do that." Perhaps if they saw firsthand the conditions, he thought, these New Hampshire women might overcome their prejudice. "If they could see the old half palsied woman in hospital who had before we took her, involuntary discharged from bowels, and has no change of clothes, they would be willing to send at least one dress and shirt."[28]

The collection and distribution of clothing required significant amounts of time and resources, beginning in earnest in 1862 and continuing into the postwar era. At a cost of $1,170,000, clothing intended for distribution was the third-highest expenditure of the Freedmen's Bureau in 1866–67, behind commissary stores and transportation.[29] "Clothing Rooms" also had designated, permanent places in the physical architecture of many freedmen's camps.[30] As the number of refugees and occupied lands grew, so too did the number of Northern men and women like Martha Schofield who sought to organize, teach, and work with them. Most came from middle-class and wealthy families, bringing with them, as Thavolia Glymph notes, "the values of the affluent and the aspiring upwardly mobile."[31] Many of those who traveled south during and immediately following the war did so with a poor outlook on formerly enslaved people's ability to take on the responsibilities of living in a free society. As Thomas C. Holt has argued, in their efforts to "strip away the mythology southern defenders had woven around slavery," abolitionists had portrayed slavery in such a way that "slaves might be objects of pity, surely, but not candidates for admission to the body politic."[32] After decades of using such rhetoric, relief workers' expectations of the people they would find in the South ranged from simple-minded "darkies" to a "race of savages."[33] White men affiliated with the military, too, often expressed negative outlooks on freedpeople's immediate prospects. Some insisted it would take a generation to achieve any positive change. "I do not think they are 'fit to take their places in society with a fair prospect of self-support and progress,'" wrote one captain.[34]

Other relief workers were more hopeful, but, as Glymph argues, they were "generally united in the belief that enslaved people were at once abused and racially inferior and lived lives of unrelieved depravity."[35] Counteracting the negative effects of slavery, these relief workers believed, required erasing the "marks of bondage" and eliminating behaviors they deemed inherent to enslavement. Formerly enslaved people needed to be instilled with new habits, routines, morals, work ethics, gender roles, and worldviews to reshape their identities and place in society, thereby enabling them to successfully navigate life as free men and women. Such views were not only held by white reformers but also espoused by free Black reformers living in the North. As Harriet Jacobs conveyed to William Lloyd Garrison, "They need to be taught the right habits of living and the true principles of life."[36] Which "habits" and "principles" were deemed most important for formerly enslaved people's education varied: While some reformers focused on the ownership of one's own body and the right to the fruits of one's own labor, others stressed the importance of marriage and familial ties. These considerations factored into relief workers' approach to aid. As Amy Murrell Taylor has argued, relief workers' "deeply ingrained expectations about the proper behavior and morals of newly freed people—ideas rooted in race, gender, and class—were channeled into nearly everything from the provision of clothing to the establishment of schools."[37]

Relief workers perceived formerly enslaved people's preparation for freedom as requiring a recalibration of their understanding of gender roles and the cultivation of traits associated with manliness and femininity—all of which were defined according to white Northern ideals. They considered the future of Black children raised in freedom to be at stake. Black women, relief workers asserted, needed to take seriously their roles as wives and mothers and actively work toward "elevating" themselves if they were to successfully rear the next generation. Martha Schofield told women they "must strive to elevate yourselves so that you may be fit to train your children for noble men and women."[38] An article in *Douglass' Monthly* asserted that Black women needed "to be taught self respect and womanly virtue, and to improve them and enable them to form desirable habits it is necessary to bring them in contact with the wise and good of their own sex." The women, the article declared, "need advice and instruction, such as only intelligent and Christian women can give."[39]

Martha Schofield traveled to Wadmalaw Island with the intention of doing just that—by teaching and setting up schools for formerly enslaved children. And she would.[40] But like many teachers she also found herself in the immediate role of relief worker as she distributed clothing, food, and other necessities to the people she sought to educate. Certainly, some people were disgruntled by the amount of relief work in which they engaged and felt their plans for educating and proselytizing were being put on hold.[41] However, others understood the provision of clothing as the crucial first step in a process of transformation. Elizabeth Hyde Botume asserted that "needles and thread and soap and decent clothing were the best educators, and would civilize sooner than book knowledge."[42] Minds were shaped by attending to bodies.

Metamorphoses

For mid-nineteenth-century Americans, the interior effects of bondage were embodied in, and evidenced by, the material appearance of formerly enslaved people who wore ill-fitting, untidy garments; "curious," amusing fabric and materials; and tattered cloth. The poor condition, inferior quality, style, and general disarray of clothing worn by formerly enslaved people were understood to reflect and produce disorder, poor habits, lack of self-respect, laziness, and degraded morals, among a host of other social ills. The ragged slave was both a reality and a visual and a literary trope employed by relief organizations, newspapers, artists, and other observers. Relief organizations drew on such imagery to their benefit, strategically presenting potential donors with an image of refugees who were in desperate need but exhibited potential for "improvement."

Descriptions of individuals as having undergone a significant change were a common trope in both Black and white observers' depictions of the process of clothing formerly enslaved people in new and secondhand garments. As in the case of Black soldiers, descriptions of civilians' transformations regularly employed words and phrases invoking contrast, including "different beings," "wholly changed," and "metamorphosis."[43] Such perceptions likely underlay the double meaning behind Julia Wilbur's observation that "they come to us for a change & we have little or nothing to give them."[44] Harriet Jacobs, upon seeing men, women and children in "clean garments," observed, "What a contrast! They seemed different beings."[45] As Amy Murrell Taylor notes, with a change of clothes, "the bodies of the refugees, in an instant, could appear to have shed their past of enslavement and suffering and take on the appearance of freedom."[46] But it was not simply *appearances* with which relief workers were concerned. They sought to embody freedom through manipulation of the material world. Clothing played a pivotal role in effecting that transformation—the replacement of ragged clothing with clean, better-fitting garments was believed to possess the power to impart new routines and perceptions of one's self, creating a basis upon which further reform and education might proceed. Dr. Greves for instance, asserted that "very little real progress can be made in reforming any people whose physique is neglected," and therefore argued that "they need to be led into correct habits of body."[47] A more ordered environment, including clothing, would serve as a corrective.[48]

Such re-clothing of formerly enslaved people must be understood within the broader context of both the historical practice of donning new clothing when one's legal status changed and nineteenth-century methods of reform. The notion that a person would begin free life with a new suit of clothing was not a product of the Civil War era and slave emancipation, but was, rather, rooted in cultural and legal practices associated with indentured servitude and apprenticeship. Until the nineteenth century, the provision of a new suit of clothing upon release from service was often one of the chief clauses in apprenticeship contracts and indentures. These legally binding contracts frequently required masters to provide one or two new suits of appropriate clothing to their white apprentices or indentured "bondsmen" upon completion of their apprenticeship or years of service.[49] The "freedom suit" was central to the process of ending one's indenture and being in full possession of one's skills and labor. These clothes, declared the protagonist of Pennsylvania author Caleb Earl Wright's novel *Two Years behind the Plough,* were "the final, crowning piece of all the benefits I had received" as an apprentice, "the festive garments in which I was to celebrate my restoration to family and friends after my two years' exile!"[50] Although such contracts were no longer common practice by 1860, the idea that new clothing came with a change in one's servile status was an accepted schema in American culture with roots in the seventeenth, eighteenth, and nineteenth centuries.[51] The predominantly white apprentices and indentured people who experienced this donning of new clothing upon completion of their years of service were not, however, viewed as requiring further transformation to take their place in society. Formerly enslaved people, on the other hand, fell within the broader class of people who were considered objects of reform.

At the center of reformers' worldview was the belief that material conditions and the physical environment affected the inward condition of a person. It was not only clothing that was implicated, but the entire built environment. And this belief applied not only to individuals, but also to the social body. In the first half of the nineteenth century, Americans, guided by this worldview, were engaged in a process of reimagining, reforming, and reconstructing various elements of the urban built environment—streets, sanitation systems, city plans, and a range of institutions, including cemeteries, government buildings, and penitentiaries—all in an effort to create more ordered spaces, and thereby a more ordered citizenry.

As attitudes toward formerly enslaved people suggest, some members of society, including Native Americans, prostitutes, criminals, and the poor, were believed to require more extensive reform than even a more organized environment could provide. Reforming people through manipulation of their clothing and environment is most succinctly articulated in late eighteenth- and nineteenth-century penal reform movements that sought to rehabilitate offenders. Prison reformers were motivated by "concern with the improvement of prisoners' souls through the everyday structuring of time, space and employment."[52] This therapeutic vision, Dell Upton has observed, was repressive, but "it was an optimistic repression, a misguided attempt to recruit republican citizens from among the downtrodden."[53]

Penal reformers were guided by a "moralism that asserted that prisoners would only recant their crimes if stripped of their former identity."[54] Clothing was central to that process. One proponent of penal reform believed that the moment when "he is obliged to take of[f] his citizen dress and to put on the convict's jacket was the one great moment in every convict's life, which might almost always be turned to good account."[55] Upon entering the penitentiary, a man's hair was cut, his face shaved, his body "thoroughly purified" of dirt and vermin, and he was then "decently clad in the clean striped dress of the prison."[56] Such a process has strong echoes in descriptions of the ritualistic stripping, washing, and uniforming of slaves who became Union soldiers. In the case of prisons, reformers frequently emphasized the necessity of washing and providing intact clothing as first steps toward destroying the criminal personality and preparing prisoners to receive lessons of reform. "The first process towards reforming a felon," noted the author of *The Art of Good Behavior*, "is to give him a thorough washing."[57] Taking this a step further, clothing prostitutes in modest garments was expected to "mend their ways."[58]

These reformers articulated a broader schema that transcended prison walls: Clothing possessed the power to both unmake and make a man or woman, to degrade and to uplift, to castigate or to "positively" transform a person to conform to social expectations. Clothing held a special power, largely because of its close association with the body. Placing relief workers' approach to clothing formerly enslaved people within this context of prison reform might seem misplaced—emancipated slaves, after all, were not incarcerated. However, they, like convicts, were perceived and described as suffering from degradation and depravity resulting from abuse and enslavement.[59] Relief workers believed that formerly enslaved people needed to be rehabilitated by developing many of the same traits that were of utmost concern to prison reformers: industriousness, religiosity, morality, and personal discipline. In short, freedpeople were among the newest members of the "downtrodden" who needed to develop "mental and corporal habits of virtuous behavior" in order to be shaped into good citizens.[60] Improve former slaves' physical conditions, Dr. Greves argued, "and they will rapidly improve in the moral and religious departments of their nature."[61]

Given the longer history of shaping people through material things, it is unsurprising that clothing played a pivotal role in relief workers' approach to effecting the transformation of the formerly enslaved. But mass wartime slave emancipation posed new challenges for ordering American society. The scale with which this effort was undertaken and what was at stake—the incorporation of millions of people into free society—were both unprecedented. Such efforts to transform formerly enslaved people through the material world shaped many people's early experiences of emancipation. Transforming people through clothing posed risks. If clothing could, quite literally, "make the man" or woman, it also held the potential to elevate Black women and men's social status to that of the white relief workers. And so Black refugees found themselves simultaneously presented with the opportunity to improve their material conditions and restricted in their choices. From the perspective of white relief workers and military officials, clothing needed to be chosen carefully such that it would correct the ills of slavery but not bring formerly enslaved people onto equal footing with white Americans. Indeed, relief workers neither sought to make Black Southerners their equals nor increase the Black population of the North. As Taylor argues, their work, along with "each shipment of money and clothing was thus an investment in containing refugees in the South, reinforcing the efforts of politicians to halt the removals of refugees to Northern states."[62] Relief workers were working under the assumption that freedom for enslaved people was still bounded by a racialized hierarchy. And it was precisely for this reason that the appearance of Black women, men, and children in finer clothing was so contentious. At stake was not merely the visual cues of status conveyed by clothing, but the inner transformation that was believed to occur.

Although some relief workers attempted to dispel the concept of an inferior "negro taste," most of them had poor opinions of the garments worn by Black refugees. While many recognized that the quality of clothing refugees wore was a direct result of conditions in the war-torn South, they were also dismayed by what they perceived as formerly enslaved people's lack of concern about the materials and styles in which they were clad. One white soldier observed a "small urchin without a rag of clothing save the basque waist of a lady's dress bristling with whalebones and worn wrong side before, beneath which his

Ingrain carpet was often patterned and colorful. Ingrain carpet, c. 1850–60. The Metropolitan Museum of Art, New York, Gift of Frances W. Geyer, 1972.

smooth ebony legs emerged like those of an ostrich from its plumage."[63] Another white man recalled a story of a boy on his way to school "in the morning, clad in a shirt of Brussels [carpet], and a pair of trowsers of ingrain carpet," likely taken from an abandoned plantation house.[64] Similarly, "many of the men," teacher Elizabeth Hyde Botume wrote, "had strips of gay carpeting, or old bags, or pieces of blanket, in which they cut arm-holes and wore as jackets. Their pants were tied below and above the knees and around the waist with pieces of rope to keep them on." The women's dresses, on the other hand, "were nothing but patches, sewed together with every variety of thread, even to coarse twine."[65] One photograph of a "contraband" depicts William Headley wearing torn pants and a cotton feed bag tied around his neck. Made into a carte de visite, this photograph was likely intended to provide evidence of slavery's degradation. More disconcerting, and particularly problematic in regard to gender, were women's use of men's clothing, the exposure of bare skin, and the use of clothing that was so ragged that it failed to communicate gender. "Some of the women," Botume observed, "had on old, cast-off soldiers' coats, with 'crocus [burlap] bags,' fastened together with their own ravellings, for skirts, and bits of sailcloth for head-handkerchiefs."[66]

That women were clad in cast-off uniform coats is unsurprising. Many refugees' first contacts with people who had access to supplies were with military officials who controlled military clothing stores. Indeed, in one area of Arkansas, clothing necessities were met through the use of deceased soldiers' clothing that was turned over by hospitals.[67] Given that military clothing was exclusively intended for distribution to male soldiers, it was limited to coats,

William Headley emancipated himself from a plantation near Raleigh, North Carolina, and arrived in New Bern, North Carolina, in 1864. On the verso of an extant carte de visite in the National Gallery of Art, Horace James described Headley's emancipation and his clothing, writing, "His cloak consisted of an old cotton grain bag, slit open on one side and raveled," giving it the appearance of having fringe. Carte de visite of William Headley, c. 1864. Library of Congress Prints and Photographs Division, Washington, DC.

pants, men's drawers, and shirts. The fundraising and shipment of clothing performed by benevolent societies, and the involvement of civilian relief workers in its distribution, were critical to obtaining women's clothing. The urgency with which such organizations responded to the need for women's clothing is telling; gender was shaped and expressed through the clothing on hand. Access only to men's clothing hindered efforts to gender formerly enslaved women through "proper" female clothing. As a result, women's and children's clothing dominated pleas for donations. One request for clothing noted that "cast-off clothes of all kinds (including summer clothing), especially such would be of use for women and children, are very much wanted."[68]

As they began the task of clothing Black refugees, relief workers were most immediately concerned with clothing's basic function: protection from the elements. Lack of proper clothing affected the rhythms of everyday life, especially during inclement weather. On one January morning Martha Schofield noted that "it is real cold now every thing freezing mercury at 30. Our school is small because they are so poorly clad."[69] Freezing weather and insufficient clothing also carried a very real risk of contributing to illness and eventually death. Indeed an 1862 appeal for donations to the National Freedman's Society asserted that "anything and everything in the shape of clothing would be most gratefully received, for unless Providence opens up some merciful way by which their needs can be supplied, the winter's chilling, blasting, wind will carry many of the half-naked contrabands to a premature grave."[70] The extreme need for clothing during cold weather was not merely a concern of the early days of emancipation, but continued as more people entered Union lines. In 1864, a teacher reminded readers of the *Christian Recorder* that "not a day passes but we are called upon by our pupils for such articles as are really necessary to shield them from the severity of the weather."[71] Flannel was particularly valued in the winter months: "The warmth obtained by wearing flannel next the body is very beneficial, and the light stimulating effect arising from its roughness tends to keep the skin in healthy action."[72]

Relief workers tackled with great earnest questions about what fabrics and forms of clothing were best suited to formerly enslaved people and how Black refugees should be instructed in "proper" modes of dress. First and foremost, they emphasized the cleanliness of bodies and clothes. Dirtiness was perceived as the "never failing sign of vulgarity." Bodily cleanliness was considered a matter of moral choice for which each individual was responsible, making it a means by which to gauge moral uprightness, civility, and even intelligence. Elizabeth Hyde Botume, for instance, referred to one person as a "clean and intelligent-looking woman."[73] In "polite" white American society, cleanliness was considered paramount to the stylishness of clothing. As one etiquette manual declared, "Better coarse clothes with a clean skin, than silk stockings drawn over dirty feet." Indeed, one advice writer recommended being "economical with your tailor" in order to be "extravagant with your laundress," for no garment, no matter how expensive or stylish, could "be pleasing unless clean and fresh."[74]

Relief workers disagreed as to whether or not cleanliness was a prerequisite for, or a goal of, refugee aid. Some proposed making cleanliness of body and clothes a requirement for receiving aid. However, this was complicated by the fact that many individuals possessed only one set of clothing—as one woman noted, "Many of the women were merely clothed in rags, and had no changeable apparel even to serve them while they washed what they had on."[75] Julia Wilbur expressed frustration with her supervisor's attempts to regulate access to clothing, particularly when he "told them [refugees] if they came there dirty they could have nothing, & they must go home & wash their clothes—He actually drove several away, when perhaps they could not wash their clothes for want of a change of garments." Wilbur waited until the supervisor left and began to distribute clothing to those who had previously been denied. She valued cleanliness, but classified it as an attribute toward which to strive, rather than an absolute requirement for aid, noting, "We intend to inculcate cleanliness, but we mean to be reasonable about it, & give the poor things a chance."[76]

Inculcating cleanliness provided a base upon which other concerns about clothing could be addressed. Levels of taste and style, fit and orderliness, and an understanding of the appropriateness of garments for particular occasions were central to relief workers' efforts to improve what they described as an inferior "negro taste" that was characterized by "curious" fabrics, odd materials, and a motley combination of mismatched garments.[77] But how, relief workers wondered, were former slaves to develop a sense of taste when their clothes had previously been purchased for them and served utilitarian means?

Relief workers' understanding of clothing worn in slavery was based upon faulty assumptions. Many of these people had never encountered enslaved people prior to the war and based their understanding of those people's clothing on abolitionist literature that depicted slaves as objects of pity.[78] When those relief workers traveled south, they met people whose access to clothing had been severely diminished. Most were not wearing the clothing they had styled for themselves, nor even the typical clothing provided by enslavers worn prior to the war. Enslaved people, too, were affected by blockades—indeed, slaveowners had previously purchased "negro cloth" and ready-made clothing from Northern manufacturers to distribute to slaves. During the war, enslavers typically clothed their own families before distributing new clothing to those they enslaved. People who lived on plantations with equipment for making cloth and clothing fared better, provided that the raw materials were still available. But many of the refugees encountered by relief workers had not been supplied with clothing since December 1860. It was little wonder, then, that clothing worn during hard labor for two or more years would be in disrepair.

Initially, some relief workers approached clothing Black refugees as though they were a blank canvas upon which they could apply their own ideas of which colors, fabrics, cuts, and styles were most suitable; they sought to define the "good taste" they deemed "fitting" for formerly enslaved people. An elusive, ever-changing concept for nineteenth-century Americans and, yet, one that held the power to permit or prohibit a person's acceptance in civilized society, "taste" implies a responsibility to actively work at refining the world in which one lived.[79] In the case of formerly enslaved people, exercising good taste was first and foremost evidence of discernment and decision-making—both skills, according to relief workers, that had been quashed by slavery and were necessary to successfully navigate freedom. Taste was not an inherent quality but, rather, one that needed to be learned. As Charles Nordhoff wrote, "Taste in these matters [of dress and home furnishings] has to be acquired slowly; they [slaves] have always been accustomed to a certain fashion of house and dress, and know nothing beyond or different."[80] They were instructed, then, to "dress well, but in cheap, plain apparel."[81] But good taste was also a situational concept tied to one's social status, race, and gender; an exhibition of good taste for one person could be a sign of vulgarity in the case of another.

Taste, rather than stylishness, distinguished slave clothing from the "costume of freedom" in the eyes of relief workers. In order for former slaves to be recognized as having begun what the white public would recognize as transformation into upright, respectable people with improved morals, they did not need to don expertly tailored clothing. Clothing's power of transformation lay in the contrast—an evolution from tattered rags to clean, crisp, more fitted, tasteful garments. The fit of clothing—or lack thereof—was of great concern, particularly taking into account the importance of posture. Judgments about a person's character and station in life were made on the basis of posture and the way in which they carried themselves. This element of nineteenth-century Americans' understanding of the relationship between clothing, the body, and character is critical to understanding perceptions of how individuals might be reformed. Erect, disciplined posture demonstrated inner self-control and moral uprightness. Relief workers were concerned, then, that refugee women's "gowns do not often fit neatly," and that their "clothes seem to hang upon a field hand, realizing the old sailor's figure of a 'purser's shirt upon a handspike.'"[82] Their clothing, in other words, was so loose fitting that it hung upon the body like a sack, offering no definition to the figure or discipline to the body.

Here lay one of the means by which relief workers understood clothing to be able to effect transformation in former slaves. As in the case of Black soldiers, replacing shapeless rags with more structured clothing was expected to confer a sense of discipline on a previously unruly body by encouraging better posture. The degree to which one required postural support had longstanding gendered dimensions. Both arbiters of fashion and physicians went to great lengths to corset and straighten women's "weaker" bodies to conform them to a particular ideal of feminine beauty that valued a diminutive waist, sloping shoulders, and a full, wide skirt. Men, by contrast, wore corsets or braces only to correct deformities. At mid-century, posture was a central goal of proper bodily management, and both women's and men's garments played an important role in molding bodies.[83] Improvements in posture that signaled an upright morality could be achieved through dress without costly, structured undergarments or refined fabrics. As detailed drawings in tailors' guides illustrate, both men's and women's clothing was cut to enhance, and help maintain, a person's posture.[84]

A pair of staged photographs depicting two children, titled "As We Found Them" and "As They Are Now," used clothing to make an argument about both the potential possessed by former slaves and the positive effect the Society of Friends could have upon refugees.[85] In the first image, both of the children have been dressed in unkempt, tattered clothing that is too large for their small frames. The boy stands with one bare foot propped upon the other. Visually, it is difficult to distinguish the line that separates the children's bodies; their tattered rags flow into one another. In the second image, the children are clothed in appropriately sized garments that correspond to those typically worn by children in the 1850s and 1860s. Clothing bears a great deal of narrative weight in terms of gendering the children in these images. The gender of one child, dressed in shapeless scraps, is not readily apparent. In the second image, however, a dark polka-dotted dress genders the child as a girl, a fact brought into greater relief through contrast with the boy's lighter-colored jacket and trousers.

Indeed, clothing played a critical role in gendering women and men—both categories of gender were artifices created through material enactments upon the body. But relief workers believed that formerly enslaved women's bodies could not be molded in the same way as white women's bodies. Culturally, Black refugee women were prohibited access to many of the sartorial elements that gendered white women's bodies, such as corsets, hoops, and fine fabrics, all of which contributed to the public image of white femininity, respectability, and discipline. Whereas silk dresses supported by crinolines were considered the epitome of good taste for elite and middle-class white women, freedwomen who donned finer clothing were criticized and even prevented from acquiring it. While at Fort Pickering, Tennessee, for instance, Henry Hayes, a New Hampshire surgeon, asserted that "the passion of the negro women for dress is excessive." One woman, he continued, "employed in some culinary employment is clothed in white muslin or something so near white that it may readily be taken for it, with three dark colored flounces, and hoops so that I do not see how she can get through the rather small door that leads into the cooking shanty."[86] For Hayes, this woman's offense was

"Virginia Slave Children Rescued by Colored Troops—As We Found Them" and "Virginia Slave Children Rescued by Colored Troops—As They Are Now," c. 1864. Virginia Museum of History and Culture, Richmond, VA.

threefold: She wore clothing that was not only elaborate, but also impractical in color for the work she performed, and that was a physical impediment to her kitchen duties. There were practical elements to this: Wearing a corset and hoops was difficult—even dangerous—for someone engaged in manual labor.[87] But it was skin color and not concern for a woman's well-being that motivated such commentary. With few exceptions relief workers asserted that smooth silk, whalebone, and rich colors were incongruous with dark skin and therefore vulgar when worn on a Black body. Some relief workers, as Amy Murrell Taylor has shown, went to great lengths to "police the boundaries between black and white women's dress and perpetuate dull, simple styles for black women."[88] They rejected donations they deemed "too good in texture," forced women to purchase calico and unbleached muslin in lieu of a desired hoop skirt, measured the width of skirts to ensure they were modest, and requested the donation of coarse fabrics, including "negro cloth."[89]

There was no universal wardrobe by which a person could be judged "well dressed"; what was proper for one person might be considered "bad dress" when worn by another.[90] Lest it be confused with being dressed in finery, to be well dressed was to be *appropriately* dressed—and what was appropriate was determined using several categories. While some of these categories were dependent upon physical features of the body, one etiquette expert emphasized that wearing clothing that one could reasonably afford was critical to dressing appropriately. The author of *The Habits of Good Society* asserted, "To be well dressed is to be dressed precisely as the occasion, place, weather, your height, figure, position, age, and remember it, your *means* require." Furthermore, appropriate dress did not exhibit "peculiarity, pretention or eccentricity" and was "without violent colors, elaborate ornament, or senseless fashions."[91] An appropriately dressed person, in other words, would not physically stand out in contrast to other members of their same social group.

The kinds of transformations and evidence of progress that relief workers expected clothing to effect are clearly revealed in discourses surrounding sartorial practices on Sundays, which played a significant role in relief workers' assessment of freedpeople's religiosity. Here, relief workers' emphasis on Sunday clothing was likely informed by approaches to reform in almshouses. In Portland, Maine, for instance, all persons were required to "put on their best apparel, and attend religious service, at the second ringing of the bell."[92] Female relief workers—many of whom were associated with Protestant organizations—were deeply troubled by a seeming lack of attention to refugees' Sunday dress because they believed that this clothing directly reflected and produced their level of piety, their respect for the Sabbath, and their religiosity more generally. In particular, relief workers were concerned by a seeming indifference toward wearing the same clothing on Sundays as on weekdays. As a result, many relief workers instructed women to wear a different dress to Sunday worship, and some made it a priority to ensure access to additional garments whenever possible. If individuals would wear nicer garments on Sunday, these relief workers believed, they would be instilled with greater reverence for God.

But enslaved people had long participated in a vibrant dress culture and had desired a "good" set of clothes, in addition to the coarser clothing in which they labored, long before any relief worker told them they should care.[93] Frederick Law Olmsted, for instance, observed in the 1850s that, in Richmond, Virginia, "the greater part of the colored people, on Sunday, seemed to be dressed in the cast-off fine clothes of the white people, received as presents, or purchased of the Jews," who were presumably willing to sell to enslaved people. Others had "a better suit of coarse blue cloth, expressly made for them evidently, for 'Sunday clothes.'"[94] Elite Southerner Mary Chesnut described enslaved women's "holiday church and outdoor get-up" as "excessive and grotesque" finery.[95] The seeming lack of attention to Sunday dress observed by relief workers was, for many refugees, likely a result of reduced access to resources.

Nevertheless, relief workers attempted to reform freedpeople's Sunday sartorial practices with direct instruction and by example. "At first," one woman wrote, "the children came to Sunday school in the same dresses they wore on a week day." After observing that their teachers wore better clothing on Sundays, however, they came "with some change in their apparel, if it was nothing but a clean apron."[96] In freedom, one woman's two daughters wore new "mazarin blue" dresses and white sunbonnets on Sunday, dresses that they had specifically purchased themselves once they had saved enough of their earnings from pulling fodder.[97] Such changes were considered material evidence of formerly enslaved people's religious improvement and recognition of the distinction between the physical labor of the week and the religious piety of the Sabbath. Of course, some relief workers looked with disdain upon formerly enslaved people's Sunday dress choices, including one woman who described them on their way to church as wearing "the most ludicrous toiletries."[98] Charles Nordhoff, however, considered it a sign of progress that men and women in the Sea Islands desired a "pair of fine shoes for Sunday and a pair of coarse shoes for working days."[99]

Relief workers shared a common goal of turning formerly enslaved people back to their own resources. They also sought to transform Black Southerners into good capitalists by instructing them in the purchase of goods. Many of those involved in the Freedmen's Bureau believed this would be best achieved through the integration of formerly enslaved men into a system of wage labor. Freedpeople's need for clothing and the desirability of other goods were employed as a means of both encouraging and coercing men and, to a lesser degree, women into working for wages. Wage labor, as Thomas C. Holt has argued of Jamaica, was a means by which former slaves might be resocialized to "accept the internal discipline that ensured the survival of the existing social order."[100] To this end, while clothing was initially provided to those with the greatest need, additional garments were available for purchase. In some areas, stores were established where refugees might purchase a variety of goods, thereby serving "as a means of stimulating industry and of teaching the freemen the value of money."[101] In other instances, clothing was exchanged for bartered goods or small sums of money.

Within the Department of the Tennessee, questionnaires sent to planters employing freedmen under the supervision of the government in 1864 revealed inconsistent approaches to clothing. While some planters provided clothing gratis, more than twenty "did not furnish it at all, seeming to have paid little attention to it." The vast majority, however, provided access to clothing and charged for it. Of the clothing that was sold to freedpeople, half was sold at cost, plus transportation; one quarter at 15 percent markup; and the remaining quarter at 25 percent markup. In another district, fully 76 percent of clothing was sold at a markup of 10 to 25 percent. While some agents reported that the clothing was good quality and supplied in sufficient quantity, others reported that they received frequent complaints from freedpeople "that they are inclined to take all, or more than all, their wages in clothes." In other words, not only were some people spending all of the earnings on clothing, but others were going into debt in order to supply themselves and their dependents with garments. The Freedmen's Bureau inquired as to whether there was a reasonable solution to such problems. Some agents said that the system worked perfectly well, but others asserted that higher wages needed to be paid. All agreed, however, that the best plan involved charging for clothing.[102]

Some relief workers and agents believed that the solution was to instruct freedpeople on how to be consumers and to integrate them into an economy. Freedpeople represented an untapped market that would bolster Northern manufacturing, if only white Northerners could teach them to be good capitalists and purchasers of goods. As James McKim wrote, reflecting on the community of freedpeople living in Port Royal, South Carolina, the distribution of clothing was not made "wholly as an act of charity," but, rather, a portion of it was sold, paid for by money earned from picking and packing cotton and from selling animals and produce to soldiers.[103] He particularly drew attention to the "*enlarged market for Northern manufactures that will be created by an enlarged area of freedom*." Certainly, the market for slave goods had been a significant boon to Northern manufacturers. But, McKim asserted, freedom would open new and greater opportunities. In slavery, he explained, masters' annual purchases for each slave were limited to "the expense of two suits of clothes, two shirts, and every six years, a pair of blankets; and, for field hands only—that is, for about one out of every three—a chip hat, or cheap cap, and one pair of shoes; and, for such as are old enough to need it, a handkerchief."[104] With emancipation, on the other hand, McKim predicted an immediate, rapid expansion of Southern purchases. He had already witnessed, upon the delivery of goods from Philadelphia, "there not being enough to supply the demand—there was almost a scramble." Experiences in Port Royal brought McKim to believe that "as soon as these people become free, their wants increase." Chief among those wants were "articles of clothing like that worn by the laborers in the North." When one calculated the potential number of new consumers—"4,000,000, the total number of slaves in the country"—McKim saw an "overwhelming economic argument" in favor of "pushing this Port Royal experiment to its logical conclusion."[105]

But relief workers also argued that formerly enslaved people did not know *how* to properly engage in the market—that they lacked taste, frugality, and restraint in making purchases. They also worried about the potential dangers and temptations posed by the freedom to choose one's clothing. In addition to accusing former slaves of dressing above their status, relief workers worried that the development of too fine of a taste could lead them into abject poverty. Henry Hayes complained that "every cent of their earnings is generally expended in finery or jewelry, rings, braclets, and gaudy glaring, colored dresses, and I should have added earrings, generally monstrous in size and shew."[106] In answers to a questionnaire sent out by the United States Freedmen's Inquiry Commission, respondents—usually military officers or male representatives of relief societies—drew attention to expenditures on clothing when asked what former slaves purchased with their wages. According to one response, they sought "to gratify the desire for gaudy dress and good things to eat, that is lifes luxuries is generally where the money goes and for those things goes freely."[107] Such items were frequently referred to as trinkets or gewgaws, terms that connoted showy, useless, worthless objects. Concern regarding the purchase of nonessential elements of fashionable dress prompted the general superintendent of the Freedmen's Bureau to inquire about its officials' roles in providing access to such items. "Have the people been led to invest much in trifles?" asked one questionnaire. More directly put, "Have you sold them any gewgaws or trinkets?" That one questionnaire was returned with "*No!*" written in response is suggestive of the absurdity with which the respondent viewed providing access to showy articles of dress.[108]

In response to what they believed to be excessive expenditures, relief workers and others took it upon themselves to educate formerly enslaved people about the importance of saving money and making wise clothing choices. One manual intended to educate freedpeople asserted that "a new coat might be very desirable, but if its purchase would create a debt, better keep the old one in good repair as possible, and stick to it another season."[109] Men were also cautioned that a woman could destroy her husband's finances "by urging him to buy for her things she could do without, and for which he is unable to pay," especially clothing and jewelry.[110] All were instructed, "For the sake of your good name, do not make a splurge in society with jewelry and fine clothes which have not been paid for, and for which you will never be able to pay."[111] Learning to exercise discretion in the purchase of clothing was considered a valuable tool for success in freedom.

Freedwomen, then, were simultaneously admonished for exhibiting a contentedness with the "tasteless" clothing worn in slavery and expected to temper their aspirations for new clothing and possessions with frugality, modesty, and respect for social rank. They were not to be satisfied with ragged, mismatched clothing, but neither should they dress above their means or attempt to fully imitate white women. So at the same time as dressing neatly and tastefully was essential to women's respectability, dressing in expensive clothing, wearing jewelry, or donning otherwise ornamental elements of dress was viewed as vain, vulgar, and wasteful. Relief workers had a particular vision of Black women's dress characterized by practicality, modesty, and easily laundered materials.

Relief workers' own sense of style and proper dress was critical to how they imagined the world in which formerly enslaved people would choose and wear new clothing. Many of the relief workers—especially women—were members of the Society of Friends, commonly known as Quakers, for whom a commitment to plainness in dress was part of their religious practice. As a religious idea, Susan Garfinkel explains, Quaker plainness was "more like a mental state than a list of rules, which are merely outward markers of the silence within."[112] Plainness did not equate to cheap or coarse fabric. Indeed, a survey of Quaker clothing in the National Museum of American History evidences the use of high-quality silks in women's clothing. Plainness, rather, was defined by solid colors and the lack of superfluous decoration. Earth tones of green, brown, and cream in solid colored fabrics—not figured or printed—defined Quaker women's aesthetic.[113] Although adherence to plainness was declining in the Quaker community, such sensibilities in relation to dress nevertheless directly influenced Quaker relief workers' perception of, and distaste for, clothing worn by enslaved people that was brightly colored or made from fabrics deemed unsuitable for clothing.[114]

Relief workers and teachers were concerned about their own clothing, too, and worked to maintain a notable difference between their own dress and that of freedpeople. They frequently wrote home requesting that a wide range of garments, fabric, and sewing supplies be sent to them. As Esther Hawks was preparing to join her husband, who was managing a plantation in the Sea Islands, she received numerous letters from him detailing the various items she should transport with her, including cotton and linen cloth, thread of various colors, handkerchiefs, linen coats, stockings, and multiple pairs of pants. The South, he declared, "is death on trousers, I assure you."[115] Martha Schofield, too, worked to maintain a hierarchy through clothing. When a box of calico, muslin, and materials for boys' pants arrived from Philadelphia, she set women to work cutting out aprons, sacques (loose-fitting garments), and chemises for girls, and coats, pantaloons, and shirts for nearly all the boys. However, when it came to her own clothing, Schofield took fabric into the closest town to have a sacque cut out and then hired a seamstress to make her silk dress.[116] Schofield's attention to her own dress and the hierarchy of clothing is clear in this photograph that was likely taken in the late 1860s or early 1870s. Second from the left, Schofield stands wearing a dress with drop sleeves and a full skirt with decorative trimming and holds a fur muff with tassels. She is dressed similarly to the other seated women, a sharp contrast to the woman standing at the right who is identified only as "Aunt Amy" and wears a checked dress and apron and carries a basket. The hierarchy is clear, yet Amy's dress is not devoid of decoration—the raised zigzag-like pattern that embellishes the skirt would have taken time and skill to apply.

Freedpeople were eager to choose garments for themselves and their families and viewed doing so as an important part of emancipation. As Thavolia Glymph has shown, freedpeople found the ability to choose and purchase their own clothing central to their idea of freedom and control over one's life.[117] They did not, however, indiscriminately adopt the sartorial practices advocated by relief workers, nor did they always select items that blended in with "the respectable raiment of society around them," which inevitably led to conflicts.[118]

The dismay and derision these relief workers expressed regarding the clothing choices of formerly enslaved people echoed those of white observers in decades before the war. One elite white woman writing in the late 1830s, for instance, described enslaved people's Sunday clothing as "the most ludicrous combination of incongruities that you can conceive," with beads, bugles, various fabrics, frills, and decorative combs.[119] What both this woman writing in the 1830s and relief workers in the 1860s failed to realize—or if they realized, refused to accept—was that the use of various fabrics and ornaments was desirable and stylish. As Stephanie Camp explains, "At least since the eighteenth century, with roots in African visual arts, black style had distinctively stressed the dynamic interplay of color and texture over the harmonies of similar elements, and surprise, movement, and argument over predictable patterns and order."[120] The boy who wore pants made from ingrain carpet may have selected that fabric precisely for its busy pattern.

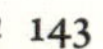

This portrait depicts (*left to right*) Jane "Jennie" Saitherwaite, Martha Schofield, Mary P. Jacobs, and Aunt Amy. Tin portrait, probably late 1860s–early 1870s. Catalog ID A00183927. Martha Schofield photograph collection, SFHL-PA-143. Courtesy of Friends Historical Library of Swarthmore College, Swarthmore, PA.

Although some relief workers, like Maria Mann, attempted to continue clothing Black bodies in drab clothing, others were eager to distribute the dress goods and garments that were donated.[121] Their focus was on practicality, modesty, and easily laundered materials. And by and large the printed cotton calicoes, muslins, and other secondhand garments that were collected and distributed to formerly enslaved people differed significantly from the heavy linen tow cloth and coarsely woven osnaburg that were closely associated with slavery. Harriet Jacobs vividly recalled the linsey-woolsey dress she was given every winter by her enslaver. "How I hated it!" she exclaimed. "It was one of the badges of slavery."[122] Many freedpeople avoided garments made from such sturdy, coarse cloth. "Yellow osnabergs," one teacher observed, "are their detestation; they are ugly in themselves, and remind people of their condition as slaves."[123] Refusing to wear donated osnaburg and linsey-woolsey garments was a material way to erase the badges of enslavement.

From teachers and others working in the South, freedpeople frequently requested, bartered produce, and exchanged manual labor for bonnets, corsets, dresses, aprons, jackets, waistcoats, and pantaloons.[124] One woman wore and saved a brown-and-cream-striped dress she likely obtained after her emancipation. While simple in style and a cotton fabric—indeed, Quaker women would largely have approved—the dress is finely stitched and corresponds to a popular silhouette in the 1860s. Similarly, a well-worn sage green dress was clearly valued by the wearer.[125] It, too, was simple in silhouette, but unlike the coarser cotton fabric of the striped dress, it was made from silk—a mark of distinction for the woman who wore it. Another dress, believed to have been worn by Alabama woman Tempy Ruby Bryant, who had once been enslaved, was made from a brown-and-tan-colored floral- and stripe-printed fabric. Great attention to detail was taken in cutting and sewing the fabric for this dress. The placket (or finished opening) of the bodice was carefully cut to align with the pattern, as were the waistband and collar. Styling one's dress had been practiced as an act of resistance within the confines of slavery. In freedom, attempts to freely exercise choice and experiment with one's style were a form of resistance to white relief workers' attempts to again place strictures on Black people's dress.

For white relief workers, clothing was an answer to one of the most pressing questions when slavery stood at the precipice of collapse: How could formerly enslaved people be incorporated into free society while simultaneously maintaining racist social hierarchies? Relief workers' efforts to transform formerly enslaved women and men were based on prejudiced, often overtly racist, assumptions about Black bodies and minds. They constructed that racism around ideas from phrenology and physiognomy, as well as assumptions about slavery's ability to quash individuality and choice. They also brought with them their own belief that white Northern culture was superior, failing to value the vibrant culture that African Americans had constructed in their resistance to slavery. Their approach to the process of clothing Black refugees tells us much more about white perspectives of how clothing functioned socially and culturally than about how formerly enslaved people perceived clothing's role in their own lives. And yet these relief workers' perspectives are critical to understanding the process of emancipation, for it is here that we see the challenges formerly enslaved people faced—the assumptions and expectations that were imposed upon them. By adopting what white relief workers believed to be correct habits of dress, cleanliness, and bodily management, formerly enslaved men, women, and children might meet the relief workers' mandate that they "*prove* yourselves *worthy* of freedom, you are free

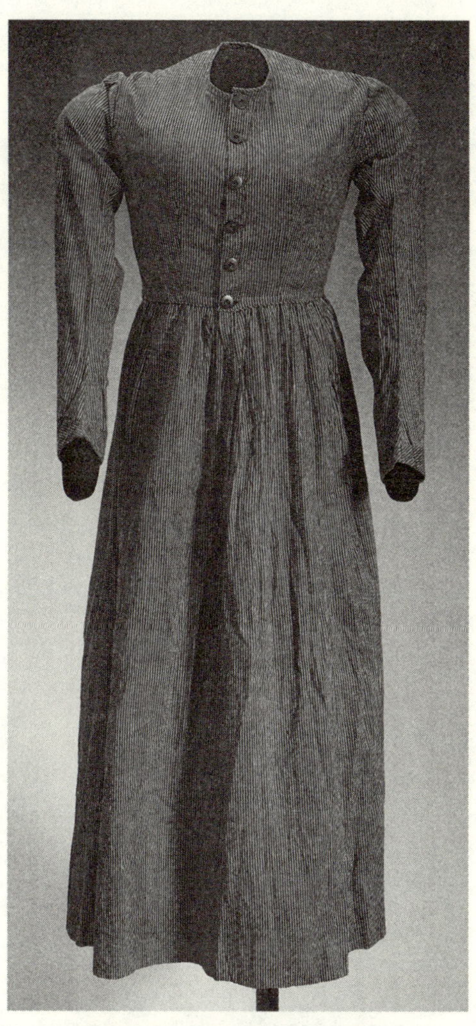

Brown-and-cream-striped day dress, c. 1865–75. Object No. 2007.3.34. Collection of the Smithsonian National Museum of African American History and Culture, Gift of the Black Fashion Museum founded by Lois K. Alexander-Lane.

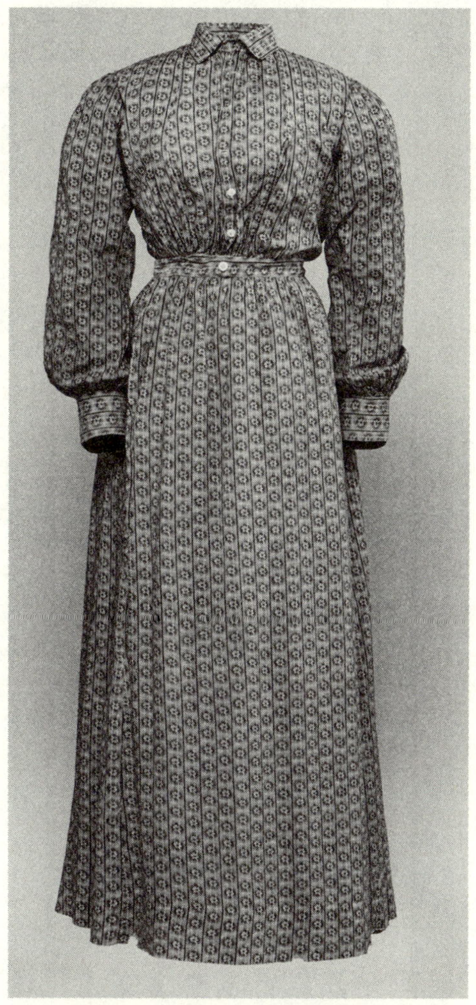

This dress has a history of having been worn by Tempy Ruby Bryant, a formerly enslaved woman. A dark brown-and-tan floral and striped patterned fabric, it was cut and sewn with attention to detail. Dress, c. 1870–90. Object No. 2018.84. Collection of the Smithsonian National Museum of African American History and Culture, Gift of Dr. Todd E. Robinson.

men & free women, responsible for every one of your acts."[126] In this context, discipline—not only in work and morality, but also in bodily management—was critical to the production of freedom.

The discourses surrounding the provision of clothing to formerly enslaved people in the years following emancipation draw attention to clothing's power to reshape the wearer. It is evident that clothing did not merely possess a symbolic, reflective role in mid-nineteenth-century culture; it also had an *active* role in shaping daily life. Nineteenth-century Americans believed that clothing not only reflected something about the wearer; it also possessed the power to transform them. And this belief—that the material environment had the power to shape a person's inner self—worked in more than one way. While relief workers viewed improvements in formerly enslaved people's clothing as positive progress, wearing clothing that was considered "above their station" threatened the racist social order.

In 1870, John Watson Alvord, the general superintendent of education for the Freedmen's Bureau, described his impressions of the changes that had come with emancipation and the end of the Civil War, drawing specific attention to the transformed appearance of formerly enslaved people in Charleston, South Carolina: "In this advancing civilization nothing is more apparent than the altered apparel of the Freedmen. From linsey wolsey, ragged garments, clumsy brogans, or bare feet of former times, we notice the change to clothes of modern material. . . . It gives the adult population in the streets and the churches an air strikingly in contrast with the menial raiment with which slavery had clothed them. It is the costume of freedom, each choosing his or her dress, according to taste, and all mainly in the respectable raiment of society around them."[127] The ability to choose one's own attire and to have access to clothing made from better-quality fabrics was, for Alvord, indicative of a much broader change—a visible testament to transformations in Southern society brought about by emancipation. African American women and men moving about in clothing of their own choosing was, he suggested, precisely what freedom looked like. Respectfully covered and heeding the lessons of respectability, properly attired Black women, men, and children evidenced their ability to meet public expectations for a civilized but subservient body in a free society. Yet in his reference to those choices conforming "mainly" to the "respectable raiment of society," Alvord's description encapsulates the continuing tension between formerly enslaved people's own clothing choices and relief workers' distribution of clothing that was, in Martha Schofield's words, "what our judgement saw fit to give." Theirs was a bounded freedom.

Part III

Destroying

Tintype of Charles C. Wheat, c. 1861. Courtesy of the American Civil War Museum, Richmond, VA.

When young C. C. "Charley" Wheat sat for his photograph, he wore a distinctive shirt. The outlines of its collar, cuffs, pockets, and placket were defined by a contrasting color of tape, along with a bow tie and a detachable white collar. Clearly, he cared about the appearance of his clothing, having paid a photographer an additional fee to have bits of gold applied to define the brass buttons on his shirt and the gold ring on his pinky finger. The clothes Charley wore no longer exist and, like so many other soldiers and civilians, evidence of what he once looked and dressed like is preserved only in this tintype. Nineteen-year-old Charley was "killed 19 Apral 1862" in Virginia by US soldiers.[1] But that was not the story that the annotator of this photograph sought to tell. Instead, Wheat's younger brother, Joseph, scrawled a remarkable set of circumstances across the carte de visite's mat: "this Picture was lossed in 61 was found on the Body of a Dead Yankey at Sharps Bourge 62." Charley gave this photograph to a relative, but it was "lossed" when Union soldiers stole it, along with other items, from her house in 1861. Years later, a Confederate soldier stopped at this woman's home for dinner and showed her his collection of battlefield "relics." Imagine her shock at discovering the stolen tintype of Charley in the soldier's bag.[2] The pleasure of having the tintype returned to her must have been diminished by the memories triggered by the knowledge that the tintype had been looted from the pockets of a dead soldier on the Antietam battlefield, for Charley's body, too, had been looted when he died. When his body was found, it "was all muddy from the red clay, and stripped of everything but the underclothes."[3]

Charley Wheat and his tintype likeness both fell victim to looting during the American Civil War: The tintype was stolen by a Union soldier from a private house; it was taken again when a Confederate soldier rifled through the pockets of that dead Union soldier; and Charley himself was stripped of his clothing, his shoes, and all his personal effects. In each instance, boundaries of property and the sanctity of the body were violated. From the stripping of soldiers' bodies to the theft of objects from their pockets, such acts of bodily violation were instrumental to the emotional and psychological means of waging war.

To be sure, the war meant the broader destruction of life and livelihood as the Wheat family had known it. In 1860, Charley's father, Horatio, was a wheat farmer who owned real estate worth $15,000 and a personal estate valued at $10,000, which included the eleven people he enslaved.[4] By 1870, the Wheat family's farming operation was severely diminished and the crops were being farmed with the help of one paid laborer. Joseph survived the war, but he had sustained a gunshot wound that resulted in the partial paralysis of his leg.[5] As the Wheat family lived through the war, all around them life was changing because of emancipation, defeat, and death. Charley had died not as a martyr on the battlefield nor in a skirmish. That Charley's body was found alone, stripped of clothing and muddied by red earthen clay, was one of the ways that the Wheat family felt war's destructiveness on a visceral level.

As Joseph Wheat sat down with his older brother's image, perhaps he found it easier to record the history of the photograph itself. There was at least some triumph in that, however small, something victorious about the photograph having been lost only to be reclaimed from the rifled pockets of a "dead Yankey." Perhaps it was easier for Joseph to preserve that story than to recount the memories stirred up by the photograph about the fate of the young man whose image it captured.

CHAPTER FIVE

Peeled Bodies

Wartime Violence, Violation, and Destruction

The story of Charley Wheat and his tintype is somewhat remarkable in terms of the series of coincidences that occurred, but the individual thefts themselves were not uncommon during the Civil War. Plundering and pilfering have historically been—and continue to be—forms of violation that accompany war. It is, then, tempting to explain Civil War theft as simply a casualty of war, and the soldiers' behavior as a wartime aberration. This explanation, however, fails to capture the connections people made between themselves and their possessions, and the powerful effects that loss could have on the human psyche. While the people involved in the theft and recovery of Charley Wheat's tintype may have temporarily deviated from their normal behavior, they were not alone in engaging in acts of appropriation, theft, and, broadly, the redistribution of clothing. Both armies captured and put into use materials seized from supply trains; bodies were stripped on the battlefield; Union and Confederate soldiers looted white and Black Southerners' homes; and formerly enslaved people took clothing from former mistresses and masters. Through these acts, Black and white Americans violated the boundaries of the body and of property, thereby shaping a wartime culture in which the threat of looting altered daily material life.[1]

Soldiers' conduct was governed by both US and Confederate army regulations and the global laws of war, which permitted both armies to seize materials that could be used to prosecute the war. They could forage for food and livestock and seize ammunition, tents, knapsacks, and clothing stores. US soldiers could refuse to return formerly enslaved people to their enslavers, claiming them as "contraband" of war. But to "plunder and pillage" was explicitly banned. "Under these rules," Aaron Sheehan-Dean explains, "it was illegal for soldiers to plunder wounded or dead enemies after a battle. The only items that could be seized from the enemy—whether combatant or noncombatant—were those that could be used for military purposes."[2] In practice, however, the war's violence—the massive taking of lives—blurred the boundaries of what soldiers considered permissible in war.

The various incidents in which clothing was taken from the original owner fall roughly into three categories: clothing that was destroyed, garments that were taken to be preserved as what nineteenth-century Americans referred to as relics, and clothes that were repurposed or used again.[3] People who took clothing and those from whom it was taken struggled with the implications of such looting. Stripping bodies, theft and appropriation of clothing, fear of looting, and the objects themselves performed powerful cultural work throughout the United States during and after the Civil War. At stake was not only the theft of property, but also the sanctity of the body. Within this context, people grappled with the blurry boundaries of ownership, theft, and violation. Those boundaries were further muddled because the war itself entailed a redefinition of the relationship between people and property through debates over confiscation and the destruction of the institution of American slavery. Human property and movable property were further linked because the looting of houses by Northern troops and enslaved people's self-emancipation often occurred in tandem. In such circumstances, slave-owning Southerners experienced the theft of their belongings as part of the larger loss of their economic status as slaveholders. The freeing of people likely influenced Union soldiers' perspectives on the theft of material objects, too. Indeed, some soldiers referenced "liberating" Southerners of their possessions, using language typically employed in describing the emancipation of enslaved people to reference material objects. Within such a context, the theft of property became all the more laden with meaning.

Exploring the theft of clothing and other objects from both bodies and homes highlights the embodied experience of wartime looting and the ways in which people's material lives were altered, either forcibly or by their own accord. Clothing, of course, was far from the only target of wartime looting, theft, and destruction. Silver, chinaware, chairs, bureaus, side tables, and even pianos were stolen from Southern homes—houses themselves were burned to the ground in their entirety. Soldiers on both sides disregarded military regulations against looting, and their motivations were as numerous as there were men: to seek a battlefield souvenir, to send a relic to a loved one at home, to exact revenge, to destroy symbols of the Southern planter class. Some men simply saw things that they liked and took them. But the theft of clothing had a more personal, critical element compared to the theft of a silver spoon. As an object that is worn against the body and central to self-fashioning, clothing is both central to a person's identity and an object capable of storing memories of a particular person. This is not to say that other possessions—or heirlooms—were not significant, but rather that there was a particularly acute feeling of violation when one's most personal possessions—those things most closely and physically connected to one's body—were taken against their will, whether on the battlefield or at home.

The language looters used to describe their actions—"taken," "obtained," "appropriated," "found"—suggests that they were engaged in an effort to understand theft within this broader context of liberating and appropriating. Rarely did looters use terminology of theft or looting in describing the objects they stole. How then should historians reference actions that led to the redistribution of possessions during wartime? The use of the term "looting" suggests a moral condemnation of the act, yet referencing objects as having simply been "taken" denies the validity of the experience of violation felt by many who lost their possessions. Historical actors themselves offered no clear consensus, as their attitudes varied depending on their relationship to the objects taken. Some expressed ethical and moral opposition to the practice. People whose objects were stolen, on the other hand, used language of violence—bodies were "peeled" or "stripped," houses were "ransacked" and "pillaged." Formerly enslaved people who took objects with them when they emancipated themselves did so with the understanding that they had earned the right to those objects through their forced labor, exercising the rightful claiming of property for which they had worked. The range of ways in which those who took objects and those whose objects were taken described those actions—the verbs they used—suggests that in the midst of war, Americans were defining a language of looting that centered on the reassignment of property. Preserving the historicity of that experience requires employing the language of looting, appropriating, and taking as it pertains to the perspective of the historical actors.

Wartime looting touched the lives of both Southerners and Northerners, though it was experienced almost exclusively on Southern soil, occurring, as it did, in connection with battles, encampments, and troop movements. Both US and Confederate soldiers stripped bodies on the battlefield, stole from dead men's pockets, took objects from Southern houses, and sent those things to their families at home. Enslaved people took with them their enslavers' clothing and other items when they liberated themselves. When battles and occupying soldiers brought the war closer to their homes, white Southern women, in anticipation of looting, altered their daily lives and material ways of being. In this context, the theft of clothing from both bodies and houses was one way in which Americans waged war against one another on both physical and psychological levels.

Peeling

On February 13, 1864, *Frank Leslie's Illustrated Newspaper* published a front-page illustration titled "Rebel Soldiers after Battle 'Peeling' (i.e. Stripping)

"Rebel Soldiers after Battle 'Peeling' (i.e. Stripping) the Fallen Union Soldiers—From a Sketch by an Officer," *Frank Leslie's Illustrated Newspaper*, February 13, 1864. From the Lincoln Financial Foundation Collection, Indiana State Museum and Historic Sites, Indianapolis, IN, and Allen County Public Library, Fort Wayne, IN.

the Fallen Union Soldiers—From a Sketch by an Officer." At the center of the illustration is a man pulling the pants off of a dead man whose body is suspended in the air. One can imagine his lifeless body jerking as the Confederate yanks on the legs of the pants. In the background, one man pulls on a soldier's pants, while another pulls off his coat, the two tugging the body between them as if it were any other object.

Leslie's asserted that such stripping was "an organized system in the armies of the Confederates" and accused them of "keeping bodies in reserve for the purpose." The newspaper further suggested that Confederates' "wretched financial condition, the difficulty of obtaining clothing, seem to be an excuse, but the whole affair is so characteristic of the rebels, so clear an example of their want of finer feelings."[4] Confederates' "organised system" of "peeling" bodies was considered glaring material evidence of their inhumanity.

The Civil War forced soldiers and civilians to contend with bodies and mass death in ways that were unprecedented for this generation of Americans. Technological changes meant not only an increasingly deadly battlefield, but also the maiming of bodies of the men who survived. As George Rable describes of the Battle of Fredericksburg, "The overwhelming presence of death at first produced horror and revulsion, but soon Yank and Reb alike psychologically closed themselves off from such sights."[5] Such "closing" oneself off helped soldiers follow commands of officers in both armies to gather items that would be useful to the army, including guns and ammunition. As they walked among bodies of dead men and horses, however, soldiers took more than military equipage. They also stripped enemy bodies of uniforms, shoes, and personal effects, gathering trinkets and better clothing with which to supply themselves. Such acts were driven by more than Confederates' desperation for supplies or a breakdown of order.[6] As evidenced by the discovery of Confederate Charley Wheat's body—stripped to the underwear and covered in clay mud—Union soldiers, too, stole the clothing off of dead men.

In the immediate aftermath of a battle, both civilians and soldiers tramped through the field, picking up objects that ranged from torn flags, tent cloth, and artillery shells to knapsacks, pocket diaries, and cartes de visite.[7] Those bits and pieces of the battlefield were sent home in letters and packages to family members—as relics of the war, objects that stored its memory.[8] Yet, although they may have obtained the same objects, there was an important distinction between the actions of relic hunters who picked up items from the ground and those who obtained their finds by searching dead and dying men's pockets. Items picked up from the battlefield after bodies had been removed and buried were items divorced from the men themselves; to loot directly from a dead body, on the other hand, was far more corporeal and violating.

After battles, the ground was strewn with gear, dead horses, and dead and dying men. One soldier described the horse-drawn ambulances carrying the wounded away from the Battle of Fair Oaks, where "thin streams of blood ran out of the sides and bottoms of these vehicles, while the drivers were lashing the horses."[9] As Michael Adams has observed, historians tend to "rush over" the clearing of the battlefield, quickly moving from surrender to "cursorily referencing the flag-draped coffin."[10] That clearing of the battlefield, and the looting and stripping that accompanied it, however, was a terribly corporeal experience. Union soldier William Nelson's statement in a letter to his wife that he "didn't touch a dead body," while his comrades looted dead Confederates, had several layers of meaning. Understanding the cultural implications of stripping and looting soldiers' bodies requires attending to the material experience of that act; it requires understanding the realities of the battlefield, with the sun beating down at the end of two days of maiming and killing. In these circumstances, men were not simply picking up clothing from the ground.

The scenes men witnessed and the horrors experienced by those who lay incapacitated on the battlefield could make the stripping of dead bodies seem inconsequential. Buzzards circled, while hogs snorted and rooted through the dead and wounded: "Intestines, heads, arms, feet, and even hearts were dragged over the ground and devoured at leisure."[11] Bodies decayed quickly in the heat; corpses swelled. Faces turned "black as charcoal and bloated out of all human semblance."[12] Indeed, some burial details found "the bodies had become so offensive that men could only endure it by being staggering drunk."[13] The rapid decomposition of bodies meant that soldiers who wanted to take belongings needed to do so quickly after the battle.[14] One Confederate described the transformation of the Fredericksburg battlefield over the course of the battle and its aftermath: "Before the fight there was just the field. Next it was covered all over with your [Union] fellows in blue clothes. Saturday night the blue clothes were stripped off, and only their white under-clothes left. Monday night these were stripped off, and Tuesday they lay all in their naked skins."[15] Words describing such stripping do not capture the corporeality of the act or experience. To take a dead man's clothes did not simply involve picking up an abandoned coat from the ground. It required the looter to pull off the man's gear; unbutton the coat, pants, and suspenders; and reach into the pockets and sift through lint, letters, knives, and trinkets. It meant wrestling to remove that clothing from a body whose limbs had begun to stiffen in the process of rigor mortis, at times exacerbated by freezing conditions.

In describing such acts, *Frank Leslie's Illustrated Newspaper* used the term "peeling"—a word that would have been read with a dual meaning in mind. On the one hand, "peeling" has been historically used to refer to robbing or stripping a person of their possessions, or seizing goods by means of violence. On the other, the term was used to describe—and evokes the image of—paring away the skin of a fruit, peeling tree bark, or removing an animal's hide.[16] Indeed, one Confederate admitted that the scene "did present something similar to a fellow drawing the hide off of a squirrel to see them, one fellow holding him at the head and the other at his feet, drawing off his overcoat."[17] The bodies of the naked Union dead, one man asserted, "looked like hogs that had been cleaned."[18] Such comparisons heightened the tangibility of stripping those men's clothing, but describing men in the context of skinning animals may also have been a subconscious effort to distance the peeled body from the man whose soul had departed.

Battlefield looting raised important questions about the sanctity of the body at a moment in which Americans were confronting death on an unprecedented scale. The manner in which dead and wounded bodies were treated was critical for cultural, emotional, and practical reasons. As Drew Faust has shown, for nineteenth-century Americans, "humanity, not just particular humans, was at stake" in the treatment of the dead. For Protestants, "redemption and resurrection from the dead were understood as physical, not just metaphysical realities, and therefore the body . . . preserved a 'surviving identity'" that required "sacred reverence and care."[19] Soldiers' journals and reflections make it clear that treating the dead with disregard could be debasing for both the dead and the living. As one soldier wrote, "They were stripped to the skin by Our soldiers who have long since lost all delicacy on the subject."[20]

The imagery of stripping dead bodies suggests that these bodies were subjected to a host of abuses. Like the Northern press, Union soldiers drew on the image of Confederates stripping Northern soldiers' bodies as evidence of Southern inhumanity and as further reason to seek revenge against rebels. As one Ohio soldier explained, "By the side of every one of our dead men you would see an old pair of shoes and a greasy, filthy pile of clothes. . . . I never hated them till now. I have now a thirst for vengeance."[21] One US officer believed Confederate acts of stripping the Union dead to be so repugnant that he ordered his men to leave all dead Confederates unburied on the battlefield in retaliation, thereby denying men the dignity of even a mass grave. Soldiers were also upset by their own armies' actions. After the Battle of Fredericksburg during a bitterly cold December, one Confederate wrote, "All the Yank dead had been stripped of every rag of their clothing. . . . It was an awful sight. I pitied these poor dead men and could not help it."[22]

Battlefield theft involving clothing is typically described in general terms of anonymity; historians convey a battlefield scene in which soldiers picked clothing and possessions off the bodies of men whom they had never before seen. Certainly, men were infrequently aware of the name of the soldier whose clothing or possessions they stole at the moment they rummaged through his pockets or pulled off his boots. However, the experience was not entirely anonymous. In some instances, soldiers stole from men they themselves had killed, as did one Union soldier who took a canteen off the body of a Confederate whom he had killed in hand-to-hand bayonet combat.[23] But even as soldiers walked the battlefield, pulling coats off of the corpses of men they neither knew nor had killed, the dead rarely remained entirely anonymous. Clothing itself offered evidence of the owner's identity. It was not uncommon for soldiers to have their names written into their clothing as a means of identifying it when sent out for laundering. Tailors, too, marked clothing as part of an inventory and laundry control system. One civilian man's coat, for instance, had the name and date "Jacob Baiz, 1864" inscribed on the inner right breast pocket.[24]

Items kept in the pockets of coats and trousers offered further information about their owners. Many looters likely did not discover the identities written and stored in these garments until after they had time to sit in camp and sort through their loot. A Union soldier, for instance, stole a cartridge box, but it was not until he returned to camp that he delightedly discovered that there were three twenty-dollar gold pieces contained in it.[25] Searching through pockets, men found Bibles, diaries, and account books with names inscribed inside. They also found letters—letters with salutations, men's names, and expressions of intimacy from loved ones. Written in the collar, on a breast pocket, or in a letter were the identities of the soldiers who had died and whose bodies had been stripped. And this made the transgression of looting all the more serious.

In stripping a man's body of clothing, soldiers did not only debase the humanity of those who had died in battle. They also stole their identity. This could have devastating consequences for many families. With the burial process often taking days after the battle, many men's bodies had decayed beyond recognition. Although names written in collars were likely intended for laundry, they could also be relied upon to pass on information to family members about a soldier's fate. Letters and papers in jacket pockets, knapsacks, and haversacks could provide clues about a soldier's identity, as well as addresses for loved ones and mementos to send home. Insignia on hats also helped to identify the companies and regiments from which men hailed, even if they did not list their names. In one instance, a soldier's skeletal remains were returned to his family when, two years after the Battle of Chancellorsville, another soldier identified him "by a tooth brush and several other articles, which were found in his clothing"—clothing that had not yet rotted away, despite the man having been buried only under a thin layer of soil.[26] When such items were stolen—the letters, the coats, the knapsacks, the hats—a body could remain unidentified. One Fredericksburg woman reported that "all the clothes had been stripped from the bodies of the Union soldiers" and she did not see how "all the corpses could be recognized" when the burial party returned a week later.[27] In these circumstances, families might never know the fate of fallen soldiers. The "peeling" of their bodies had erased their ability to be identified—and therefore their identities themselves.

Wounded men, too, were stripped of clothing. A Union army nurse described the deplorable condition in which one Confederate soldier entered the hospital. He had been stripped of his clothing by his own comrades, she explained: "Before they left him they stripped off all his clothes; they could not afford to leave even those."[28] One imagines the struggle faced by the wounded as the enemy—and perhaps comrades—walked the battlefield, stripping clothing from nearby dead, and their own attempt to hold on to both their life and their possessions. Confederate soldier John Wyeth recalled an incident after the Battle of Chickamauga in which the wounded soldier was not as lucky. A Texas soldier demanded the boots worn by a captured Union cavalry officer who had been shot through the foot. "I want your boots," the Texan declared. The officer "sat down and held up the sound foot while the Texan pulled that boot off and tried it on." It fit. He motioned for the other, but the wounded man asked if he would split the boot so that it could be removed without further injuring his foot. The Texan remarked, 'You reckon I'm going to spoil that boot?'"[29] And he yanked it off.

Both Confederate and Union soldiers attributed such stripping to the need for supplies and a callousness toward bodies that developed from repeated wartime exposure. One Union soldier noted that "the corpses that lay farthest forward [on the battlefield] had been stripped white; the rebels must have needed clothes."[30] Writing his memoirs thirty years later, Union chaplain William Corby acknowledged the stripping of bodies that occurred, noting that "Southern historians apologize for this by saying that the Confederates were in rags and could not secure a supply of clothing 'for love or money.'"[31] Similarly, former Confederate John Wyeth claimed that, earlier in the war, thefts from the dead or the living would never have occurred. But "men had become callous and indifferent, and then the necessities of the Southern troops, half starved and poorly clad as they were, justified to some extent the wholesale appropriation of all the belongings of their prisoners."[32]

There were instances in which ill-supplied Confederate companies entered battle in full knowledge that victory would mean the opportunity to resupply themselves. Confederate soldier Richard Lewis described the quality of the clothing taken after the Battle of Fredericksburg, writing, "The Yankees are very well clad, being provided with sufficient warm clothing for the winter and it is of the very best material." Indeed, the soldiers' stripping of the battlefield dead was so successful that he firmly believed that "if we meet the Yankees a few more times on such fields as this we will be very well provided for."[33] As Lewis suggested, the prospects for obtaining better clothing were a central motivator for many soldiers who stripped dead bodies.

But to assume that this was an act of desperation fails to acknowledge the complexity of soldiers' motivations—to desire better clothing one need not be ill supplied or wearing rags. Looting bodies—living and dead—to improve one's own circumstances was so common that Jim McFall wrote to his sister, "You say Ma is going to send me a coat. Tell her not to do it. I will get a Yankey coat."[34] A year later, he again "captured a fine Yankee over coat the other day therefore I will not want my over coat at all do not send it." Meanwhile, his brother bragged to those at home that he had "made a pretty good Hall off the Yanks," having "captured . . . one pair of fine shoes pocket books & knifes."[35] The theft of pocketbooks and knives required searching through dead men's gear, pants, or coat pockets. The McFalls were not motivated by necessity in stripping Union soldiers of their clothing; their family kept them well supplied throughout the war. So well, in fact, that in late 1864 Jim McFall received a new uniform, complete with brass buttons and gold cord, as well as a silk cravat, just months before the war's end. McFall's efforts to make a "good Hall off the Yanks," then, seem to have been motivated by convenience and perhaps a sense of conquest, not a state of desperation.[36]

There was a significant difference in how men thought about and described reaching into the coat pockets of their dead comrades versus when the enemy stole from those same pockets. Many soldiers believed it to be their last duty to a friend who fell on the battlefield to notify his family of how he had died and to send his belongings home. They were motivated, in part, by the desire to reassure families that the soldier had died a "Good Death," a concept firmly entrenched in mid-nineteenth-century Protestant American society. A Good Death required one to show clear signs of salvation: to outwardly demonstrate on their deathbed a consciousness of their impending death, signs of repentance, and a belief in their soul's redemption.[37] In other words, to die a Good Death, a man needed to be *ready* to die. This readiness to die was so essential to determining the "goodness" of a death that soldiers often tried to convince themselves that their comrades had been well prepared for death, even when they died suddenly or alone.[38] In the context of a culture in which anticipating and accepting imminent death was interpreted as an outward sign of a man's salvation, exhibiting fear, anger, or cowardliness before death, or even having a scowl upon one's face, was distressing evidence of a man's impenitent soul. As they assessed the manner in which a comrade had died, and searched their bodies for items to send home to families, soldiers also risked the possibility of discovering information that they did *not* want to pass on to the soldier's family—evidence that suggested the man did not die a Good Death. That evidence occasionally took the form of body armor.[39]

Numerous war memoirs relate incidents in which men, walking the field after a battle for signs of life, discovered dead, armor-clad soldiers. Lucius Chittenden found one such soldier leaning against a tree: "I placed my hand on his chest to detect any sign of life. It encountered a metal substance. I opened his clothing, and took from beneath it a shield of boiler-iron, moulded to fit the anterior portion of his body, and fastened at the back by straps and buckles." It was then that Chittenden saw the reason for the soldier's demise: "Directly over his heart, through the shield and through his body, was a hole large enough to permit the escape of a score of human lives."[40]

Soldiers knew that their bodies would be searched if they died; many had performed the act themselves many times. That knowledge likely affected their decisions against wearing body armor. Given the critical role played by manly resolve and sacrifice in ideas about death, to be found clad in a bullet-proof vest or another form of body armor could be interpreted as a material symbol of a man's *unpreparedness* to die. At a moment in which the hint of a smile on a dead man's mouth was interpreted as evidence of his heavenly ascent, to find a dead comrade sheathed in metal suggested precisely the opposite. "The best way" to confront the possibility of death in battle, Union colonel Charles Johnson explained to his wife, was to "take your chances without *skulking* behind a '*bullit proof vest*' that is not worth a continental curse at that."[41] A man who overtly attempted to defy death was a man who had reservations about dying; he exhibited a desire to resist the will of God and an unwillingness to sacrifice his life for the nation. For this reason, then, many soldiers agreed with Johnson and forewent wearing such vests, leaving no possibility for body armor to be discovered upon their bodies when searched after battle.

When the bodies had been removed from the field, the material detritus of battle remained, leading to another wave of scavenging. At Gettysburg, the ground was "almost carpeted with knapsacks, haversacks, canteens, hats, caps, blankets, in fact everything that goes to make the horrors of a battlefield." One might obtain a blanket or cap, but as one soldier explained, "Many of the hats and caps are besmeared with brains" and the blankets, "dotted with blood."[42] Nevertheless, one man regularly went to the communities near Chancellorsville and the Wilderness, where he bought boxes of salvaged clothing to trade. That clothing was from families who had picked up soldiers' clothes from the battlefields: "Some was flung away, and some, I suppose, was stripped off the dead. Any number of families jest lived on what they got from the Union armies in that way. They'd pick up what garments they could lay hands on, wash 'em up and sell 'em."[43] In this way, soldiers' gear and clothing made its way onto the secondhand clothing market and into the homes of civilians. Although this likely occurred more frequently in Southern communities, such clothing could also make its way into Northern homes, through shipments, in areas in which Union troops were stationed, or when battles took place on Northern soil, as in the case of Gettysburg, Pennsylvania.

Both soldiers and civilians, then, might find themselves wearing the pants of a dead soldier—during or after the war. While on his "tour" of the South's "battlefields and ruined cities," John Trowbridge encountered a man who told him:

> "Ye see that apple-tree? I got a right good pair o' pants off one o' your soldier's under that tree once."
>
> "Was he dead?"
>
> "Yes. . . . Shot through the head. The pants wa'n't hurt none."

Trowbridge turned to another man and asked, "Did you rob a dead soldier of those [pants] you have on?" The man replied that he had bought them in Fredericksburg and had never robbed a dead man. Trowbridge pressed him, asking, "How do you know they were not taken from a corpse?" The man replied that they might be, but it couldn't be helped: "A poo' man can't be choice."[44]

John Trowbridge's account of his conversation with these two former Confederates raises a significant question about the afterlives of looted clothing: What did it mean to wear the clothing and use the personal effects found in the pockets of the dead? In the mud and mire of many soldiers' lives, it may have made little difference. Yet, others seem to have been haunted or repulsed by the experience. Few soldiers seem to have written reflections on what it meant to wear a dead man's clothes. But one imagines that when putting on a coat previously worn by a dead soldier, a man might have considered how it had been obtained.

Alexander Hunter was proud of the coat he wore. So proud, in fact, that he later donated his coat to the Smithsonian. The coat was that of a dead man, but Hunter did not steal it. Rather, that dead man's sister gave it to him when she saw that he was wearing a tattered jacket.[45] In contrast, Charles Pluemacher's reaction to the discovery that the pocket watch he purchased secondhand had been looted from a dead man's body suggests that some men found the prospect of wearing such items repulsive. After the war ended, Pluemacher purchased a watch, not knowing where it had come from. However, he was "told later by comrades of the very thief that this time piece had been stolen from an officer" who was shot down "16 paces from the cannons mouth" at the Battle of Antietam. Underlying this statement is the knowledge that the officer would have been severely wounded, possibly mutilated. The soldier who stole the watch likely rifled through the bloody pockets of a man whose organs were exposed. The thought of this disgusted Pluemacher. He never wore the watch again and seems to have tried to atone for what he considered a disgraceful act by sending the watch to the governor of Virginia, not knowing the name of the man who owned it.[46] Eventually it became part of the Museum of the Confederacy in Richmond, Virginia (now the American Civil War Museum). Although both Pluemacher and Hunter owned and used, at least for a time, articles taken from a dead man's body, they had opposite reactions to that experience. That contrast suggests that what mattered to their sensibilities was not the act of wearing something removed from a dead soldier but, rather, *how* those objects of personal adornment had been taken off of that dead man—whether they had been removed lovingly by a sister or seized from the bloody pockets of a soldier maimed by a cannonball.

Some officers worried about the practical consequences of wearing stolen clothing. In the winter of 1864, for instance, Confederate officer G. M. Sorrel distributed a cautionary circular among the troops under General James Longstreet's command, ordering them to avoid "using all Federal clothing."[47] It was a bitterly cold winter, "enough to friz the River Styx in Purgatory," according to one man, and many Confederates had readily welcomed the extra layers of clothing and replacements for worn garments that they obtained by seizing the property of Union prisoners of war.[48] Sorrel suggested that the "impropriety of depriving prisoners of war of their clothing" should be enough to dissuade soldiers from such theft. But in January 1864, he was concerned not with the ethics of his men's actions, but with an invisible danger lurking in the creases and folds of Union soldiers' uniform coats: smallpox. The recent appearance of the telltale fever, rash, and pustules on the bodies of Confederate soldiers, Sorrel reported, was "directly traceable to the use of Yankee clothing taken from a prisoner."[49]

Disease was not the only concern at stake—so, too, was the misidentification of soldiers and the risk of firing at one's own comrades. It was not uncommon for both Union and Confederate forces to seize supply trains as a means of thwarting the success of the opposing army. In the course of such seizures, commanding officers might choose to distribute the supplies among their men. In other instances, men simply took what they wished. "We got a good deal of yankey plunder," one Confederate described. "We took 2000 overcoats of the finest quality." He also "got a fine yankee cap I have it on <u>now</u> and several pairs of Shoes."[50] When such seizures occurred, commanding officers needed to weigh the costs and benefits of using enemy uniforms. The Lieber Code provided specific instructions to the Union army in this regard, requiring all enemy uniforms put into circulation be noticeably marked to prevent misidentification and friendly fire.[51]

Marking seized uniforms posed a particular problem for Confederates. Under ideal circumstances, captured enemy uniforms would be made to look like one's own uniform. But captured Union blue uniforms could not be easily dyed gray. The blue dyes would first need to be bleached out of the fabric, and the cloth then dyed again—often requiring materials that were not readily available. Instead, Confederates typically used Union uniforms just as they were. It is easy to imagine the confusion that could occur after Confederates reoutfitted themselves in Union uniforms: "Our men at Plymouth were all stripped, and in an hour every Rebel was dressed in our uniform."[52] Indeed, one Confederate soldier noted that at Harper's Ferry, "the whole ground... was pretty well covered in places with old clothes which our soldiers had thrown off, substituting new ones."[53] Another noted that if it had not been for the battle flags that designated their company, the Confederates might have been mistaken "for a brand new Brigade from Boston."[54]

Objects in museums and private collections evidence not only the stripping of bodies but also the ways in which looting bodies and stealing from prisoners of war could be used to wage war by stripping men of their brass manhood. As historian Teresa Barnett rightly points out, by stripping buttons, "soldiers asserted their enemies' failures as soldiers and appropriated a token of their own prowess."[55] Furthermore, the forced removal of buttons by a prison guard was humiliating to captives.[56] But there was more to these actions. In a wartime culture that celebrated brass manhood, taking those buttons effectively stripped a man of the material objects required for him to enact that manhood.

To understand how men experienced the theft of those trappings of brass manhood, it is necessary to consider that stripping a man of brass manhood was precisely what was intended in military punishments. Divesting a soldier of his uniform, buttons, or insignia was a method of public shaming and punishment in both the Union and Confederate armies, and part of the ritual of "drumming out of camp" those soldiers who had been dishonorably discharged.[57] Given the broader significance of the removal of insignia in the military context, soldiers viewed and experienced the stripping of buttons, sashes, and other insignia as a form of humiliation and emasculation.

Both Union and Confederate soldiers kept buttons stolen from dead or imprisoned enemies as trophies of war. The act of collecting buttons as war trophies was part of a performance of one's manhood in which the emasculation of one man increased the masculinity of the other—at times quite literally in the removal of brass buttons from one man, and the sewing of those buttons onto the uniform of another. In some instances men wrote with bravado their stories about taking brass buttons and insignia; others sent the buttons to family members; still others sewed them onto their uniforms and wore them proudly. George Wilson, for instance, "captured" crossed-cannon insignia

Vest. This US soldier's vest was taken by a Confederate soldier on the battlefield. Its history was handwritten with ink onto the linen lining: "CAPTURED FROM Milroy, BATTLE OF Winchester." Courtesy of the American Civil War Museum, Richmond, VA.

from a federal artillery captain at the Battle of Winchester in 1863, and then wore them on his own uniform until he himself was captured two years later.[58] Similarly, coats in the collection of the American Civil War Museum have both Union eagle and Confederate state buttons sewn to their breasts. One soldier stole not merely buttons, but one-half of a vest, as a trophy. He removed one front breast panel on which the brass buttons were sewn, writing on the inside of the lining "CAPTURED FROM Milroy, BATTLE OF Winchester."

While the soldier who took this vest kept the entire breast panel and buttons, New York soldier Fred Mather curated his button collection after the war by mounting it on a cardboard backing. He included handwritten descriptive notes detailing where and from whom the buttons had been taken. One Georgia button was taken "from dead at Harris House," an infantry button was taken from "dead at Spottsylvania," and a South Carolina militia officer's

Confederate Buttons.

gathered by Companion Fred Mather

1st Lieut, 7th N.Y. Heavy Artillery

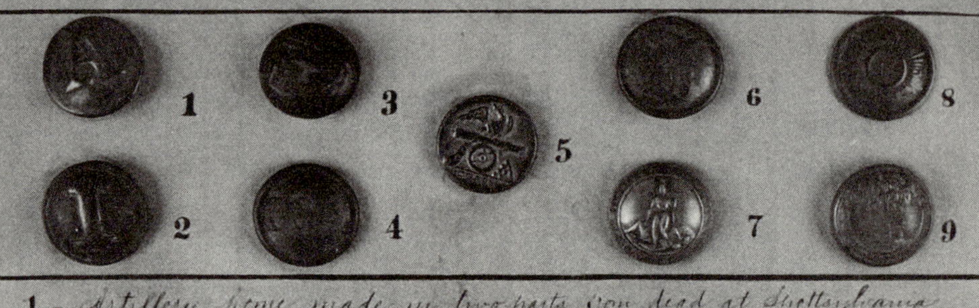

1- Artillery, home made, in two parts, from dead at Spottsylvania

2- Infantry, home made, cast solid, from dead at Spottsylvania

3- Georgia, home made, in two parts, from dead at Harris House.

4- C.S.A., made by S. Buckley & Co., Birmingham, from prisoner at Milford Station, Va., May 21st, 1864.

5- Artillery Corps, made by Scovills & Co. Waterbury, Conn., from prisoner at Cold Harbor, June 3d.

6- Infantry, Officer's button, no makers name, at Cold Harbor, June 3d.

7- Virginia Militia, Scovill Mfg. Co. Waterbury, Conn.; Cold Harbor

8- North Carolina, home made, cast solid, from guard in Macon, Ga. Prison, July, 1864.

9- South Carolina Militia, Officer's button, made by Schuyler, Hartley and Graham, N.Y., cut from Officer's coat in prison at Charleston, S.C., August, 1864.

Lieut. Fred Mather (First New York Heavy Artillery) took these buttons from Confederate prisoners and the Confederate dead. Mather noted where he obtained each button and, when identifiable, the button's manufacturer. Military buttons mounted on card, 1860–64. Collection of the New-York Historical Society.

button was "cut from Officer's coat in prison at Charleston, S.C."—all presumably taken from coats that were still upon the men's bodies.[59] This collection, then, was assembled through a willingness to disobey army codes: by stealing from prisoners of war, humiliating them in the process; and by desecrating Confederate bodies, stripping them on the battlefield.

Battlefield looting blurred lines about property and the sanctity of the body, and some men seemed unbothered by the process. "Our men strip the Yankees naked before burying them," Confederate Hall McGee wrote. He then described reading through the letters, presumably taken from those same soldiers: "I pull up and actually blush," he wrote, "to think a woman could write such disgraceful letters as I read." He seemed nonplussed when it came to the naked dead and their private letters, but in the next sentence of his dairy wrote with disgust about the house he camped in that same night. It had "been occupied three nights before by beast Butler as hdqrs—everything in the house totally destroyed, furniture smashed up, clothing torn to pieces."[60] Looting was well and good for soldiers like McGee, as long as Confederates were doing it. But when the same act turned to Southern civilian spaces, looting took on new valences.

Concealing

Disobedience of army orders extended far beyond the battlefield, as soldiers took the acts of looting to which they had become accustomed on the battlefield into the homes of Southern civilians. The looting of homes and foraging on Southern land are typically situated within an effort to understand the US Army's hard war.[61] But considering such thefts alongside the looting that took place on the battlefield reveals broader conceptions of people's attitudes toward the sanctity of the body. As the Union and Confederate armies traversed the South, civilians—white and Black—made efforts to conceal their belongings. Enslaved women hid their quilts and other belongings in the rafters of cabins or under floorboards. Elite white women buried silver and ordered enslaved people to conceal other valuables in wells or in the woods. One woman, "determined to trust none of the servants," planned to hide her family's provisions and valuables herself, but finding that she could not handle a shovel, had three enslaved persons bury them for her. When US soldiers were approaching their house, she and four other women put on all of their best clothing, "for we had determined to meet them in our best as if all else was destroyed we would still have something; we descended and all five of us stood on the piazza to receive, and if possible, prevent their entrance."[62] They were unsuccessful and

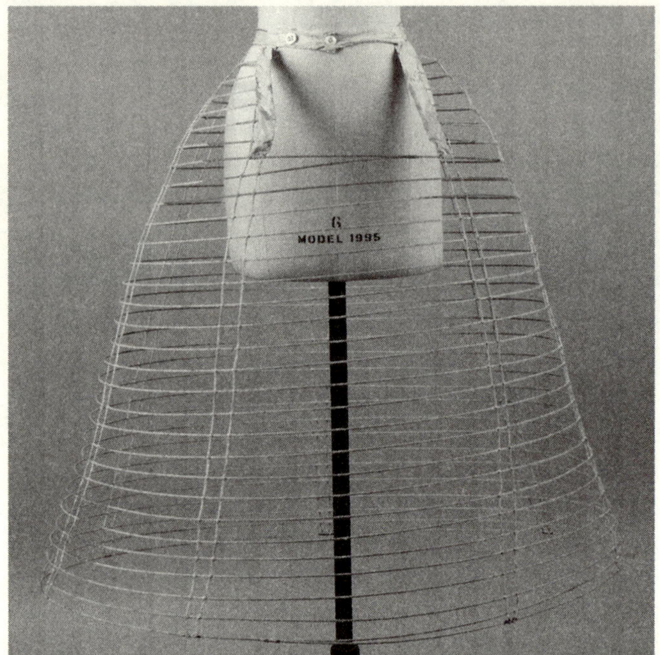

Crinoline, c. 1860. The Metropolitan Museum of Art, New York, Irene Lewisohn Bequest, 1986.

the soldiers searched the house extensively. Many white women felt compelled to hide their valuables on their persons and in their bedrooms, believing, as Lisa Tendrich Frank has argued, that the "feminine sphere was off limits to invaders" and assuming that "anything on their body would remain untouched."[63] Stories of women hiding valuables beneath their skirts are common, but this experience was largely class based, in terms of both the items that were hidden and the manner in which it was done. The experience of clanking silver hidden under one's dress required owning both objects of value and the fashion to conceal them. This practice of hiding items under skirts meant that fear of looting was expressed as an embodied, sartorial practice.

While items could be hidden beneath skirts of any kind, the cage crinoline, or hoop skirt, offered a greater means of concealment due to the space created by the crinoline between the body and the dress fabric. Such crinolines were made from a series of graduated steel hoops connected by fabric tape—stiff, woven strips of cotton. Some women described tying objects to the steel hoops themselves, allowing the objects to dangle from the hoop. Although made from steel, these hoops were necessarily thin and incapable of supporting a significant amount of weight. Hiding several objects required an alternative approach, such as that taken by Susan Blackford, who, at the news of the Union army's

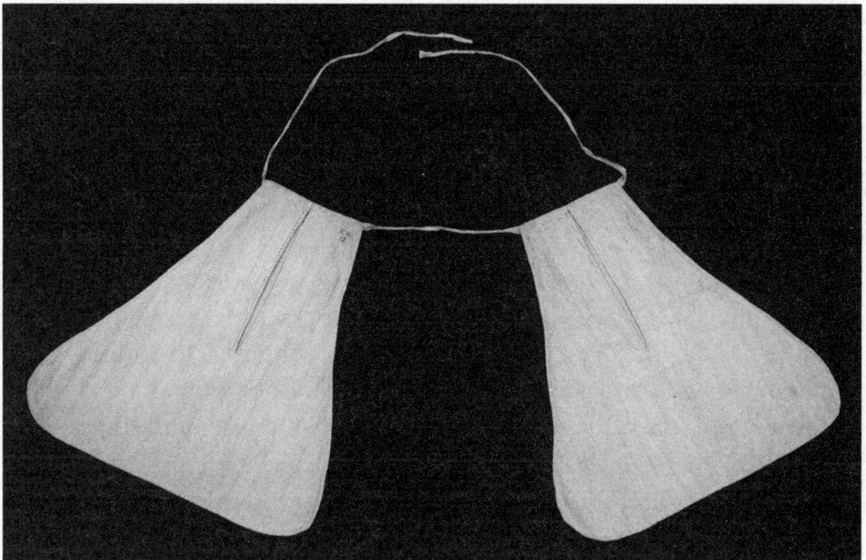

Pockets like this one were worn beneath a woman's dress and accessed through slits in the skirt. Cotton pocket, c. 1860. Brooklyn Museum Costume Collection at the Metropolitan Museum of Art, New York, Gift of Mrs. Samuel Gilford, 1944.

impending arrival, gathered up the family's silver, including the sugar dish, cream pot, bowl, forks, and spoons. She put the items into the legs of a pair of her husband's long underwear, "tying up each leg at the ankle and buckling the band around my waist" so that the objects hung under the crinoline.[64]

A material culture of improvisation and repurposing of outdated dress practices emerged in response to the threat of looting. Blackford's impromptu decision to use her husband's underwear to hide silver could be easily reversed. When the threat of looting passed, she could unbuckle the waist, untie the legs, and return the drawers to their original use. Other women, however, fashioned bags specifically for the purpose of hiding valuables. Some women turned to the use of an outdated article of women's dress—the pocket, a large, flat bag that was tied around a woman's waist and worn underneath the crinoline. At the height of its fashion in the eighteenth century, this bag was accessed through slits along the seams of skirts and petticoats. By the 1840s, dress patterns show the incorporation of pockets sewn into the seams of skirts, but working-class women continued to wear pockets that tied around the waist. Elite women's use of pockets to hide their valuables, then, involved both the resurrection of an old dress practice and the use of what was, by then, a largely lower-class accessory.[65]

The simple construction of a pocket meant that it could be quickly assembled. At midnight, in the midst of the evacuation of Richmond, Judith McGuire sat down to sew large pockets "and filled them with as many of our valuables as we could suspend from our waists."[66] Certainly, carrying items under one's skirts was not unfamiliar to women. However, whereas pockets were traditionally used to carry small amounts of money, a watch, scissors, or other small implements to keep them close for daily use, now women loaded them with jewelry, silverware, and other valuables to keep them from the hands of looters.

The physical weight of the pockets stuffed with objects to hide under women's skirts was a material reminder of the threat of looting and conflict; the experience was laden with physical emotion and often anxiety. In some instances, women coped with the experience through humor. Susan Blackford wrote to her husband describing her preparation for the arrival of Union soldiers. The items under her hoop could not be seen, but as she walked, the silver clanked, the absurdity of which caused her to laugh, an expression of her nervousness. Her anxiety was not unfounded and many women worried that, while soldiers might not physically remove their valuables from under their skirts, they would threaten and force them to do so themselves.[67]

Fear of discovery when walking with metal valuables beneath their skirts in the presence of soldiers motivated some women to devise ways to silence the clanking. One method involved hiding valuables in fabric, including pockets and garments. Sewing small pockets into a bag had long been employed in the construction of women's pockets as a means of offering extra protection for fragile objects. Instructions for making a pocket noted that "sometimes an inner pocket or pockets are made for a watch, &c. and this is done by sewing a square piece of the material inside the pocket. The top is left open, but the sides and bottom of it are firmly sewed down."[68] Some women took an extra step to completely sew the valuables into fabric, such that it would require a seam ripper or scissors to remove the objects. One Richmond family, for instance, had both a fabric pocket and a "money belt" made from basic, unbleached utilitarian cotton fabric.[69] Folding back this now-disassembled belt reveals circular rust stains of various sizes and snipped threads—evidence that the owner had once sewn coins of various denominations into the fabric.[70]

This removable belt could be worn under any dress, or exchanged between members of the family. However, other women sewed coins into garments themselves. Susan Blackford's sister, for instance, unstitched "some flannel strips, which decorated her homespun linsey balmoran skirt" in order to "sew coins at intervals under it all around."[71] This technique served multiple purposes, with an eye toward both strategy and comfort. Coins that were individually stitched would not come into contact with one another, thereby silencing them and decreasing chances of discovery. It also meant that the weight of the coins could be distributed throughout a single garment, both making it easier for the wearer to walk and offering a smoother silhouette.

In using their clothing to hide valuables, women expressed a confidence that their spherical skirts created a bodily boundary that would not be trespassed. Indeed, women who left behind diaries seem to have less frequently expressed a presumption that sexual assault was part of war, compared to later conflicts. In her anticipation of Sherman's arrival in Columbia, South Carolina, Emma LeConte was "hastily making large pockets to wear under my hoopskirt" because she believed "they will hardly search our persons."[72] Yet sexual violence was part of the Southern wartime experience. While social mores of this time period may have valued the sanctity of women's bodies, not all men respected the physical boundaries created by women's skirts.[73] One soldier noted that "both officers and men appear to have cast off all the restraints of home & indulge their passions to the fullest extent."[74]

Explicit references to the violation of women's bodies are infrequent—likely in part due to the social stigma attached to sexual intercourse outside of wedlock—and yet such violations occurred. Elite women expressed expectations that they would be treated with respect by enemy soldiers, but those soldiers did not necessarily regard women with respect, enemy or otherwise. Prior to his enlistment, Union soldier Joel Bouton viewed women as disposable objects, writing, "I go with one for a while, then discard her for another." He also referred to women as "pretty expensive property."[75] Bouton took that attitude with him to war, writing to a friend, "We have a peculiar drill to go through when we meet a female down here. It is this. Present arms—close (clothes) up,—lie down,—draw rammer,—ram cartridge. There is one time and two motions to each command but the last when the recruit makes as many motions as he has a mind to. Yo can guess how each command is exicuted. Such is military."[76] While his friend may have been able to guess the specifics of these interactions, Bouton does not make clear whether or not this "drill" was consensual or an act of rape. Soldiers frequently used innuendo in describing sexual interactions with women—both forcible and consensual. In other instances, however, actions were quite clear, as when Albert Lane was convicted of forcing himself on one woman "then and there forcibly and against her will, feloniously did ravish and carnally know her."[77] Women like Emma LeConte who believed their persons would hardly be searched assuaged their fears of looting by hiding their belongings on their person, but the surety of their bodily protection was, in fact, uncertain.

Women expressed feelings of violation when their homes were looted, conveying their distress most intensely when their bedrooms and wardrobes were broken into. Caroline Hill was incensed by male soldiers rifling through her family's garments. "The horrid creatures stole many of the clothes & other things broke into the wardrobe & trunk & strewed what they did not steal, all over the floor."[78] One year later, Hill again found her home under attack, noting that it had been "ransacked from 'head to foot' seven times." She found the experience dehumanizing, comparing soldiers' treatment of her to that of a dog.[79]

Hill was angered when men threw her clothing out of the wardrobe, but other women looked on while soldiers destroyed their belongings. "There was no place, no chamber, trunk, drawer, desk, garret, closet, or cellar," one woman declared, "that was private to their unholy eyes."[80] At one Gettysburg, Pennsylvania, house, Confederate soldiers dragged silk dresses through the mud, stomped on them, and then left them hanging on a fence.[81] Silk was a difficult fabric to clean under normal circumstances, and even if the silk dresses were still intact after such treatment, they would have been virtually impossible to revitalize.

Such incidents were not only about the theft or destruction of property, but also part of a gendered struggle that centered on clothing and related accoutrements. Taking or destroying women's dresses was one way for Union soldiers to attack the South and the slaveholding class.[82] Soldiers themselves recognized that the theft of women's clothing and other objects of adornment transgressed a gendered boundary. Union soldier Levi Bryant explained, "I never had face enough on me to go into a house & step up to a young girl & demand her rings or [threaten to] Blow out her Brains. & I thank God for the hart I have it is not so hard as some I find. When I can Stoop to Rob the wimin of their Little keepsakes I must have my hart hardend & case hardend first."[83] Although Bryant likely saw bodies looted on battlefields, he drew a stark line between men at war and civilian women and their possessions.

There is a significant difference between destroying dresses and taking them. Whereas a destroyed dress might remain in the abstract an important symbol of violation or triumph, the material object itself was gone or ruined to the extent that it could no longer function as a dress. Stolen dresses, however, continued to retain the ability to be worn—even if the wearer was no longer the original owner. Union and Confederate men took dresses for practical purposes—tearing them to make cartridges or bandages, or as disguises in which to desert the army.[84] Soldiers' theft of dresses with the intention of shipping them to women at home, however, has likely been underestimated.

Confederate nurse Kate Cumming implicated Northern women in the looting of Southern homes, charging them with plaguing soldiers with insistent requests for looted objects. "I do not suppose the men would rob us as they do," she asserted, "if they were not incited by the importunities of their women." Elaborating, Cumming wrote, "Many letters, taken from dead Federals on the battle-fields, contain petitions from the women to send them valuables from the South. One says she wants a silk dress; another, a watch; and one writer told her husband that now was the time to get a piano, as they could not afford to buy one."[85] Cumming's charge against Union women's desire for stolen valuables might be an exaggeration intended to insult the propriety of Northern women. But there was truth to her words and she may very well have read such "petitions" in the letters found in dead Union soldiers' coats. Whether or not Cumming was correct in her assumption that Northern women requested Southern silks, those Northern women did, indeed, receive such silks.

Not all thefts were dramatic encounters between women and soldiers. In the aftermath of the Battle of Fredericksburg, for instance, soldiers looted houses that were abandoned by their inhabitants at the army's approach. A sketch of Fredericksburg shows the chaos of looting, with parasols, bureaus, and rocking chairs laying in the street. Some of those items were transported by Union soldiers to Norfolk, Virginia, where soldiers made arrangements to ship them north via express package services or by naval ship. Such shipments were illegal, however, and some soldiers' boxes were confiscated. One such box, intended for a Philadelphia grocer's address, contained a "valuable Silk Dress pattern" as well as books, china, and a silver tea urn. Another box, sent to a Pennsylvania doctor, contained "Two Silk Dresses, Webster's Dictionary, One Parasol, one Ladies Shawl, &c."[86] But what would a grocer or doctor want with a silk dress pattern, a dress, or a ladies' shawl?

These particular packages never made it to their destination, having been confiscated by a commanding officer, but similar shipments were, indeed, opened by the intended recipients. The theft and shipment of such items defies a categorization of stolen goods as relics or mementos of war. Certainly, a dress could function as such, but it is far more likely that these items were intended to be reused. The box of looted ladies' clothing shipped to Anna Kelly of Blairsville, Pennsylvania, for instance, was likely for Kelly herself to wear. As the daughter of a farmer whose personal estate was worth only one hundred dollars, it is unlikely that Kelly had an expansive wardrobe.[87] The report

Arthur Lumley traveled with the US Army of the Potomac as a special artist. He captured the disarray of wartime looting in this image that depicts furniture in the streets of Fredericksburg. Pencil sketch by Arthur Lumley, *Halt of Wilcox's Troops in Caroline Street Previous to Going to Battle,* December 13, 1862. Courtesy of the Library of Congress Prints and Photographs Division, Washington, DC.

on the confiscation of these articles does not detail the contents of the box, but given the frequency with which silk dresses were stolen, it is likely that these, too, were made from this expensive fabric. Elite women's dresses could include between ten and thirty-five yards of fabric. A Southern woman's bell-shaped hoop skirt dress could be remade to fit the recipient, or the fabric repurposed and used for multiple dresses worn without hoops. Such fine silk would have served as a status symbol in one's community.

The incorporation of elite women's dresses into another person's wardrobe took on added meaning when that person was a formerly enslaved woman. Many slaveholding women lost their clothing when those they had enslaved seized it and left, striking out on their own path to freedom. Enslaved women took "ribbons and trinkets" and bows; others left plantations wearing silk dresses. They did not only take the outer garments of fashion, however. They also took the undergarments that were critical to creating the popular silhouette of the 1860s, including petticoats and crinolines. Kate Stone, for instance, lost "most of our underclothes and dresses, all my fine and pretty things, laces, etc., except one silk dress."[88] "A joyful feeling of freedom," Stephanie Camp notes, was "embodied in women's claims on their owners' symbolic dress."[89] Unlike soldiers who stole, however, when enslaved women took clothing they typically did so with the understanding that such property was rightfully theirs; it was payment for years of enslaved work. Slaveholding women, however, decried such actions as theft. Although the formerly enslaved women considered such possessions to be theirs for the taking, they nevertheless understood the implications the loss of such clothing would have for former mistresses. At the sight of "saucy negro women" in Richmond, one white woman lamented, "the eye is offended by all it sees."[90]

Clothing theft was one means by which people waged war against their enemies—a way by which they deprived them of not only their bodily coverings but, at times, their identity as well. The act of using one's clothing to prevent theft was a means by which people, and especially elite women, combatted the demoralizing uncertainty of enemy occupation. The relationship between looted clothing and culture, then, was shaped by experiences both on the battlefield and in civilians' houses. War taught men that they could not expect that their own bodies would be treated as inviolable. This was quite unlike the expectations of elite Southern women, who hid their valuables beneath their skirts under the assumption that men would not dare violate the privacy of their bodies. The threat of looting—whether of one's home or of one's body—resulted in actions taken by both civilians and soldiers that affected their physical experience of the material world in which they lived. Women sewed pockets to wear beneath their skirts; men decided not to wear body armor for fear of its discovery upon their death. Soldiers left belongings with friends out of fear that their body would be robbed, or shipped home items that they valued and did not wish to lose.

The stripping of clothing from the wearer was powerful in a society that not only embraced a public gender construction enacted through clothing—the manhood and womanhood that were tied to wartime brass—but also believed in the transformative power of clothing. Stripping clothing and failing to replace it with other garments violated ideas about transformation that were bound up in the process of divestiture, nakedness, and re-clothing that was central to understandings of rebirth and identity. The body and soul, or inner self, were entangled in the nineteenth-century imaginary. By extension, garments worn upon the body were tied to the inner self as well. Indeed, in the mid-nineteenth century, some health reformers were actively contesting medical and religious notions of the body's weakness by describing the body as unified with the soul.[91] Physician Elizabeth Blackwell argued, "In the wonderful whole of creation no part is separated from the rest, mind and matter, body and soul, substance and form, are essentially related."[92] Although Blackwell's motivation in writing was to elevate the importance of women's health, her assertions pointed to the broader belief that the material world in which the body lived had powerful effects upon not only the body, but also the soul. These understandings of the body-soul-material world relationship influenced how people thought about clothing's transformative qualities. The act of divestiture was central to clothing's ability to transform—one needed to remove one's old clothes to shed their old self. But that transformation also hinged on covering that naked body with new clothing. What, then, were the implications when a body was never re-clothed?

When men put on a military uniform, they clothed themselves in brass manhood, and public culture reaffirmed that expression of manhood. When that clothing was forcefully peeled from their body—living or dead—their manhood, too, was publicly stripped away. The adjectives with which men described the appearance of the looted dead—"naked skins," "sheaves in a harvest field," "hogs that had been cleaned"—conveyed their acknowledgment that manhood, indeed humanity, had been stripped away. Furthermore, descriptions of the dead suggest not only that men were repulsed at the actions of the enemy, but also that they no longer looked upon the stripped dead as enacting brass manhood—they expressed pity and disgust for them. Indeed when Daniel Holt saw his naked, dead friend, he used the words "all that remained of so pure and worthy a man as he," suggesting that the stripping of the man's body had simultaneously stripped him of manhood to the point that the evidence of the man that he had once been was nearly obliterated.[93] Even in the eyes of comrades who had seen them march into battle, a stripped man could make little claim to the brass manhood that was bound up in his clothing.

Those elite women whose houses were looted and dresses stolen experienced such acts as a violation of their status as women. They lost the trappings of elite clothing culture through which they themselves conveyed their wealth and status. When that clothing was destroyed, it entered a realm of the symbolic lost. When it was stolen and reappropriated, however, either by Northern white or formerly enslaved women, that clothing could take on a subversive quality. In a society that believed in clothing's transformative qualities, enslaved women could potentially elevate their own status by wearing elite women's dresses. Certainly, they were accused of "playing the lady," but those accusations stemmed from white women's fear that in "playing" the lady, a Black woman might become one. Such loss and the possibilities of its consequences were even more potent because elite white women's clothing could not be easily replaced in the blockaded South.

Knowledge of these acts was central to the broader context in which soldiers and civilians confronted the loss and destruction of both clothing and the sanctity of men's and women's bodies. Yet writers rarely addressed peeled bodies and pillaged dresses in connection to one another at the time. Indeed, when Kate Cumming charged Northern women with responsibility for the looting of Southern homes because of their "petitions" to soldiers to acquire valuables and dresses, she failed to note the irony in the fact that her knowledge of such requests for valuables came about because of the looting of clothing and letters from the bodies of "dead Federals." Such looting was all the more destructive in a society whose sartorial practices were coming undone.

CHAPTER SIX

The Unraveling of White Southern Dress Culture

Clothing in the Wartime South

At the same time as men struggled with the implications of battlefield stripping, women stuffed valuables into pockets, and relief workers were beginning to imagine freedpeople as new consumers, many white Southerners were experiencing the upending of their dress practices. In an undated wartime letter, Margaret Hudlow, a white woman in her early thirties with four children and a disabled husband, summoned her limited grasp of spelling and grammar to pen a letter to the governor of Georgia. In it, she drew attention to her family's struggle to support themselves in the face of rampant speculation and unequal access to clothing and fabric, calling upon the governor to take action to alleviate the suffering of Georgia's women and their families:

> i now through the kind mercies of god drop you a few lines to inform you how we are geting a long in this part of the cuntry truly hopeing you will assiste us in tellin the speculaters how trifling they ar treating the soldiers wives an that they are now whiping our soldiers in the field wors than the yankies when they hear how there families is having to go an beg an pay one month wage for 2 bushels of corn. . . . we cant get thredd to cloth our men i have sent to rawswell factory an had to pay 13 dollars a bunch they sayed i did not get thare in time. . . . i have four children my health is so bad i cant spin. . . . maby will make 10 pounds of cotton not a nuff to clothe my family eaven. . . . soldiers may pay tar fight blead an die for thare rights but will not get them.[1]

Hudlow's letter could be easily classified among those written by white Southerners who were becoming increasingly disenchanted with wartime conditions on the home front. But more was at stake. Here, Hudlow joined women from a broad range of economic and social backgrounds who found themselves unable to buy cloth at local textile mills or purchase the implements and raw materials to make their own clothing and felt that their best recourse was to demand that the governor fulfill his responsibilities to his citizens.

The landscape of wartime Southern textiles is typically understood as being defined by the scarcity of raw material, the paralyzing effects of reliance on Northern and British imports, rampant speculation, the undeveloped state of

Southern manufacturing, reliance on homespun fabric, and the disappearance of the silk-attired Southern belle.[2] This interpretation is so pervasive that for modern Americans one of the most iconic images of the South's decline is the romanticized transformation in dress undergone by Vivien Leigh portraying Scarlett O'Hara in David O. Selznick's 1939 production of Margaret Mitchell's *Gone with the Wind*. Having worn a delicate, voluminous white-and-green floral dress with hoops prior to the war, O'Hara is reduced to a ragged pink calico covered with a drab, makeshift apron and wrapped in a coarse brown shawl, before attempting to reclaim her former image of wealth by transforming the plantation parlor's velvet portieres and gold tiebacks into the now-iconic "Green Curtain Dress." And, indeed, there was some truth to Selznick's portrayal of elite Southern women's dress and the repurposing of fabric. However, as Margaret Hudlow's letter indicates, there was far more at stake in the shifting state of Southern dress practices than questions of self-presentation, social status, or loss. Citizens' understanding of their relationship to the government was also being tested as they experienced and, at times, invited increased state intervention in their daily lives—intervention that contributed to the disruption of Southern dress practices. A public culture of brass manhood had been celebrated in efforts to shape shared identities in a Confederate South that was fractured along political, economic, and racial lines. Cockades, ribbons, and aprons had been donned by civilians. Yet while celebratory in the context of the early wartime surge of patriotism, clothing became one of the most tangible ways in which Southerners suffered war's toll, making it a key site through which their support for the government was eroded.

The circumstances of war dictated, but government authorities and actions took part in shaping, the changing landscape of Southern fabric and clothing production and consumption, extending the state's reach not only into the plantation houses and mansions of the elite, but also into yeoman farmers' houses, poor whites' shacks, and enslaved people's cabins. The US federal government, the central Confederate government, and individual state governments were all intimately, if not always explicitly, involved in the everyday sartorial practices of Black and white Southerners during and immediately following the war through the emancipation of enslaved people; enactment of tariffs, policies, and blockades; the enforcement of pseudo-sumptuary laws; and mandates and incentives for army textile production. At stake was not only access to basic necessities, but also the perpetuation of cultural norms and social hierarchies created and embodied by dress.

Tensions on the home front were fueled by the challenge of accessing cloth and clothing, by competing efforts to create and express political identities through clothing, and—in the case of Union and Confederate sympathizers—through the use of clothing as a form of subversion. The emancipation of enslaved people, who performed so much textile production and clothing care, directly affected their enslavers. Civilian clothing—and lack of it—shaped people's bodies and daily lives and thereby shaped both how civilians contributed to the ways war was waged and how they experienced war's effects. These material experiences conditioned their approach to interpersonal relationships, involvement with the government, and the politics of daily life.

When Black women walked out of their enslavers' houses or off a plantation, they took with them their skills in textile production and clothing care. They took with them the washing, drying, starching, and ironing; and the carding, spinning, dyeing, weaving, sewing, and mending. Other women, though they remained enslaved, denied their enslavers the use of those skills, emboldened by the transformations brought by the war. With great contempt, one enslaver claimed that Beckie "makes me a great trouble ironing days. She is so careless and stupid."[3] Beckie, like many enslaved women, had begun refusing to perform the backbreaking work of laundry days. Laundry, including washing, starching, and ironing, was such a hated chore that it was almost exclusively relegated to the work of enslaved women. Indeed, nonslaveholding white women in cities who had the means to do so hired out their washing to Black and white laundresses.[4] But it was not only laundry that enslaved women spurned. "Household slaves," Thavolia Glymph shows, "discovered new openings through which to claim personal time or to flee the household entirely. Whether they left or stayed put during the war, they obliged their mistresses to take on the work of slaves."[5]

White women were not altogether lacking in their ability to perform these tasks of clothing care and production. Indeed, clothing production was often a joint enterprise between female enslavers and enslaved women, functioning as a piecework system of sorts, with white women making patterns and cutting out the cloth and Black women sewing and finishing the garments. The experiences of women enslaved on Kate Stone's Louisiana plantation offer an example of the complexity of Black and white women's interactions related to clothing production. On various occasions, Stone's mother chalked patterns on uncut cloth, which were then cut out by the enslaved seamstresses. In other households, white women cut the cloth, suspecting that enslaved women would waste cloth when laying out patterns for cutting fabric. Stone's mother also "basted for the seamstress," meaning that she took cloth that had been cut into a pattern and tacked it with loose stitches for sewing. Similarly, Stone did the machine work on some chemises but had the seamstress finish them.[6] Stone considered chalking out patterns and supervising the cutting to be hard work. "After a day or so of this work," she noted, "Mamma would go to bed quite broken down and Aunt Lucy, the colored housekeeper, would finish the superintending."[7]

The work of clothing production was dependent on the ability to access cloth, of course. The Union blockade of the rebellious states disrupted cotton export and limited the importation of supplies, but it was also porous, allowing Confederate runners to slip through carrying both essential and luxury goods.[8] This permeability offered a distinct advantage to white Southerners with personal connections and a means to travel—or purchase goods—from beyond the blockade. But that was a double-edged sword. Meeting a friend on the street, South Carolinian Frederick Porcher noted that "her dress was not fresh and she was at a loss to know how to [hide] her torn and faded silk gloves." "In short," he continued, "she looks like most ladies whom you meet now that are not wives or daughters of blockade runners and great speculators."[9] In this context, the everyday politics surrounding the material trappings of the Southern social hierarchy became increasingly complex, creating tension within the social order, even among friends, thereby testing relationships between people. The clothing that a white person wore in public could materially display one's mercantile connections and ability to pay high prices for new dress goods, but it could also mark one as a war profiteer. Clothing could belie a person's adaptive repurposing of possessions or signal their declining financial situation or abject poverty.

Confederate civilians experienced declining quality in dress, difficulty in obtaining new items, and increased use of homespun materials over the course of the war. These changes have been primarily situated within broader paradigms of Confederate women's patriotism, the deterioration of their economic status, and home front morale.[10] Such analysis provides only a limited glimpse into the ways in which civilians, and especially women, experienced, confronted, and ascribed meaning to disruptions in—and, in some instances, the destruction of—their accepted dress practices. Material goods shaped women's bodies and daily lives, affecting how war conditioned their approaches to interpersonal relationships, involvement with the government, and the everyday politics of life. In conflicts surrounding clothing we see also the maintenance of the state by virtue of women's efforts to enforce, through appeals for its protection, what they perceived as a contract between the state and its citizens.[11]

When the South emerged from the war, clothing played a pivotal role in shaping postemancipation identities and in how an unraveled nation began to knit itself back together.[12] Scholars have tended to analyze clothing—frequently understood as a "social skin"—within the context of constructing a public image. And, indeed, outward appearance was critically important to middling and elite Southern women's construction of their social selves. However, by pushing beyond the interpretation of clothing as a "skin" worn for the purpose of conveying messages to other people, to also consider people's physical experiences of wearing their clothing, it becomes apparent that what a person wore had far deeper implications for their sense of self. The circumstances created by—and responses to—cloth shortages offer a window into how people thought about their clothes. This was particularly evident in Southerners' reflections on the disparity between what they had once worn and that to which they now had access.

The significance and extent of the wartime disruption of white Southern sartorial practices become more evident when we consider objects alongside women's personal narratives. Indeed we gain new perspective on the effects of blockades and shortages in the Confederacy when we consider just what it was that people were trying to maintain in the realm of dress—the quality of goods to which they were accustomed, the feel of cloth, its cleanliness, the amount of fabric required to produce garments, the tools necessary to manufacture cloth at home, and the skills that it required. In what ways did the government insert itself into the sartorial practices of white Southerners, and how did people understand this entanglement of the state and dress culture? What, in other words, was the full import of Margaret Hudlow's assertion that her cotton crop was "not a nuff to clothe my family eaven"?

"Plucked Peacocks"

Elite Southern women had embraced homespun goods as a form of patriotism at the start of the war, but in the midst of fighting, death, and the threat of occupation, many women of all social classes clung to prewar sartorial practices in an attempt to maintain a semblance of their prewar lives and to steady their resolve in the context of such uncertainty. Elite women went to great efforts to stay current with fashions and maintain a "pleasing toilette," frequently judging their wardrobes in light of those worn by friends and acquaintances. Some expressed great pleasure in the knowledge of the superiority of their own appearance, while others lamented their inability to maintain the dress practices to which they were accustomed. In their effort to maintain not only their social status, but also a recognizable sense of their own selves, women formed informal networks of exchange among family and friends, experimented with substitute materials, reworked old garments, traveled "beyond the blockade" to buy goods at premium prices, made cloth, and purchased Southern-manufactured fabric. These women were not shallowly concerned with social appearances. Nor did they wholeheartedly embrace homespun fabric with patriotic fervor. Rather, women's impetus for sustaining prewar sartorial practices and their use of homespun went much deeper, reaching into the depths of their being.

The significance of one elite young Georgian's assertion that she felt "like a plucked peacock" only becomes recognizable when we consider what, precisely, was involved when it came to women's clothing.[13] Throughout the United States, the higher a woman's social rank, the less physical labor she likely performed, the more layers of clothing she likely wore, and the more likely she was to rely on either enslaved or wage labor for the care of her clothing. By the late 1850s, elite and middle-class white women throughout the United States were wearing clothing styles that required more layers of undergarments and foundation garments than had earlier styles. Their typical daytime, public attire included five or six layers: undergarments, foundational garments, another layer to cover foundational garments, a dress, a finishing layer, and a sixth layer of outer garments, depending upon the season. This layering was essential not only to achieve the popular bell-shaped silhouette, but also to create a physical barrier between a woman's body and her finer garments that needed to be protected from sweat and bodily odors because of the difficulty in laundering them.[14] Indeed, to thoroughly clean a silk dress, it needed to "be entirely taken to pieces" by detaching the skirt and sleeves from the bodice. Even then, some housekeeping manuals advised, "Unless the silk is of very good quality, it will not be worth while to take the trouble of cleaning it."[15] Protecting delicate fabrics, then, was essential to maintaining cleanliness.

Women's first layer of clothing included a loose-fitting chemise and long stockings held up by garters that were worn either just above or just below the knee. The next layer included a pair of drawers, which were frequently slit between the legs to simplify women's use of chamber pots or outhouses. A long chemise, which could be easily washed, protected a woman's fabric corset—often made from cotton or silk—that was stiffened with strips of whalebone or metal, usually referred to as "boning." In addition, women wore a crinoline consisting of either tiered metal hoops held together by fabric tape, or a cloth skirt with casings for wire. Over these foundational garments, women wore either a long-sleeved shirt or false sleeves/undersleeves, a corset cover (a short-waisted shirt), and a petticoat that covered the hoops.

Over these, a woman wore either a dress, or a bodice and skirt. Undersleeves and petticoats served multiple purposes: Undersleeves both provided

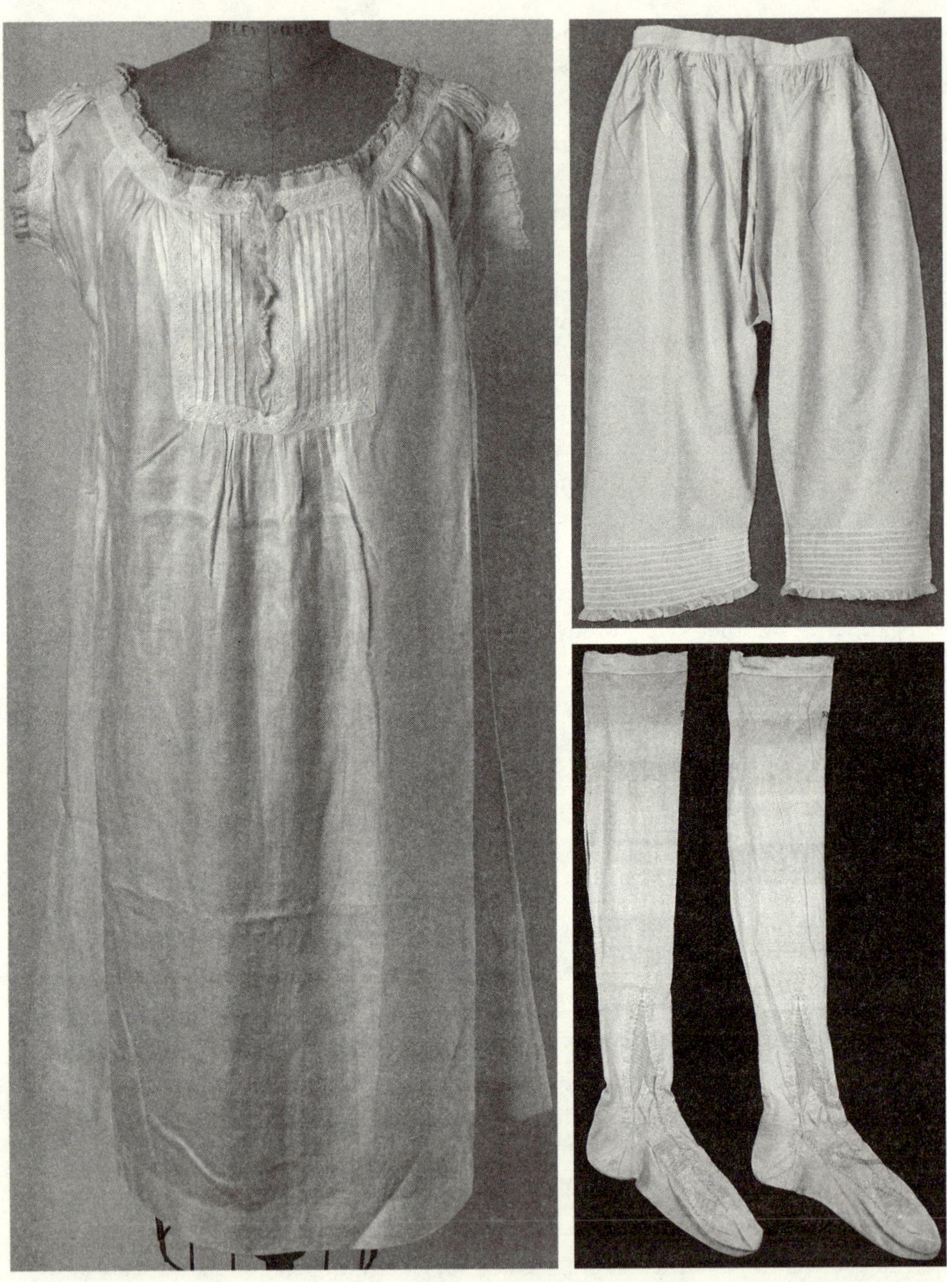

(*left*) Linen chemise, c. 1860s, American. The Metropolitan Museum of Art, New York.
(*top right*) Drawers, c. 1866, American. The Metropolitan Museum of Art, New York.
(*bottom right*) Silk stockings, c. 1850–60, American. Brooklyn Museum Costume Collection at the Metropolitan Museum of Art, New York.

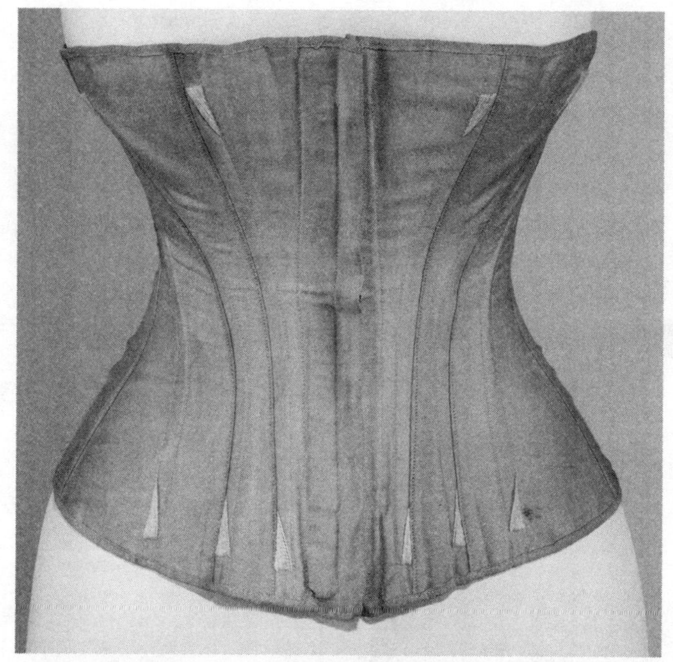

Corset, 1861–63, Worcester Skirt Company, American. Brooklyn Museum Costume Collection at the Metropolitan Museum of Art, New York.

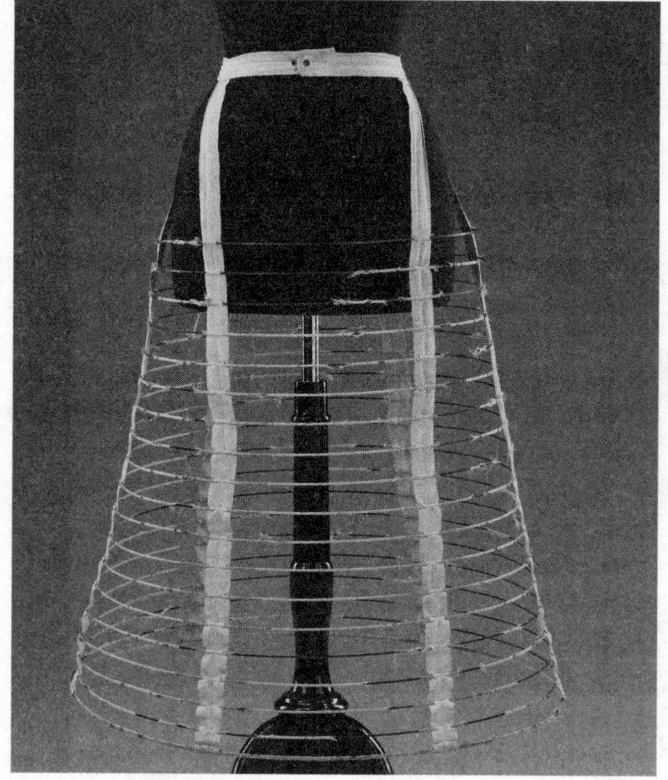

Cage crinoline, 1862–63, Royal Worcester Corset Company, American. Brooklyn Museum Costume Collection at the Metropolitan Museum of Art, New York.

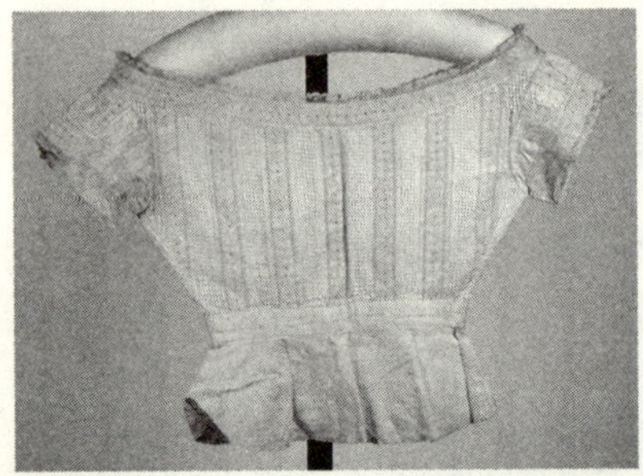

Cotton corset cover, 1860, American. Brooklyn Museum Costume Collection at the Metropolitan Museum of Art, New York.

Cotton petticoat, 1850–60, American. Brooklyn Museum Costume Collection at the Metropolitan Museum of Art, New York.

Undersleeves, c. 1860, American or European. The Metropolitan Museum of Art, New York, Gift of Mrs. Albert S. Morrow.

Afternoon dress, c. 1862, American. Silk cotton, wool. Brooklyn Museum Costume Collection at the Metropolitan Museum of Art, New York.

an additional degree of modesty by adding cuffs and protected dress sleeves from sweat. Petticoats, on the other hand, smoothed the appearance of corsets and hoops, provided additional volume to a skirt, and created a protective barrier between corsets and hoops and the more delicate dress fabric. Women often pinned a separate collar to their dress, and brooches, necklaces, earrings, and bracelets were used as accessories. Finally, women wore leather shoes, thin calfskin leather gloves, and a hat or bonnet. Depending upon the weather, she might complete her outfit with a cloak, coat, or mantle.

Whether at public functions or entertaining at home, elite women compared their wartime dresses to those of their peers, making judgments about the wearer's character based upon their clothing choices. Sarah Morgan resented the fact that her friend wore her finest dress to a social gathering despite the knowledge that doing so would highlight the deficiency of Morgan's own clothing: "Nothing would do but she must dress up fine; so she put on her handsomest organdie. In vain I pointed to my simple pink muslin with a white body that I had worn all day, and begged she would not make the contrast between us more striking than ever, as I felt I could not change it without exciting remark. She was obdurate; dressed herself in gorgeous array, and, as usual, I looked like her lady's maid."[16] Morgan deemed her friend obstinate, chastising her for wearing a fine dress that demarcated through its materiality an increasing chasm within the ranks of the planter elite. Here, in the context of an everyday activity, were two women experiencing the material unraveling of the planter class. In the disruptive context of war, these women—both of whom were part of the prewar planter elite—found themselves navigating the shifting social landscape of Southern sartorial practices. A person's prewar social status could not be sustained in the absence of the material trappings of class and the ability to dress like one's peers. Morgan's unease with clothing's ability to blur the lines of social rank was not uncommon. Eliza Andrews, an elite young Georgian, was jealous of one woman who, having just returned home from "beyond the lines," wore "beautiful dresses [that] were a revelation to us dowdy Confederates, and made me feel like a plucked peacock."[17] Once a woman who dressed in comparative luxury, Andrews felt stripped of her ability to maintain such dress practices.

At times, women went to great measures to ensure they had the elements of proper dress. When the house in which she was staying was under bombardment, Morgan did not immediately respond to calls to "Take to the fields! Take to the woods!" Instead, she "was putting on my hoops and hastily catching up any article that presented itself to me in my speed." Her mother yelled, "Sarah! You will be killed! Leave your clothes and run!" In her haste, she managed to save "the most useless of articles with the greatest zeal, and probably left the most serviceable ones." Her "running-bag" contained only one dress that also had sentimental value: "a white linen cambric with a tiny pink flower—the one I wore when I told Hal good-bye for the last time." The remainder of her wardrobe was left behind.[18]

As was the case for Morgan, white refugees fleeing from the Union army's advance faced a particularly difficult situation in maintaining their prewar sartorial practices. Refugees found it difficult to maintain not only a presentable wardrobe, but also their cleanliness.[19] Some lacked the enslaved labor to launder their clothes or money to hire a laundress; others wore the same dresses more frequently. When Sarah Morgan, with no clothing except the dress she wore, encountered some acquaintances after fleeing Baton Rouge in 1862, she admitted that she was "ashamed" by her appearance: "every one as dirty as possible; I had on the same dress I had escaped in, which, though then perfectly clean, was now rather—dirty."[20]

Still, Morgan, as a member of the planter elite with wide-reaching connections, was in a far superior position to most women who were displaced by advancing armies. Indeed, aid societies for white Southern refugees, including the Refugee Relief Commission of Ohio, found themselves providing women's and children's apparel of all kinds to white "refugees whose homes have been destroyed by the effects of war, or who, from the necessity of obeying military orders, were obliged to seek aid and homes among strangers" in towns located across Tennessee, Kentucky, Mississippi, Arkansas, and Louisiana.[21] These were not monied white female refugees but, rather, people hailing from yeoman or poor backgrounds.[22] "Three quarters of them have been trained to till the soil," noted one relief worker, "obtaining a scanty living among the hills of Tennessee and Georgia." Now, she continued, hundreds of these women and children were living on the outskirts of Nashville "in fields or hovels, scantily clad in garments ill suited to the season and daily dying from exposure and want."[23] These people's material circumstances could be similar to those of formerly enslaved people living in "contraband" camps.

At the same time, prices for new fabric were becoming increasingly inflated. In Kingston, Georgia, in July 1863, Kate Cumming bought "a pretty calico dress for three dollars per yard, and a pretty gray homespun for a dollar and seventy-five cents per yard."[24] By November 1864, she was paying "five dollars for ten common hairpins, and three dollars for a ball of common homespun thread."[25] Another woman in Mobile, Alabama, paid "eight dollars per yard for a calico dress, ten for a gingham, twenty for a common delaine; children's boots fifty dollars; ladies,' seventy-five."[26] In rural Camden County, Georgia, Julia Fisher noted that her friend wore "a course homespun dress that cost her $42.00," but even that exorbitant rate was better than she herself was able to negotiate in January 1864. Her own husband was dressed "very shabbily," and Fisher had resorted to using "bedticking—sheets—curtains and the linings of my dresses to clothe him and now we know not where to get anything more." When a family friend sent six yards of striped homespun so that she could make shirts for her husband, Fisher praised it as "a rich and welcome gift," for her husband would no longer need to be clothed in textiles intended for household use.[27]

Having money to afford goods at inflated prices was only half the battle—location and personal connections were also critical. Dolly Lunt Burge lamented that there were "hundreds of thousands" of "homesteads left with only the sad & lonely wife & mother" who could not "obtain what is absolutely needful." And yet, she noted, it was "not the poor alone" who could not access necessities, but women in her own position as well. As early as January 1862, Burge observed that her own cloth would "have to be made at home this year as it cannot be bought." She was frustrated that she had "hundreds of dollars in my pocket book & yet I cannot buy a yard of calico to make my [daughter] Sadai a sunbonnet it cannot be had. For weeks she has been wearing a bunch of rags for her bonnet is nothing else." Like many women of her status, Burge was resourceful in her attempts to sustain both her and her daughter's level of dress as long as possible. When calico could not be purchased, she devised another solution: using a piece of her aunt's dress to make up a bonnet to replace six-year-old Sadai's ragged one.[28] The decline in sartorial practice represented by her inability to provide her daughter with a new bonnet weighed on Burge. And the reason becomes especially apparent when we consider a prewar photograph of Sadai.[29] Pictured with Rachel, an enslaved nurse, Sadai wears a cape and an elaborate hat with delicate trimmings.

Women like Burge mobilized their networks of extended families and friends, establishing their own informal economies through which they worked to sustain prewar sartorial practices. Living in an isolated area of Camden County, Georgia, near the Florida border and over 100 miles from Savannah, Fisher relied upon friends living elsewhere for access to items for purchase as well as a market for secondhand clothing. In at least a few instances, Fisher sent a friend "cast off clothing" to exchange for other goods in another town. She relied upon that same friend to send supplies for her and her husband, including "six yards of striped homespun for shirts."[30] Such exchanges were not simple favors, but rather transactions that created hierarchies of benevolence between friends.

Other women bartered for dress goods. "Indeed barter has become the order of the day," Catherine Edmonston declared in September 1864. "We pay for our weaving in Lard! Two lbs of Lard pays for the weaving of 2 yds of coarse cloth."[31] Similarly, Gadwell Jefferson Pearce, president of LaGrange Female College, instructed one woman to "get all the thread you can. It is an article of necessity and good currency vastly better than Confederate" money.[32] At the Sweetwater Cotton Factory outside Atlanta, people bartered their best produce for factory goods since "the operatives much preferred produce to worthless Confederate money."[33] Anne Shannon Martin recalled one woman who "had a pair of single homemade corsets, that she was willing to let Mrs. Howard have for six yards of calico. That, at ten dollars a yard, would be sixty dollars, quite a respectable sum for a pair of homemade corsets. Mrs. Howard very prudently declined to bargain."[34] Such opportunities for barter created a noncash nexus around clothes and fabric, simultaneously complicating relationships among friends and neighbors by muddling the social hierarchy and creating new kinds of dependencies. Having access to goods in such a quantity that one was able to serve as an intermediary for friends and neighbors reinforced a woman's social standing in the community, but engaging in barter also had the potential to tarnish that standing.

Catherine King was in a much more privileged position as the wife of one of the owners of Roswell Mills and used her connections to textile manufacturing—and her own wardrobe—to supply clothing for her daughter and grandchildren who lived in another town. But even her status as a textile mill–owner's wife could not ensure access to the goods she desired. King sent a package to her daughter that included "a flannel skirt of mine," noting that she had two other flannel skirts "and can do very well without." She also sent "a morning dress, which I have just finished making hope they will not be too short for you." King's efforts to obtain clothing or dress goods for her grandchildren were less fruitful, and while she felt relatively successful in solving her daughter's immediate clothing problems, she was anxious about the onset of colder weather. "What we are going to do for winter clothes," she worried, "I do not know."[35]

The correspondence King and other elite women maintained is instructive, offering evidence of not only women's concern with fabric availability, variety, and cost, but also merchants' ability to control to their advantage the circumstances and conditions upon which cloth and other dress goods were sold.[36] One woman expressed frustration toward merchants who refused to sell items in exchange for Confederate scrip.[37] Catherine Edmonston encountered a similar situation in which she was quoted forty-five dollars per yard if she purchased an entire piece of cloth, but would be charged fifty dollars per yard if she only wished to purchase a portion of the cloth. Edmonston refused the offer, declaring that she was "not willing to wear the price of three barrels of corn in one chemise."[38] Catherine King's father, on the other hand, found it necessary to buy a bolt of black wool delaine measuring 100 yards in order to secure what she claimed was "the only nice piece we could find," because the merchant would not cut the bolt of cloth into shorter lengths. A fine woolen fabric, wool delaine was durable and affordable while still notable for its "sightliness."[39] King's extended family divided the 100 yards of fabric into lengths suitable for several dresses for multiple family members.[40]

As the experiences of King, Edmonston, and their acquaintances suggest, women frequently went to great lengths to obtain finer fabrics like wool delaine, silk, and calico before resorting to the use of "homespun" cloth. Burge, for instance, set "the women to spinning" only when it became clear that cloth had become one of the "things money cannot buy in this Confederacy!"[41] Catherine King, whose husband's textile mills were actively producing thousands of yards of fabric for Confederate army use until their destruction in the summer of 1864, was willing to pay exorbitant prices to provide an alternative to homespun—even for children. In a letter to her daughter, King included a scrap of black-and-red-checked fabric to which she pinned a note: "This is for our precious boy who possessed but two home spun dresses. I got two yards and paid $53 for it—a *big* price but all wool."[42] Obtaining wool, a sturdier, more comfortable fabric, was a victory for King.

The language of compulsion women used to describe the turn to making or wearing homespun illustrates their dissatisfaction. Emma Cullens noted, "Now that factory thread is selling at such exorbitant rates," she would "be compelled to manufacture clothing for my family."[43] Writing under the pen name Elzey Hay in 1866, Eliza Andrews noted that, even as some women believed they "were following in the footsteps of our revolutionary ancestresses, who, we had been told, were mighty at the spinning-wheel and knitting-needle," the actual experience of wearing homespun put a damper on their initial "burst" of patriotic fervor. Putting on an "outward show and parade" wearing homespun was "well enough while the novelty lasted, but that wore off in a season, and when summer came, we found our homespuns insufferably hot."[44]

As this summertime experience suggests, women were concerned not merely with the way their clothing was publicly perceived, but also with the physical experience of wearing that clothing. And the quality of that experience was increasingly difficult to maintain over the course of the war. As with soldiers, quality, comfort, practicality, and refinement factored into women's understanding of their garments. For those previously accustomed to the smooth feel of finely woven linen, wearing coarse fibers was disconcerting. And it was not merely their dresses with which they were concerned, but their undergarments as well.

The state of their underclothing was particularly unsettling for some women. The knowledge that she wore coarse undergarments was far more distressing to Eliza Andrews than was the use of bits of old garments to freshen the old dress she wore over them. Indeed, she was clear that she could "stand patched-up dresses," and could "even take a pride in wearing Confederate homespun, when it is done open above board." But she felt "vulgar and common in coarse underclothing." Andrews was swept with a wave of emotion when she had the opportunity to wear embroidered linen undergarments again after two long years of wearing "coarse Macon Mills homespun." Even though she had only temporarily borrowed them from her cousin, Andrews "was so overpowered at having on a decent piece of underclothing . . . that I could hardly go to sleep." Instead, she lingered in front of the mirror, and "looked at myself undressed just to see how nice it was to have on a respectable undergarment once more."[45] For Andrews, wearing homespun was an acceptable political statement when worn publicly "above board in the open." Wearing coarse undergarments, however, physically felt to her to be a necessity rather than a choice, making the sensation of unrefined cloth against her bare legs and chest as she walked, sat, and went about tasks a daily reminder not of her patriotic fervor for the Confederacy, but rather of her declining economic and social circumstances.

"Not A Nuff to Clothe My Family Eaven"

Once the initial patriotic fervor marked by homespun balls had passed, producing and wearing homespun was often portrayed as a last resort in elite women's diaries. Yeoman and poor white women often found themselves unable to access even the coarsest of cloth, or the tools and raw materials necessary to card, spin, weave, and ultimately sew their own clothing. To spin, weave, and dye fabric on one's own required both specialized implements and skill. Elite women's ability to rely on family connections, trade networks, and the spinning and weaving skills of enslaved workers gave them a distinct advantage in combatting cloth shortages. As the civilian population began to feel the negative effects of legislation, regulations, and restricted sources of raw materials, women called upon state governments to rectify the problem. The governor, they argued, had the power to intervene—whether through direct aid to individuals, or by mediating their dealings with factory owners. One woman addressed Georgia's governor directly, asserting, "You are the representative of the yeomanry of the land—who ar near helpless."[46]

Although similar stories could be told across the South, Georgia offers a particularly elucidating case study of women's efforts to find recourse through the state government. At the center of women's letters to Governor Joseph Brown were questions about the state's responsibility to them, and its ability to regulate the economy and the circulation and accessibility of goods. From their perspective, the state government had not only called and conscripted their male family members into service, but had also disrupted—and even closed off—local access to goods by redirecting businesses and factories to mobilize for war, while simultaneously failing to curb the harmful effects of speculators and inflation. In this context, homespun could be nearly impossible to purchase or even manufacture in one's own home.

The significance of women's specific demands related to the manufacture of clothing requires understanding what it took to transform clumps of dirty, oily wool or a bale of twisted cotton fibers into wearable garments—the methods of production and the amount of cloth required to produce typical garments. A "common calico dress," for instance, required ten yards of cloth.[47] Producing cloth at home required numerous specialized implements, including cotton or wool cards—which were used to disentangle, clean, and align fibers to prepare them for spinning—a spinning wheel, a handloom, needles, scissors, and patterns, not to mention the skills required to use them. If a person lacked any one of these items, making cloth would be impossible.

This was a very real problem for many women, as some of the materials required to manufacture these implements were themselves affected by blockades and the requisition of materials for army use. Producing cotton or wool cards, for instance, required wood, leather, and fine wire. While wood was readily available, leather could be had only at a premium due to military demand for shoes, horse equipage, and other military equipment. Wire was another problem entirely, as the South suffered from a general shortage of affordable metal. Indeed, Julia Fisher remarked that "nails are so scarce that whenever a building is burned there is a quick demand for nails."[48] In some communities, by the end of the war, sewing needles themselves had become a form of currency. Emma Cullens spoke for many women when she noted that she was "compelled to manufacture clothing" for her family, but would only be able to do so "if cards can be procured."[49]

Women wrote to Governor Brown, some to request—others, to demand—that he aid them in procuring either cloth or the cotton cards necessary to produce it at home. The women who wrote to Brown ranged from educated, formerly monied women to those who were marginally literate or required others to write on their behalf. While some writers drew upon the rhetoric of patriotism and loyalty to plead their cases, others vehemently argued that the state had a responsibility to protect, support, and aid them in their efforts to clothe their families—or else.

Sustained criticism from individuals and the press eventually prompted Brown and the Georgia state legislature to attempt to relieve the cotton card problem. In 1864, $200,000 was appropriated from the state treasury "for the purpose of purchasing cards, and procuring the necessary materials for carrying on the work of manufacturing wool and cotton cards, and card clothing for factories."[50] Furthermore, the state penitentiary and its inmates were required to manufacture cotton cards, and other manufacturers were given explicit instructions on policies governing the making and distribution of cards. In an effort to simultaneously appease cash-poor citizens and obtain the leather necessary for making the cards, Brown instituted a policy in which cards could be obtained in exchange for either leather or animal hides suitable for making it. The government was flexible in terms of hides, accepting those of sheep, goat, deer, and dogs, the last of which was intended to combat Georgia's overpopulation of feral dogs.[51]

Recognizing that destitute families would be incapable of paying cash for cards, Brown allowed county courts to purchase cards using funds distributed to the county for the benefit of soldiers' families. The court was then "required to distribute the cards among the most needy families of soldiers (who will use them) in place of their value in money." Each family was permitted one pair, and cards were to be supplied to a family "in the order in which its name comes in the list, beginning at A and going through the alphabet" in order to "show partiality to none."[52]

Despite government efforts to institute manufacturing, barter, and distribution systems, Georgia women still experienced difficulty in obtaining cotton cards. Some women may have lived far from the Milledgeville factory and lacked funds to prepay for the delivery of a package of hides, as required. Others may have only had access to hides that would have been rejected by the manufacturer as unfit to make good leather. Emma Cullens appealed to Brown, "emboldened by [his] well known sympathy for soldiers families," relaying that her "income forbids the purchase of cards as retailed. Should you be so kind as to allow me to procure a pair from the factory, rest assured I know *how* to be grateful." Cullens's gratefulness would, she implied, take the form of her husband's vote in the ballot box in support of Brown.[53] Other women, despite their desperate tone, offered to pay for cards—if only the governor could help locate them, reserve a pair, or send them directly: "pleas sir if their is any cotton cards to bee had I would be thankfull and willing to pay a reasonable prise if you would provide som way for me to get a pair if you cant help such a poor woman as me I dont no what wee will do [to] keep cloaths. . . . pleas send me a pair of cards if posable."[54]

Margaret Harris, a widowed soldier's wife with a two-year-old son living in Hogansville, Georgia, encountered difficulty with the distribution system. While she had the money to purchase cards, she needed the governor's help obtaining them from the state factory. "I have had my name down for a year for a pair of cards," she wrote, but at the last distribution—likely according to the alphabetical system—the county "gave only three to a district." And yet, despite her reliance on the state's support of her as a soldier's widow, she admitted that she knew she was "better off than many, too many in our widowed land." Better off, in part, because she knew that her neighbors, who were also in desperate need of cards, "were not blessed with education and coult not make known their wants as easily as myself." She enclosed money for the cards and a certificate attesting to her identity, and requested that the governor send a pair by express.[55] Whether or not the cards were sent to Harris is unknown. According to the agent in charge of distributing aid to indigent soldiers' families, however, given the "present high prices of clothing," "she can not cloth her self and child unless she had a pair of cards to assist her."[56]

Women did not only draw on the state's responsibility to them as soldiers' wives and mothers. Lizzie Bachelder's circumstances were not uncommon. "You must know dear Governor," she wrote, "that I am one of the many in these troubled times, who are sorely puzzled by the question 'wherewith shall you be clothed?'"[57] Bachelder emphasized her own role in the reproduction of Confederate culture—"as teacher, 'mind fashioner' to a few of our juvenile Confederates"—thereby reminding Brown of her own value to the Confederate cause. Her teacher's salary, however, was "too meager to allow the purchase of factory spun thread, at its present price, consequently must devote all the spare moments to spinning." She found it "very mortifying to one's delicacy or rather pride to thus beg, but alas plain necessity has trampled these down, or kindly hushed them to sleep."[58] She asked Brown to assist her in procuring a pair of cards from the factory.

Women argued that they had the ability to assist the state in the war effort, if only they were provided with the opportunity. Some women identified the valuable services they could render to the state in exchange for assistance in procuring textile implements. Cotton cards, they asserted, would enable them to clothe not only their families, but also Georgia's soldiers. As one woman wrote, "I will call your attention to the fact that numbers of our women are destitute both of cards and the skins which are demanded for them. Now if they could be furnished with the former, at a *reasonable price in money* it would add hundreds of yds. to the clothing bureau of our state, which you know are much needed by our destitute soldiers."[59] Indeed, Brown recognized the value of these women's potential contributions, noting that if "the women of Georgia . . . were supplied with Cotton Cards, they would not only clothe their families, but would, by untiring industry, contribute largely to the supply necessary for our gallant troops."[60]

Certainly women could aid the Confederacy through their textile work, but they also possessed the power to harm it if the state failed to fulfill its responsibilities to them. Bachelder, for instance, who referred to herself as a "mind fashioner," had the power to inculcate Confederate pride in her students, but what went unsaid was that she could also undermine the Confederacy. More frequently, letter writers connected men's Confederate loyalty to women's access to cloth and the material conditions of Georgia's increasingly impoverished civilians—conditions, they argued, that were both created and exacerbated by "the great scarcity of Cotton yarns," the "almost impossibility of procuring Cotton Cards," and "the limited means of soldiers wives and families." The government's failure to respond to women's requests, then, could have serious consequences for the secessionist project. "Let it be remembered," one woman asserted, "that without the aid of Factories, thread cannot be obtained, and the destitute poor cannot be clad. Let the families of our soldiers be fed and clothed, and they will more cheerfully and patiently bear the toil and suffering of camp, and more gallantly meet the assaults of the enemy." But she cautioned, "Let them be neglected, and dissatisfaction and desertion will inevitably follow."[61]

While the government created a distribution plan, a means of obtaining leather to make cards, and designated state-run card factories, without the ability to make enough cards to supply demand, such plans were immaterial. Just a few months after establishing requirements for acquiring cards, Brown admitted that card manufacture was being "impeded for want of suitable card wire." With wire selling at what he deemed "enormous prices"—thirty dollars per pound—Brown proposed that the government engage a Milledgeville resident who was about to go to Europe to purchase and import a quantity of wire for state use.[62] Despite these efforts, Governor Brown and the Georgia state legislature never adequately addressed the cotton card problem—women in need of cloth and supplies continued to write letters until the final days of the war.

Making and Remaking Clothing

Even as the clothing culture they knew began to crumble around them, elite Southern women fought to maintain their sense of etiquette by finding ways to obtain particular forms of clothing, if not always of the same quality. When coarser fabrics were used, attention to detail and efforts to articulate current styles were still highly valued. Women eagerly sought out copies of contemporary fashion periodicals. One Richmond woman recalled that "despite the rigor of the blockade, the latest mode [of fashion] would now and then struggle through in *Godey's Lady's Book*, or *Frank Leslie's Magazine*, or *Le Bon Ton*."[63] These issues, Eliza Andrews later recalled, were passed between friends until they became "so bethumbed and crumpled that one could scarcely tell a fashion-plate from a model cottage."[64] But here, too, one's access to fashion periodicals that made their way through the blockade depended upon location and connections. As Julia Fisher noted from her isolated home in Camden County, Georgia, "For three long years the world has been comparatively lost to us. We know nothing of the changes that have taken place during that time. In dress we are just where we were in 1860—for fashion, but rags and wrinkles are more plentiful."[65]

Although women gained access to fashion plates, most struggled to obtain the materials necessary to re-create the latest fashions portrayed in these periodicals. In July 1864, for instance, *Godey's* featured five voluminous dresses, which included a "white grenadine dress, trimmed with graduated ruffles edged with a fancy gimp. Puffs of violet silk cross the ruffles at intervals. The corsage is in the Pompadour style, and trimmed with a puff of violet silk and narrow graduated ruffles. A very narrow scarf mantle, of the same material as the dress, is trimmed to match."[66] While a woman could have a dress sewn from homespun or calico that roughly replicated this silhouette, the same light, gauzy quality of grenadine fabric could not be replicated without a jacquard loom, which allowed for the control of individual warp yarns.

Grenadine might have been difficult to come by, but imported fabric frequently slipped through Union blockades and could be accessed by those with money and proximity to ports. One North Carolina family, for instance, purchased block-printed floral cloth made from English wool and cotton. Further embellished with embroidery—likely after purchase—the cloth was made into a child's dress with a matching jacket in the popular Zouave style. Other blockade-run fabrics were more modest, including a pink-and-gray-striped floral fabric used to make a bodice.[67]

Inability to access ideal materials did not prevent Southern women from attempting to keep up with fashions. Kid gloves, for instance, were praised by *Godey's Lady's Book* as "a suitable complement to an elegant toilet."[68] Lacking access to a fine pair of these soft goatskin gloves, one Virginia girl used a stiff paper pattern to cut and sew her own gloves from linen, finishing them with dark thread by stitching three decorative lines on the back of the hand and two borders encircling the wrist.[69] The gloves closely resemble the description of those highlighted in an 1862 edition of *Godey's*, which noted that "the best [kid gloves] have three rows of stitching on the back, and two narrow borders of pinked kid at the wrist; they are fashioned by two buttons. The stitching is in black, or some color contrasting with the glove."[70]

A sleeve pattern made from an 1864 edition of the New Orleans *Daily Picayune* suggests that, even with this makeshift newsprint pattern, the maker was attempting to execute a popular sleeve shape for a dress bodice. Likewise, a young girl's dress was made from cotton grown, spun, and woven by a family member. And yet, the plain fabric did not negate the maker's desire for ruffled

Child's dress and jacket, made in England and brought through the Wilmington, NC, blockade in 1864. Acc. No. 19XX.110.1. Courtesy of the North Carolina Department of Natural and Cultural Resources.

sleeves, a pocket, trim, and the popular wide, horizontal neckline favored for girls' garments. Similarly, a vest with a history of having been worn by a white South Carolinian was made from cotton grown, spun, and woven by enslaved workers on his plantation and corresponded to conventions of men's style.[71]

Women also patched and repurposed old clothing, at times making entirely new garments. One woman "wore a dress made of some old lace curtains found at a Jew's store. They were fifty years old, very yellow and shop-worn. My costume was greatly admired and the Jew had a run on the store the next day."[72] Eliza Andrews, on the other hand, reworked an old garment: "My dress was a masterpiece though patched up, like everybody else's, out of old finery that would have been cast off years ago, but for the blockade. I wore a white barred organdy with a black lace flounce round the bottom that completely hid the rents made at dances in Montgomery."[73]

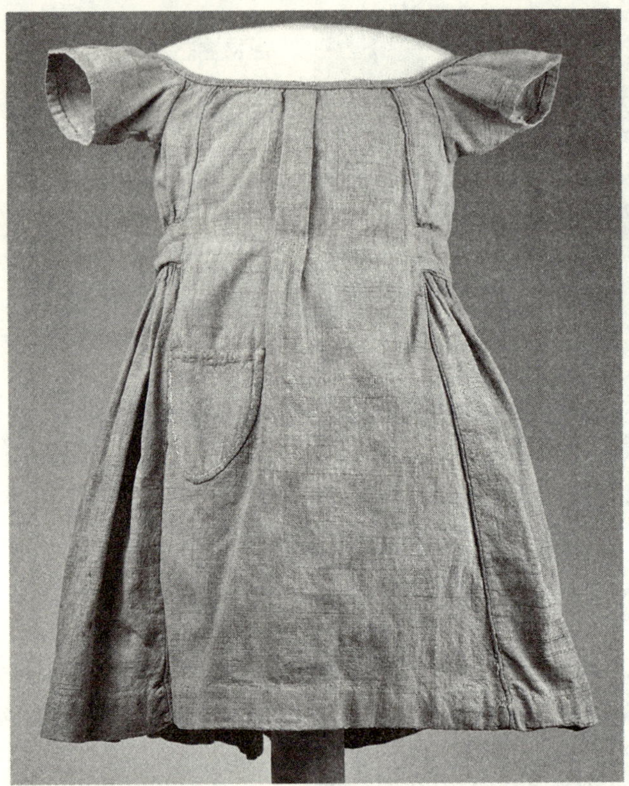

The cotton for this dress was grown, spun, and woven near Lynchburg, Virginia, by the Rudd family. It was worn by Sarah Virginia Rudd, who was born in 1862. Child's dress, c. 1864. Courtesy of the American Civil War Museum, Richmond, VA.

In other instances, women tore up their old dresses, cutting them into strips, unraveling the fabric, and mixing it with cotton. One woman mixed silk with fine cotton lint and passed it "through the cotton cards two or three times, so as to have the mixture homogeneous." She spun it very fine to remove unevenness in the threads so that when "woven into cloth, it was soft and silky to the touch, and a beautiful color. It was corded with the best pieces of the worn silk, and trimmed with pasteboard buttons covered with some of the same silk." The result was, as a neighbor put it, "an elegant dress for the times."[74] The use of home-produced cloth, then, did not mean that all sense of fashion and style was abandoned.

Despite these often-successful efforts to maintain fashions using alternative fabrics, many women looked back on their former wardrobes with nostalgia and made an effort to preserve the good clothing that remained. By war's end, Eliza Andrews found herself altering her own daily practices in an effort to save her best dresses, fearing her inability to purchase new clothing when it wore out. Once accustomed to wearing finery, Andrews now found herself going about in a state of undress, "in déshabille most of the time . . . keeping a dress and coiffure ready to fling on at a moment's notice, when visitors are seen coming up the avenue."[75] She thought it "dreadfully vulgar to go dowdy about the house," but saw few other options. The departure of the people her father had enslaved resulted in new tasks requiring physical labor for which her usual daytime attire was unsuitable. Given the nature of the work, she worried that "our clothes would not last a month if we were to wear them around all the time, when there is no one here."[76] And that clothing could not be easily replaced. With the end of the war, blockades were lifted and Southerners stood on the verge of again having access to much-needed materials and dress goods, but many white Southerners' finances were in a state of distress, bound up in worthless Confederate scrip or reserved for more pressing needs related to reestablishing a family's livelihood. "What is one to do," Andrews asked, "when one has hardly clothes enough to be respectable when one goes out, and no money to buy any more?"[77] This was a conundrum faced by not only civilians, but also Confederate officers and soldiers as they returned to their homes in defeat.

The struggle to maintain dress practices or even to access the tools by which to produce thread and cloth significantly shaped many white Southern women's experiences of war across the social spectrum. Such experiences came to bear on white Southerners' reactions and experiences in the immediate postwar era, when the United States government sought to complete the process of suppressing the rebellion by controlling the sartorial practices of returning Confederate soldiers. In this context—while the North and South began to transition into postwar life and confront the work of Reconstruction—clothing took on intense political meaning as people debated and protested, sometimes violently, ways to cover and display the body.

CHAPTER SEVEN

The Garb of Treason

Struggles over Clothing at War's End

Through the challenges of obtaining cotton cards, frustration with policies and tariffs related to importation, and unreliable access to basic clothing, white Southerners had intimately experienced Confederate and state government intervention in their sartorial practices. That intervention, however, became even more explicit as the United States federal government resumed control of the states in rebellion. It was then, in June 1865, that Susan Bradford found herself walking the streets of Tallahassee, growing increasingly emotional at the scene around her—over the orange thorns skewered through buttonholes, the brass buttons covered in black fabric as though in mourning, and the gold braid ripped from gray uniforms. These were the sights that made her "blood boil."[1]

In April 1865, just weeks into his presidency, President Andrew Johnson issued an executive order removing trade restrictions in the former Confederate states, excepting articles deemed "contraband of war," notably "gray uniforms and cloth."[2] Southern clothing firms were required to turn over stocks of gray cloth, and former Confederate soldiers who continued to wear uniforms were subject to arrest.[3] At the same time, many white Southerners lashed out at formerly enslaved people for dressing "above" their station, as well as at Black and white Union soldiers, whose uniforms were material reminders of defeat and occupation.

Whether men took off their uniforms at the end of war voluntarily or because wearing them was prohibited is not a trivial detail. It is central to how the war and postwar were experienced throughout the nation. The end of the war brought contestation and ambivalence about Union policy, reconciliation, and the status of African American men and women. Those struggles played out at the level of the everyday through conflicts over who had the right to wear what clothing. Union soldiers wore their uniforms as victors while advocates for Black men's rights seized on the image of the uniformed United States Colored Troops (USCT) to argue for equality. Meanwhile, the forced removal of Confederate uniforms and the subsequent donning of ill-fitting, out-of-style clothing played into the image of the war-torn, ragged South. The cultural cachet attached to homespun dresses, Confederate uniforms, and brass buttons was important to the mythmaking of Lost Cause ideology. The material world was not merely a backdrop upon which legal, political, and cultural disputes played out, but central to shaping the end of the war and its many contestations.

At war's end, the federal government faced a dilemma: Should the South be punished and humiliated for seceding and provoking this bloody war? Or should the government embark on a policy of reconciliation? Ulysses S. Grant, in allowing Lee and his soldiers to retain their weapons upon surrender, set a reconciliatory tone for the end of war. And the federal government embraced it—quickly holding out an olive branch to incorporate the former Confederacy back into the Union.

Military commanders, however, saw recurring conflicts that made punishment seem necessary to maintain order. For them, it was not simply the *idea* of the Confederacy that was problematic in the occupied South; it was also the continued, visible *materiality* of its presence. In the year following Lee's surrender, military reports, citizens' correspondence, and local newspapers detailed numerous incidents involving former Confederate soldiers who refused to accept defeat. Material elements of the Confederacy—and the continued presence of uniforms in particular—were frequently cited as one of the most contentious elements of such encounters. An article published one month after the war's end, for instance, detailed the "indignation of the loyal citizens of Covington, Kentucky," who had "lately been worked up to a boiling pitch by the conduct of the returning rebel soldiers, many of who assert defiantly that they are not yet subdued, and who wear their rebel uniforms and use the most insulting and tantalizing language to Union men."[4]

In response to such affronts, commanding officers across the South and border states enacted bans, under penalty of imprisonment, against the wearing of Confederate uniforms or military decoration. General Orders issued May 5, 1865, for the District of East Tennessee, for instance, stated, "Hereafter any person found within the limits of this command, wearing or having about his person the badges, insignia, or uniform of an officer of the late Confederate armies, will be considered as guilty of an act of hostility toward the United States Government and will subject himself to arrest and imprisonment."[5] Although officers were singled out in this Tennessee order, in West Virginia, the prohibition was further reaching: "No person will be permitted to wear the rebel uniform or any insignia designating rank or position in the late rebel army."[6]

Military officials were not alone in pursuing efforts to quell the material presence of the former Confederacy—they were joined both by state legislatures and by the federal government. US attorney general James Speed, speaking on behalf of the administration, asserted that "the stipulation of surrender permits no such thing, and the wearing of such uniforms is an act of hostility against the Government."[7] Similarly, the Tennessee legislature supported "prohibiting resident citizens, who have taken the oath [of allegiance], from wearing the rebel uniform on penalty of from $5 to $25." Although this was a significant fine, supporters of this measure clearly did not believe that it would sufficiently deter repeat offenders, as they further stipulated that "for second and succeeding offences," the fine would be doubled.[8] Missouri legislators went so far as to recommend not only forbidding uniforms and insignia, but also prohibiting the sale of "any picture of officers wearing the Rebel uniform, under the penalty of $20."[9]

As suggested by these measures, the Confederate uniform was one of the most powerfully charged symbols of secession. Although in actuality uniforms ranged in color from a crisp gray to a drab chestnut brown, "gray" and "blue" had quickly become substitute identifiers for "the Confederacy" and "the Union," for "Reb" and "Yank." The color of a uniform, theoretically, if not always in practice, distinguished one's comrades from the enemy. But it was not merely gray cloth that was of concern at war's end. The trappings of brass manhood—the gold braid, shoulder straps, epaulets, and especially brass buttons—quickly displaced US officials' initial focus on restricting the availability and use of gray cloth. As one Confederate soldier observed, "In order to remove these uniforms out of sight as much as possible, the military authorities issued an order that the brass buttons on the coats and jackets of the late Confederate soldier must come off by a certain day." In many instances, men were given "the choice of covering the buttons with some material that would hide the shining brass or cut them off." Regardless of a soldier's decision, their brass buttons were required to "be off or hidden from sight," or they faced the threat of arrest and imprisonment.[10] Stripping uniforms of their decoration was not only a more expedient means of demilitarizing the material culture of the South; it was also a more potent one.

Postwar prohibitions regarding Confederate soldiers' military clothing have not gone unnoticed.[11] However, explanations for US government motivations generally assume such restrictions were a natural step forward in extinguishing any remaining embers of rebellion and suppressing Confederate memory. Yet, to strip a man of his clothing was to commit more than a physical offense—it also symbolically stripped a man of his public identity, humanity, and manhood. Former Confederate soldiers understood the act of having their buttons cut from their uniforms—especially when performed under arrest or on the street—within this broader context of military discipline, public shaming, and methods of violence and humiliation enacted against Black soldiers. Given buttons' centrality in defining wartime manliness, requiring former soldiers to strip their uniforms of buttons also undermined soldiers' ability to visibly and materially display claims to sexual desirability through their military service. Indeed, Eliza Andrews, a young elite Georgia woman, lamented that the "beautiful Hungarian knot, the stars, and bars, the cords, the sashes, and gold lace, are all disappearing. People everywhere are ransacking old chests, and the men are hauling out the old clothes they used to wear before the war, and they do look so funny and old-fashioned, after the beautiful uniforms we had all gotten used to!" She found it "pitiful, as well as comical, to see the poor fellows looking so dowdy."[12]

Such associations added cultural significance to policies regarding Confederate uniforms. Indeed, John Worsham, a Virginian, expressed surprise and disgust at the policy, precisely for its public nature: "Some of our men thought this such a foolish order for the great United States government to issue, that they paid no attention to it; and many were stopped in the streets of Richmond and their buttons were cut off!"[13] This shaming was very personal, requiring a Union soldier to physically restrain an ex-Confederate, grasp a button, and slash it from his coat, likely with a knife.

As Worsham's Virginia comrades' actions convey—and the Tennessee legislature perhaps anticipated in its policy for repeat offenders—many former Confederate soldiers boldly and repeatedly defied such orders as a material protest to US military occupation. Women defiantly wore cockades emblazoned with brass, and a newspaper reported, "The conduct of these men is modified only by necessity. The paroled men still flaunt their rebel uniform—still wear, as Gen. Gordon styles it, at Norfolk, 'the garb of treason'—or did till he stopped it."[14] Other soldiers were more blatantly insolent. In the court case *United States v. Joe W. Davis*, a US officer testified that Davis was arrested for "wearing [a] gray uniform with brass buttons." Upon his arrest, the buttons were cut off and he was released. Davis "requested the buttons, saying they were his property and the Provost Marshal gave them to him," after first obtaining "a promise that he would not wear them again." After being released, Davis went on his way, but only thirty minutes later, the officer again encountered Davis on the street, "with similar buttons sewed on his coat and vest. I rearrested him and took him to the Provost Marshal."[15]

Joe Davis was adamantly defiant in his insistence on being allowed to own and wear his brass military buttons. Henry Kyd Douglas, on the other hand, put his uniform back on for a lark and ultimately landed himself in a prison

This frock coat was worn by Confederate staff officer Henry Kyd Douglas. He was arrested for wearing his military uniform on the streets of Shepherdstown, West Virginia, in May 1865. Uniform coat owned by Confederate staff officer Henry Kyd Douglas. Courtesy of Antietam National Battlefield, National Park Service.

cell next to Lincoln assassination conspirator Mary Surratt. In early May 1865, Douglas, a Confederate major and assistant adjutant general, sold his mule to buy civilian clothing to abide by Johnson's order, but then agreed to have a photograph taken in uniform with a woman in Shepherdstown, West Virginia. He walked out of the photographer's studio and back to his lodgings wearing his complete uniform. It would have been hard not to notice the major, wearing his gray frock coat with stars on the collar, double-breasted rows totaling fourteen brass buttons, and gold braid on the sleeves.[16]

The next day, according to Douglas, a US officer "came with much of the pomp of war, raided the photographer's and carried off the picture, and then demanded my surrender." Among his charges was appearing "in the streets of Shepherdstown in Confederate uniform—'a badge of treason and rebellion, intended and designed to encourage and incite rebellion, against the government.'"[17] Douglas was sentenced to Fort Delaware for two months, which he deemed a "most lame and impotent conclusion" to the ordeal. In explaining the decision, General John Stevenson stressed that the material trappings of Confederate uniforms—"wearing or display of any badge of treason"—were the material enactment of "a spirit of hostility to the established government. The purposes of the Government and the whole purposes of the war, are (*sic*) to utterly eradicate such feeling in the country. Acts savoring of treason, of themselves, cannot be palliated—this is one of them."[18] Douglas was on his way to Fort Delaware when he was diverted instead to Washington, DC, because rumors surfaced that he might have information about Lincoln's assassination.[19] What had begun as a trip to a photographer to capture his likeness in his uniform ended for Douglas at Old Capitol Prison—wearing his citizen's clothes—in a cell next to Surratt and called as a witness in the conspirator's trial. In the end, Douglas served out his sentence at Fort Delaware. He declared that it was upon his release in August 1865 that "for me, the War was over, at last!"[20]

While Douglas had been able to purchase civilian clothing by selling off a mule, for some former soldiers, obeying general bans on gray Confederate uniforms proved infeasible. In the early weeks after war's end, many had little access to new clothing. In response, some of these prohibitions were relaxed to allow men to continue wearing gray coats and pants—as long as they were stripped of any further identifying military markers, especially the brass buttons and gold braid. This leniency helps to explain why Joe Davis's buttons were removed, but his uniform coat not confiscated, upon his arrest. As one Georgia woman wrote, "I went to see Mrs. Elzey and found her cutting off the buttons from the general's coat. The tyrants have prohibited the wearing of Confederate uniforms. Those who have no other clothes can still wear the gray, but must rip off the buttons and decorations." Mrs. Elzey replaced her husband's "striking brass" with understated buttons covered in plain gray cloth.[21] Indeed, as evidenced by surviving uniforms, the covering of brass buttons and removal of gold braid produced a marked change in the aesthetic of a uniform coat. Diminished in fanciness and decorative nature, coats lacking brass buttons appeared quite ordinary, and even drab. The sleeve buttons on a Confederate uniform in the Smithsonian's collection, for instance, are covered in fabric, the brass peeking through only where the fabric has been torn. Such material objects could no longer carry the cultural power of brass manhood attached to them earlier in the war.

Most soldiers "submit[ted] in dignified silence to the humiliating decree."[22] Robert E. Lee, for instance, was frequently seen in his "rebel uniform, without insignia of rank."[23] However, other men abided by the requirement

Made from a wool and cotton blend, this jacket was originally a cadet gray. It includes nine brass buttons. Shell jacket, 1863–64. Worn by John C. Speck, Thirty-Ninth Battalion, Virginia Cavalry. Courtesy of the American Civil War Museum, Richmond, VA.

Made from wool jean cloth, this coat, in contrast to the jacket on the left, has four brown composition buttons. Sack coat, 1864. Worn by Thomas Vaden Broke, Third Co. Richmond Howitzers. Courtesy of the American Civil War Museum, Richmond, VA.

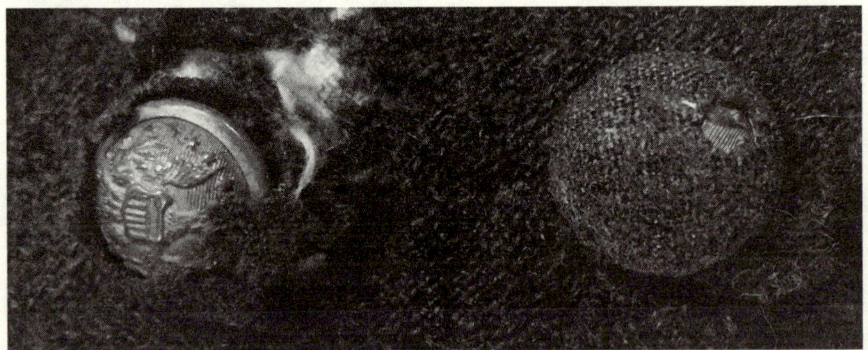

Fabric-covered sleeve buttons on Confederate uniform, c. 1865. Division of Military History, National Museum of American History, Smithsonian Institution.

to remove brass buttons but did so in such a way as to mock the orders. Eliza Andrews delighted in the fact that "some of our boys put their discarded buttons in tobacco bags and jingle them whenever a Yank comes within earshot. Some will not replace them at all, but leave their coats flying open to tell the tale of spoliation. Others put ridiculous tin and horn buttons on their military coats."[24] Jingling brass buttons or wearing garish replacements was clearly meant to insult occupying troops, but the disinclination to abandon the Confederate uniform could also take a far more sinister, violent turn, becoming a means of intimidation against those who had remained loyal to the Union, African Americans, and especially members of the United States Colored Troops. "It is quite in order," a newspaper correspondent reported from Kentucky, "to wear Rebel uniforms with C.S.A. waist-belts, and plenty of pistols to shoot loyalists on sight."[25] Similarly, when serving on a Texas jury in 1866, one man noted that "Confederate uniforms (privates and officers) were the rule; lawyers, witnesses and hangers-on all armed to the teeth, and of the attorneys, every one who had by his services gained the right of wearing a rebel uniform, was sure of parading the same." The trial resembled, he observed, a Confederate court martial more than anything else.[26]

Other men complied without resistance when ordered to strip their uniforms of rank. A news article described one such scene in Nashville: "'Now colonel,' says the Provost Martial, 'cut off these insignia of rank. You too, Major. Cut your buttons off also.' A couple of officers get out their penknives and reciprocate services . . . and off come the stripes of gold braid from the collar, and the C. S. A. Buttons from the double-breasted coat. 'That's right,' says the Federal officer, 'Now I'd advise you to get some other clothes as soon as you can.'"[27] Policies restricting the material culture—and particularly clothing—associated with the Confederacy had deep cultural implications, given the broader context of the significance of buttons as symbols, war trophies, and objects that played a role in creating brass manhood. One man declared "that the Government should supply him and his family with farming impliments, horses &c., claiming a restoration of his citizenship rights, and complaining of his sufferings and losses during the war, and that his sons were not allowed to wear their rebel uniforms."[28] For this man, the ability to continue wearing the Confederate uniform was placed alongside the importance of his property and citizenship rights.

In some instances, women, like Susan Bradford, reacted to the prohibition of military insignia with greater vitriol than did men. Elite white women's own sense of wartime gender identity was tied to that of men, for they played a central role in creating and celebrating military brass manhood. Many had

The veteran's jacket is laid down in the right foreground of the painting. Winslow Homer, *The Veteran in a New Field*, 1865. The Metropolitan Museum of Art, New York, Bequest of Miss Adelaide Milton de Groot, 1967.

sewed uniforms, bought gold lace, mailed clothing to soldiers, saved men's buttons, fashioned jewelry from them, and wore military-inspired styles themselves. As a result, they understood this policy not only as stripping Confederate men of their brass manhood, but also as prohibiting women's role in the gendering of Confederate men—and thereby denying them the ability to shape their own identities in relationship to those men. And this—the denial of their ability to participate in the dominant culture through which gender had been defined for four years of war—is why seeing soldiers with missing gold braid and black buttons made Susan Bradford's blood boil.

The Victor's Uniform

The end of the war and the abandonment of uniforms raised important questions about postwar life throughout the United States. As the discarded uniform and canteen suggest in Winslow Homer's now-iconic painting of *The Veteran in a New Field* (1865), Union soldiers voluntarily removed their uniforms and returned to comparatively drab civilian attire. In this context, Northern men and women were adjusting to a postwar reality in communities where many faces would never be seen again and where many of those who returned, returned changed—both physically and mentally. What did the voluntary abandonment of uniforms mean for how these men and women conceived of gender in the postwar era?

Union soldiers wore their uniforms as victors. On May 23 and 24, 1865, one month after President Johnson's order banning Confederate uniforms, more than 200,000 US soldiers marched through Washington, DC, from the Capitol to the White House in a Grand Review of the Armies.[29] Those present—Ulysses S. Grant's Army of the Potomac and William Tecumseh Sherman's armies of the Tennessee and Georgia—represented only a portion of the army. Hundreds of thousands of soldiers remained dispersed in the western theater and no USCT companies were included in the processions. Sherman's soldiers, arriving from the hard war campaign through Georgia and the Southern coast, were joined by Black men marching with spades, a pack-mule train carrying camp equipage, gamecocks, and "a brace of young coons." They were accompanied by "half-a-dozen contraband females on foot; a dozen contraband males leading the mules," and "a white soldier or two on horseback to see that everything was all right."[30]

Tens of thousands of visitors flocked to the city to see the spectacle and to celebrate the US Army's victory. They stood several people deep along the parade route, leaned out windows from which they threw flowers, and waved handkerchiefs and American flags. Recently resupplied, the Army of the Potomac's "dark and light blue uniforms gave a fine effect to the spectacle.... These troops did not, as to dress, present a war-worn appearance; they were all well and cleanly clad."[31] "The Western boys," on the other hand, "looked *hard*," according to one observer. "They were dingy, as if the smoke of many battles had dyed their garments, and the dust and mud of the sacred soil of a dozen insurrectionary States had adhered to them."[32] Tens of thousands of uniformed men marched through Washington that day and, as Lincoln's secretaries John Nicolay and John Hay later reflected, "The whole country claimed these heroes as part of themselves."[33] Many soldiers did not feel much like heroes. They simply wanted to be home where, as William Willoughby wrote, they could "live a life of civilization to be able to get some thing to eat once more that may be considered food for man."[34] Yet as victors, Willoughby and his comrades could both voluntarily take off their uniform coats and voluntarily put those uniforms back on for a special event without consequence—the same act that was a crime when performed by a former Confederate.

Not all US soldiers who survived the war immediately mustered out. More than 100,000 US soldiers remained in the rebellious states for a year after war's end, with 20,000 or more remaining for the next few years.[35] While US troops who returned home voluntarily removed their own uniforms, those soldiers who remained in the South in the 1860s and 1870s continued to wear theirs, and thus continued to embody brass manhood in the presence of rebels. When Confederate men were denied the ability to participate in that kind of manhood, it was all the more bitterly borne because of the presence of those occupying federal soldiers, and especially Black troops, in their brass-buttoned uniforms. As a result, at the end of the war, references to "brass buttons" became firmly associated with the dark blue uniforms of occupying US soldiers. In some Southern communities, where they were once a sight to be treasured, brass buttons became the equivalent of a cuss word.

The US uniform marked USCT soldiers for repeated abuse and even outright murder. It was a dangerous mark upon a Black man's body in the postwar South. As one newspaper reported in regard to Kentucky, "It is worth noticing that the most exasperating offense of a freedman is to have borne arms in defense of the Government. Should a colored soldier dare to retain any marker of his service in the Union armies, he is shot down." This violence was, in part, a continuation, and often an escalation, of the wartime treatment of Black soldiers.[36]

Hubbard Pryor, who had once posed for photographs of his transition from enslaved man to Union soldier, experienced neither a victor's welcome nor a ceremonious removal of his uniform. Pryor was captured in Dalton, Georgia, in October 1864 and worked on Confederate labor gangs in Alabama, Mississippi, and Southwest Georgia for the remainder of the war. He described how, in 1865, he was abandoned by the Confederates and "walked his way back to his old home in a sick, broken down, naked and starved condition, the country being everywhere full of returned Confederate soldiers, that he traveled after night and was fearful of being killed by them."[37] Pryor had escaped slavery in Georgia, mustered into the US Army in Tennessee, and marched with that army back to Georgia, only to be captured within seven months and forced into hard labor for the Confederate army. Pryor had worn the US Army uniform. And yet, at war's end, he was uncertain as to his relationship to that army. In 1890 he wrote to the War Department to inquire as to whether he had been listed at war's end as a deserter or a prisoner of war. He had been recorded as a prisoner, but he died before he could apply for the pension benefits that he had earned by donning a uniform.[38]

The removal of uniforms by Black soldiers was complex. Wearing that uniform was a material stake in the ground, a declaration that they had earned the right to citizenship through military service. Removing it ushered in a new chapter in their fight to secure rights as citizens. As these debates played out in the 1860s, Black men in US uniforms played a central role in propaganda iconography advocating for the extension of Black men's rights. Unlike the images of their formerly enslaved counterparts that were used to support Black enlistment in the early 1860s, however, these veterans were not standing upright in crisp uniforms with a hopeful gleam in their eyes. Instead, they leaned on wooden crutches, their once-stately uniforms now distorted by amputated limbs. The use of the war veteran and the "empty sleeve" in postwar political rhetoric was a common trope in a wide range of causes to benefit both Black and white soldiers, including the funding of pensions and medical care and the support of "Soldiers' Homes." In the case of Black men's rights, however, the image of the African American veteran amputee was intended to illustrate the nation's debt to them for their sacrifice to the Union cause and to highlight the hypocrisy of denying them full citizenship and rights.

White artist Thomas Waterman Wood's triptych *A Bit of War History: The Contraband, the Recruit, and the Veteran*, painted during 1865 and 1866, offered a vivid argument about the government's treatment of its Black veterans. Whereas earlier photographs and prints depicted the transition from slave to soldier, Wood offered an image of the logical end of that transformation: the Black veteran. Like earlier images, Wood depicts the man in the same location in each phase of his transformation: standing outside the Provost Marshal's office. In the first image, he appears as a formerly enslaved refugee in shabby, patched clothing with his meager belongings tied up in a handkerchief and secured to a stick. Unlike the downtrodden image of Hubbard Pryor, however, this man's expression conveys elation at having reached Union lines where he offers his services to the army. The next image shows the man dressed in full uniform, with brass buttons and a US belt buckle, a gun resting on his shoulder, ready for the march. The final image in the triptych depicts the man as he has returned from war, his once-bright blue uniform now faded, a red, white, and blue bandage peeking out from under his kepi, suggesting a head wound. He leans on crutches and, yet, still salutes, despite having lost his leg in the war. Wood, like other postwar artists, drew on the uniform as the key symbol of this man's identity, reasserting the continuing relationship that existed between the federal government and Black soldiers in order to illustrate the government's failings.

By donning a suit of clothing that white Americans recognized as their own symbol of virile manhood, sacrifice, and the preservation of the Union, Black men had forced society to recognize, if not to respect, their claims to belonging to the nation. In their writings, photographs, and sketches, abolition-minded

Thomas Waterman Wood, *A Bit of War History: The Contraband, the Recruit, and the Veteran,* 1866. The Metropolitan Museum of Art, New York.

Americans, both white and Black, had imbued uniforms with transformative power, the power to cover the scars of slavery and undergo an inner rebirth that transformed the slave into a man in full possession of himself. And yet, that uniform also marked Black men for physical and verbal abuse by white Southerners and Northerners alike, increasing the sacrifices made by Black men to secure their own freedom, ensure the destruction of slavery, and preserve the Union. Despite the violence they endured because of wearing Union blue, the uniform—as a material object, as a visual image, and as a symbol—did help to usher Black men along the path to citizenship, though not the clear path that Frederick Douglass had hoped. It was, instead, a thorny path mired with political snags and racist barriers.

Embracing the Ragged Rebel

Former Confederates' experiences contrasted sharply with the victorious laying down of arms (and buttons) in the North—victorious Union men could embody their manhood differently, and Northern women could imagine it differently, in the context of victory. The ban on Confederate uniforms, by contrast, humiliated and denied Confederate men their manhood at an intimate, *visceral* level in front of one another and women—they were not only defeated in the war, but they were emasculated after it. Banning uniforms literally banned the objects that—for four long years—had defined Confederate men as *men*. Yet they harnessed their anger over this process of emasculation to seize control of the narrative, and it is that process that helps to explain how—and why—the Lost Cause took hold.

The Lost Cause nurtured a public memory of the Confederacy that described slavery as a benevolent institution, secession as constitutional, and the cause as righteous. Stories of glorious victories despite severe undersupply and privation buoyed the Lost Cause.[39] In this context the war-worn ragged rebel became a potent material symbol that presumed to embody Confederate soldiers' experiences throughout four years of war. Historians have peeled away the layers of the Lost Cause, revealing it to be a distortion of history that romanticizes the Old South and the Confederate cause.[40] But the image of the hard-fighting ragged rebel has persisted. There were moments throughout the war in which Confederate (and Union) soldiers were severely undersupplied, and by its end there were certainly Confederate soldiers lacking shoes and wearing worn-out pants. The Union's hard war and breaks in supply chains delayed and prevented soldiers' resupply. Yet many Confederate soldiers continued to be supplied throughout the war. In December 1864,

South Carolinian Jim McFall put on a new uniform coat complete with gilt brass buttons, gold cord, and gold lace.[41] Susan Bradford's cousin donned a "splendid new uniform" in 1865.[42] The Richmond Clothing Depot continued operation until its capture in April 1865, with gray woolen goods still available to be seized and put to use in sewing cloaks at the Freedmen's School. Nevertheless, stories of glorious victories despite severe undersupply buoyed the Lost Cause, which emphasized that military defeat resulted from the Union army's advantage in number of men and resources, including clothing.[43] The stripping of uniforms and the subsequent donning of ill-fitting, out-of-style clothing played into the romanticized image of the war-torn, ragged, but honorable South.

Rather than a sign of defeat, then, the image of the "ragged Rebel soldier" must be understood as evidence of elite white Southerners' intransigency in the postwar era—of their refusal to accept defeat. Not only men, but women, too, embraced a more ragged womanhood—one defined by homespun dresses, everyday sacrifice, and the ability to survive with few resources. The gallantry associated with Confederate uniforms and women's sacrifice would last far beyond the war, making its way into turn-of-the-century literature and a "moonlight and magnolias" view of the Old South. In a fictional account of a postwar ball, the author of *The Clansman: An Historical Romance of the Ku Klux Klan* (1905) invoked both the ragged beauty and pride of women in homespun and the wartime manhood embodied by shining brass buttons, while vilifying Union soldiers for desecrating the Confederate uniform.

Women like Eliza Andrews, Catherine King, and Dolly Lunt Burge had gone to great lengths to avoid wearing homespun, paying high prices to clothe their families in imported fabric and repurposing their prewar finery for new garments. Those elite women who did embrace homespun worked to make it "pretty," using vibrant dyes, woven patterns, lace embellishments, and elements of fashionable styles. And yet, the image of the girl in homespun cloth presented in *The Clansman* was so bland that it was uncharacteristically plain and drab—and praised because of it: "He saw that her dress was of coarse, unbleached cotton, dyed with the juice of walnut hulls and set with wooden hand-made buttons. The story these things told of war and want was eloquent, yet she wore them with unconscious dignity. She had not a pin or brooch or piece of jewellery. Everything about her was plain and smooth, graceful and gracious. . . . The coarse black dress that clung closely to her figure seemed alive when she moved, vital with her beauty."[44] Nowhere present in this story is women's frustration with dye that stunk and washed out of the fabric, the unsettling feeling of wearing coarse underwear, or their longing for finer fabrics. Neither does the author reference the jubilant patriotism promoted in wartime Confederate propaganda, nor do the characters sing, "Three cheers for the homespun dress the Southern ladies wear!" Preserved here is only the wartime sacrifice and suffering endured by Southern women.

Later in this fictional story, to the delight of all in attendance, Ben Cameron, the grand dragon of the Ku Klux Klan, appeared at a ball in his Confederate colonel's uniform: "Its yellow sash with the gold fringe and tassels was faded and there were two bullet holes in the coat." The applause, sighs, and exclamations in praise of the uniform were quickly overshadowed when a federal

> military commandant suddenly confronted them with a squad of soldiers.
> "I'll trouble you for those buttons and shoulder-straps," said the Captain.
> Elsie's amber eyes began to spit fire. Ben stood still and smiled.
> "What do you mean?" she asked.
> "That I will not be insulted by the wearing of this uniform to-day."
> "I dare you to touch it, coward, poltroon!" cried the girl, her plump little figure bristling in front of her lover.
> Ben laid his hand on her arm and gently drew her back to his side: "He has the power to do this. It is a technical violation of law to wear them. I have surrendered. I am a gentleman and I have been a soldier. He can have his tribute. I've promised my father to offer no violence to the military authority of the United States."
> He stepped forward, and the officer cut the buttons from his coat and ripped the straps from his shoulders.[45]

Ben's poised response was far removed from descriptions of the men who, forty years before the publication of *The Clansman,* had rattled buttons in tobacco bags at passing Union soldiers and sewn garish buttons onto their uniforms as a mockery of government officials' policies. No longer a flashpoint focused on the continued presence of Confederate material culture and the emasculating implications of defeat, brass buttons cut from a uniform coat had instead fully entered into the myth of the Lost Cause.

Confederate uniforms stripped of their insignia were central to creating the myth of the Lost Cause, but so, too, were those uniforms that had initially been removed immediately after the war, only to be resurrected a few years later. In 1873, Jubal Early took the stage at a gathering of the Southern Historical

Society wearing his gray lieutenant general's uniform, including cuff links with the Confederate flag. Early, who, refusing to surrender, initially exiled himself to Canada after the war, had returned to the United States where, Caroline Janney explains, he "crowned himself as the spokesman for all things Confederate and quickly became one of the most vocal proponents of the Lost Cause."[46] In later years, as reconciliation evolved and reunions brought together Confederate and Union veterans, gray uniforms and rebel flags continued to be used. But it was not only uniforms that were of concern in the postwar South. The clothing of civilians, Black and white, was also central to how people experienced and, in some cases, protested the outcome of the war.

War's end marked a new chapter in formerly enslaved people's clothing possibilities. When enslaved women emancipated themselves, some took with them the clothing of their enslavers. They wore and packed bags with everything ranging from dresses and undergarments to ribbons, lace, and bows. "Women secured the clothing out of need," explains Stephanie Camp, "and accessorized with glee; pragmatic concerns were not necessarily separable from merriment."[47] With earned wages they saved money to purchase clothing of their own choosing. Virginia Newman's "idea of freedom," Thavolia Glymph notes, was "a blue guinea with yaler spots"—her first "bought dress."[48] Sarah Tate, who had been enslaved in Texas, shared Newman's sentiment.

Forty-one years old when the war ended, Tate remained in the household of her former enslaver, working as a domestic servant. With her first wages, she purchased ten yards of white cotton cross-barred fabric that she sewed into a long-sleeved dress with fashionable drop sleeves and cuffs that would have fit neatly around her wrists. A simple yet elegant applied band, along with a deep hem, gives the white dress a sense of movement. Although the dress's style is not extravagant, its making was clearly intended to be a statement and even an indulgence of sorts.[49] Made from a high-quality cotton, the dress has a full skirt with decorative tucks, a style that required more fabric and, thus, more expense to make. Purchasing fabric for a nice gown was an exercise of Sarah Tate's freedom. Tate preserved the dress, which was clearly a meaningful purchase, made from cloth purchased with her first wages earned as a free woman.[50]

Faced with seeing Black women in finer dresses, the end of slavery, and a new social order, white Southerners began to question the sartorial practices that had governed social hierarchies prior to the war. As Andrews expressed, "As soon as we became tired of any article, we would give it to some of our servants, and often, towards the close of the war, have I seen my 'mammy' or my maid in cast-off dresses that I fairly grudged them." She wondered how

"Marriage of a Colored Soldier at Vicksburg by Chaplain Warren of the Freedmen's Bureau," *Harper's Weekly*, June 30, 1866. Library of Congress, Washington, DC.

she could ever have been so foolish as to give away anything that had been "so little worn."[51] Emma Holmes, a twenty-six-year-old South Carolinian, expressed revulsion at seeing Black women dressed "in the most ludicrous and disgustingly tawdry mixture of old finery, aping their betters most nauseatingly—round hats, gloves and even lace veils."[52]

And it was precisely for this reason that the appearance of Black women, men, and children in finer clothing was so contentious. It was not merely the visual cues of status that were at stake, but the inner transformation that was expected to occur. Her Confederate perspective influenced Holmes's disdain, but Northerners, too, commented on such displays of dress, and the gaudily dressed, caricatured Black woman became a stereotype in popular culture. Certainly, there were exceptions to the portrayal of Black women's dress as "excessive." In an 1866 *Harper's Weekly* image of the marriage of formerly enslaved people, for instance, the women are depicted with diminutive waists achieved through corsetry, gloved hands, and bell-shaped skirts.[53]

This image clearly offered a visual argument about Black women's ability to achieve expectations of femininity. However, unlike the "Poor Oppressed"

Sheet music cover. E. A. Benson, "Poor Oppressed, or the Contraband Schottisch" (Nashville, 1862). Library of Congress, Washington, DC.

"Contraband" woman portrayed on an 1860s sheet music cover, who wore flamboyant colors, a voluminous, tiered skirt, and a bonnet complete with multicolored feathers, these women were clad in simple, patternless, yet elegant garments lacking jewelry or decoration. It is significant that this depiction of Black women exhibiting middle-class standards of gentility takes place at a wedding. The somber orderliness of the gathering and the neatly dressed people gave credence to the assertion that African American men and women valued marriage, directly countering critical beliefs about Black familial ties.

Although Black men and women wearing nicer clothing in public was not uncommon, many more lacked the ability to purchase such clothing as they started free lives with little to no money or property. They wore what they had, secondhand garments they acquired through relief organizations, and items they could purchase. They wore white cotton dresses, guineas with yellow spots, and brown-and-cream-striped dresses. Some former enslavers delighted when formerly enslaved people presented a drab appearance. One white woman, for instance, spewed hatred toward any freed person who did not remain in the service of their former enslaver. She mocked the circumstances of a man who had been enslaved by her family, writing, "He hawks fish about the streets and takes advantage of his new gained liberty to go very dirty and shabby." "He has not ascended in the social scale," she scoffed. And she hoped he never would. She considered it a "blessing," she wrote, "that the race will not last long for they are dying at 95 per week in the city and the mortality on the Islands is equally great all sorts of horrid diseases . . . are raging among them."[54]

With Black people wearing finer clothes and Yankee blue around them, former Confederates used their own clothing to protest defeat, the end of slavery, and occupation by federal soldiers. Certainly, they had already used this tactic during wartime. In Winchester, Virginia, women wore secession bonnets in the presence of Union soldiers; in Memphis, rebel women abandoned hoops; in New Orleans, women paraded in front of Union officers wearing secesh symbols. But during wartime, those actions signaled loyalism to the Confederate cause and registered their objection to Union soldiers' presence in their communities. In the postwar era, using clothing as a means of protest took on added valences. When the outcome of the war still hung in the balance, patriotic clothing was an expression of hope for which army would prevail. In the postwar era, wearing such symbols was a sign that the wearers would not willingly accept defeat. Instead, many people used clothing to enhance their vehement defiance of the new social order and to express their rage, while others used it as a means of silent protest.

In Richmond, some women quietly objected to loss by wearing mourning clothing in the presence of Union soldiers.[55] At a church service, where "nine-tenths" of the women "were dressed in deep mourning," one woman "had two rows Confederate buttons upon a black silk sack" dress, "while another wore upon her sleeves the gold braid" of a colonel.[56] But in Salisbury, North Carolina, Justina Chambers chose a much more striking means of protest, dressing her five-year-old son in a green wool flannel jacket emblazoned with Second National Confederate flags, trimmed with red tape and braid. The Chambers's Confederate sentiment ran strong. When war broke out, Justina Chambers's husband, Pinckney, raised a company and served as a major in the Forty-Ninth North Carolina Regiment.[57] She went to great expense to clothe her young son in Confederate symbols, paying forty-eight dollars per yard in 1864 for fabric that was made in England and ran the blockade. Now in the collection of the American Civil War Museum, the jacket was accessioned with a history of having been "severely commented on when worn in the presence of Federal soldiers stationed in Salisbury, North Carolina."

Justina Chambers made this jacket for her five-year-old son. The olive-green wool flannel cloth is printed with a Second National Confederate Flag. Its collar and hem are trimmed with red tape and two rows of braid. The fabric was made in England, cost forty-eight dollars per yard, and ran the blockade at Wilmington, North Carolina, in 1864. Courtesy of the American Civil War Museum, Richmond, VA.

Given that Salisbury did not come under federal control until April 1865, the Chambers continued dressing their son in Confederate garb at war's end. And indeed, for the Chambers family, who had enslaved more than seventy people in 1860, that end was devastating. Many of those whom they had enslaved remained nearby, divided into family groups (at least four of whom took the last name of Chambers), and worked as farmhands, but the white Chambers family's way of life was significantly altered.[58] Walking through Salisbury with their small son in a coat of Confederate-flag fabric was a material way in which the Chambers family could register their protest of the war's outcome.

While mourning dress, cockades, homespun, and Confederate flags were all holdovers from wartime, new forms of clothing were also created as part of the violent, deadly response to defeat. The Ku Klux Klan began in Pulaski, Tennessee, in 1866 and 1867, and quickly spread its violence to other states, becoming by 1871 a national movement. The first iteration of the Klan used "violence not to define themselves as masters and black men as slaves, but to define themselves as dominant and their victims as compliant within the new postslavery order."[59] They employed clothing, primarily in the form of costumes and masks, to terrorize Black Southerners. These were not the uniformly dressed groups of Klansmen of *Birth of a Nation* fame, but, rather, groups of men wearing every manner of costume, ranging from grotesque horned masks to red paper hats with square stars tacked on them to white robes and hoods. While such costumes concealed Klan members' identities and instilled fear in their victims, they also linked them to performance and popular culture.[60] Such costumes, Katharine Lennard argues, "enlarged the stakes of encounters between attackers and victims, highlighting the degree to which such encounters were brutal performances of domination in addition to the more tangible damage they inflicted upon victims and their homes."[61] Although they clearly wore costumes and not daily clothing, the Klansmen employed forms of dress in their intimidation, violation, and murder of Black Southerners.

Wartime deprivation and sartorial restrictions created deep resentment among white Southerners—and the reminders of those experiences were everywhere around them. As Eliza Andrews wrote, "I feel like crying whenever I think of the change and all that it means. . . . We are a poverty-stricken nation, and most of them [former soldiers] are too poor to buy new clothes. I suppose we are just now at the very worst stage of our financial embarrassments."[62] Material reminders of their defeat took the form of not only the blue uniforms worn by occupying US soldiers, but also the clothing worn by their white neighbors, friends, and family as they walked in the streets, paid visits to one another, and began to come to terms with postwar life. They also used their clothing as a means of protest, and indeed, that attire stood, Thavolia Glymph argues, "as potent and visible symbols of the ideological threat to freedom." And yet, such clothing "had a motive but no practical purpose."[63] The Confederacy was defeated. Enslaved people were free. Wearing a secesh bonnet, dressing a child in the Second National Confederate Flag, or continuing to wear a gray coat could revivify neither the Confederacy nor their "beloved" South.

Part IV
Saving

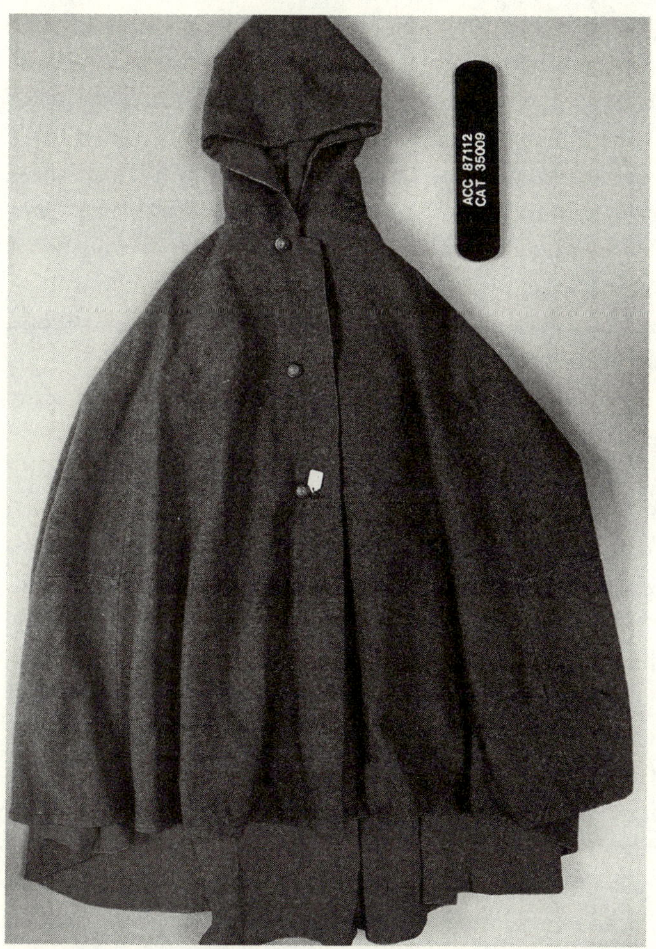

This woman's cloak, made by a freedwoman from gray Confederate army cloth and sold to a white Northern woman, was, for many years, mistakenly described by the museum as a "Confederate Woman's Cloak." Here, the cloak is depicted not on display but, rather, as it was photographed for museum cataloging purposes. Woman's cloak, c. 1865. Courtesy of the Division of Military History, National Museum of American History, Smithsonian Institution.

From the heavy cloth used for army uniforms to the contrasting red and gray associated with the Confederate artillery to the brass buttons used to secure it, this hooded cloak looks every bit like the name under which it was originally cataloged: "Confederate Woman's Cloak." One can easily picture a "secesh" woman walking through Richmond or Baltimore, using her cloak to declare her allegiances to the Confederacy. Except, upon closer inspection, the buttons don't depict the seal of Virginia, palmettos, or any other Confederate symbol. Instead, the gilding was applied over stamped eagles worn by the US Army. The buttons hint that this cloak might be parading as something it is not, but it wasn't unusual for a US button to appear on the breast of a Confederate—some soldiers even sewed them on as trophies of their conquests. The object itself is a conundrum. And that's where its provenance matters.

This cloak is, indeed, made from Confederate Army woolen goods—textile analysis can help confirm that—but it was neither made by or for, nor even worn by, a secesh woman. In fact, it was made by a recently emancipated woman to be sold to and worn by a white Northern woman—circumstances that could only exist because of the end of slavery, the seizure of Richmond by US forces, and the defeat of the rebellion.

Many stories can be told through this cloak. In 1865, Black women at the Freedmen's School in Richmond, Virginia, were set to work by white teachers who instructed them to make these heavy, hooded cloaks that would be sold to "Northern ladies." The cloaks were made from "Confederate Grey" woolen goods that had been captured at the end of the war, making them more profitable when sold because the outlay for fabric was minimal. The cloaks' proceeds supported the school, simultaneously enabling the purchasers to feel gratified by their philanthropic gesture.

So, too, might the cloak be read in the context of the work of the freedmen's schools. Efforts to teach women to sew and mend were part of a broader project of instructing formerly enslaved women in household duties and other skills that relief workers believed necessary to make them "virtuous women, dutiful wives, and devoted mothers."[1] Relief workers saw sewing classes as meeting multiple goals: Black women were expected to gain valuable skills, develop pride in work and the products of that work, and establish their ability to support themselves, thereby reducing the need for charitable relief. The cloak's owner described its making as part of a broader effort to gather "vagrant colored women into such places as could be provided and set them to some useful employment."[2] But if we rely only upon the written stories attached to the preservation of this cloak, we would be led to believe that it was the product of attempting to teach a woman how to sew. It's only when we unbutton the flaps, turn back the hood, and examine the seams that we see that this cloak holds another story. Finely stitched with an even hand and the lining expertly applied, it defies the stories told about it—it is evidence of a skilled seamstress at work.

This cloak is a reminder of just how critical it is to both analyze objects on their own accord and read them against other forms of documentation: a reminder to use information gleaned through object analysis to ask different questions of the texts, and to read those texts to reconsider the objects, all the while reading against the grain for misperceptions, half-truths, and new clues. It is also an opportunity to simply ask, why? Why was this cloak saved? What story did its owner hope to preserve by donating it to the National Museum? Understanding *that* story matters, too. It matters not only for the histories that we tell, but also for identifying how the process by which something came to be saved may have obscured other histories that have yet to be told: for questioning the power that narrative holds.

CHAPTER EIGHT

Every Rent and Hole Spoke Words

Clothing as Relics and Narratives of War

Three weeks after Robert E. Lee's surrender at Appomattox, Judith McGuire described a friend's reaction to the end of the war. The woman had placed some items into a Confederate-made envelope, sealed it, and wrote, "In memory of our beloved Confederacy." McGuire admitted that she felt like doing the same, "treasuring up the buttons, and the stars, and the dear gray coats, faded and worn as they are, with the soiled and tattered banner, which has no dishonouring blot." But not yet! She could not "feel that all is over yet."[1]

But all was, indeed, over. General Joseph Johnston had surrendered to General William Sherman in Durham, North Carolina, just a few days prior. During the preceding few months, in a slow process of disintegration, the Confederate armies, government, and labor system had collapsed.[2] Did McGuire seal up buttons and stars, or the "dear" gray coats? These trappings of wartime brass manhood? Her diary does not say but, rather, ends abruptly: "My native land, good-night!"[3] Others, however, did pack up the buttons, stars, and uniform coats—not only the gray coats, but also the blue, green, and Zouave coats worn by men at various points during the war. The accoutrements that defined brass manhood—the buttons, braids, and lace—were preserved, but so too were socks, drawers, shirts, cockades, dresses, body armor, and swatches of fabric, all of which contained memories and meanings of wartime experience.

This book could be written only because at some point in the 1860s, the owners, looters, or recipients of this clothing made the decision to save that clothing and they, or someone else, saw reason to continue to preserve it—in museums, historical societies, and private collections. Their motivations for doing so were wide and varied; some likely could not articulate their reasons. As objects that are worn against the body and central to self-fashioning, clothing is both tied to a person's identity and capable of storing memories of the particular person who made or wore it. "Clothing reminds," as Ann Rosalind Jones and Peter Stallybrass note.[4] It materializes memories of a person or their experience, memories that can be activated through sight, touch, and smell. The clothing that was saved at the end of the war stored and evoked such memories, but it also played critical roles in shaping postwar life.[5]

Much of the clothing included in this book now resides in museum collections, protected by acid-free tissue paper and stored in archival boxes. American museums had their origins in cabinets of curiosities and the impulse to understand the natural world, but by the late nineteenth century, as Steven Conn argues, "the intellectual architecture" used to build museums was "predicated on the assumption that objects could tell stories 'to the untrained observer,'" if they spent time studying and observing those objects.[6] The objects on which this history is based entered collections as early as 1861 and up to the present moment. People's impulse to preserve and document the war intensified in the 1880s and 1890s as the nation moved into new phases of reconciliation. Veterans' organizations were founded, "Blue and Gray" reunions were organized to bring together Union and Confederate soldiers with greater frequency, and veterans of the war began to die in greater numbers. Museums were founded to preserve artifacts and relics of the war, ranging from the Libby Prison War Museum in Chicago, to Confederate museums in Richmond and Charleston, to museums housed in the Grand Army of the Republic's Hall in Chicago and regimental memorial halls like that of the Fifth Maine in its regimental cottage on Peaks Island, Maine. Their founders used objects to narrate their versions of the war, imbuing those objects with meaning and making "their beliefs material."[7] Such objects also played a powerful role in the mania for Southern memorialization and the cult of the Lost Cause, itself a manifestation of public memory.

Many articles of clothing in museum collections now lack provenance connecting them to the original owners. Uncovering their stories requires situating them among an array of other objects, images, and texts; at times, we are only able to make reasoned conjectures. But some people did document those connections, writing and telling histories about individual objects. As these objects passed between time and circumstance, they created and took on new meanings, resulting in a multilayered material culture that transcended the moment in which that clothing was sewn or worn, saved or exhibited. The materials themselves were critical actors in that process: Brass eventually tarnished; moths infested coats and ate holes through wool; crimson-red blood turned a deep shade of reddish-brown; white cloth yellowed; thread rotted, making seams give way. Some objects are still in remarkably stable condition, but others have fallen victim to years stuffed inside a musty trunk. In many people's eyes, the decay of these objects elevates their status to that of relics; their dank odor serves as a portal to the past, generating romanticism about the American Civil War and the people who once made or wore them. Relics, Peter Carmichael reminds us, "possessed tremendous emotional power because they had the capacity to assign meaning to life's experiences."[8]

But not all objects are relics—they must be imbued with that status through human narratives. The power of objects in history far surpasses their uses by or meanings for individual people. Objects are central to the stories that communities and societies tell about themselves and their past—they are the building blocks of collective memory. Saved, collected, preserved, exhibited, and interpreted, often in museums, they are characters in the histories we narrate.

Wartime produced a general impulse for collecting and preserving objects, whether they were collected on the battlefield, from a house in which one had camped, or from the knapsack carried home from war. Such objects validated people's participation in and experience of war.[9] One woman saved a pair of knitted socks, attaching to them a note that read, "Socks of Gen. R. E. Lee's given to me by Mrs Lee his wife for my sons during the war. E. Preston."[10] Articles of dress that were typically worn out and discarded or recycled, these socks were deemed worthy of preservation, complete with—and perhaps more prized for—their rents and stains. In another instance, a Union soldier kept scraps of fabric torn from upholstered chairs in the Confederate legislature and later donated them to the Massachusetts Historical Society. These bits of textiles and articles of clothing served to document the owners' connection to the war—to establish both their presence at significant events, such as the seizure of Richmond, and their relationships to important people. Objects like Lee's socks have something of a celebrity status in the realm of Civil War relics. Items owned by US and Confederate generals, Abraham Lincoln, Jefferson Davis, and other well-known figures hold prominent positions in museum collections. But what about the stuff? The ordinary old clothing and fabrics worn by ordinary people?

In addition to their own clothing, or that worn by loved ones, people saved scraps of fabric to document their material presence at certain events and locations, to assert dominance in their ability to loot, and to chronicle what they believed were conditions peculiar to wartime. The ability to save a wartime coat, shirt, or pair of underwear marked a certain degree of privilege. To save an item of clothing meant removing it from daily use, ending its circulation. Clothing—and cloth in general—held its value long after it was made or purchased. Even if the clothing was no longer useful to the wearer, it retained value through secondhand clothing and rag markets. The ability to pack away coats, shirts, pants, socks, and underwear into a trunk meant that the wearer already owned enough garments or had the means to purchase additional cloth and clothing. Indeed, many coats were not preserved precisely because the clothing worn on their return from the war front was, for some men, the only clothing they owned. For others, that clothing was so dirty or louse infested that its destruction seemed necessary.

One Union soldier wrote to a family member about his regrets about the military clothing that he could not save. Having recently thrown away his old clothes, he reflected that "when I parted with them I wished several times that I might send them to you." His motivation to do so was in part to preserve them as relics and to preserve the stories held within those clothes. "Every rent and hole spoke words that I shall never forget," he wrote. "I wish you would have seen them."[11] The rips and holes in this clothing chronicled his experience of the war in ways that relaying those experiences through words could not. For some people, objects preserved memories that were difficult—perhaps impossible—to express in words. But absent objects, too, as this reference to his discarded clothing suggests, stored memories of his war.

Objects, clothing among them, that were packed away, stolen, or lost entirely were removed from daily use, affecting people's everyday movements. When Judith McGuire described the uncertainty and fear that accompanied leaving her home during wartime, she reflected on the familial and historical value and memories of the things she left behind: "Oh, that I could know what is going on in those walls, all encompassed by armies as it is. With my mind's eye I look into first one room and then another, with all the associations of the past; the old family Bible, the family pictures, the library, containing the collection of forty years, and so many things which seemed a part of ourselves. What will become of them? Who are now using or abusing them?" Both memories and identity were bound up in those objects—"so many things," McGuire emphasized, "which seemed a part of ourselves."[12] As McGuire suggests, people's ability to traverse through the "mind's eye" the houses, camps, and landscapes they inhabited during the war—to conjure up images of the clothes and objects that made up those material worlds—allowed for those absent objects to preserve memories of the war. Though he could not put his fingers through the holes or trace the fabric's rents, a soldier could revisit that uniform through his mind's eye to prompt the words describing experiences he could "never forget."[13]

When soldiers took off their uniforms, what became of their brass manhood? In the immediate postwar era, former Confederates were banned from wearing their insignia and brass buttons.[14] And so, for a time, brass manhood, once a national, public culture, became a manhood reserved for the victors. As modern United States museum collections attest, many of those Union soldiers preserved their brass buttons, epaulets, and "sword-belted manhood," voluntarily packing their uniforms away. Photographs saved by formerly enslaved men-turned-soldiers documented their quest to be granted the right not only to partake in brass manhood, but to be recognized as men in full possession of their bodies—men with rights to citizenship. Black men saved the insignia that had adorned their uniforms: the belt buckle stamped "US" and buttons with eagles.[15] But Confederate soldiers also kept their uniforms, and Confederate women, their jewelry and cockades, many of which retained those same elements of brass manhood. Northern women, too, saved mementos from the war, creating scrapbooks filled with photographs, storing out-of-fashion dresses, and setting aside scraps of fabric. An array of patriotic Union fabrics printed with flags, stars, and abolitionist symbols are now preserved in multiple collections.[16]

Wartime had produced conditions in which brass manhood was questioned and challenged: conditions that prompted some men and women to ascribe to other, at times competing, definitions of wartime gender conventions. The death, destruction, and inhumanity of war—the stripping of dead bodies and the looting of homes—had tarnished the glory of brass manhood for some and denied its embodiment to others. It is not surprising, then, that brass manhood was not the only form of manhood preserved through surviving material culture. The undershirts, drawers, and socks stored memories of battlefront style and retained a history of a more intimate kind of manhood that was predicated on relationships to women in one's family. Body armor, too, preserved a manhood that valued survival for the sake of one's family over martyrdom.

Ohioan Henry Heinmiller saved not only the bullet removed from his left hip, but also the drawers he was wearing when he was shot in March 1865. Heinmiller transported the drawers over 500 miles, from a North Carolina field hospital back to his home in Columbus, Ohio. They were not saved for future use; if they had been, they would likely have been discarded when they wore out. No attempts appear to have been made to remove the now rust-colored bloodstains spattered across them. Instead, Heinmiller kept the drawers as a relic of the war, and his family continues to preserve them into the present day, both as evidence of their ancestor's role in the war, and as something once connected to his physical body. These were not simply the drawers of a Union soldier; they were the drawers of a 6′4″ Ohioan who had suffered a gunshot wound to the left hip. While his body is gone, the evidence of his wound remains, in the form of the bloodstained hole in his drawers. Heinmiller's drawers do not preserve his brass manhood—though he had gained the rank of first lieutenant. Instead, they preserve a coarser manhood

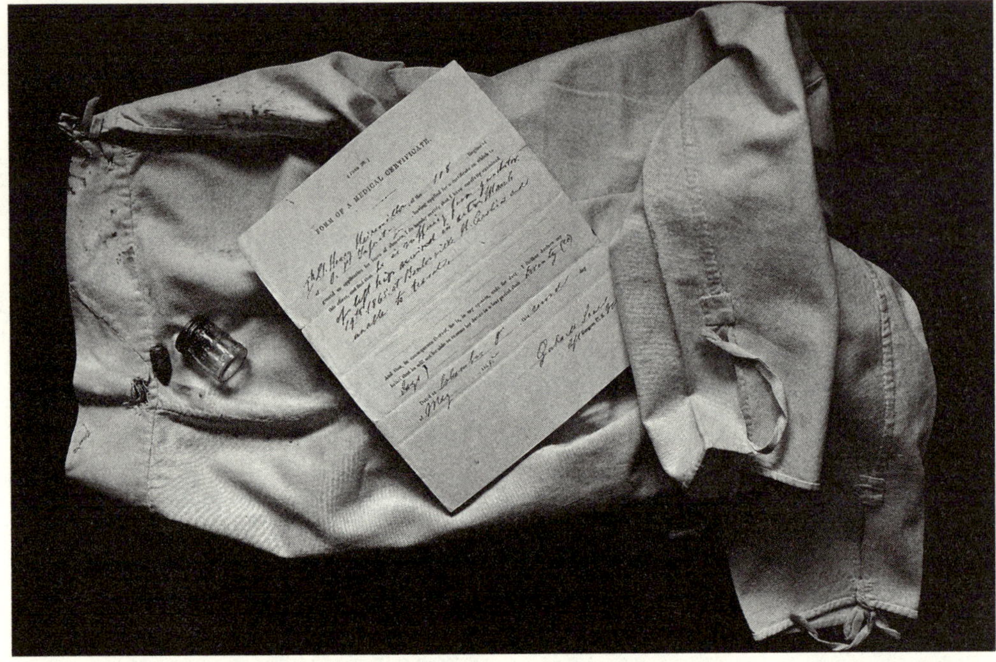

Drawers worn by Henry Heinmiller, c. 1865. Private collection.

defined by survival and his ability to return home to his family, having performed his duty for both them and the nation.[17]

While Heinmiller's drawers remain in his family's possession, many other such objects made their way into museums in the 1880s and 1890s as Grand Army of the Republic and regimental memorial halls frequented by veterans, ladies' memorial societies, and the United Daughters of the Confederacy actively collected and displayed objects that had been kept by soldiers and their families. In 1886, within this context, an article in a Washington, DC–area newspaper conveyed that the US National Museum (now the Smithsonian Institution) was seeking Confederate uniforms for its collection. The timing of the National Museum's efforts to collect Confederate items is somewhat surprising. It would be several more years, in 1894, until the Confederate Memorial Literary Society in Richmond, Virginia (now the American Civil War Museum), would begin soliciting donations and its "Relics Committee" would start collecting objects and documents for its museum.[18] A few former Confederate soldiers wrote directly to the National Museum as a result of that newspaper article.

At the time he wrote to the National Museum, O. W. Barrow, a former Confederate captain, had long since become a manufacturer of fine plug and twist tobacco in Danville, Virginia. Writing to a curator, he noted that he "saw from a paragraph in a News Paper a few days since, that you want to get a Captains Confederate Uniform Coat." The curator, seeking to foster this potential donation, wrote back, noting that he would eagerly embrace "such a specimen" that "would fill a gap in our collections which up to present time we have found impossible to fill." The curator noted that the museum "fully recognize[d] the desirability and importance of preserving such relics of the war," although he did not elaborate why.[19] Barrow, too, thought it important and sent his coat.

I. E. Nagle was also eager to preserve his own relics, donating to the National Museum his Confederate surgeon's uniform, along with a few additional "mementoes of the war." He explained why he thought they would be valuable additions to the museum's collection, noting that he believed "that there are none others in existence, for all the inquiries that I have made from old comrades, failed to discover that any other person, has thought so far in the long ago, as to save any of these mementoes of a dead empire." He offered, for example, his shirt, noting that he did not "know of any of the kind in any other hands." As a survey of modern museum collections suggests, Nagle was far from alone in having kept his shirt. But underlying his justification for the museum's acquisition of his uniform was a certain desire to feel that his possessions were rare and therefore more culturally valuable. Indeed, he claimed to inhabit a collector's identity that was, in part, grounded in a fascination with rarity. Reflecting on why his shirt had survived and others had not, he mused, "I suppose if I wasnt something of an antiquarian in my habits and fancies, it too and all the other things would have gone into oblivion."[20]

These men were not merely performing a public service by donating or loaning objects to the museum; they were actively involving themselves in the construction of a collective narrative of war and reconciliation. The clothing they sought to deposit in the National Museum held personal memories, but it was also the stuff of collective memory. According to sociologist Maurice Halbwachs, even seemingly very personal memories are shaped by social circumstances, making "nearly all personal memories, learned, inherited, or at least informed by a common stock of social memory."[21] As uniform donors deposited their clothing in the national collection, they moved that clothing from the realm of their personal memory—that memory of their own wartime experience—and into that of the collective. They were creating "attics of memory" composed of physical objects.[22]

When former Confederate George Wilson, once a prisoner of war, sent his coat to the National Museum, he did so with reconciliation in mind. He felt "confident that the National Government of our re-united [illegible] country will care for and treat, as kindly these well worn and moth eatin relics as her soldiers did the wearer after his capture in April 1865." In donating the clothing to the National Museum, he hoped "that they may help to keep alive the friendly feelings of the true soldiers who wore the gray or blue."[23] Wilson saw his donation not only as a means of preserving his wartime mementos beyond his own lifetime, but also as an act of atonement for the part he had played in the war. Having once been involved in rebelling against the United States, he now sought to help to heal those wounds with his "moth eatin" coat.

By donating the coat, Wilson was also attempting to ensure that ordinary soldiers were represented in the National Museum. He had read that officers' coats had been sent to the museum, but noted that "the privates of the late war seem scarce." His coat was a basic, single-breasted gray wool shell jacket with nine buttons—five marked "A" for artillery and four marked "I" for infantry. The jacket, then, preserved the brass manhood he had embodied during the war. But in its mix of buttons—one could not be both an infantry *and* an artillery soldier—the coat also attested to the fact that such manhood could be difficult to maintain. Wilson successfully incorporated his history into the national collection in a way that Union soldiers of his rank did not. Although today Union uniforms far outnumber Confederate uniforms in the Smithsonian's collection, the majority of those uniforms entered the collection in the twentieth century through a large transfer of objects from the War Department—many of which have no wearer's name attached. Union uniform coats that made their way into the collection in the nineteenth century were typically those of notable officers—such as Grant, Sherman, McClellan, and Custer. Julia Grant, for example, provided a large collection of her husband Ulysses S. Grant's possessions associated with his presidency and military service.[24] This difference in the way in which items entered the National Museum is further evidence that the removal and preservation of uniforms at the end of the war—the voluntary versus forced removal of the trappings of brass manhood—were experienced differently by the victors and the defeated.

While some uniform donations were made in an effort to continue to patch up a country recently torn by war, others contributed to the creation of an alternative narrative of loss. Consider for example, the donation of Alexander Hunter, a former private in the Confederate army. The jacket he donated was a meaningful object to him with a deep history. Another soldier originally owned the jacket, but when that man was killed in August 1862, the man's sister took it from him and gave it to Hunter, who, she saw, was wearing a tattered jacket at the time. The gray wool shell jacket lasted Hunter the du-

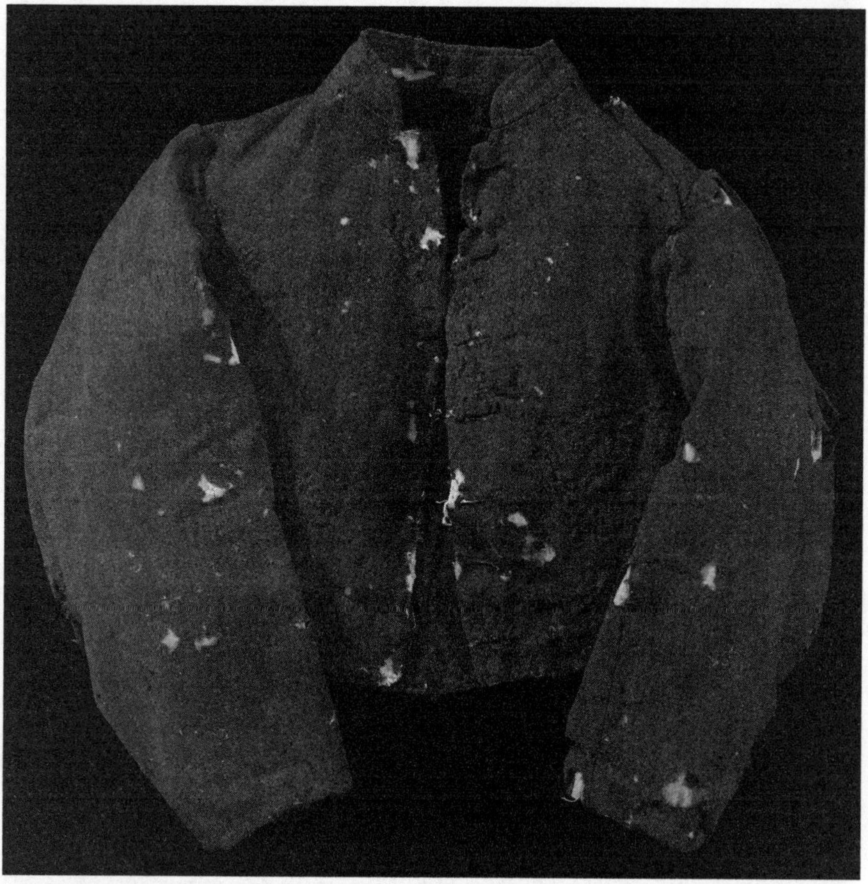

The holes and tears in Alexander Hunter's jacket were part of the material culture of the ragged rebel soldier. Jacket, worn by Alexander Hunter, c. 1861–65. Courtesy of the Division of Military History, National Museum of American History, Smithsonian Institution.

ration of the war. Indeed, he may have considered it a talisman of sorts—for he was wounded twice while wearing it, but not fatally. For the past 140 years, Hunter's jacket has been in the Smithsonian's collection, unable to be displayed because of its poor condition (at least since the time when records of exhibition began to be kept). And for those 140 years, it has been assumed that Hunter had simply donated a tattered jacket. But when we piece together this object, its acquisition history, and other forms of evidence, this tattered jacket reveals much more.

Nineteen years after he donated the jacket, Hunter published *Johnny Reb and Billy Yank*—a novel based on his own wartime diaries and experiences.

He was motivated to write it, he claimed, because well-ranking officers had published the majority of war literature. A private soldier, he asserted, "can afford to tell the truth as to what he saw, heard and thought without fear or favor. And above all, a private in the ranks, having no grievance, can be fair and just." But was Hunter fair and just? It is unlikely, for the book, it is important to note, is dedicated to

> "Johnny Reb"
> that tattered son of fortune and the nursling
> of many a dark and stormy hour

"That tattered son" was the ragged rebel soldier, a symbol of the Lost Cause of the Confederacy.[25]

A myth, according to theorist Roland Barthes, talks about things: "It purifies them, it makes them innocent, it gives them a natural and eternal justification, it gives them a clarity which is not that of an explanation but that of a statement of fact."[26] Talking and writing about the Lost Cause were critical to the process of making it a "statement of fact," of replacing the causes and events of the war with fabricated memories. So, too, were the donation and collection of objects and the creation of museums. Hunter's *Johnny Reb and Billy Yank* was his contribution to the creation of the image of the ragged rebel, his way of talking about things. Indeed, Hunter's novel describes many ragged and barefooted soldiers, frequently employing the terms "rags," "ragged," and "tatters." But his donation of his uniform coat nearly twenty years prior was also a public act in physically creating that image. Hunter's donation can be seen as an effort—conscious or not—to materially document in the National Museum the ragged Southern manhood embraced as part of the myth of the Lost Cause.[27]

The wider mythmaking process in which Hunter engaged through his writing and the donation of his jacket gained incredibly powerful traction in the postwar era and the early twentieth century. Its success was due, in part, to the establishment of collections like that of the Confederate Museum of the Confederate Memorial Literary Society in Richmond. Women took a leading role in this and other Confederate museums. In Richmond's Confederate Museum, individual rooms were devoted to each of the Confederate states, and a "Solid South" room displayed relics from across the South and from donors across the nation to "the glory of the whole."[28] Portraits and uniforms celebrated Confederate officials, while thousands of everyday items ranging from hardtack to sewing kits memorialized the experience of common soldiers.

Donated to the Confederate Memorial and Literary Society in Richmond, Virginia, this bodice was likely owned by Mary Gooch. Its 1905 label read "My Mother's / Ran Blockade to Charleston from Louisa and ugly as it is it cost $18.00 per yard." Bodice, c. 1861–65. Courtesy of the American Civil War Museum, Richmond, VA.

The stories that people attempted to preserve through objects in museums were not, of course, only focused on the battlefield. Others were intended to preserve or protest the changes that war had wrought. Southern women frequently saved articles of clothing or fabric, noting how much they cost, how they were obtained, and the process by which they were made. Numerous pieces of cloth were preserved within letter collections—cloth that was used to show friends or family samples of the fabric from which their clothing was to be made. Others retained cloth specifically as examples of what they had worn, of the sacrifices they had endured. The daughter of a woman who made a bodice from printed cotton noted that the fabric had run the blockade and "as ugly as it is cost $18.00 per yard." This bodice, other examples of women's and children's clothing, and items ranging from palmetto hats to sleeve patterns made from newspaper were also donated to and displayed in the Confederate Museum. There, they were presented as "examples of material privation, women's labors on the home front, and badges of honor in the face of a blockade of Yankee goods"—interpretations that obscured elite women's wartime hatred of rough cloth, much of which was produced by the hands of enslaved women.[29]

Formerly enslaved people saved clothing items owned in slavery, continuing to wear them or altering them to wear in their free lives, and passed them on to future generations. A white cotton skirt with a small pattern print with a single flower surrounded by a stippled frame was stored in a chest for many years after it was last worn. The skirt had been mended many times and was so well used that its fabric is now thin and soft to the touch. Now in the National Museum of African American History and Culture, this garment was described by the donor's grandmother as her "mother's mother's grandmother's mother's mother's clothing that she wore during slavery." That woman had kept the skirt, once her everyday garment worn as an enslaved woman, when she was emancipated—perhaps she continued to wear it as part of her life in freedom. Eventually, it made its way into a trunk to be passed down through generations—the history it contained was to be respected; the memories it stored, preserved.[30]

White people's work of creating memory around enslavement began before it ended and included not only textual accounts of enslaved people and the conditions in which they lived and labored, but also the taking and saving of material objects associated with enslavement. The process of remembering is, of course, also one of forgetting—often, a willful process of forgetting. Remembering has as much to do with identity, power, and authority as it does with the act of conserving and recalling information.[31] This is particularly apparent in the case of objects tied to slavery that were given by white donors to museums in the Jim Crow South. When slave-made cloth was presented as a gift to the Confederate Memorial and Literary Society, it was often described only as "plantation made" during the Civil War. Even when the work was attributed to an enslaved person, their name was erased. At the same time, effort was taken to identify the donor's full name and location, usually including the name and/or owner of the plantation. The 1905 catalog description for samples of "Homespun, made in 1863 by a slave belonging to Miss Mary Pilgram," for instance, reasserts Miss Mary Pilgram's identity as a slave owner and her dominant position in Woodruff, South Carolina, society while simultaneously reducing, once again, the person whose skill produced this cloth to a category of property. The maker's name, gender, and age are absent from this entry.[32] The label helped to reassert white Southern dominance in the Jim Crow South by documenting a named master's continued possession of the work of an unnamed slave and by

Printed floral skirt worn by an enslaved ancestor of Janett Sharee Galloway, 1850–75. Object No. 2011.52. Collection of the Smithsonian National Museum of African American History and Culture, Washington, DC.

Cloth made by an enslaved person on a Woodruff, South Carolina, plantation, 1863. The 1905 catalog entry read, "Homespun, made in 1863 by a slave belonging to Miss Mary Pilgram, Woodruff, S.C. Given by her." Courtesy of the American Civil War Museum, Richmond, VA.

suggesting slaves' continued loyalty to masters; it attempted to mitigate the upending of Southern social hierarchy that accompanied emancipation.

Not all cloth made by enslaved people was saved by former Confederates. One Union soldier saved scraps of coarse brown, blue, tan and cream-colored fabric both for himself and to send to a friend, labeling it "Confed Cloth woven on plantation, St. Johns . . . the only cloth I have seen."[33] His impetus for saving it seems to have been situated within a desire to document that such a thing as this coarse plantation-made cloth had once existed. Although differently motivated in their desire to save homespun cloth woven during the war, Union soldiers and former Confederates told a similar story. Rarely did they praise the quality of the cloth, even though much of it is quite well made. Instead, it was saved as a curiosity of the war or to document destitution and supply scarcity.[34] In some cases, that cloth was saved as physical evidence of white women's wartime work, as physical evidence of what Southerners had endured.

When we extract these bits of cloth from the textual narratives in which they have been embedded by their donors, and look at the cloth itself, we instead see the skill of often-enslaved artisans: people who possessed the knowledge and ingenuity to card and spin cotton and wool; to dye yarn using a variety of natural materials, ranging from bark to berries; and the skill to weave cloth into a wide range of plaids, stripes, and checks. These were fabrics that were well made, even as wartime conditions made cotton cards, dyes, mordants, and spare parts for looms difficult to obtain. Looking at the textile itself reveals that the person—or people—who produced these pieces of cloth had an eye for creating vibrant colors; skill in tight, even weaving; and the ability to map out the warp and weft using several colors to create both small and large, evenly spaced patterns. This cloth was made by skilled weavers.

The saving of objects is critical to our ability to interpret the past through the material world. And yet the remembering and documenting that often happen in the process of saving can confound later efforts to interpret objects. Saving is itself a selective process. It involves the decision to keep one thing—or to acquire one object for a collection—over another. This in itself can skew our sense of an object's representativeness or uniqueness in the material world it once inhabited, something that can be mitigated by building out that object's historical context through additional objects, texts, images, and other sources. Add to this the documenting of stories attached to the object—when, where, and who made it, wore it, used it, took it—and that object's identity can be reduced to written words, often in the form of a museum catalog entry, which becomes the object's primary identifier for people in the present.

If, then, we use one of the Confederate Museum's original catalog entries as our sole guide to viewing a piece of "homespun," we see only a rough piece of cloth. But when we begin with the cloth, its vibrancy begins to reemerge and the memories of skilled hands that are embedded within it begin to be released. What we see here is a complicated intertwining of text and object. When we allow ourselves to privilege words over things—as historians typically do, since, as Leora Auslander notes, "words are our stock-in-trade"—we allow those words to dictate the memory and the historical value stored within the things themselves.[35] Yet, we might begin to recover the memory these objects store of the individuals who made, used, sold, and saved these things. By refocusing our attention onto the things themselves, to really understand the physical clues embedded in objects, we can begin to mediate the power of those words, allowing people's stories to emerge, even though they are no longer here to narrate them.

The stories that we, like Civil War–era Americans, tell about things—the memories we create and verbalize for them—are not always accurate. Yet, the objects have their own ways of telling their story—from a synthetic fabric revealing that a "nineteenth-century slave blanket" could not have been made before 1970, to a piece of cloth showing the skill of the artisan who wove it on the plantation on which she was enslaved. This involves reading against the grain and between the lines of what people had to say about their clothes, but it also requires examining the seams and tears of the objects themselves.

Conclusion

Albert W. Bacheler was eighteen years old when he marched to war with a New Hampshire company. He was wounded at Chancellorsville and again at Gettysburg before being captured as a prisoner of war in Bermuda Hundred, Virginia, and taken to the infamous Libby Prison in Richmond.[1] His fellow Union prisoner John Babb, a Marylander whose community sent men to both armies, benefited from a network of family and friends who managed to have a Confederate deliver new clothing to him. But Bacheler was not similarly connected.[2] In December 1864, upon escaping through a tunnel dug under the foundation of his cellar prison, Bacheler wore only a pair of pants and a torn shirt. When he reached the home of African Americans along his escape route, one man gave him a coat and wished him safe travel back to Union lines. Bacheler made it—and so did the coat, which he kept throughout his life, parting with it only upon his death in 1929, nearly sixty-five years later.[3]

The meanings ascribed to this coat, as with other objects, shifted over the course of its life, changing according to the stage of its life cycle and people's relationship to it. No documentation tells the first iteration of this coat's history, but analyzing the coat itself in light of the broader context of clothing from this period hints at what that history might have been. Double-breasted, with two rows of four fabric-covered buttons and a full skirt, this civilian coat was no longer in style in 1864; it was likely made in the early 1850s. Although it is in poor condition now, its skilled construction suggests that it was likely cut by a tailor and sewn by a seamstress. The coat is made from wool with a cotton lining. The sleeve lining—a brown-and-white fabric with a zigzag pattern—appears to be of the quality that could have been made from cotton carded, spun, dyed, and woven on a plantation or manufactured as "negro cloth." Lined with cotton, not silk, as was typical of men's dress coats of this period, the coat would not have been considered finery but was relatively fashionable, nevertheless. An enslaved man may have worn it as part of his livery; it might also have been owned by a white man who gave it to an enslaved man when he no longer desired to wear it himself.

This coat contains multiple stories, offering insight into the labor of a woman who carded and wove cotton, men and women who cut and sewed, and its daily

An African American man gave this coat to US soldier Albert Bacheler, after he escaped from Libby Prison in 1864. Courtesy of Museum Textiles Services, Inc.

use by a man who had likely once been enslaved. While the coat has degraded due to the conditions of its display in the twentieth century, the tears are likely from an earlier period—perhaps evidence of its long-term use by the African American man, or the result of incidents along Bacheler's route back to Union lines. The coat documents, too, Bacheler's struggle to escape Confederate captivity and the importance of the coat to him in his postwar life.

Bacheler did not simply pack away the coat after returning to New Hampshire. Periodically, he took the coat out. According to the label accompanying the coat's display, he contemplated it "when things went wrong and future looked dark." A teacher and later principal, Bacheler was known for showing it to students "when they became discouraged as a symbol that there is a way of escape from every difficulty." The coat was so tied to Bacheler's postwar identity that when he died it was presented to a former student. For more than eighty years, the coat has been displayed in a case at Bacheler's former teaching post in Massachusetts, along with his photograph and a brief history. It continues to have significance for the school and the community. In 2015, two eleven-year-old boys began raising funds to conserve and rehouse the coat in a protective case.[4]

This single coat changed hands multiple times, and with each change its meanings shifted. For one woman, its fabric was an object of labor; for one tailor, a welcome commission. For one man, it was likely an everyday object that he valued for both its usefulness and his self-presentation. For another, it was both the means and symbol of his successful survival of an escape from Libby Prison. To still another, the coat stored the memory of a cherished teacher; for a textile conservator, it proved a rewarding challenge. Today, it is an object around which a community has come together to engage in both preservation and an understanding of their own community's broader history—a history whose many layers matter.

The students who pass the display case containing Bacheler's coat today live, by comparison, in a world of fast fashion. Trends change quickly and retro styles creep back onto clothing store racks every so often, typically to the chagrin of those who were teenagers during the era that has been newly declared trendy. When a shirt gets a hole or a pants seam rips out, Americans more often than not throw the clothing out, donate it in hopes that their trash becomes someone else's treasure, or mail it to a clothing recycling program, that twenty-first-century version of the work of nineteenth-century ragpickers. Articles of clothing typically don't last as long in our daily lives as they did in the mid-nineteenth century.

And yet, like nineteenth-century Americans, many of us continue to ascribe meanings and memories to our own and other people's clothes. We carefully select outfits for special occasions or important events. Sometimes, we endure discomfort to ensure our clothing meets society's dress code. We wear a favorite sports team's logo to indicate our allegiances. We innovate to clothe soldiers in protective gear and athletes in performance wear. We save clothing that marks our experiences and belonging, and that which reminds us of important moments or people significant to our lives.

Often only one, if any, of the moments of an object's life can be recovered using direct textual evidence. Yet, as with Bacheler's coat, analyzing and situating that object within a broader array of sources—with texts and images and other objects—can resurrect those meanings, if only as conjecture. Such conjecture is worthwhile, for it reveals the overlapping lives of people and things, their intersecting historical contexts, and the contingency of history itself.

I have attempted to reconstruct such uses, meanings, and memories tied to clothing for Americans who lived through, died in, and survived the Civil War. This history reveals clothing as both a battlefront on which the war was fought and a tool for living through this conflict. The clothes in this book tell histories of people's deeply personal confrontation with the Civil War and its aftermath, of how they learned to wage war against one another and how they confronted new anxieties produced in wartime.

In 1862, newspaper headlines across the North and South were filled with triumphal announcements of army victories and accounts of war's "awful carnage."[5] *Shiloh. Antietam. The Second Battle of Bull Run. Fredericksburg. Stone's River*. Claiming together over 100,000 casualties, these battles proved some of the deadliest and costliest of the war. As US and Confederate soldiers confronted mass death and Americans' initial fervor for war faded, the reach of the military and the government—both federal and Confederate—continued to expand, setting the stage for the emergence of a modern national state. Governmental power, military tactics, political ideologies, loyalty, the economic costs of war, the future of American slavery—these were among the issues that dominated national debates in 1862. But for Black and white women and men across the North and South, and in the eastern and western theaters of battle, the everyday experiences of war and the government's role in civil society were shaped and felt in far more material, often subtle, ways—ways that could not always be fully explained in or accounted for by words or captured in newspaper headlines.

In Philadelphia, Pennsylvania, the Lockwood Manufacturing Company was preparing to produce "Ladies' Patent Electro 'Union' Collars and Cuffs"—paper collars and sleeve cuffs printed with stars and the American flag. On her Georgia farm, 800 miles south, Dolly Lunt Burge was experiencing the effects of a deteriorating marketplace constricted by the pressure of Union blockades.[6] In Ellijay, Georgia, 200 miles away, "wash woman" and seamstress Mahalay Hyatte was facing her own struggles as she penned a letter to Georgia governor Joseph E. Brown, requesting fifty dollars to pay for necessities—she thought "the government . . . [ought] to help me until I get help," given that she had "done a great deel of work [to ma]ke clothing for the soldiers."[7]

That same winter, two weeks' ride to the northwest in St. Louis, the US Army was actively working to standardize the appearance of its forces. Strongly worded General Orders from the Department of the Missouri advised all Union officers that they would "be arrested and tried for disobedience of orders and neglect of duty" if they wore gray or mixed uniforms in the field. Any Union soldier with gray garments was ordered to immediately turn them in to the

Quartermaster's Department, at which time they would be issued clothing "of the proper color"—dark blue—at no expense.[8] Meanwhile, a seamstress in Cincinnati walked from the Clothing Depot to her home, carrying a bundle of precut fabric to sew into those blue uniforms. The Confederate army, too, was struggling with problems in uniforming its troops. As Virginian Joseph Waddell observed, "There is no such thing as 'uniform'—all sorts of coats, pants, hats and caps—but they are alike in dustiness, dirtiness, and general shabbiness."[9]

In Northern towns and Union encampments, Union soldiers and their friends and families were inundated with advertisements and sales pitches for bulletproof vests that promised to save thousands and make soldiers more powerful and valuable to the nation. On the battlefield of Shiloh in western Tennessee, Confederate soldiers looted the bodies of those dead Union soldiers, taking with them not only clothing and shoes but also pieces of body armor worn by men and their officers, saving them as trophies of war.[10] While some soldiers could afford to purchase and wear such questionable technology into combat, Union soldier John Babb was struggling to procure a pair of boots while encamped in Hampton, Virginia. Not having been paid for his army service in five months, he had no cash with which to purchase them himself, but he hoped his father would help ameliorate his current plight.[11]

That same month, with Abraham Lincoln's preliminary Emancipation Proclamation on the horizon, New York general W. K. Strong wrote to Secretary of War Edwin Stanton in Washington, expressing concern—and detailing his plan—"for the most economical mode" of providing clothing for soon-to-be-freed slaves: a plan that involved the US government's purchase of "negro goods designed for the southern market."[12] Formerly enslaved people were working to clothe themselves in styles, cuts, patterns, and colors of their own choosing. At the same time, a Boston relief organization was already engaged in gathering "cast-off clothes of all kinds" for the destitute, self-emancipated freedpeople who had placed "themselves under the protection of the United States government" 1,000 miles to the south in Port Royal, South Carolina.[13] White relief workers deemed the tattered clothing freedpeople wore as unacceptable for free men and women, a point that photographers attempted to poignantly convey through the dissemination of images depicting newly outfitted freedpeople alongside those of their former ragged selves.

In these disparate places—from Cincinnati to Philadelphia; Ellijay, Georgia, to Pittsburg Landing, Tennessee; Boston to Port Royal, South Carolina; St. Louis to Hampton, Virginia—the clothing that people made and wore was a contested site through which Americans confronted broader questions about war and emancipation. The political, social, and economic disruptions that war made in everyday life demonstrate just how critical clothing was for basic survival, comfort, social engagement, political expression, and cultural continuity. The war heightened the importance of everything from fine silks to soiled rags, causing men and women to reflect on and express their relationships to clothing through both their actions and writing. They grappled with, challenged, and defined their understanding of violence, race, gender, and their relationships to one another and to the government through the clothing they made, wore, destroyed, and saved.

Clothing was central to making war, both as a critical form of supply and as a means of shoring up the shared identities and patriotism that enabled families and communities to send men into battle. Its production was a space in which women challenged their relationships to the government and by which officials came to recognize women's textile work as political. For formerly enslaved people, clothing was a material way in which they created their freedom, but it was also a site through which they struggled with predominately white relief workers over what precisely freedom and free people looked like. The clothing individuals wore—and that which they could no longer access—affected their daily lives, how they navigated interpersonal relationships, how they engaged with the government, and, at a visceral level, how they experienced their own bodies in wartime.

Struggles to create, shore up, and resist identities made clothing a powerful weapon to wield in both physical and emotional warfare. Clothing-related looting and violation on the battlefield, as well as the unraveling of those Southern dress practices upon which social hierarchies had been based, proved intimate means by which US and Confederate soldiers and Southern civilians experienced the violent reality of war. As they moved through this war and beyond it, people saved not only garments but also bits and pieces of material, using it to craft memories and legacies of war that ranged from personal introspection to the powerful collective memory of the Lost Cause. War's end ushered in not only the political Reconstruction of the South, but also the need for an entire nation to be woven back together into a new pattern—a pattern with new kinds of conflicts and frayed edges.

The politics of Civil War–era dress culture continue to permeate American society—indeed, the clothes themselves do. They are part of our memorial landscapes, our popular culture, our public memory. Uniformed Civil War soldiers appear in town squares throughout the nation, cast in bronze or carved in stone. Gift shops at National Park Service Civil War sites sell kepis and calico bonnets for children. The division between Union blue and Confederate gray continues to have cultural resonance in American life. That stark division was never a reality, but since the mid-twentieth century, people clad in a mix of blues, grays, and browns have regularly gathered in battlefield and recreational parks to reenact the war's battles.

Among many, though not all, reenactors, attention to the authenticity of war-related reproductions—especially clothing—is akin to the precision of connoisseurs. As one reenactor explained, "I mean, I could care less what I wear in the rest of my life, but out here I'm obsessed with my clothes. It's like I'm searching for the Holy Grail, except it's not a cup, it's a bit of gray cloth with just the right amount of dye and the exact number of threads."[14] For reenactors, the precision of their clothing is about performance, the authenticity of experience, and, for some, a desire to escape the modern world through a romanticized version of the past. Their self-proclaimed obsession speaks to the multifaceted levels of clothing and its pivotal role in shaping both broader social and cultural developments, and humans' understanding and expression of them.

Such an enduring romantic vision of the Civil War era exists in part because of the care with which former soldiers and their families packed up their brass-buttoned uniforms, the impulse to save bits and pieces of wartime culture, and former Confederates' successful work in crafting a Lost Cause mythology that embraced a ragged masculinity.

A "moth eatin" coat.
Scraps of coarse fabric.
Photographs of a slumped, recently enslaved man alongside him
as an upright soldier.
A brown-and-cream-striped dress worn in freedom.
A pair of brass button earrings.
A bulletproof vest.

These objects created and contained intimate experiences and memories of war, emancipation, and reconciliation. Some of these objects speak to clothing's transformative capacity to affect and manipulate the body and inner self—whether through the disconcerting texture of homespun cloth or the postural support provided by a bulletproof vest. Others speak to competing and complementary visions of manhood and womanhood, and still others to contentious understandings of the meaning of freedom in the material world. Together, they reveal an entangled and violent history of the immediacy and intimacy with which people lived out—and with—the American Civil War. Such clothing transcended the boundaries of home front and war front, offering people across the United States not only the means of waging war but also the materials for weaving back together this nation that had come unraveled.

Notes

Abbreviations

The following acronyms are used in the notes to refer to archives.

AAS	American Antiquarian Society
FHL	Friends Historical Library of Swarthmore College
GSA	Georgia State Archives
MARBL	Stuart A. Rose Manuscripts, Archives, and Rare Books Library, Emory University
MHS	Massachusetts Historical Society
NARA	National Archives and Records Administration
NMAAHC	National Museum of African American History and Culture
NMAH	National Museum of American History
NPS	National Park Service
RG	Record Group
RHS	Roswell Historical Society
SCHS	South Carolina Historical Society
USCT	United States Colored Troops
VMHC	Virginia Museum of History and Culture
WPA	Works Progress Administration

Introduction

1. "Diary of Susan Bradford Eppes," June 1865, in Eppes, *Through Some Eventful Years*, 288–89.

2. Eppes, *Through Some Eventful Years*, 288–89.

3. For studies that look at clothing as a reflection of identity, see Haltunnen, *Confidence Men and Painted Women*; and Bushman, *Refinement of America*.

4. Upton, *Another City*; Mauro, *Art of Americanization*.

5. Examples of historians' published works that address material culture and the Civil War include Cashin, "Trophies of War"; DeGruccio, "Letting the War Slip through Our Hands: Material Culture and the Weakness of Words in the Civil War Era," in Berry, *Weirding the War*, 15–35; Beilein, "The Guerrilla Shirt"; Byrd, "Loot, Occupy, and Re-envision: Material Culture of the South Carolina Plantation," and Knowles, "No Cotton in the Kingdom: Textiles in the Civil War South," both in *The Civil War and the Material Culture*, 57–86, 87–109; Shaw and Bassett, *Homefront and Battlefield*; Luskey and Phillips, "Material Culture"; Cashin, *War Matters*; Cashin, *War Stuff*; Phillips, *Looming Civil War*; Broomall, *Private Confederacies*; Cashin, ed. special issue, *Ohio Valley History* 22, no. 4; and Cox, *Fabric of Civil War Society*.

6. Consider, for instance, Leora Auslander's discussion of the role of clothing in the English, American, and French Revolutions, in *Cultural Revolutions.*

7. Studies of military-civilian relations have helped to bridge the division between military and social history. Focusing on the conflicts between soldiers and the people who lived in the path of the armies, these studies have been driven in part by the question of whether or not the Civil War was a "total war" in terms of destruction. At the heart of these studies, most of which focus on either Sherman's campaigns of 1864 and 1865 or guerrilla warfare, is an attempt to understand civilian resistance and to assess how successful Sherman's strategy was at demoralizing Southerners. In this context, historians have considered the motivations behind Union policies toward civilians, generals' orders, and soldiers' willingness, or refusal, to obey them. See Royster, *Destructive War*; Grimsley, *Hard Hand of War*; Bailey, *War and Ruin*; Neely, "Total War?"; and Ramold, *Baring the Iron Hand.*

8. In 1989, Maris Vinovksis argued that social historians had neglected the Civil War as a topic of study, as evidenced by how little was known about everyday life during the war. At that time, the most extensive studies of common soldiers remained Bell Wiley's *The Life of Johnny Reb: The Common Solider of the Confederacy* and *The Life of Billy Yank: The Common Soldier of the Union*, published in the 1940s and 50s. Social historians have suggested that a focus on battles has skewed our understanding of the far-reaching consequences of war. However, military historians have countered with the argument that an overwhelming focus on the home front has taken the "war" out of war. See Vinovskis, "Have Social Historians Lost?"; Vinovskis, *Toward a Social History*; and Faust, "Civil War Home Front."

9. See, for instance: Bensel, *Yankee Leviathan*; and Balogh, *Government Out of Sight.* Some historians have focused on the relationship between the Civil War, Reconstruction, and changes to the US Constitution, especially the three constitutional amendments adopted between 1865 and 1870. Among these works are Belz, *Reconstructing the Union*; Hyman, *More Perfect Union*; Benedict, *Compromise of Principle*; Paludan, *A Covenant with Death*; Nelson, *Fourteenth Amendment*; Stanley, *From Bondage to Contract*; Vorenberg, *Final Freedom*; Tsesis, *Thirteenth Amendment and American Freedom*; and Hamilton, *Limits of Sovereignty.* For studies of the Confederacy and nation, see Rable, *Civil Wars*; Freehling, *South vs. the South*; Gordon and Inscoe, *Inside the Confederate Nation*; and McCurry, *Confederate Reckoning.*

10. Haulman, *Politics of Fashion*, 7.

11. Orpheus T. Lanphear cited in Rockman, *Plantation Goods*, 9–10.

12. Bederman, *Manliness and Civilization*, 7; Foote, *Gentlemen and the Roughs*, 4.

13. Glymph, *Women's Fight*, 4.

14. I use fashion in terms of both changes in dress trends and as a concept—what Kate Haulman has described as "a shape-shifting vessel of an idea that people fill up with various meanings depending on time, place and circumstance." Haulman, *Politics of Fashion*, 3.

15. For more on the rise of the lithograph, see Griffiths, *Prints and Printmaking.*

16. For more on the expansion of markets and railroads, see Cronon, *Nature's Metropolis.*

17. In the early 1860s, despite the onset of war, American fashion writers continued to report on the latest styles in France and England. Wide dresses supported by hoops remained *la mode*, though this style was increasingly difficult for Southern women to maintain when hoops were broken and unable to be replaced as a result of blockades that prevented con-

sumer goods from reaching many areas of the South. Fischer, *Pantaloons and Power*, 17. For more on *Godey's Lady's Book*, see Winkler, "Influence of Godey's 'Lady's Book.'"

18. Zakim, *Ready Made Democracy*; Kuchta, *Three-Piece Suit*.

19. Severa, *Dressed for the Photographer*, 84; Fischer, *Pantaloons and Power*, 22.

20. For more on Civil War–era photography see Fox-Amato, *Exposing Slavery*; Rosenheim, *Photography*; and Zeller, *Blue and Gray*.

21. "Dawn's Early Light: The First Fifty Years of American Photography," online exhibit, Carl A. Kroch Library, Cornell University, accessed August 2015, http://rmc.library.cornell.edu/DawnsEarlyLight/exhibition/celebculture/index.html.

The receipt of a friend's carte de visite prompted William Lloyd Garrison to say, "How wonderful is the photographic art! What a world of enjoyment and pleasure it has been opened! How it will help to cement friendship, quicken recollection, inspire esteem, and solace bereavement! Nature, assisted by art, reproducing herself in all her varied manifestations!" William Lloyd Garrison to Esteemed Friend, July 24, 1865, African American History Collection, box 3, William Clements Library, University of Michigan–Ann Arbor.

22. Quoted in Zakim, *Ready Made Democracy*, 2. Original quote from an 1853 circular addressing appropriate attire for American diplomats: "Extract from circular, dated Department of State, June 1, 1853," 36th Cong., 1st Sess., Exec. Doc. No. 31.

23. Zakim, *Ready Made Democracy*, 2.

24. For detailed histories of the development of textile manufacturing and clothing production in the United States, see Walsh, "Democratization of Fashion"; Dublin, *Women at Work*; Malone, *Waterpower in Lowell*; and Eaton, *Amoskeag Manufacturing Company*.

25. An increasingly scientific approach to dyeing and finishing cloth occurred over the course of the eighteenth and nineteenth centuries. See, for instance, Berthollet and Berthollet, *Art of Dyeing and Bleaching*; Napier, *Chemistry Applied to Dyeing*; and Love, *Art of Cleaning*.

26. The ready-to-wear clothing industry initially focused on the production of men's clothing and simpler garments for women. The more complicated construction of women's clothing, particularly high fashion, required handwork until near the turn of the twentieth century.

27. For a studies of enslaved people and clothing in the prewar South, see Knowles, "Fashioning Slavery"; and Foster, "*New Raiments of Self.*"

28. For more on the role of the sewing machine, see Breakwell, "Nation in Extremity."

29. Edwards, *Only the Clothes on Her Back*, 5–7.

30. Strasser, *Waste and Want*, 39.

31. For more on pawning, see Woloson, *In Hock*; and Tebutt, *Making Ends Meet*.

32. Nearly all of a bankrupt person's property was passed to a court-appointed assignee; only "necessary clothing," along with bedding, tools, and kitchen implements, was exempted. In Connecticut, for instance, bankrupts were permitted to retain clothing, bedding, and tools worth up to $500 in 1849 and $700 in 1860. Coleman, *Debtors and Creditors*, 77; Balleisen, *Navigating Failure*, 120. See also Warren, *Bankruptcy in United States History*; and Mann, *Republic of Debtors*.

33. With the increasingly widespread use of manufactured cotton cloth, the amount of household laundry increased. Cotton, unlike silk and wool, was easily washed in water. Cowan, *More Work for Mother*, 65; Strasser, *Waste and Want*, 81.

34. Walsh, *Economical Housekeeper*, 407–8.

35. Cowan, *More Work for Mother*, 65.

36. Glymph, *Out of the House*, 71–72.

37. During the Civil War, the high price of rags created financial difficulty for a number of paper manufacturers. While some mills suspended operations, others responded to the problem by forming new partnerships. Some manufacturers began to use scrap paper more extensively in order to continue production. By 1866, the price of linen and cotton rags had quadrupled due to wartime demand for all forms of cloth, resulting in the importation of rags from Europe to sustain paper production. By 1880, wood pulp had become the primary material for newspaper production. Zimring, *Cash for Your Trash*, 20, 23; Valente, *Rag Paper Manufacture*, 107.

38. Historians have primarily used textiles and clothing as a *lens* through which to explore other questions, rather than as an object of analysis. While works by Michael Zakim, Kate Haulman, and Adam Mendelsohn take clothing into the political realm, most studies involving clothing focus on production, labor relations and organization, technological development, or business. As such, clothing itself appears as an abstract idea. The material objects are typically not examined, in terms of either their tactile qualities or their use. In most studies, in other words, the fabric, style, trimmings, and often the circumstances of the consumption of clothing have little bearing on the analysis. Zakim, *Ready Made Democracy*; Haulman, *Politics of Fashion*; Mendelsohn, *Rag Race*.

39. Joanna Cohen defines emotional value as the ability of an object to constitute a personal identity. Cohen, "Reckoning with the Riots," 69.

40. A number of scholars have likened clothing's communicative abilities to a form of language, a suggestion that has important theoretical implications. I do not refer to clothing in this way, because it suggests a close affinity between the types of information that clothing and textual sources communicate. For more on the debate about clothing as language, see Baumgarten, *What Clothes Reveal*; McCracken, *Culture and Consumption*, chap. 4; and Lurie, *Language of Clothes*.

41. I borrow this definition from Ann Jones and Peter Stallybrass, who, in their study of the Renaissance, define clothing as "all that is worn, whether shoes or doublet or armor or ring." Jones and Stallybrass, *Renaissance Clothing*, 3.

42. A military uniform, for instance, does not simply identify an officer's rank—its insignia actively helps to create that rank by asserting their position of authority in a visible, material way, commanding the deference of lower-ranking soldiers. Auslander, "Beyond Words," 1017.

43. "Material culture," Henry Glassie argues, "records human intrusion in the environment." People alter nature to their liking—shaping, reshaping, and arranging things throughout their lives. Underlying this approach is the theoretical assertion that objects are constantly being culturally redefined; as objects move in time, space, cultural circumstance, and form of representation, their meanings and ability to act shift. This is not to say that objects' actions are always a causal force, or that they do things instead of human actors. Glassie, *Material Culture*, 1; Woodward, *Understanding Material Culture*, 103; Latour, *Reassembling the Social*, 72, 80.

44. Igor Koptyoff has argued that objects go through a process of commodification-decommodification-recommodification. He posits that these transformations can be lik-

ened to a type of biography, suggesting that things have social lives. This trajectory of an object's existence can be further elaborated to include advertisement, display, sale, gift, loan, and legacy. Neil Harris has also discussed architecture using the language of "life stages," drawing distinctions between conception and birth, growth and maturity, and aging and death. Auslander, *Taste and Power*, 26; Woodward, *Understanding Material Culture*, 103–4; Kopytoff, "Cultural Biography of Things"; Harris, *Building Lives*, 4. See also Appadurai, "Introduction," in *Social Life of Things*, 3–63; and Prown, "Mind in Matter."

45. This project builds on object-based studies of clothing that analyze details like construction and materials, and whose analysis often begins and ends with a single object; histories of fashion in the United States, Britain, and Europe that focus on changing modes of dress and their cultural implications; and an emerging scholarship on social and political histories of dress. These studies provide an important point of departure for thinking about the influence of fashion changes, transformations in production methods, the organization of labor, and the theoretical implications of clothing. However, most of these studies are ultimately either more concerned with the connoisseurship of a particular group of objects (in the case of object studies) or with what clothing *reflects* about the world, rather than how it *acts* upon people and society. Scholars of Britain and Europe have engaged with the study of clothing and fashion to a greater degree than have those who study the United States. See, for instance, Crowston, *Fabricating Women*; Jones, *Sexing La Mode*; Jones and Stallybrass, *Renaissance Clothing*; Kuchta, *Three-Piece Suit*; Breward, *Hidden Consumer*; Roberts, "Samson and Delilah Revisited"; and Matlock, "Masquerading Women, Pathologized Men."

Part I

1. Kennedy Palmer, US Civil War Service Records, M324, NARA.

2. *Catalogue of the Confederate Museum* (1905), 87.

Chapter One

1. William Willoughby to Nancy Willoughby, July 5, 1863, William Willoughby Papers, AAS.

2. W. Willoughby to N. Willoughby, November 16, 1863, Willoughby Papers, AAS.

3. Stamper and Condra, *Clothing through American History*, 72; Fine, *World of Consumption*, 98.

4. For example, Robert E. Lee, Ulysses S. Grant, Braxton Bragg, Henry Halleck, Joseph Hooker, George B. McClellan, George Sykes, William T. Sherman, P. T. G. Beauregard, A. P. Hill, Thomas J. Jackson, James Longstreet, and George Pickett reemerged on the national stage to lead the US and Confederate armies during the Civil War. Newell, *Regular Army*, 21.

5. On the American militia, see Rowe, *Bulwark of the Republic*.

6. Newell, *Regular Army*, 8.

7. United States Army regulations of 1858–60 established the uniform that defined the Union soldier of the regular army—sky blue trousers, deep blue frock coats, blue woolen sack coats, and forage caps. Prior to the Civil War, as Frederick Adolphus has observed, state militias

wore cadet gray, a light shade of bluish-gray, which came to symbolize the sovereign states, in contrast to the dark blue of the federal government. This association with the state rather than the national government contributed to the Confederacy's adoption of gray as its official uniform color. Confederate States of America War Department, *Uniform and Dress*; Cole, "Survey of U.S. Army Uniforms," 5, 11, 22; and Frederick Adolphus, "Basics about Confederate Uniforms," Adolphus Confederate Uniforms weblog, accessed June 21, 2016, http://adolphusconfederateuniforms.com/basics-of-confederate-uniforms.html.

8. Turner Ashby to Richard H. Horner, December 5, 1860, VMHC.

9. This was a long-standing tradition in the American military with roots dating back to the Revolutionary War in which officers—who tended to be from wealthier families—supplied their uniforms at a time when the fledgling nation was cash strapped. This tradition expanded in the nineteenth century, as both regular army officers and militias purchased their own uniforms. In the modern United States military, uniform regulations are issued and officers are required to supply themselves with uniforms matching those regulations. "American Revolution Impact on Clothing," in Doering, *Pre-colonial Times*, 22; Emerson, *Encyclopedia*, 6–7.

10. General Orders No. 59, Dept. of the Missouri, March 10, 1862, RG 92, box 1170, NARA.

11. Lieber, "General Order No. 100," Article 64.

12. The range in uniforms is not surprising given that, historically, a distinction existed between the appearance of regular and volunteer American soldiers. As in the case of the Mexican-American War, this difference was due, in part, to the federal government's repeated failure to plan for wartime supply. Such repeated failures likely contributed to the tendency of uniforms to follow civilian styles. Winders, *Mr. Polk's Army*, 112.

13. According to Charles Newell, prior to the Civil War it took, on average, forty-four years for an officer to reach the rank of colonel in the artillery, thirty-seven years in the infantry, and twenty-one in the cavalry. Newell, *Regular Army*, 49.

14. Eppes, July 28, 1861, in *Through Some Eventful Years*, 157.

15. "Insignia of Rank in the Federal Army," *Wisconsin Daily Patriot*, October 1, 1861.

16. The copy from which sleeve insignia and shoulder straps have been removed is in the holdings of the American Antiquarian Society, Worcester, MA. The complexity of the materiality of brass manhood increased in 1863, when the Union army introduced "Corps Badges" that were worn on caps or the left breast of a coat. These badges served a practical purpose—the easy identification of stragglers and deserters—but they also became a source of pride for soldiers. A chart provided information on the color and symbol combinations and their corresponding divisions and corps. Cole, "Survey of U.S. Army Uniforms," 21.

17. "Insignia of Rank, and Regulation Swords of the United States Army," *Philadelphia Inquirer*, September 14, 1861; "How to Read Shoulder Straps," *Fincher's Trades Review*, October 3, 1863.

18. "Automaton Regiment" (1863), AAS.

19. For more on mid-nineteenth-century understanding of metal qualities, see Holland, *Treatise*.

20. Produced in a time-intensive process, gold thread was made by coating a solid rod of silver with numerous layers of thin gold leaf. The rod was then drawn through a series of graduated circles in a hot steel plate to reduce its diameter to the size of fine wire. This wire

was flattened between rollers and wrapped around threads of yellow silk, giving the threads a coil-like appearance. Bigelow, *Elements of Technology*, 401; "Gold Embroideries and Lace," *Godey's Lady's Book and Magazine*, July–December 1864, 189.

21. Jonathan F. Plimpton Collection of Civil War Buttons and Insignia, MHS.

22. As historian Kate Haulman has shown, fashion became ideologically feminized in the eighteenth century. This was based on three related premises: "First, [that] the consumption of fashionable goods was women's activity; second, that attention to dress and display was not merely an observable but an inherently female preoccupation due to women's natural vanity and insatiable appetite; and, finally, that the very concept 'fashion' possessed symbolically 'feminine' traits such as unpredictability and fickleness." Yet, as Haulman notes, there was a divide between theory and practice. Haulman, *Politics of Fashion*, 49.

The importance of appearance to men is routinely dismissed or underestimated. In their recent survey of clothing in American history, for instance, Anita Stamper and Jill Condra have suggested that the "male relationship with fashionable dress was . . . somewhat detached." Stamper and Condra, *Clothing through American History*, 155.

23. Henry Lee Higginson to Mary Lee Higginson Blake, May 20, 1862, reprinted in Perry, *Life and Letters of Henry Lee Higginson*, 160.

24. Josiah Marshall Favill, August 25, 1862, in *Diary of a Young Officer*, 182.

25. "Diary of Malvina Sarah Black Waring," March 15, 1864, in Taylor and Conner, *South Carolina Women*, 1: 282.

26. Kate Stone, March 9, 1862, in Anderson, *Brokenburn*, 99.

27. Eppes, July 28, 1861, in *Through Some Eventful Years*, 157.

28. Ella Rodman, "Capt. Torwood's Experience," *Peterson's Magazine*, February 1864, 144.

29. Union playing cards, American Card Company, c. 1862, AAS.

30. Douglass, *Addresses*, 7.

31. Frederick Douglass, in Rice, *Reminiscences of Abraham Lincoln*, 317.

32. David Hunter was commander of the Department of the South. He began recruiting enslaved men for a regiment of Black troops in April and May 1862, later issuing Order No. 11, which declared freedom for slaves in South Carolina, Georgia, and Florida. Lincoln, however, declared Hunter's proclamation void. Hunter to Stanton, quoted in Hargrove, *Black Union Soldiers*, 38–39; Tomblin, *Bluejackets and Contrabands*, xx.

33. L. Thomas to Stanton, May 20, 1863, in United States War Department, *War of the Rebellion*, ser. 3, vol. 3, 214.

34. Douglass, in *Reminiscences of Abraham Lincoln*, 317.

35. Of USCT soldiers, 19 percent were recruited in Northern states, 24 percent in border states, and 57 percent in the Confederate states. Ultimately, formerly enslaved men made up the majority of the 180,000 African American men who served in the Union army. John David Smith, "Let Us All Be Grateful We Have Colored Troops Who Will Fight," in Smith, *Black Soldiers in Blue*, 8.

36. Robert Dale Owen to Abraham Lincoln, August 5, 1863, Abraham Lincoln Papers, Library of Congress, Washington, DC.

37. Cowden, *Brief Sketch*, 45.

38. Jacob Bruner to Martha J. Bruner, April 28, 1863, Bruner Letters, Ohio Historical Society, Columbus.

39. The Civil War coincided with both the rapid expansion of the press and improvements in photographic technology, allowing for visual and textual representations of wartime experiences to be voraciously consumed by the American public, especially in the North. Slaves' "transformations" from chattels to soldiers were among the many images circulated in the popular press, as cartes de visite, and in a range of ephemeral paper objects. Richards, "U.S. Civil War Print Culture," 349–50. For more on the depiction of African Americans during wartime, see Fox-Amato, *Exposing Slavery,* 160–214; and Fahs, *Imagined Civil War,* 163–69.

40. Weicksel, "Quand l'uniforme fait l'homme libre," 141–42; Smith, "Let Us All Be Grateful," 7.

41. Photography and prints drew upon a broader visual language and were important means of disseminating both abolitionist and Black enlistment messages. Mary Niall Mitchell has argued that these images were effective as propaganda precisely because of their apparent realism rendered through the daguerreotype. They expressed both the "perceived reality" of a sitter's improved appearance and "the rhetoric of progress inherent in the spectacle of transformation." In the words of an editor at the *New York Independent* in regard to a photograph of a former slave, such an image "tells the story in a way that even Mrs. Stowe cannot approach, because it tells the story to the eye." Mitchell, *Raising Freedom's Child,* 120; quoted in Jackson, *Violence, Visual Culture,* 14.

42. Here, the writer refers to Confederates' use of enslaved men to build fortifications and perform other military tasks. Wilson, *Black Phalanx,* 109.

43. James A. Seddon to Gen. G. T. Beauregard, November 30, 1862, reprinted in Berlin et al., *Freedom,* 57.

44. Johnson deposition, July 11, 1864, in Berlin et al., *Freedom,* 589.

45. Rollin, *Life and Public Services,* 9.

46. "Assault on Corporal Ross," *Philadelphia Inquirer,* June 6, 1863.

47. A. T. Augusta, "The Late Outrage Upon Surgeon Augusta, in Baltimore," *Christian Recorder,* May 30, 1863, 1.

48. Wilson, *Black Phalanx,* 132.

49. For an example of stripping as military punishment see Wilder, *Practicing Medicine,* 75.

50. General Orders No. 20, Army of the Ohio, June 5, 1862, RG 92, box 356, NARA; Charles H. Van Wyck, "Government Contracts," *Congressional Globe,* February 7, 1862, 710; "Song of the Shoddy," *Vanity Fair,* September 21, 1861, 142; Robert Fairfax to Nim, October 31, 1861, Fairfax Family of Alexandria, VA, Letters, 1861–1899, Collection of the Confederate Memorial Literary Society (hereafter CMLS), VMHC; Jones, *Rebel War Clerk's Diary,* 188. For a detailed analysis of wartime contracting see Wilson, *Business of Civil War.*

51. John Babb to Father, September 2, 1862, John D. Babb Family Papers, 1862–65, MSS 360, MARBL.

52. John Babb to Father, Mother, and Sister, October 3, 1862, Babb Family Papers, MARBL.

53. John Babb to Parents and Sister, October 20, 1862, Babb Family Papers, MARBL.

54. John Babb to Father, November 19, 1862, Babb Family Papers, MARBL.

55. Theodore Livingston to Father, June 19, 1864, Livingston Family of Madison County, FL, Papers, 1862–1865, Mss2 L7624 b 1–17, CMLS, VMHC.

56. Whereas white privates earned thirteen dollars per month *plus* an additional three dollars' clothing allowance, Black soldiers—even noncommissioned officers—received ten dollars, *minus* a three-dollar clothing allowance. If a Black soldier needed new shoes or pants, in other words, the cost was *deducted* from his monthly pay, leaving him with only seven dollars. White men could conceivably receive sixteen dollars in pay per month by foregoing their clothing allowance. John F. Marszalek, "Marching to Freedom: The U.S. Colored Troops," in Holzer and Gabbard, *Lincoln and Freedom*, 121.

57. *Revised United States Army Regulations of 1861*, 47.

58. Quoted in Matthews, *149th Pennsylvania Volunteer Infantry*, 50.

59. Berlin et al., *Freedom*, 657.

60. James S. Wadsworth, *Report to the Adjutant General, U.S. Army*, December 1863, MS Am 647, Houghton Library Special Collections, Harvard University.

61. James McFall to Sister Creak, November 21, 1864, McFall Letters, MARBL.

62. Cutters' manuals and tailors' guides provided detailed instructions on measuring, calculating, and cutting military clothing. Military cutting, Scott asserted, generally required several lessons, as there were "few good military tailors in our cities." Scott, *Cutter's Guide*, 11.

63. Shell Jacket worn by Henry Gansevoort, 1861, Acc. No. 53757, NMAH.

64. Ward, *Philadelphia Fashions & Tailors' Archetypes*, 3; Glencross, *True Guide to Practical Cutting*, 20–22.

65. Account book entry, November 27, 1863, Gruter and Gerecke Account Book, Petersburg, VA, VMHC.

66. James Helme Rickard, May 31, 1864, Civil War Letters, AAS.

67. James McFall to Lucretia McFall Anderson, November 14, 1864, McFall Letters, MARBL.

68. James McFall to Sister Creak, November 29, 1864, McFall Letters, MARBL.

69. W. McFall to Ma, December 11, 1862, McFall Letters, MARBL.

70. Zakim, *Ready-Made Democracy*, 92.

71. Seth Rogers in Higginson, *Letters of Major Seth Rogers*, 344.

72. Mason to Wife, December 3, 1864, Mason Family Papers, 1825–1902, Mss1 M3816 d, VMHC.

73. Washington, North Carolina, was occupied by Union soldiers beginning in 1862. George W. Bowen Diary, Southern Historical Collection, University of North Carolina at Chapel Hill.

74. In lieu of asking families for clothing, some men turned to an alternative source: sutlers, the civilian merchants who sold provisions to men in the field or in camp. Soldiers had a problematic relationship with sutlers. Many relied upon them for additional supplies, but they also worried about being cheated by "Sutlers and other *Sharks*." Charles F. Johnson, November 22, 1861, in Pelka, *Civil War Letters*, 113; James Helme Rickard, August 28, 1864, and September 5, 1864, Civil War Letters, AAS.

75. Robert Fairfax to Jeanie, October 23, 1861, Fairfax Letters, VMHC.

76. Mason to Wife, November 11, 1864, Mason Family Papers, 1825–1902, Mss1 M3816 d, VMHC.

77. Whites, "Forty Shirts and a Wagonload of Wheat."

78. Theodore Livingston to Father, June 19, 1864, Livingston Family Papers, VMHC.

79. W. Willoughby to N. Willoughby, July 8, 1862, Willoughby Papers, AAS.

80. W. Willoughby to N. Willoughby, August 24, 1862, Willoughby Papers, AAS.

81. W. Willoughby to N. Willoughby, August 9, 1864, Willoughby Papers, AAS. For a more complete account of Nancy and William Willoughby's business, see Weicksel, "'Make Up a Box to Send Me.'"

82. Beilein, "Guerrilla Shirt," 156.

83. Shirt, Edwin G. Booth, 0985.13.00580, ACWM.

84. Shirt, Luther Wright Jerrell, 0985.13.00494b, ACWM; Shirt, William Terry, 0985.13.00581, ACWM.

85. Shirt, Edward W. Crozier, 0985.07.00183, ACWM.

86. Shirt, Andrew Thomas Beam, 0985.10.00020, ACWM.

87. Beilein, "Guerrilla Shirt," 162.

88. Shirt, Confederate army, AF*1886(C), NMAH.

89. Mason to Wife, December 3, 1864, Mason Family Papers, VMHC.

90. J. H. Jones to M. G. Meigs, August 17, 1862, RG 92, entry 225, box 1170, NARA.

91. Portions of this section were previously published as "Armor, Manhood and the Politics of Mortality."

92. Linderman, *Embattled Courage*, 156–60.

93. Billings, *Hardtack and Coffee*, 275.

94. Walker, *Eighteenth Regiment, Conn. Volunteers*, 21.

95. "Attention, Soldiers!," *Columbian Register*, August 23, 1862, 3.

96. "Attention, Soldiers!"

97. "Attention, Soldiers!"

98. Johns, *Forty-Ninth Massachusetts Volunteers*, 53.

99. *Town of Wayland*, 436.

100. Rhodes, *All for the Union*, 112.

101. "Attention, Soldiers!"

102. "Attention, Soldiers!"

103. John T. Cheney to Mary, March 23, 1862, in *Illinois Artillery Officer's Civil War*, 24.

104. Thaaddeus Reynolds quoted in Dunkelman, *Brothers One and All*, 120.

105. William Vermillion to Dollie, quoted in Hess, *Rifle Musket*, 81.

106. *Charles Stokes and Co.'s Illustrated Almanac*, 26.

107. "Secret Steel Breastplate," *Scientific American* 5, no. 17 (October 26, 1861): 264.

108. Advertisement for "The Soldiers' Bullet Proof Vest," *Harper's Weekly*, March 15, 1862.

109. De Velling, *History of the Seventeenth Regiment*, 119.

110. "The Soldier's Bullet Proof Vest," *Philadelphia Inquirer*, March 14, 1862, 3.

111. Granville Stokes, "Hints to the Drafted," *Philadelphia Inquirer*, October 22, 1862, 5.

112. "The Soldier's Bullet-Proof Vest," *Frank Leslie's Illustrated Newspaper*, March 8, 1862, 252.

113. Moore, *Rebellion Record*, 5:232.

114. Sandage, *Born Losers*, 56.

115. Weicksel, "Quand l'uniforme fait l'homme libre," 143.

116. *Charles Stokes and Co.'s Illustrated Almanac*, 26.

117. "State Items," *Connecticut Courant*, November 30, 1862, 2.

118. Quoted in Heineman, *Civil War Dynasty*, 160.

119. Linderman, *Embattled Courage*, 135–38.

120. "Secret Steel Breastplate," *Scientific American* 5, no. 7 (October 26, 1861): 264.

121. Bartol, *Nation's Hour*, 20.

122. Sidney Willard cited in Bartol, *Nation's Hour*, 37.

123. Bartol, *Nation's Hour*, 20.

124. For more on the notion of the Good Death, see Faust, *This Republic of Suffering*, 3–31.

125. Fahs, *Imagined Civil War*, 10–11.

126. James McFall to Lucretia McFall Anderson, November 21, 1864, McFall Letters, MARBL.

127. J. McFall to L. McFall Anderson, December 21, 1864, McFall Letters, MARBL.

Chapter Two

1. James Roswell King transferred an interest in the Ivy Woolen Mills to Theophile Roche, a French national, believing that this would render the mill neutral and save it from destruction. *Roche vs. U.S.*, Case 466, in Petite, *"The Women Will Howl,"* 70.

2. Robert Kennedy to Darius Livermore, July 6, 1864, in Petite, *"The Women Will Howl,"* 79; Silas C. Stevens, July 7, 1864, in Hitt, *Charged with Treason*, 7.

3. W. T. Sherman to Garrard, July 7, 1864, in *War of the Rebellion*, ser. 1, vol. 38, pt. 5, 76–77.

4. References to women's work sewing army uniforms appear in nearly every scholarly work on women and the war, although there is no sustained study of these efforts. In the twentieth century, historians' questions were largely directed by Civil War–era women's own reminiscent interpretations of their involvement with clothing production. Women's work sewing uniforms has generally been viewed as expressions of patriotism and is firmly situated in what Drew Faust has described as a politics of sacrifice. However, such patriotic contributions of elite and middle-class women were only part of women's involvement with the much broader system of supply—one to which laboring women were central, and for whom necessity could easily overshadow patriotic fervor. Two notable exceptions include work by Judith Giesberg and Stephanie McCurry, both of whom address working-class and yeoman women. McCurry has offered another interpretive framework through which to understand women's wartime actions—a "politics of subsistence" firmly grounded in women's self-identification as soldiers' wives who believed themselves to be entitled to the support and protection of the government that their husbands, fathers, and brothers served. In the context of clothing we see at work both Faust's politics of sacrifice and McCurry's politics of subsistence. Faust, *Mothers of Invention*, 17; McCurry, *Confederate Reckoning*, 133–77.

For women's reminiscences of wartime work, see Brockett and Vaughan, *Woman's Work*; and Moore, *Women of the War*. Also see Faust, *Mothers of Invention*; McCurry, *Confederate Reckoning*; Leonard, *Yankee Women*; Silber, *Daughters of the Union*; and Giesberg, *Army at Home*.

5. The following studies of seamstresses also provide important departure points for thinking about the relationships between seamstresses, clothing, and broader social and cultural changes. Their focus, however, has been on labor. Clare Crowston's *Fabricating Women* is a notable exception in her attention to what clothing construction can tell us about the women who made garments. See also Foner, *Women and the American Labor*

Movement; Stansell, "Origins of the Sweatshop"; Gamber, *Female Economy*; and Walsh, "Democratization of Fashion."

6. McCurry, *Confederate Reckoning*, 141.

7. See, for instance, Whites and Long, *Occupied Women*; Frank, *Civilian War*; Campbell, *When Sherman Marched North*; and Grimsley, *Hard Hand of War*.

8. Portions of this chapter draw upon Weicksel, "Confederate Cultures of Military Clothing Production."

9. Wilson, *Business of Civil War*, 2.

10. Wilson, *Business of Civil War*, 5–6.

11. Newell and Shrader, *Of Duty Well and Faithfully Done*, 139, 143.

12. It is estimated that during the course of the war ten million pairs of pants and six million woolen blankets were supplied to the Union army. Newell and Shrader, *Of Duty Well and Faithfully Done*, 153; Wilson, *Business of Civil War*, 1.

13. Wilson, *Confederate Industry*, 99–100. Surviving uniforms made in Europe suggest limited importation to the North. See, for instance, a coat made by A. P. Rago in Portugal held in the Brooklyn Museum Costume Collection at the Metropolitan Museum of Art. The Confederate government, too, contracted with overseas suppliers. See Adolphus, *Imported Confederate Uniforms*; and Cox, *Fabric of Civil War Society*, 30–32.

14. For more on the Northern textile industry, see Rivard, *New Order of Things*.

15. Dunaway, *First American Frontier*, 151.

16. Histories of the Southern textile industry usually begin in the postwar era. But Southern textile production was not a postwar development. As Michelle Gillespie has accurately observed, "Historians tend to relegate the development of antebellum southern manufacturing to second-class status, insisting on the primacy of the cotton economy and plantation agriculture in their continual quest to explain the region's uniqueness." Gillespie, "Building Networks of Knowledge: Henry Merrell and Textile Manufacturing in the Antebellum South," in Delfino and Gillespie, *Technology, Innovation, and Southern Industrialization*, 97.

On the antebellum Southern textile industry, see Russel, *Economic Aspects of Southern Sectionalism*; Lander, *Textile Industry in Antebellum South Carolina*; Hearden, *Independence and Empire*; Glass, *Textile Industry in North Carolina*; and Evans, *Conquest of Labor*.

17. Dunaway, *First American Frontier*, 148.

18. Wilson, *Confederate Industry*, 102–3.

19. Originally from Windsor, Connecticut, Roswell King left New England for Georgia in 1788, where he eventually became the overseer of Major Pierce Butler's lucrative Sea Island cotton plantations. Leaving Butler's plantation under the oversight of his son, King moved to north Georgia, where he laid out plans for the mill town of Roswell, founding the Roswell Manufacturing Company along Vickery Creek in 1839 and ultimately leaving its management in the hands of his son, Barrington. A number of Southern mill villages were founded on paternalistic principles motivated by religious principles and a desire for social reform among poor whites, who made up the majority of mill employees. These villages were tied to particular manufacturing companies. Among these were the Prattville Manufacturing Company, in Prattville, Alabama (founded by Daniel Pratt); Henry Merrell's Clarke County, Arkansas, mills; and to a lesser extent, Roswell. Most of these towns were founded by New Englanders who had migrated south. Petite, *"The Women Will Howl,"* 9–12; Evans, *Conquest of Labor*, 74–75.

20. 1860 US Federal Census, Cobb County, Georgia, Ancestry.com. Henry Merrell, a New Yorker with textile manufacturing experience, was employed by Roswell. Merrell went on to form his own company and mill town in Arkansas.

21. The Kings were not alone in their efforts to hire people to expand their network of Northern and Southern connections. As Michelle Gillespie has explained, Northern mechanics and entrepreneurs who moved south in search of manufacturing opportunities were "critical bridges for the introduction of cotton manufacturing's attendant new technologies in the region." Gillespie, "Building Networks of Knowledge," 106.

22. Petite, *"The Women Will Howl,"* 23.

23. Galloway, *Dear Old Roswell*, 4.

24. Such transactions quickly came to an end with the outbreak of war. A few months later, King noted that the company had a large stock of yarn in Philadelphia but it could not be sold "until we have peace—this will cramp us very much." Barrington King to William Baker, February 22, 1861, Barrington King Letters, RHS; Barrington King to William Baker, May 4, 1861, Barrington King Letters, RHS.

25. Barrington King, letter, May 1861, Barrington King Letters, RHS.

26. Barrington King, undated letter (probably before September 1862), Barrington King Letters, RHS.

27. Kenner Garrard to William T. Sherman, July 6, 1864, *War of the Rebellion*, ser. 1, vol. 38, pt. 5, 68.

28. Shaw and Bassett, *Homefront & Battlefield*, 78.

29. Silber, *Daughters of the Union*, 18.

30. "Gov. Brown to the People of Georgia," *Macon Daily Telegraph*, May 23, 1861, 3.

31. "Editor, Plattsburgh Republican," *Plattsburgh Republican*, May 18, 1861, 2.

32. Mary Henderson cited in Glymph, *Women's Fight*, 136.

33. Livermore, *My Story of the War*, 138.

34. For a broader study of enslaved women's wartime work and experiences, see Glymph, *Out of the House*; and Testimony of Nancy Johnson, March 22, 1873, Southern Claims Commission, in Berlin et al., *Freedom*, 151.

35. In many instances, WPA interviewers recorded or imposed dialect upon the interviewees' recollections. Calvin Moye in Mellon, *Bullwhip Days*, 167.

36. Eppes, *Through Some Eventful Years*, 147.

37. Such erasure of enslaved women's work was common for many tasks. Glymph, *Out of the House*, 186.

38. This woman also implied that enslaved women's compulsory work on these drawers for Confederate soldiers was evidence of their support of their enslavers. She wrote, "The negroes were faithful and kind. They did not believe our troops would ever be beaten." Taylor and Conner, *South Carolina Women*, 1: 79.

39. Susan Bradford Eppes was the daughter of Dr. Edward Bradford, owner of the Pine Hill plantation near Tallahassee. According to the 1850 census, Bradford enslaved over 100 people. The family lost their wealth as a result of the war. Bradford married Nicholas Ware Eppes in 1866 at the age of twenty. After her husband was murdered in 1904, Eppes lost her home. A member of the United Daughters of the Confederacy, she began to write her memoirs at the age of seventy-nine. Her books included *The Negro in the Old South*, *Through Some*

Eventful Years, and *Verses from Florida*. As Tracey Revels has noted, "all were heavily soaked in moonlight and magnolias." Revels, *Grander in Her Daughters*, 142.

40. Eppes, *Through Some Eventful Years*, 179; Eppes, *Negro of the Old South*, 108.

41. Glymph explains, "During slavery, they [white women] had presided over the production of jams, and their grammatical construction of this work, 'made jam today,' had erased the labor of bondswomen on whom the actual making had devolved." Glymph, *Out of the House*, 186.

42. Eppes, *Through Some Eventful Years*, 179.

43. Glymph, *Women's Fight*, 136.

44. Glymph, *Women's Fight*, 137.

45. Louisa McCord Smythe, "Recollections of Louisa McCord Smythe," 47, Louisa McCord Smythe Papers, 1862–c. 1920 (1209.03.02.05), SCHS.

46. Jane Weaver, "How to Transfer Patterns," *Peterson's Magazine*, February 1861, 174.

47. John J. Hinchman and Company, "Pattern for Army Mittens" (New York, c. 1861–65).

48. "Hospital Slippers for the Sick and Wounded Soldiers of the Union" (Philadelphia, 1861).

49. Shaw and Bassett, *Homefront & Battlefield*, 83.

50. "Hospital Slippers," *Peterson's Magazine*, February 1862, 172.

51. The rate was not to exceed that of "similar materials purchased by the 'Department' and the quantity allowed for each garment shall be the same as used in our Manufacturing Bureau." S. S. Glover, "Circular: To the Soldiers' Aid Societies of S.C.," *Camden (SC) Confederate*, March 28, 1862, 4.

52. Henry T. Clark, "A Good Example," *Fayetteville (GA) Observer*, August 19, 1861, 1.

53. S. S. Glover, "Circular: To the Soldiers' Aid Societies of S.C." *Camden (SC) Confederate*, February 21, 1862, 4.

54. "Gov. Brown to the People of Georgia."

55. Mrs. Sarah T. Bugg to Joseph E. Brown, September 9, 1861, Joseph Emerson Brown Governor's Incoming Correspondence, GSA.

56. Julia M. Fisher to Joseph E. Brown, October 6, 1862, Joseph Emerson Brown Governor's Incoming Correspondence, GSA.

57. US Sanitary Commission, Circular No. 54, October 22, 1862 (New York, 1862), 1.

58. Clark, "A Good Example."

59. Diary of Sarah Rousseau Espy, August 27, 1861, Alabama Department of Archives and History, Montgomery, accessed June 28, 2025, https://digital.archives.alabama.gov/digital/collection/voices/id/15912/rec/2.

60. The US Army's clothing allowance also included a fatigue forage cap, a hat with trimmings, pompon, and an eagle and ring. *Revised United States Army Regulations of 1861*, 170; *Regulations of the Army of the Confederate States*, 108.

61. Jones, *Confederate Odyssey*, 359.

62. Ward, *Philadelphia Fashions & Tailors' Archetypes*, 3.

63. Wilson, *Confederate Industry*, 99–100.

64. Wilson, *Business of Civil War*, 86.

65. For studies of women sewing within the home, see Burman, *Culture of Sewing*; and Boydston, *Home and Work*.

66. Wilson, *Business of Civil War*, 5.

67. In operation since 1799, the Schuylkill Arsenal was originally part of the Commissary General of Purchases, which was subsumed by the Quartermaster's Department in 1842 as it took responsibility for procuring uniforms, boots, and other equipage for the regular army. Wilson, *Business of Civil War*, 5.

68. For more on depot systems, see Wilson, *Confederate Industry*; and Wilson, *Business of Civil War*.

69. For more on the postwar interactions between white Southern women who sewed and African American women, see Glymph, *Out of the House*.

70. Wilson, *Business of Civil War*, 84.

71. Giesberg, *Army at Home*, 73.

72. Wilson, *Business of Civil War*, 86.

73. For clarity, the letter reads, "My friend and me have gone out to the arsenal for employment but we have not got it. I think it is time now that there was something done for the suffering soldiers' wives at home. It is some time since our husbands were paid off and we have not sometimes anything to eat." Mary Morris and Elizabeth Moore to Edwin Stanton, March 23, 1863, Records of the Quartermaster General, RG 92, box 1004, NARA.

74. The clerk noted on the front of the letter that it was to be "referred to the quartermaster general to report how many women are employed in the within named arsenal how many wives of soldiers, and what especial reason exists why this woman should not be employed. By order of the secretary of war." Mary Morris and Elizabeth Moore to Edwin Stanton, March 23, 1863.

75. "Who Pockets the Difference?," *Fincher's Trades Review*, September 5, 1863, 54.

76. "Philadelphia Seamstresses: Meeting of Women Employed in the U.S. Arsenal," *Fincher's Trades Review*, August 8, 1863, 38.

77. Giesberg, *Army at Home*, 137–38.

78. "Philadelphia Seamstress: Meeting of Women Employed in the US Arsenal," *Fincher's Trades Review*, August 8, 1863, 38.

79. Historian Judith Giesberg has emphasized the role of the Protestant Union League's scrutiny of working-class, predominantly Irish Catholic, women's loyalties in the hiring practices of the Schuylkill Arsenal. Giesberg, *Army at Home*, 139.

80. Taylor et al., eds., *South Carolina Women in the Confederacy*, 79.

81. For studies addressing the Southern Claims Commission, see Lee, *Claiming the Union*; Penningroth, *Claims of Kinfolk*; and Klingberg, *Southern Claims Commission*.

82. Martha Ledbetter Claim, List of "Standing Interrogatories," Southern Claims Commission Records, 1871–73, M1470, NARA, Fold3 Database.

83. Lockley, in *Neither Lady Nor Slave*, 113.

84. Elizabeth W. Grubb Claim, Fulton County, Georgia, Southern Claims Commission Records; 1860 US Federal Census, Atlanta Ward 5, Fulton County, Georgia, Ancestry .com.

85. Lusana Muselwhite Claim, Cobb County, Georgia, Southern Claims Commission Records.

86. Sarah S. Baldwin, Cobb County, Georgia, Barred and Disallowed Claims, Southern Claims Commission Records.

87. Carrie Hambrick, DeKalb County, Georgia, Southern Claims Commission Records.

88. Bailey, *Private Chapter of the War*.

89. George Bailey, Testimony on behalf of Mrs. Carrie Hambrick, Decatur, Georgia, Southern Claims Commission Records.

90. Stoker, *Grand Design*, 36.

91. For more on the destruction of railroads, see Glatthaar, *General Lee's Army*, 137.

92. Lieber, "General Order No. 100." For an in-depth study of the Lieber Code, see Witt, *Lincoln's Code*.

93. "Destruction of Rebel Cotton Factories," *Daily National Intelligencer* (Washington, DC), July 27, 1864, 2.

94. "Destruction of Rebel Cotton Factories."

95. Conyngham, *Sherman's March*, 145.

96. W. T. Sherman to H. W. Halleck, July 9, 1864, in *War of the Rebellion*, ser. 1, vol. 38, pt. 5, 92.

97. Bates to Parents, July 19, 1864, Bates Collection, section 7, folder 2, VMHC.

98. "From the South," *Richmond Examiner*, August 9, 1864, reprinted in *Crisis* (Columbus, OH), August 31, 1864.

99. Sherman to Halleck, July 9, 1864.

100. W. T. Sherman to Gen. Webster, July 9, 1864, in *War of the Rebellion*, ser. 1, vol. 38, pt. 5, 92–93.

101. W. T. Sherman to Garrard, July 7, 1864, *War of the Rebellion*, ser. 1, vol. 38, pt. 5, 77. General George Thomas reported that "the Roswell Hands, 400 or 500 in number, have arrived at Marietta. The most of them are women. I can only order them transportation to Nashville where it seems hard to turn them adrift." "What," he asked, "had best be done with them?" Sherman replied, "I have ordered General Webster in Nashville to dispose of them. They will be sent to Indiana." Gen. George Thomas to W. T. Sherman, *War of the Rebellion*, ser. 1, vol. 38, pt. 5, 104; W. T. Sherman to Gen. George Thomas, *War of the Rebellion*, ser. 1, vol. 38, pt. 5, 104.

102. Not all of the women appear to have been sent north—at least a few were put to work in support of the Union. General Dodge purportedly told the Union surgeon in charge of hospitals in Marietta "to hire as many of these women as could, as nurses, with pay, rations, etc., allowed such, by the Army regulations." James Snell, quoted in Hitt, *Charged with Treason*, 57.

103. Andrew Johnson to George H. Thomas, July 29, 1864, in *War of the Rebellion*, ser. 1, vol. 39, pt. 2, 210.

104. "The War upon Women," *Daily Constitutional Union* (Washington, DC), July 25, 1864, 2.

105. "The War upon Women," *Macon Daily Telegraph*, August 12, 1864, 2.

106. "More War upon Women," *New York Commercial Advertiser*, July 21, 1864, 2.

107. Henry G. Stratton to Sister, July 9, 1864, in Hitt, *Charged with Treason*, 41.

108. Hitt, *Charged with Treason*, 74.

109. Hitt, *Charged with Treason*, 121.

110. *Daily Ledger* (New Albany, IN), December 29, 1864, in Petite, *"The Women Will Howl,"* 129.

Part II

1. 1860 US Federal Census, New Bethlehem Borough, Clarion County, PA, accessed June 16, 2023, Ancestry.com.

2. "Clearspring Still Ahead," *Hagerstown Herald of Freedom & Torch Light*, May 29, 1861.

Chapter Three

1. For more on advertising and marketing commercialized identities, see Kreiser, *Marketing the Blue and Gray*, 21–22.

2. Haulman, *Politics of Fashion*, 6.

3. McDonnell, *Performing Disunion*, 120.

4. William Broun to Edwin Broun, Charlottesville, VA, November 16, 1860, Broun Family Civil War Letters, 1860–1864, Valdosta State University Archives and Special Collections, Valdosta, Georgia.

5. "About the Southern Cockades," *Jeffersonian Democrat* (Chardon, OH), January 4, 1861, 1.

6. "The Cockades," *Evening Star* (Washington, DC), December 19, 1863, 3.

7. Cockade, 1860, Cat. No. 0985.10.00224, ACWM; Secession cockade, c. 1862, Tennessee State Library & Archives, Gerald Branch Howard Papers, accessed April 3, 2023, https://digital.mtsu.edu/digital/collection/shades/id/77/rec/1.

8. "Editor's Easy Chair (for August)," *Harper's New Monthly Magazine*, June–November 1861, 411.

9. Advertisement, *New York Daily Tribune*, April 23, 1861.

10. Advertisement, *Portland (ME) Advertiser*, January 11, 1861, 2.

11. "The Latest News," *Holmes County Republican* (Millersburg, OH), January 10, 1861, 1.

12. "Excitement in Baltimore," *Alleghenian* (Ebensburg, PA), April 18, 1861, 2.

13. "Editor's Easy Chair (for August)," 411.

14. Ladies' patent collars and cuffs, Lockwood Manufacturing Company, c. 1863, Library Company of Philadelphia.

15. Jane Stuart Woolsey, cited in Glymph, *Women's Fight*, 133.

16. "Dear Spectator," *Staunton (VA) Spectator and General Advertiser*, June 11, 1861, 1.

17. "A Female Rebel in Baltimore—An Everyday Scene," *Harper's Weekly*, September 7, 1861, 1.

18. Janney, *Burying the Dead*, 35–36.

19. Laura Lee, Diary entry, May 16, 1862, in Mahon, *Winchester Divided*, 35.

20. Cited in Ott, *Confederate Daughters*, 53.

21. Shaw and Bassett, *Homefront & Battlefield*, 178–79.

22. Silk handkerchiefs made by W. H. Tucker Kayess, London, Cat. nos. 0985.13.01633–01634, ACWM.

23. Dress fabric, Ribbons and Textiles Collection, McA10090.F, Library Company of Philadelphia.

24. Shirt, Edwin G. Booth, 0985.13.00580, ACWM.

25. Collins, *Threads of History*, 166; 1870 United States Federal Census, Edgar County, Illinois, Ancestry.com.

26. Parkinson, "Edgar County, Illinois," 79–85.

27. Child's Confederate artillery uniform, Acc. No. 0985.7.137, ACWM; Thomas "Tad" Lincoln Portrait, c. 1864, NARA.

28. Both objects are in the collection of the Confederate Museum, Charleston, South Carolina.

29. "Chitchat upon New York and Philadelphia Fashions for June," *Godey's Lady Book*, June 1861, 574.

30. For a study of Zouave military fashion see Harrison and Brown, *Zouave Theaters*.

31. Mrs. Sylvester Bleckley, "Recollections of the War," in Taylor and Conner, *South Carolina Women in the Confederacy*, 1:364.

32. Caroline Cowles Richards Clarke, May 1861, in Clarke, *Village Life in America*, 225.

33. Vivandières' dress was well known in America as a result of the popularity of Donizetti's opera *La Fille du Regiment*. One need not have attended the opera to encounter this image. For instance, a full-length illustration of Cora De Wilhorst as Marie from the opera was published in an 1857 issue of *Frank Leslie's Illustrated Newspaper*. Mary W. Blanchard, "The Manly New Woman," in Connor, *Off the Pedestal*, 139; Kagan and Hyslop, *Smithsonian Civil War*, 98; "Madame Cora De Wilhorst as 'The Daughter of the Regiment,'" *Frank Leslie's Illustrated Newspaper*, March 28, 1857, 264.

34. Cohen, *Luxurious Citizens*, 184.

35. Ulrich, *Age of Homespun*.

36. Frank, *Women in the American Civil War*, 1:333.

37. *Oxford English Dictionary*, "homespun," accessed May 16, 2016, https://www.oed.com/dictionary/homespun_adj?tab=etymology.

38. "Homespun," *Augusta Chronicle*, January 18, 1861.

39. Importantly, the company's advertisement noted that all of its stock was purchased "before the Tariff went into effect," and therefore his imported fabrics could be sold for less. John N. Kein & Company advertisement, *Macon Daily Telegraph*, April 9, 1861.

40. "Homespun," *Augusta Chronicle*; "Patronising Home Industry," *Daily Constitutionalist* (Augusta, GA), February 2, 1861.

41. "The exorbitant cost and scarcity of an array of household items, including fabrics, lace, ribbons, and stockings, forced women of all classes to revert to home manufacturing. Frank, *Women in the American Civil War*, 1:333.

42. "Homespun Party," *Augusta Chronicle*, April 3, 1861.

43. Ott, *Confederate Daughters*, 53.

44. "Homespun Party."

45. Auslander, *Cultural Revolutions*, 86.

46. Auslander, *Cultural Revolutions*, 87.

47. "Home Industry," *Daily Constitutionalist* (Augusta, GA), March 31, 1861.

48. Clayton, *Requiem for a Lost City*, 30–31.

49. Kate Cumming, January 11, 1864, in Cumming, *Journal of Hospital Life*, 121.

50. "Homespun Party," *Augusta Chronicle*, April 3, 1861.

51. In 1860, J. J. McIver enslaved forty-six people. 1860 US Federal Census Slave Schedules, Darlington, South Carolina, Ancestry.com.

52. A. C. Cooper, "Days That Are Dead," in *Our Women in the War*, 437.

53. Florida Saxon, "Unto the Bitter End," in *Our Women in the War*, 71.

54. Smith, *Sensing the Past*, 93.

55. Confederate dye refers to a range of natural dyes, including gray (myrtle bushes), blue (indigo), brown (oak bark, walnut hulls), red (poke berries), green (hickory, alum), yellow (cocklebur leaves), orange (sassafras), and black (sumac berries), among others. Cumming, *Journal of Hospital Life*, 171; Tortora and Johnson, *Fairchild Books Dictionary of Textiles*, 140.

56. C. T. Hinckley, "Dyeing," in *The Ladies' Companion*, vol. 7, ser. 2, 234; Napier, *Chemistry Applied to Dyeing*.

57. A mordant is a substance, usually an inorganic oxide, that combines with a dye or stain and thereby fixes it in a material.

58. Berthollet and Berthollet, *Elements of the Art of Dyeing*, 327–33. See also Love, *Art of Cleaning*.

59. As Parnell notes, calicos could also be glazed by hand with a hot iron, but with the invention of glazing machinery in the nineteenth century, the process was increasingly mechanized. Parnell, *Dyeing and Calico-Printing*, 111.

60. Cumming, *Journal of Hospital Life*, 171.

61. Cumming, *Journal of Hospital Life*, 81.

62. Saxon, *War Time Reminiscences*, 18–22.

63. A sleeve from Thomas's dress (Cat. no. 0985.13.01176) is in the collection of the American Civil War Museum. Napier, *Art of Dyeing*; and Napier, *Chemistry Applied to Dyeing*, 408.

64. Cumming, *Journal of Hospital Life*, 59.

65. "Removal," *Daily Picayune* (New Orleans, LA), August 7, 1861, 4.

66. For more on blockade running and economic policy in the Confederate States, see Andreas, *Smuggler Nation*.

67. Beatty, *Alamance*, 80.

68. Cotton production slowed during the war and blockades made it difficult to export or trade what was being produced. Furthermore, Southern textile mills were forced to divert their production to meet the needs of the army, leaving consumers with few options. By the end of the war, needles were so scarce in some areas that they were used as a form of currency. Gordon, "Textiles and Clothing," 41.

69. Beatty, *Alamance*, 80.

70. "Atlanta Markets," *Augusta (GA) Chronicle*, January 14, 1863.

71. She further asserted, "Extortion is carried on at a high rate," and feared "that we have not seen the worst." Julia Johnson Fisher, Diary, January 3, 1864, call no. 1757, Documenting the American South, University of North Carolina at Chapel Hill, http://docsouth.unc.edu/imls/fisherjulia/fisher.html.

72. Bensel, *Yankee Leviathan*, 223–24. As Bess Beatty writes of North Carolina, "A four-way struggle developed as the Confederate government, the North Carolina government, and the state's civilian population all claimed a share of the goods mill owners produced." Beatty, *Alamance*, 80.

73. These items included, at 20 per centum ad valorem: beads, bracelets, braids, curls or ringlets, composed of hair, "epaulettes, galloons, laces, knots, stars, tassels, tresses, and wings of gold or silver, or imitations thereof." At 15 per centum ad valorem: "articles of clothing or apparel, including hats, caps, gloves, shoes and boots of all kinds, worn by men, women or children, of whatever material composed, not otherwise provided for"; braces, suspenders, webbing, or other fabrics composed wholly or in part of Indian rubber, not otherwise provided for"; "buttons and button moulds of all kinds"; "caps, hats, muffs, and tippets, and all other manufactures of fur, or of which fur shall be a component part; caps, gloves, leggins, mits, socks, stockings, wove shirts and drawers, and all similar articles worn by men, women and children"; "cotton laces, cotton insertings, cotton trimming, laces, cotton laces and braids"; Delaines; items used for making hats and bonnets; materials for making shoes; manufactures of silk, wool, worsted, cotton, flax, hemp, bone, shell, horn, ivory, leather, velvet, angora, mohair; "needles of all kinds, for sewing, darning and knitting." At 10 per centum ad

valorem: precious stones and imitations set in gold or silver, or other metal. For a full list of imports affected by this act, see "An Act to Provide Revenue from Commodities Imported from Foreign Countries," May 21, 1861, in Matthews, *Statutes at Large*, 127–35.

74. Glymph, *Women's Fight*, 12

75. Glickman, "'Through the Medium of Their Pockets,'" 29–30.

76. Jefferson Davis to House of Representatives, December 20, 1864, in *War of the Rebellion*, ser. 4, vol. 3, 949.

77. Confederate States of America, "Act to Prohibit the Importation of Luxuries," February 6, 1864.

78. Cohen, *Luxurious Citizens*, 196.

79. Cohen, *Luxurious Citizens*, 200.

80. Cohen, *Luxurious Citizens*, 203–5.

81. Cong. Globe, "An Act to Provide for the Payment of Outstanding Treasury Notes, to Authorize a Loan, to Regulate and Fix the Duties on Imports, and for Other Purposes," or "Tariff of 1861 (Morrill Tariff)," 36th Cong., 2nd Sess. Ch. 68, March 2, 1861: 184–86; 191–92, accessed January 31, 2024, https://fraser.stlouisfed.org/title/5871?start_page=2.

82. Cong. Globe, "An Act to Provide Internal Revenue to Support the Government and to Pay Interest on the Public Debt," 37th Cong., 2nd Sess. Ch. 119, 1862: 465–66, accessed January 31, 2024, https://fraser.stlouisfed.org/title/revenue-act-1862–6137; Irwin, *Clashing over Commerce*, 212–13.

83. Cohen, *Luxurious Citizens*, 210.

84. For more on the free produce movement, see Holcomb, *Moral Commerce*.

85. *Women's Patriotic Association*, 6.

86. "The Ladies Non-Importation Association at Washington—Articles of Association," *Daily Age* (Philadelphia, PA), May 4, 1864, 2.

87. "The Latest News," *Daily Age* (Philadelphia, PA), May 4, 1864, 2.

88. Scranton, *Proprietary Capitalism*, 276.

89. *Women's Patriotic Association*, 10–15.

90. *Women's Patriotic Association*, 11.

91. Daly, *Diary of a Union Lady*, 297.

92. *Women's Patriotic Association*, 17.

93. Daly, *Diary of a Union Lady*, 306.

94. "Ladies' Covenant," *Deseret News*, May 25, 1864, 273.

Chapter Four

1. I use "relief workers" to encompass those people who were actively working to aid freedpeople and manage the transition to freedom. In some respects, the use of the term "relief worker" is anachronistic—it did not come into use until the late 1870s. However, these individuals understood themselves to be working toward the provision of relief. It is not my intention to elide the differences between the goals of various individuals, secular and religious organizations, and government agencies, nor to suggest that their work was always positive; much of their work was characterized by racist assumptions about African Americans. Rather, I employ this term in order to refocus our attention on one of the collective tasks these organizations faced: providing various kinds of aid.

2. Martha Schofield to Mother and Sisters, October 16–17, 1865, Letter extracts, Martha Schofield Papers, SFHL-RG5–134, FHL; Schofield, October 16–19, 1865, and December 2, 1865, Diary, 1865–66, Schofield Papers, FHL. A transcription of Schofield's diary is also in the Southern Collection, University of North Carolina, Chapel Hill.

3. Litwack, *Been in the Storm So Long*, xi.

4. Elsewhere I have explored more broadly the built environment and material culture of communities formed by formerly enslaved people. See Weicksel, "Fitted Up for Freedom."

5. Camp, *Closer to Freedom*, 62.

6. Knowles, "Fashioning Slavery," 71.

7. Rockman, *Plantation Goods*, 185. See *Plantation Goods* for an extensive study on the production of goods, including clothing, for plantation use.

8. For a broader analysis of property ownership see Penningroth, *Claims of Kinfolk*.

9. Cited in Rockman, *Plantation Goods*, 245.

10. Stephanie Camp provides an in-depth analysis of the making, meaning, and use of enslaved people's clothing. See *Closer to Freedom*, 60–83.

11. Camp, *Closer to Freedom*, 80.

12. Annie Groves Scott in Baker and Baker, *WPA Oklahoma Slave Narratives*, 374.

13. Knowles, "Fashioning Slavery," 115.

14. Enoch M. Duley, "Two Hundred Dollars Reward!," broadside, Livingston Co., Kentucky, May 9, 1860, Gilder Lehrman Collection, New York Historical Society; "Notice," *Semi-Weekly Standard* (Raleigh, NC), November 27, 1860, 4.

15. Hopley, *Life in the South*, 147. For additional instances, see Gross, *What Blood Won't Tell*; "Notice," *Carolina Observer* (Fayetteville, NC), November 19, 1860, 4; "Runaway," *Richmond Whig*, November 16, 1860, 1; and "$200 Reward!!" *Alexandria (VA) Gazette*, July 21, 1860, 3.

16. Kemble, *Journal*, 58.

17. Camp, *Closer to Freedom*, 80–84.

18. McKim, *Freedmen of South Carolina*, 29.

19. "Dealings with the Contrabands and Slavery: Facts, Scenes, and Incidents," *Douglass' Monthly*, December 1861, 564–65.

20. Cited in Jones-Rogers, *They Were Her Property*, 193.

21. Botume, *First Days among the Contrabands*, 32.

22. Holt, *Children of Fire*, 141.

23. Alonzo Potter, in *Report of the Proceedings*, 7.

24. Harriet Buss to Parents, June 11, 1863, in Harriet Buss Papers, Ms. Coll. 8, fol. 7, Kislak Center for Special Collections, Rare Books, and Manuscripts, University of Pennsylvania.

25. Nordhoff, *Freedmen of South Carolina*, 17–19.

26. W. K. Strong to Edwin Stanton, "Contraband Clothing," Records of the Quartermaster General, RG 92, box 399, NARA.

27. Taylor, *Embattled Freedom*, 159–60.

28. J. M. Hawks to Esther Hawks, August 3, 1862, Library of Congress.

29. "Howard Investigation," in *Index of Reports of Committees*, 463.

30. Lucy Chase to "Home Folks," January 28, 1863, Lucy Chase Papers, AAS.

31. Glymph, *Women's Fight*, 171.

32. Holt, *Children of Fire*, 141.

33. Emancipation League, *Facts Concerning the Freedmen.*

34. O. Brown, December 31, 1862, in Emancipation League, *Facts Concerning the Freedmen*, 7.

35. Glymph, *Women's Fight*, 166.

36. Harriet Jacobs, "Life among the Contrabands," *Liberator*, September 5, 1862, 3.

37. Taylor, *Embattled Freedom*, 14.

38. She continued, "You are responsible for every child that God has given you—& you neglect your duty when you do not use every means in your power to train them in a way that will make them good & true men & women." Schofield, April 22, 1866, Diary, 1865–66, Schofield Papers, FHL.

39. "An Appeal," *Douglass' Monthly*, January 1863.

40. Schofield eventually founded the Schofield Normal and Industrial School in Aiken, South Carolina.

41. See, for example, the experiences of American Missionary Association missionaries Abisha Scofield and W. S. Bell. Taylor, *Embattled Freedom*, 162–63.

42. Botume, *First Days*, 236.

43. As one teacher wrote, "We fitted these people out with clothing and gave them a piece of soap. The next day they all appeared at school with hands and faces clean and shining as if polished. They looked like another 'gang.'" Botume, *First Days*, 139; Cowden, *Brief Sketch*, 46.

44. Julia Wilbur to Anna Barnes, October 2, 1863, Rochester Ladies Anti-Slavery Society Papers, William Clements Library, University of Michigan, Ann Arbor.

45. Jacobs to Garrison.

46. Taylor, *Embattled Freedom*, 167.

47. Greves quoted in McKim, *Freedmen of South Carolina*, 30.

48. Upton, *Another City*, 268.

49. In Maryland, for instance, masters were legally required to provide men with "one new hat, a good suit, one new shift of white linen; one new pair of bench-made shoes and stockings." Women, on the other hand, received "a waist-coat and petticoat, a new shift of white linen, shoes and stockings; a bib apron; two caps of white linen." Indenture contracts were not always this specific. Gabriel Ginings, for instance, was to be provided "two suits of apparel." Quoted in Staples and Shaw, *Clothing through American History*, 69; Indenture of Gabriel Ginings, 1663, in Demos, *Remarkable Providences*.

50. Wright, *Two Years behind the Plough*, 202.

51. For more on indentured servitude see Tomlins, "Indentured Servitude in Perspective."

52. Ash, *Dress behind Bars*, 13.

53. Upton, *Another City*, 243.

54. Ash, *Dress behind Bars*, 14.

55. Quoted in Upton, *Another City*, 259.

56. Upton, *Another City*, 259.

57. *Art of Good Behavior*, 23.

58. Clothing provided to prisoners was initially intended to be humiliating, but by the mid-nineteenth century, some reformers worried that such clothing would have an injurious effect. As educator Samuel Gridley Howe argued, forcing prisoners to "wear a uniform

which is purposely contrived to be grotesque as to be an unmistakable badge of degradation" was "unkind, unjust, and pernicious." Donning such dress, Howe continued, would strip a man of his pride and self-respect, thereby injuring his "moral nature." Such uniforms were abandoned in Massachusetts in 1865 precisely because they were "calculated to drive [the prisoner's] manhood from [him]." Ash, *Dress behind Bars*, 17; Howe, "Essay," 42–43, quoted in Upton, *Another City*, 268.

59. This depravity, however, was attributed to a lifetime of enslavement and abuse, rather than criminality.

60. Upton, *Another City*, 268.

61. Greves quoted in McKim, *Freedmen of South Carolina*, 30.

62. Taylor, *Embattled Freedom*, 162.

63. Higginson, *Army Life*, 172.

64. Nordhoff, *Freedmen of South Carolina*, 9.

65. Botume, *First Days*, 58.

66. Botume, *First Days*, 58.

67. "Clothing Provided," *Report of the General Superintendent of Freedmen*, 12.

68. Child, "The Port Royal Free-Black Community."

69. Schofield, January 8, 1866, Diary, 1865–66, Schofield Papers, FHL.

70. "The Condition of the Contrabands in Washington," *Christian Recorder*, November 1, 1862.

71. "An Important Letter from a Teacher of the Freedmen," *Christian Recorder*, April 16, 1864.

72. Cooley and Brough, *Cooley's Cyclopaedia of Practical Receipts*, 457.

73. *Art of Good Behavior*, 11; Brown, *Foul Bodies*, 5–6, 11; Botume, *First Days*, 139.

74. *Habits of Good Society*, 156–57.

75. "Condition of the Contrabands."

76. Julia Wilbur to Emily Howland, February 5, 1863, in Yellin, *Harriet Jacobs Family Papers*, 439.

77. McKim, *Freedmen of South Carolina*, 31; Nordhoff, *Freedmen of South Carolina*, 9.

78. Holt, *Children of Fire*, 141.

79. As Richard Bushman further notes, there was no effort to define taste in everyday discourse, and yet it was always admired and required for a refined personality. Bushman, *Refinement of America*, 83, 96.

80. Nordhoff, *Freedmen of South Carolina*, 17.

81. Fisk, *Plain Counsels for Freedmen*, 17.

82. A phrase meant to convey loose-fitting clothes. *Naval Encyclopaedia*, 670; Nordhoff, *Freedmen of South Carolina*, 17.

83. Stearns, *Battleground of Desire*, 76.

84. Scott, *Cutter's Guide*.

85. "Virginia Slave Children Rescued by Colored Troops—As We Found Them" and "Virginia Slave Children Rescued by Colored Troops—As They Are Now," c. 1864, VMHC.

86. Henry Hayes Journal, June 10, 1864, William Clements Library.

87. Yet, this was also a problem for working-class white women who, despite being unable to achieve the level of womanhood of elite and middle-class women, were nevertheless gendered as "white women."

88. Taylor, *Embattled Freedom*, 169.

89. Taylor, *Embattled Freedom*, 167–70.

90. *Habits of Good Society*, 170.

91. *Habits of Good Society*, 171.

92. "Rules and Regulations for the Government of the Portland Alms-house," reproduced in Wagner, *The Poorhouse*, 42–45.

93. For more on enslaved people's clothing, see Foster, "*New Raiments of Self*."

94. Olmsted, *Journey*, 27–28.

95. Chesnut, *Diary from Dixie*, 166.

96. Quoted in Hoy, *Chasing Dirt*, 55.

97. Pulling fodder referred to the stripping of corn stalks for cattle feed. Caroline Putnam, November 9–16, 1868, Caroline F. Putnam Papers, William Clements Library.

98. Catherine P. Noyes cited in Glymph, *Women's Fight*, 194.

99. Nordhoff, *Freedmen of South Carolina*, 20.

100. Holt, *Problem of Freedom*, 53.

101. Taylor, *Embattled Freedom*, 165.

102. *Report of the General Superintendent of Freedmen*, 29, 44, 59.

103. McKim, *Freedmen of South Carolina*, 20.

104. According to McKim, "the average cost of maintaining a slave, independent of his food has been computed at $13.50 per annum for a field-hand, or $4.50 a head all around." McKim, *Freedmen of South Carolina*, 21.

105. McKim, *Freedmen of South Carolina*, 27.

106. Henry Hayes Journal, June 10, 1864.

107. D. B. Nichols to the Commission, September 8, 1863, United States American Freedmen's Inquiry Commission, Houghton Library, Harvard University.

108. Nichols to the Commission.

109. Fisk, *Plain Counsels for Freedmen*, 55–56.

110. Fisk, *Plain Counsels for Freedmen*, 56.

111. Fisk, *Plain Counsels for Freedmen*, 57.

112. Garfinkel, "Quakers and High Chests," 68.

113. The 1695 advice on plainness advised against wearing "superfluous Buttons, or broad Ribbons about hats" and to be "careful about making, buying or wearing (as much as they can) striped, or flowred stuffs [fabrics], or other usefulness or superfluous things." Philadelphia Yearly Meeting Discipline, cited in Garfinkel, "Quakers and High Chests," 64; Quaker Clothing Collection, Division of Home and Community Life, NMAH.

114. For more on changing Quaker aesthetics, see Frost, "From Plainness to Simplicity," 16–40.

115. J. M. Hawks to Esther H. Hawks, July 27, 1862, Esther Hill Hawks Papers, Library of Congress.

116. Schofield, March 16, 17, 23, 25, 26, 1869, Diary, 1869-71, Schofield Papers, FHL.

117. Glymph, *Out of the House*, 204.

118. Alvord, *Letters from the South*, 7.

119. Kemble, *Journal*, 58. For further interpretation of Frances Kemble, see Camp, *Closer to Freedom*, 84.

120. Camp, *Closer to Freedom*, 84. See also White and White, *Stylin'*, 17–19.

121. Taylor, *Embattled Freedom*, 168–70.

122. Jacobs, *Life of a Slave Girl*, 20.

123. McKim, *Freedmen of South Carolina*, 31.

124. See, for instance, Caroline F. Putnam Papers; Martha Schofield Diary; and Julia Wilbur Papers, Haverford College, Quaker & Special Collections, Haverford, PA.

125. Both dresses are in the collection of the National Museum of African American History and Culture, Smithsonian Institution, Washington, DC.

126. Schofield, April 22, 1866, Diary, 1865–66, Schofield Papers, FHL.

127. Alvord, *Letters from the South*, 7.

Part III

1. Handwriting analysis of the script on the tintype and another photograph identifying himself suggests that Joseph wrote the history on the front of his brother's tintype. Tintype, C. C. Wheat, donated by "Col. W. L. Timberlake," ACWM; Joseph N. Wheat, Robert E. Lee Camp Confederate Soldiers' Home Applications for Admission, 1884–1941, Library of Virginia, Richmond, VA; "William Lewis Timberlake," Mobile County #49, *Alabama Census of Confederate Soldiers*, 1907.

2. Postcard, Joseph N. Wheat, ACWM; 1850 US Federal Census, Page County, Virginia, population schedule; Wheat, Soldiers' Home Applications.

3. Charley Wheat's gravestone identified him as a member of the Seventh Virginia Cavalry. The story of Wheat's death was recounted by Joseph Wheat and later published in the "Do You Remember?" column of the November 7, 1941, issue of the *Page News and Courier*. Also see Robert H. Moore II, "Sesqui'fying April 20, 1862—Luray Learns of Charley Wheat's Fate," *Cenantua's Blog*, April 20, 2012, https://cenantua.wordpress.com/2012/04/20/sesquifying-april-20-1862-an-unpleasant-surprise-in-luray/.

4. 1850 US Federal Census Slave Schedules, Clarke County, Virginia, Ancestry.com; 1860 US Federal Census Slave Schedules, Clarke County, Virginia, Ancestry.com; US Selected Federal Census Non-Population Schedules, 1850, District 12, Clarke County, Virginia, Ancestry.com; 1870 US Federal Census, Luray Township, Page County, Virginia, Ancestry.com.

5. Joseph N. Wheat, August 26, 1909, "Application of Soldier, Sailor or Marine for Disability by Reason of Disease or the Infirmities of Age," Confederate Pension Records, Ancestry.com.

Chapter Five

1. Portions of this chapter are included in the following publication, which explores the acts, experiences, and meaning of looting and material culture more broadly: Weicksel, "'Peeled' Bodies, Pillaged Homes."

2. Sheehan-Dean, *Calculus of Violence*, 54; Lieber, "General Order No. 100." For more on the Lieber Code, see Sheehan-Dean, *Calculus of Violence*, 180–86; and Witt, *Lincoln's Code*.

3. For a detailed exploration of relics in the nineteenth century, see Barnett, *Sacred Relics*.

4. "Rebel Soldiers after Battle 'Peeling' (i.e. Stripping) the Fallen Union Soldiers—From a Sketch by an Officer," *Frank Leslie's Illustrated Newspaper*, February 13, 1864.

5. Rable, *Fredericksburg! Fredericksburg!*, 277.

6. See, for instance, Drew Faust's description of stripping. Faust discusses cultural anxieties regarding the dead, dehumanization, and attempts to provide proper burial, but only briefly refers to the implications of clothing theft. Faust, *This Republic of Suffering*, 74–75.

7. The Museum of the Confederacy (now the American Civil War Museum) in Richmond, Virginia, included many of these relic hunters' finds in its collection.

8. Cashin, "Trophies of War," 339; Barnett, *Sacred Relics*, 81.

9. Robert Knox Sneden, in Adams, *Living Hell*, 85.

10. Adams, *Living Hell*, 85.

11. John Edwards to Joseph Shelby, December 7, 1862, in Adams, *Living Hell*, 88.

12. Thomas Meyer, quoted in Adams, *Living Hell*, 100.

13. Samuel Compton, quoted in Adams, *Living Hell*, 102.

14. "Rebel Soldiers after Battle."

15. Trowbridge, *The South*, 107.

16. *Oxford English Dictionary*, "peeling," accessed May 16, 2016, https://www.oed.com/dictionary/peel_v1?tab=etymology.

17. Lewis, *Camp Life of a Confederate Boy*, 37.

18. Quoted in Glatthaar, *General Lee's Army*, 175.

19. Faust, *This Republic of Suffering*, 61–62.

20. Quoted in Glatthaar, *General Lee's Army*, 175.

21. George Landrum, quoted in Noe, *Perryville*, 323.

22. Quoted in Glatthaar, *General Lee's Army*, 175.

23. Henry I. Bowditch, "Bowditch Memorial Cabinet Catalog," 1877, MHS.

24. Jacket worn by Jacob Baiz, Armed Forces History Collection, NMAH.

25. William C. Nelson to Maria C. Nelson, October 10, 1861, in Ford, *Hour of Our Nation's Agony*, 65.

26. Schroyer App Diary, May 15, 1865, cited in Carmichael, *War for the Common Soldier*, 297.

27. Martha Stephens, quoted in Gallagher, *Fredericksburg Campaign*, 106.

28. Mary Phinney, February 25, 1864, in *Army Nurse*, 139.

29. Wyeth, *With Sabre and Scalpel*, 248.

30. Small, *Road to Richmond*, 70.

31. Corby, *Memoirs of Chaplain Life*, 90.

32. Wyeth, *With Sabre and Scalpel*, 248.

33. Lewis, *Camp Life*, 37.

34. James McFall to Sister, November 29, 1863, McFall Letters, MARBL.

35. W. McFall to Sister, October 9, 1864, McFall Letters, MARBL.

36. J. McFall to L. McFall Anderson, December 21, 1864, McFall Letters, MARBL.

37. For more on the soul, see Abruzzo, "Sins of Slaves."

38. Faust, *This Republic of Suffering*, 18.

39. Portions of this section were published as Weicksel, "Armor, Manhood and the Politics of Mortality."

40. Chittenden, *Recollections of President Lincoln*, 419–20.

41. Johnson, in Pelka, *Civil War Letters of Charles F. Johnson*, 113.

42. Quoted in Barnett, *Sacred Relics*, 81.

43. Trowbridge, *The South*, 115.

44. Trowbridge, *The South*, 132.

45. Confederate shell jacket worn by Alexander Hunter, NMAH.

46. Charles Pluemacher, Pocket Watch and Accession Files, ACWM.

47. Letter, G. M. Sorrel to James Longstreet, January 25, 1864, Civil War Collection, 1861–66, AAS.

48. Jones, *Tennessee in the Civil War*, 129.

49. Sorrel to Longstreet, January 25, 1864. For my more detailed interpretation of clothing and disease, see Weicksel, "Dress of the Enemy."

50. John W. Holloway to Bettie, January 28, 1862, John William Holloway Papers, 1861–72, Mss1 H72865, VMHC.

51. Lieber, "General Order No. 100."

52. Mary Phinney, May 6, 1864, in *Army Nurse*, 142.

53. Andrew B. Wardlaw diary, September 13, 1862, quoted in Bohannon, "Dirty, Ragged, and Ill-Provided For," 114.

54. John Keely in Bohannon, "Dirty, Ragged, and Ill-Provided For," 114.

55. Barnett, *Sacred Relics*, 82.

56. Holzer, *Civil War in 50 Objects*, 149–53.

57. Marshall, *Army Life*, 83–84; Wilder, *Practicing Medicine*, 75; Watson, *Civil War Surgeon*, 75.

58. Cross Cannons, George Wilson, Armed Forces History Collection, NMAH.

59. "Military Buttons Mounted on Card, 1860–1864," Unidentified makers, New-York Historical Society, New York, NY.

60. Hall T. McGee Diary, May 17, 1864, Hall T. McGee Diary Transcription, 43/2223, SCHS.

61. For more on looting and the built environment, see Cashin, *War Stuff*, 108–30.

62. Maria Johnstone Porcher to Clelia, May 25, 1865, Porcher Family Papers, 1082.00, 11/315/4, SCHS.

63. Frank, "Bedrooms as Battlefields," 33, 40. For more on this gendered interpretation of male soldiers and female civilians, see Frank, *Civilian War*.

64. Susan Blackford to Charles Blackford, March 6, 1865, in Blackford and Blackford, *Letters from Lee's Army*, 281.

65. Shaw and Bassett, *Homefront & Battlefield*, 154.

66. McGuire, April 3, 1864, in *Diary of a Southern Refugee*, 344.

67. Susan Blackford to Charles Blackford, March 6, 1865, in Blackford and Blackford, *Letters from Lee's Army*, 281–82.

68. *The Workwoman's Guide*, 73.

69. Money belt and pocket, c. 1864, The Valentine, Richmond, VA.

70. Shaw and Bassett, *Homefront & Battlefield*, 154.

71. Susan Blackford to Charles Blackford, March 6, 1865, in Blackford and Blackford, *Letters from Lee's Army*, 281.

72. Emma LeConte, February 14, 1865, Diary transcription, 1864–65, Southern Historical Collection.

73. Crystal Feimster, "Rape and Justice in the Civil War," *New York Times*, April 25, 2013; Sheehan-Dean, *Calculus of Violence*, 306–11.

74. Emory Sweetland to Mary Sweetland, January 20, 1865, quoted in Dunkelman, *Brothers One and All*, 186.

75. Joel Bouton to Stephen Hoyt, January 7, 1862, quoted in Dunkelman, *War's Relentless Hand*, 9.

76. Joel Bouton to Stephen Hoyt, March 29, 1863, quoted in Dunkelman, *Brothers One and All*, 185.

77. Quoted in Feimster, "Rape and Justice."

78. Caroline Kean Hill Diary, June 1, 1863, VMHC.

79. Caroline Kean Hill Diary, June 12, 1864, VMHC.

80. "Diary of a Woman of Fayetteville, March 22, 1865," in Jones, *When Sherman Came*, 284–86.

81. Creighton, "Gettysburg Out of Bounds," 77.

82. Cashin, "Torn Bonnets," 355.

83. Levi Bryant, quoted in Dunkelman, *Brothers One and All*, 185.

84. Cashin, "Torn Bonnets," 355.

85. Kate Cumming, July 17, 1864, in *Kate*, 211.

86. "Report of L. C. Baker About Property (Stolen) and Sent from the South to Parties in the North," January 4, 1863, *US, Case Files of Investigations by Levi C Turner and Lafayette C Baker, 1861–1866*, NARA M797, accessed May 10, 2016, https://www.fold3.com/publication/626/us-civil-war-subversion-investigations-1861–1866.

87. "Report of L. C. Baker," January 4, 1863; 1860 US Federal Census, Indiana County, Pennsylvania, accessed May 10, 2016, Ancestry.com.

88. Stone, *Brokenburn*, 203.

89. Camp, *Closer to Freedom*, 122.

90. Emma Mordecai, quoted in Camp, *Closer to Freedom*, 177.

91. Skinner, *Women Physicians*, 94.

92. Blackwell, *Laws of Life*, 61–62.

93. Daniel M. Holt, May 17, 1863, in Greiner, Coryell, and Smither, *Surgeon's Civil War*, 103.

Chapter Six

1. Margaret Hudlow to Gov. Joseph Brown, Joseph Emerson Brown Governor's Incoming Correspondence, 1861–65, GSA.

2. Scholarship on Union and Confederate textile procurement has traditionally been rooted in the study of the American economy. These studies are driven by an attempt to understand both the Civil War's effect on the modernization of the American economy and the connections between the outcome of the war and each government's ability to supply its armies. For studies of Confederate procurement, see Wilson, *Confederate Industry*; DeCredico, *Patriotism for Profit*; and Goff, *Confederate Supply*.

3. Hunter, *To 'Joy My Freedom*, 16.

4. For an in-depth study of laundresses in the postwar era, see Hunter, *To 'Joy my Freedom*.

5. Glymph, *Out of the House*, 131.

6. Stone, *Brokenburn*, 7, 32, 58.

7. Stone, *Brokenburn*, 7.

8. The effects of these policies on British textile production have been well documented in terms of cotton production. Indeed, the inability to import sufficient quantities of South-

ern cotton led British manufacturers to seek out new sources of cotton. For more on cotton, see Schoen, *Fragile Fabric of Union*; and Beckert, *Empire of Cotton*.

9. Frederick Augustus Porcher to My own Darling, July 1, 1864, Porcher Family Papers 1082.00, 11/315/1, SCHS.

10. Historians remain divided over whether the social and economic realities of the Southern home front or military losses were the causal forces behind declining support for the Confederate project. Civil War scholarship has clearly shown that the Confederate South was fractured—economically, racially, politically—and that the Southern experience of the war is difficult to define using generalities. Some scholars, including Drew Gilpin Faust, Paul Escott, and William Freehling, argue that from the beginning of the war, white Southerners had a lack of will and a faltering commitment to Confederate nationalism. Other historians, including Gary Gallagher, James McPherson, and Stephen Ash, argue that battlefield losses led to the decline of an originally strong Southern morale among both civilians and soldiers. For studies of Confederate nationalism, morale, and defeat, see Faust, *Creation of Confederate Nationalism*; Escott, *After Secession*; Freehling, *South vs. the South*; Beringer et al., *Why the South Lost*; Ash, *Middle Tennessee Society Transformed*; McPherson, "American Victory; American Defeat"; and Gallagher, *Confederate War*.

11. For more on the state, see Rao, *National Duties*; Edling, *Hercules in the Cradle*; and Balogh, *Government Out of Sight*.

12. On the Lost Cause, see Janney, *Burying the Dead*; Blair, *Cities of the Dead*; Gallagher and Nolan, *Myth of the Lost Cause*; and Foster, *Ghosts of the Confederacy*. For works that contributed to Lost Cause ideology, see Davis, *Rise and Fall*; and Pollard, *Lost Cause*.

13. Andrews, February 10, 1865, in *Wartime Journal*, 87.

14. As Ruth Schwartz Cowan explains, "When cotton replaced linen and wool as the most frequently utilized fabric, laundering increased; indeed, one of cotton's attractions as a fabric was that it could be washed fairly easily." Cowan, *More Work for Mother*, 65.

15. Walsh, *Economical Housekeeper*, 407–8.

16. Sarah Morgan Dawson, October 1, 1862, in *Confederate Girl's Diary*, 244.

17. Andrews, February 10, 1865, in *Wartime Journal*, 87.

18. Dawson, August 10, 1862, in *Confederate Girl's Diary*, 164.

19. Cashin, "Into the Trackless Wilderness," 43.

20. Dawson, May 30–31, 1862, in *Confederate Girl's Diary*, 48.

21. The refugees came from Tennessee, Georgia, Arkansas, Virginia, North Carolina, Kentucky, Alabama, Mississippi, Louisiana, and South Carolina, with the vast majority originating from eastern Tennessee. Refugee Relief Commission of Ohio, *First Semi-Annual Report*, 3.

22. See, for instance, Cashin, "Into the Trackless Wilderness."

23. Refugee Relief Commission of Ohio, *First Semi-Annual Report*, 6–7.

24. Cumming, July 30, 1863, in *Journal of Hospital Life*, 79.

25. Cumming, November 20, 1864, in *Journal of Hospital Life*, 151.

26. Cumming, March 3, 1864, in *Journal of Hospital Life*, 122.

27. Julia Johnson Fisher Diary, January 3, 1864, call no. 1757, Documenting the American South, University of North Carolina at Chapel Hill, http://docsouth.unc.edu/imls/fisherjulia/fisher.html.

28. Dolly Lunt Burge, June 3, 1862, in *Diary*, 128.

29. Photograph of Sadai and Rachel, 1858, accessed March 20, 2016, http://www.burgeclub.com/OurHistory/TheBurgeStoryfull.aspx; "Sadai Burge and her slave nurse, Rachel," Burge Family Papers, no. 266, box 3, folder 17, MARBL.

30. Fisher Diary, January 4, 1864.

31. Catherine Ann Devereux Edmonston, September 19, 1864, in *Journal of a Secesh Lady*, 617.

32. Gadwell Jefferson Pearce, quoted in Williams, *Rich Man's War*, 86.

33. "Exile of the Sweetwater Operatives," *Nashville Times*, August 20, 1864, quoted in Hitt, *Charged with Treason*, 87.

34. Anne Shannon Martin Diary, March 12, 1864, cited in Stamper and Condra, *Clothing through American History*, 84.

35. Catherine M. N. King to daughter Catherine M. N. King Correspondence, RHS.

36. The common practice of sending scraps of fabric in personal correspondence took on a heightened function during the war. The correspondence and fabric scraps of Catherine King offer a glimpse of the cost and variety of fabrics accessible to a moderately wealthy family. Included in one letter were scraps from which various garments were made in a variety of patterns and colors, including blue-and-white plaid, black-and-white striped, black with white dot and flower pattern, black with white diamond pattern, plain black, and a red-and-black check. Fabric scraps, Catherine M. N. King Correspondence, RHS.

37. Fisher Diary, April 11, 1864.

38. Edmonston, February 26, 1865, in *Journal of a Secesh Lady*, 673.

39. Montgomery, *Textiles in America*, 215.

40. Fabric scrap with attached note, Catherine M. N. King Correspondence, RHS.

41. Burge, June 3, 1862, *Diary*, 128.

42. Fabric scrap with attached note, Catherine M. N. King Correspondence, RHS.

43. Emma Cullens to Gov. Joseph Brown, November 18, 1863, Joseph Emerson Brown Governor's Incoming Correspondence, GSA.

44. Elzey Hay [Eliza Andrews], "Dress under Difficulties; or, Passages from the Blockade Experience of Rebel Women," *Godey's Lady's Book*, July 1866, 33.

45. Andrews, *Wartime Journal*, March 8, 1865, 110–11.

46. Anonymous letter to Gov. Joseph E. Brown, Joseph Emerson Brown Governor's Incoming Correspondence, GSA.

47. Fisher Diary, April 11, 1864.

48. Fisher Diary, January 3, 1864.

49. Emma Cullens to Gov. Joseph Brown, November 18, 1863, Joseph Emerson Brown Governor's Incoming Correspondence, GSA.

50. "An Act to provide for raising a revenue for the political year 1864, and to appropriate money for the support of the Government during said year, and to make certain special appropriations, and for other purposes therein mentioned," in *Acts of the General Assembly*, 8.

51. Brown explained: "We must have leather to make the cards, or our machinery will avail us nothing. As the supply of leather is very limited, probably nothing but cards will bring what we need. We will, therefore, give the preference to all persons who bring you leather, or hides suitable to make leather, fit for use in this business." Anyone who brought in "one good skin, whether tanned or not, will be permitted to purchase on pair of cards at six dollars, and pay the difference in money." This policy was later changed so that cards could be "had at the sale room at the old price of six dollars a pair, half in skins, and the

other half in money." Joseph E. Brown to T. T. Windsor, February 9, 1863, State Papers of Governor Joseph E. Brown in Candler, *Confederate Records*, vol. 2, 361; "Cotton Cards," *Daily Constitutionalist* (Augusta, GA), February 6, 1864.

52. Brown to Windsor, February 9, 1863, State Papers, 361.

53. Cullens wrote: "Did not good taste forbid would whisper to you that when my husband goes to the ballot box to deposit his vote for Gov. Brown that his wife only regrets that her four boys are not old enough to and do likewise." Cullens to Brown, November 18, 1863 Joseph Emerson Brown Governor's Incoming Correspondence, GSA.

54. Mary Carns to Gov. Joseph Brown, March 21, 1863, Joseph Emerson Brown Governor's Incoming Correspondence, GSA.

55. Harris's husband, Augustus S. Harris, enlisted for the duration of the war on February 16, 1862, as a private in Co. A of the Fourteenth Alabama Infantry. He received a severe wound in the back at the Battle of Gaines Mill and died on July 31, 1862. After his death, Margaret Harris sought to claim the wages due to him, but ran into difficulty. While she believed that he was due four months of wages, she ultimately received approximately twenty dollars. Record of Augustus S. Harris, "Compiled Service Records of Soldiers Who Served in Organizations from the State of Alabama," M311, NARA.

56. M. V. Harris to Joseph E. Brown, November 21, 1863, Joseph Emerson Brown Governor's Incoming Correspondence, GSA.

57. Here, Bachelder drew on a well-known Biblical passage from the book of Matthew that urged people to set aside their worldly needs and focus on God, who would provide all things: "Wherefore, if God so clothe the grass of the field, which to day is, and to morrow is cast into the oven, shall he not much more clothe you, O ye of little faith? 31 Therefore take no thought, saying, What shall we eat? or, What shall we drink? or, *Wherewithal shall we be clothed?* 32 (For after all these things do the Gentiles seek): for your heavenly Father knoweth that ye have need of all these things. 33 But seek ye first the kingdom of God, and his righteousness; and all these things shall be added unto you." Matthew 6:30–34 (KJV).

58. Lizzie C. Bachelder to Gov. Joseph Brown, November 22, 1862, Joseph Emerson Brown Governor's Incoming Correspondence, GSA.

59. Lucinda K. Hillsman to Gov. Joseph Brown, March 25, 1865, Joseph Emerson Brown Governor's Incoming Correspondence, GSA.

60. Joseph E. Brown to T. T. Windsor, February 9, 1863, State Papers.

61. "Cotton Spinners Convention," *Southern Banner* (Athens, GA), May 20, 1863.

62. Joseph E. Brown, June 8, 1863, State Papers.

63. Putnam, *Richmond during the War*, 315.

64. "Now and then a Godey's or a Bon Ton would makes its way through the blockade, and create a greater sensation than the last battle. . . . I remember walking three miles once to see a number of the Lady's book, only six months old; then learned that it had been lent out, and, after chasing it all over town, found it at last, so bethumbed and crumpled that one could scarcely tell a fashion-plate from a model cottage." Hay, "Dress under Difficulties," 33.

65. Fisher Diary, January 3, 1864.

66. "Description of Steel Fashion-Plate for July," *Godey's Lady's Book*, July 1864, 94–95.

67. This bodice is in the collection of the ACWM, cat. no. 09085.13.01080.

68. "Chitchat upon New York and Philadelphia Fashion for June," *Godey's Lady's Book*, June 1862, 618.

69. These gloves and glove pattern are in the collection of the ACWM.

70. "Chitchat upon New York and Philadelphia Fashions for February," *Godey's Lady's Book*, February 1862, 210.

71. These items are in the collections of the ACVM.

72. Margaret Loughborough, "Reminiscence, undated, of Margaret Loughborough concerning her experiences during the Civil War," Mss2 L9285 a 1, CMLS, VMHC.

73. Andrews, February 16, 1865, *Wartime Journal*, 95.

74. Hague, *Blockaded Family*, 93–94.

75. Andrews, July 21, 1865, in *Wartime Journal*, 338.

76. Andrews, July 21, 1865, in *Wartime Journal*, 339.

77. Andrews, May 27, 1865, in *Wartime Journal*, 271.

Chapter Seven

1. Eppes, *Through Some Eventful Years*, 288–89.

2. Andrew Johnson, "Executive Order," April 29, 1865, *The American Presidency Project*, accessed May 5, 2014, http://www.presidency.ucsb.edu/ws/?pid=7205.

3. Blair, *Cities of the Dead*, 52.

4. "Kentucky Rebels," *Raftsman's Journal* (Clearfield, PA), May 24, 1865.

5. *War of the Rebellion*, ser. 1, vol. 49, pt. 2, 638.

6. "An Order Concerning Rebel Soldiers in West Virginia," *Daily Intelligencer* (Wheeling, WV), June 15, 1865.

7. James Speed to Edward M. Staunton, April 22, 1865, in *War of the Rebellion*, ser. 1, vol. 46, pt. 3, 918.

8. "Tennessee Legislature," *Nashville Daily Union*, April 29, 1865.

9. In addition, the bill proposed "that any person violating the provision of the first section shall be fined not less than $10, nor more than $50. Section third forbids the wearing of any uniform or insignia, denoting an official position in the Rebel service, or offering for sale any picture of officers wearing the Rebel uniform, under the penalty of $20. The fines and penalties of these offenses shall go, one-half to the informer and the other to the school fund. Section fourth makes null and void all process served by any special constable, who has served in the Rebel army, except he subsequently served in the Union army and was honorably discharged thereupon." "Legislation in Missouri," *Fayetteville Observer*, December 21, 1865.

10. Worsham, *One of Jackson's Foot Cavalry*, 293.

11. See, for instance Blair, *Cities of the Dead*; Bradley, *Bluecoats and Tar Heels*; and Marten, *Sing Not War*.

12. Andrews, May 27, 1865, in *Wartime Journal*, 270.

13. Worsham, *One of Jackson's Foot Cavalry*, 293–94.

14. Rev. Alonzo H. Quint, "Beaten, but Unchanged," *Caledonian*, June 9, 1865.

15. "Provost Court—Judge Benedict," *Daily Picayune* (New Orleans, LA), December 10, 1865, 6.

16. For an examination of Douglas's case in the context of paroles, see Janney, *Ends of War*, 199–202.

17. Douglas, *I Rode with Stonewall*, 336–39.

18. Douglas, *I Rode with Stonewall*, 339.

19. Douglas, *I Rode with Stonewall*, 340.

20. Douglas, *I Rode with Stonewall*, 349.

21. Andrews, May 27, 1865, in *Wartime Journal*, 270.

22. Andrews, May 30, 1865, in *Wartime Journal*, 276.

23. "All Sorts of Paragraphs," *Daily State Sentinel* (Indianapolis, IN), June 14, 1865, 2.

24. Andrews, May 30, 1865, in *Wartime Journal*, 276.

25. "Kentucky Loyalty," *Evening Telegraph* (Philadelphia, PA), April 28, 1866.

26. "From Texas," *Fremont (OH) Journal*, March 9, 1866.

27. "The Federals in the South-West," *Manchester Guardian*, June 5, 1865, cited in Bradbury, *While Father Is Away*, 273.

28. "Complaints of John A. Wise," *Dayton (OH) Daily Empire*, June 9, 1865.

29. For extensive overviews of the Grand Review, see Gallagher, *Union War*, 7–32; and Royster, *Destructive War*.

30. "Review of the Armies," *New York Times*, May 25, 1865.

31. "Review of the Armies," *New York Times*, May 24, 1865.

32. Lucas, *99th Indiana Infantry*, 82.

33. Cited in Royster, *Destructive War*, 417.

34. Willoughby Diary, October 8–9, 1864, Willoughby Papers, folder 19, AAS.

35. Downs, *After Appomattox*, 9.

36. "Kentucky Loyalty."

37. Hubbard Pryor, cited in Coddington, *African American Faces*, 128.

38. National Humanities Center, Resource Toolbox, The Making of African American Identity, vol. 1, 1500–1865, 2007, accessed July 31, 2024, https://nationalhumanitiescenter.org/pds/maai/identity/text7/pryor44thcolored1864.pdf. Pryor's service is summarized in Davis, "A Soldier's Story."

39. Caroline Janney, "The Lost Cause," *Encyclopedia Virginia*, Virginia Humanities, accessed November 18, 2024, https://encyclopediavirginia.org/entries/lost-cause-the/.

40. Janney, "The Lost Cause."

41. James McFall to Sister Creak, November 21, 1864, William McFall Letters, MARBL.

42. Eppes, *Through Some Eventful Years*, 288–89.

43. Janney, "The Lost Cause."

44. Dixon, *The Clansman*, 62.

45. Dixon, *The Clansman*, 256–57.

46. Janney, *Remembering the Civil War*, 142.

47. Camp, *Closer to Freedom*, 121.

48. Glymph, *Out of the House*, 204.

49. Knowles, "Fashioning Slavery," 209; Tate emancipation dress, Witte Museum, San Antonio, Texas.

50. Lonn Taylor, "Sallie Tate's Emancipation Dress: A Rare Glimpse into Texas Slavery and Freedom," *Texas Monthly*, April 2014, https://www.texasmonthly.com/the-culture/sallie-tates-emancipation-dress/.

51. Elzey Hay, "Dress under Difficulties," 32.

52. Emma Holmes, quoted in Litwack, *Been in the Storm*, 116.

53. "Marriage of a Colored Soldier at Vicksburg by Chaplain Warren of the Freedmen's Bureau," *Harper's Weekly*, June 30, 1866.

54. Maria Johnstone Porcher to Clelia, June 11, 1865, Porcher Family Papers, 1082.00, 11/315/4, SCHS.

55. Janney, *Burying the Dead*, 42.

56. "Church Service" and "Secesh Impudence," *Philadelphia Inquirer*, April 12, 1865.

57. Chambers Family Papers #2828, Southern Historical Collection, University of North Carolina at Chapel Hill.

58. *Catalog of the Confederate Museum* (1905), 209; Child's Jacket, Cat. no. 0985.09.00057, ACWM; 1860 US Federal Census Slave Schedules, South Part, Iredell County, North Carolina, Ancestry.com; 1870 US Federal Census, Chambersburg Township, Iredell County, North Carolina, Ancestry.com.

59. For a detailed study of the first Ku Klux Klan and its costumes, see Parsons, *Ku Klux*, 78.

60. Parsons, *Ku Klux*, 72–108.

61. Lennard, "Uniform Threat," 46.

62. Andrews, May 27, 1865, in *Wartime Journal*, 270.

63. Glymph, *Out of the House*, 138–39.

Part IV

1. Farmer-Kaiser, *Freedwomen and the Freedmen's Bureau*, 34.

2. Margaret Hillhouse to Curator of the Smithsonian Institute, April 20, 1925, accession file 87112, NMAH.

Chapter Eight

1. McGuire, April 28, 1865, in *Diary of a Southern Refugee*, 360.

2. Sternhell, *Routes of War*, 155–56.

3. McGuire, May 4, 1865, in *Diary of a Southern Refugee*, 360.

4. Jones and Stallybrass, *Renaissance Clothing*, 3.

5. For studies of Civil War memory more generally, see Blight, *Race and Reunion* and *Beyond the Battlefield*; Blair, *Cities of the Dead*; Brundage, *Southern Past*; and Janney, *Remembering the Civil War*.

6. Conn, *Museums and American Intellectual Life*, 4.

7. Hillyer, "Relics of Reconciliation," 37; Stevenson, "Vacationing with the Civil War."

8. Carmichael, *War for the Common Soldier*, 281.

9. Carmichael, "Trophies of Victory," 199.

10. Socks, Robert E. Lee, Confederate Miscellany Collection, MARBL.

11. Carter, *Four Brothers in Blue*, 450.

12. McGuire, *Diary of a Southern Refugee*, 54–55.

13. Carter, *Four Brothers in Blue*, 450.

14. *War of the Rebellion*, ser. 1, vol. 49, pt. 2, 638; "An Order Concerning Rebel Soldiers in West Virginia," *Daily Intelligencer* (Wheeling, WV), June 15, 1865.

15. Items in each of these categories are now in the collection of the Smithsonian Institution's National Museum of African American History and Culture.

16. See, for instance, collections held by the Library Company of Philadelphia and the National Museum of American History.

17. Correspondence with Descendants of Henry Heinmiller, private collection. Special thanks to Sara Hume for putting me in touch with the family.

18. John M. Coski, "The American Civil War Museum," *Encyclopedia Virginia*, Virginia Humanities, accessed November 4, 2024, https://encyclopediavirginia.org/entries/museum-of-the-confederacy/.

19. Correspondence with O. W. Barrow, March 29, 1886, Accession File 17332, Armed Forces History Collection, NMAH.

20. Correspondence with I. E. Nagle, November 30, 1886, Accession File 18342, Armed Forces History Collection, NMAH.

21. Halbwachs, *On Collective Memory*; Brundage, *Where These Memories Grow*, 3.

22. Brundage, *Southern Past*, 3.

23. George Wilson, September 1886, Accession File 17942, Armed Forces History Collection, NMAH.

24. Accession File 18528, Armed Forces History Collection, NMAH.

25. Hunter, *Johnny Reb and Billy Yank*, preface.

26. Barthes, *Mythologies*, 255–56.

27. Hunter, *Johnny Reb and Billy Yank*.

28. *Catalogue of the Confederate Museum* (1905), 9; Hillyer, "Relics of Reconciliation," 53.

29. Hillyer, "Relics of Reconciliation," 56.

30. Skirt worn by an enslaved ancestor of Janett Sharee Galloway, Object Number 2011.52, NMAAHC.

31. Brundage, *Southern Past*, 4.

32. An earlier version of the catalog from 1898, however, stated that the maker was a woman. Catalog #228, *Catalogue of the Confederate Museum* (1905) and *Catalogue of the Confederate Museum* (1898).

33. Cloth, 1861–65, MSS 20, box 3, fol. 3, Confederate Miscellany Collection, MARBL.

34. For textual portrayals of homespun's relationship to white women's sacrifice, see Taylor and Conner, *South Carolina Women*, 1:364.

35. Auslander, "Beyond Words," 1015.

Conclusion

1. Albert W. Bacheler was born in Midnapore, India, to American Free Baptist missionaries Otis and Catherine (Palmer) Bacheler. After Catherine died in India, Albert, his father, and his stepmother returned to the United States in 1852. Stacy, *Otis Robinson Bacheler*, 245, 475.

2. Babb Family Papers, MARBL.

3. Special thanks to Camille Breeze for bringing this coat and its story to my attention and for sharing her conservation reports with me.

4. Julie Pattison-Gordon, "Communities Rallied to Save Civil War Coat, Now Asked to Vote," *Bay State Banner* (Boston, MA), July 6, 2016, accessed August 8, 2016, http://baystatebanner.com/news/2016/jul/06/communities-rallied-save-civil-war-coat-now-asked-to-vote/.

5. "The Latest News," *Hartford Courant*, September 19, 1862, 3.

6. Burge, June 3, 1862, *Diary*, 128.

7. Mahalay Hyatte to Joseph E. Brown, January 22, 1862, Joseph Emerson Brown Governor's Incoming Correspondence, GSA.

8. General Orders, No. 59, Department of the Missouri, Records of the Quartermaster General, March 10, 1862, RG 92, entry 225, box no. 1170, NARA.

9. Joseph Addison Waddell, May 7, 1862, "Augusta County: Diary of Joseph Addison Waddell (1855–1865)," Valley of the Shadow: Two Communities in the American Civil War, https://valley.newamericanhistory.org/diaries/AD1500.

10. George G. Bryson, "Handcuffs on Manassas Battlefield," *Confederate Veteran* 14, no. 1 (January 1906): 304.

11. John Babb to Father, September 2, 1862, John D. Babb Family Papers, 1862–65, MSS 360, MARBL.

12. W. K. Strong to Edwin Stanton, "Contraband Clothing," Records of the Quartermaster General, RG 92, box 399, NARA.

13. F. J. Child, for Boston Education Commission, "The Port Royal Free-Black Community," October 27, 1862, MHS.

14. Robert Hodge, quoted in Horwitz, *Confederates in the Attic*, 388.

Bibliography

Manuscript Collections

Ann Arbor, MI
  William Clements Library, University of Michigan
    African American History Collection
    Caroline F. Putnam Papers
    Church of the Covenant Collection
    Dayton Orphan Asylum Photograph Album
    E. Augustus Garrison Diary
    Elizabeth Rous Comstock Papers, 1740–1929
    Frank H. Stearns Papers
    Henry Hayes Journal
    James S. Schoff Civil War Collection
      John C. Beattie Family Correspondence
      H. H. Gillum
      Simon Peterson Papers
      Edward Cahill Collection, 1863–65
    Point Lookout Prison Collection
    Raymond Family Letters, 1864–65
    Simmons Sketchbook
    Simon Peterson Papers
    Soldiers' Relief Society Papers, Haverhill, Massachusetts
    Women's History Collection
Atlanta, GA
  Atlanta History Center
    Captain Francis DeGress Papers
    Perry Family Correspondence
  Georgia State Archives
    Joseph Emerson Brown Governor's Incoming Correspondence
  Stuart A. Rose Manuscript, Archives, and Rare Books Library, Emory University
    Burge Family Papers
    Confederate Miscellany Collection
    C.S.A. Quartermaster W. Frank Ayer Records, 1861–65
    James Burton Diary
    John D. Babb Family Papers, 1862–65
    William H. Ivey Papers
    William McFall Letters

Boston, MA
Massachusetts Historical Society
Bowditch Memorial Cabinet
Charles Henry Calhoun Brown Diary, 1864
Edmund Miles Papers
Education Commission Records, 1862–74
Edward Lillie Pierce Volumes, 1852–73
Frank C. More Papers, 1825–1941
Frank C. Morse Diaries, 1855–76
Jonathan F. Plimpton Collection of Civil War Buttons and Insignia
Cambridge, MA
Baker Library, Harvard University
R. G. Dun and Company Papers
Houghton Library, Harvard University
James S. Wadsworth, *Report to the Adjutant General, U.S. Army*, December 1863
United States American Freedmen's Inquiry Commission Papers
Chapel Hill, NC
Southern Historical Collection, University of North Carolina
Cadwallader Jones Iredell Papers, 1856–65
C. D. Epps Papers, 1862–1915
Charles Howard's Family Domestic History, c. 1910
David Franklin Thorpe Papers, 1854–1944
Emma LeConte Diary, 1864–65
George W. Bowen Diary, 1863–81
Habersham Elliott Papers, 1820–98
Harriet Jacobs Family Papers Project Records, 1890s–2005
Henry A. Huntington Papers, 1862–64
Hermitage Plantation Papers, 1864
Howard Family Papers, 1856–1917
James Hervey Greenlee Diary, 1837; 1847–1902
John H. Crowder Papers, 1862–73
Margaret E. Blackwell Papers, 1861–65
Martha Schofield Papers, transcription, 1865–69
McLaurin Family Papers, 1861–99
Paul Turner Vaughan Papers, 1862–65
Peter Evans Smith Papers, 1738–1944
Richard F. Langdon Papers, 1863
Roach and Eggleston Family Papers, 1825–1905
Samuel Agnew Diary
Samuel H. Hines Papers, 1864–71
Shotwell Family Papers, 1829–1930
Springs Family Papers, 1772–1924
William King Diary
Charleston, SC
South Carolina Historical Society
Hall T. McGee Diary

Louisa McCord Smythe Papers, 1862–c. 1920
Porcher Family Papers
Columbus, OH
Ohio Historical Society
Jacob Bruner Letters, 1861–63
Haverford, PA
Haverford College Quaker & Special Collections
Julia Wilbur Papers, 1843–1908
Montgomery, AL
Alabama Department of Archives
Diary of Sarah Rousseau Espy
Nashville, TN
Tennessee State Library & Archives
Gerald Branch Howard Papers
New York, NY
New-York Historical Society
Gilder Lehrman Collection
New-York Historical Society Broadsides Collection
Philadelphia, PA
Historical Society of Pennsylvania
Charles Henry Coxe Letters
Frank T. Bennett Diary, 1862
Helen S. Grier Diary, 1862–63
Horstmann-Lippincott Family Papers, 1724–1963
Jefferson Justice Papers, 1862–91
Society of Union Army Records
William Olcott Papers
Wister and Butler Families Papers, 1700–2005, Collection 1962, *Camp Views of the War of the Rebellion*, 1861–64
Kislak Center for Special Collections, Rare Books, and Manuscripts, University of Pennsylvania
Georgiana Miller Johnson Diary, 1861–70
Georgietta W. Savage McLaughlin Diaries, 1860–67
Harriet Buss Papers
Library Company of Philadelphia
Cartes-de-Visite Collection
Civil War Miscellanies Collection
Civil War Poems and Songs Collection
Civil War Scrapbook of Envelopes and Portraits
Civil War Volunteer Saloons and Hospital Collection, 1861–68
Confederate States of America Collection
McAllister Civil War Prints, Ephemera, and Scrapbooks
Richmond, VA
Library of Virginia
Robert E. Lee Camp Confederate Soldiers' Home Applications for Admission, 1884–1941

Virginia Museum of History and Culture
Bates Collection
Booker Family of Mecklenburg County, VA, Papers, 1861–65
Caroline Kean Hill Diary
Fairfax Family of Alexandria, VA, Letters, 1861–99
Gruter and Gerecke Account Book, 1862–64
James Madison Brannock Papers, 1862–65
John N. Cadwallader Letters
John William Holloway Papers
Livingston Family of Madison County, FL, Papers, 1862–65
Margaret Loughborough Reminiscence
Mason Family Papers, 1825–1902
Turner Ashby, Letter, December 5, 1860
Roswell, GA
Roswell Historical Society
Barrington King Letters
Catherine M. N. King Correspondence
Swarthmore, PA
Friends Historical Library of Swarthmore College
Martha Schofield Papers, 1853–1944
Martha Schofield Photograph Collection
Valdosta, GA
Valdosta State University Archives and Special Collections
Broun Family Civil War Letters, 1860–64
Washington, DC
Library of Congress
Abraham Lincoln Papers at the Library of Congress
Alfred Mordecai Papers, 1790–1948
Black History Collection
Esther H. Hawks Papers
Frederick Douglass Papers
John N. Ferguson Diaries, 1861–66
Liljenquist Family Collection
Lydia J. Stull Papers, 1865
Marshall M. Miller Papers, 1862–1903
Mary Ann Bickerdyke Papers
William A. Gladstone Collection of African American Photographs
William A. Gladstone Papers
National Archives and Records Administration
Records of the Adjutant General, RG 94
Records of the Bureau of Refugees, Freedmen, and Abandoned Lands, RG 105
Records of the Judge Advocate General (Army), 1792–2010, RG 153
Records of the Quartermaster General, RG 92
US Civil War Service Records, M324

Worcester, MA
American Antiquarian Society
Barton Family Civil War Letters, 1862–68
Cartes-de-Visite Collection
Civil War Collection, 1861–66
Haverhill and Bradford (MA) Soldiers Relief Society Records, 1861
Henry A. Huntington Papers
Instructional Games Collection
James Helme Rickard Civil War Letters, 1864–66
John E. Anderson Collection
John Francis Gleason Papers, 1860–96
John G. Gough Papers, 1827, 1843–86
Lucy Chase Papers
Samuel E. Staples Papers, 1849–1900
William Augustus Willoughby Papers, 1861–65

National Archives Records Digitized on Fold3.com

Civil War Subversion Investigations
Confederate Citizens File
Southern Claims Commission Records
Union Citizens Files

Object Collections

American Civil War Museum, Richmond, VA
Atlanta History Center, Atlanta, GA
Chicago History Museum, Chicago, IL
Confederate Museum, Charleston, SC
Kent State Museum, Kent, OH
Massachusetts Historical Society, Boston, MA
Metropolitan Museum of Art, New York, NY
Minnesota Historical Society, Minneapolis, MN
National Civil War Museum, Harrisburg, PA
National Museum of African American History and Culture, Smithsonian Institution, Washington, DC
National Museum of American History, Smithsonian Institution, Washington, DC
New York Historical Society, New York, NY
Pitt Rivers Museum, Oxford, UK
Roswell Historical Society, Roswell, GA
Smith Plantation, Roswell, GA
South Carolina Historical Society, Charleston, SC
US National Park Service Database
Antietam National Battlefield, Sharpsburg, MD
Gettysburg National Military Park, Gettysburg, PA

National Park Service Museums and Collections Database
The Valentine, Richmond, VA
Virginia Museum of History and Culture, Richmond, VA

Digitized Letters and Diaries

Agnew, Samuel Andrew. *Diary, 1863–1864*. Documenting the American South, UNC–Chapel Hill.
Clark, H. C. *Diary of the War of Separation*. Documenting the American South, UNC–Chapel Hill.
Cormany, Rachel. *Diary, 1863*. The Valley of the Shadow, UVA.
Emerson, Nancy. *Memoranda of Events, Thoughts, &c, 1862*. The Valley of the Shadow, UVA.
Fisher, Julia Johnson. *Diary, 1864*. Documenting the American South, UNC–Chapel Hill.
Gallaher, DeWitt Clinton. *Diary, 1864–1865*. The Valley of the Shadow, UVA.
King, William. *Diary, 1864*. Documenting the American South, UNC–Chapel Hill.
Niles, Jason. *Diary, 1861–1864*. Documenting the American South, UNC–Chapel Hill.
Wadley, Sarah Lois. *Diary, 1859–1865*. Documenting the American South, UNC–Chapel Hill.
Wallace, Frances Woolfolk. *Diary, 1864*. Documenting the American South, UNC–Chapel Hill.
Withers, Anita Dywer. *Diary, 1860–1865*. Documenting the American South, UNC–Chapel Hill.

Newspapers and Periodicals

Alexandria (VA) Gazette
Alleghenian (Ebensburg, PA)
Army Argus and Crisis (Mobile, AL)
Arthur's Home Magazine (Philadelphia, PA)
Augusta (GA) Chronicle
Black Republican (New Orleans, LA)
Boston(MA) Recorder
Caledonian (St. Johnsbury, VT)
Camden (SC) Confederate
Carolina Observer (Fayetteville, NC)
Christian Recorder (Philadelphia, PA)
Cincinnati (OH) Daily Enquirer
Columbian Register (New Haven, CT)
Confederate Veteran (Nashville, TN)
Congressional Globe (Washington, DC)
Connecticut Courant (Hartford, CT)
Daily Age (Philadelphia, PA)
Daily Columbus (GA) Enquirer
Daily Constitutionalist (Augusta, GA)
Daily Constitutional Union (Washington, DC)
Daily Intelligencer (Wheeling, WV)
Daily Ledger (New Albany, IN)
Daily National Intelligencer (Washington, DC)
Daily Picayune (New Orleans, LA)
Daily Sentinel (Indianapolis, IN)
Dayton (OH) Daily Empire
Deseret News (Salt Lake City, UT)
Douglass' Monthly (Rochester, NY)
Evening Star (Washington, DC)
Evening Telegraph (Philadelphia, PA)
Fayetteville (GA) Observer
Fincher's Trades Review (Philadelphia, PA)
Frank Leslie's Illustrated News (New York, NY)
Fremont (OH) Journal
Godey's Lady's Book and Magazine (Philadelphia, PA)

Hagerstown (MD) Herald of Freedom & Torch Light
Harper's New Monthly Magazine (New York, NY)
Harper's Weekly (New York, NY)
Hartford (CT) Daily Courant
Holmes County Republican (Millersburg, OH)
Illustrated Exhibitor and Magazine of Art (London, England)
Jeffersonian Democrat (Chardon, OH)
Liberator (Boston, MA)
Macon (TN) Daily Telegraph
Nashville (TN) Times
New York Commercial Advertiser (New York, NY)
New York Daily Tribune (New York, NY)
New York Times (New York, NY)
Peterson's Magazine (Philadelphia, PA)
Philadelphia (PA) Inquirer
Plattsburgh (PA) Republican
Portland (ME) Advertiser
Raftsman's Journal (Clearfield, PA)
Richmond (VA) Dispatch
Richmond (VA) Examiner
Richmond (VA) Whig
Scientific American (New York, NY)
Semi-Weekly Standard (Raleigh, NC)
Southern Banner (Athens, GA)
Staunton (VA) Spectator and General Advertiser
Vanity Fair (New York, NY)
Wisconsin Daily Patriot (Madison, WI)

Selected Books, Pamphlets, and Treatises

Abbott, John Stevens Cabot. *The History of the Civil War in America: Comprising a Full and Impartial Account of the Origin and Progress of the Rebellion*. Springfield, MA: G. Bill, 1863.

Acts of the General Assembly of the State of Georgia Passed in Milledgeville at an Annual Session in November and December, 1863; Also Extra Session of 1864. Milledgeville, GA: Boughton, Nisbet, Barnes, & Moore, State Printers, 1864.

Alvord, John Watson. *Letters from the South*. Washington, DC, 1870.

American Freedmen's Inquiry Commission Report. 1863.

Andrews, Ethan Allen. *Slavery and the Domestic Slave-Trade in the United States*. Boston: Light & Stearns, 1836.

Annual Reports of the Asst. Commissioner, Bureau of Refugees, Freedmen and Abandoned Lands. Washington, DC, 1865–69.

Arming the Slaves in the War for the Union: Scenes, Speeches, and Events. New York: Rogers and Sherwood, 1875.

The Art of Good Behavior. New York: Huestis and Cozans, 1850.

Austin, Jane G. *Dora Darling: The Daughter of the Regiment*. Boston: J. E. Tilton and Company, 1865.

"The Automaton Regiment, or Infantry Soldiers' Practical Instructor." New York: D. Van Nostrand, 1863.

Baker, T. Lindsay, and Julie P. Baker, eds. *The WPA Oklahoma Slave Narratives*. Norman: University of Oklahoma Press, 1996.

Barrow, Sarah. *Red, White, and Blue Socks*. 1862.

Berthollet, C. L., and A. B. Berthollet. *Elements of the Art of Dyeing and Bleaching*. Translated by Andrew Ure. London: Thomas Tegg, 1841. First published 1791.

Bigelow, James. *Elements of Technology*. Boston: Hilliard, Gray, Little, and Wilkins, 1831.

Blackwell, Elizabeth. *The Laws of Life: With Special Reference to the Physical Education of Girls*. New York: George P. Putnam, 1852.

Brown, William Wells. *The Negro in the American Rebellion: His Heroism and His Fidelity*. Boston: Lee and Shepard, 1867.

Califf, J. M. "To the Ex-members and Friends of the 7th USCT." Fort Hamilton, NY: 1878.

Candler, Allen D. *The Confederate Records of the State of Georgia*. 2 vols. Atlanta: Chas. P. Byrd, 1909.

Carter, Robert Goldthwaite. *Four Brothers in Blue: A Story of the Great Civil War from Bull Run to Appomattox*. 1913. Reprint, Norman: University of Oklahoma Press, 1999.

Cartwright, Samuel. "Diseases and Peculiarities of the Negro Race." *De Bow's Review* 11 (1851): 64–69.

Catalogue of the Confederate Museum. Richmond: I. N. Jones, 1898.

Catalogue of the Confederate Museum of the Confederate Memorial Literary Society. Richmond: Ware and Duke, 1905.

Charles Stokes & Company's Illustrated Almanac of Fashion for 1863. Philadelphia, 1863.

Child, F. J., broadside for Boston Education Commission. "The Port Royal Free-Black Community." Boston, October 27, 1862.

Child, Lydia Maria. *The Freedmen's Book*. Boston: Ticknor and Fields, 1865.

Chisholm, Julian John. *A Manual of Military Surgery: For the Use of the Surgeons of the Confederate States Army*. 1861. Reprint, San Francisco: Norman Publishing, 1989.

Chittenden, Lucius. *Recollections of President Lincoln and His Administration*. New York: Harper & Brothers, 1891.

Confederate States of America. "An Act to Prohibit the Importation of Luxuries, or of Articles Not Necessaries or of Common Use." Richmond, VA: Parrish and Willingham, February 6, 1864.

Confederate States of America War Department. *Uniform and Dress of the Army of the Confederate States*. Richmond, VA: Wynne, 1861.

Cooley, Arnold J., and J. C. Brough. *Cooley's Cyclopaedia of Practical Receipts, Processes, and Collateral Information in the Arts, Manufactures, Professions, and Trades*. London: John Churchill and Sons, 1864.

Cowden, Robert. *A Brief Sketch of the Organization and Services of the Fifty-Ninth Regiment of United States Colored Infantry, and Biographical Sketches*. Dayton, OH: United Brethren Publishing House, 1883.

Dalton, William. *Gutta Percha: Its Discovery, History, Remarkable Properties, Vast Utility and Application to Scientific and Ornamental Purposes*. London: J. O. Clarke, 1849.

Davis, Jefferson. *The Rise and Fall of the Confederate Government*. 1881. Reprint, New York: Barnes & Noble, 2010.

Dixon, Thomas, Jr. *The Clansman: An Historical Romance of the Ku Klux Klan*. New York: Doubleday, Page and Company, 1905.

Douglass, Frederick. *Addresses of the Hon. W. D. Kelley, Miss Anna E. Dickenson and Mr. Frederick Douglass*. Philadelphia: July 4, 1863.

Emancipation League. *Facts Concerning the Freedmen, Their Capacity and Their Destiny*. Boston: Press of Commercial Printing House, 1863.

Fay, Eli. *Discourse, at the Funeral of Hans P. Jorgensen, Capt. of Co. A, 15th Regiment, Mass. Volunteers*. Fitchburg, MA: Caleb C. Curtis, 1863.

Fisk, Clinton B. *Plain Counsels for Freedmen: In Sixteen Brief Lectures*. Boston: American Tract Society, 1866.

"Game of Visit to Camp." New York: McLoughlin Brothers, between 1863 and 1870.

General Orders from the Adjutant-General and Inspector's Office, CSA. Richmond, VA, 1862.

General Orders from the Adjutant-General and Inspector's Office, CSA. Richmond, VA, 1863.

Glencross, William. *Manual; or True Guide to Practical Cutting*. New York: William Glencross, 1866.

Gould, Benjamin Apthorp. *Investigations in the Military and Anthropological Statistics of American Soldiers*. New York: Published for the US Sanitary Commission by Hurd and Houghton, 1869.

The Habits of Good Society. New York: Carleton, 1864.

Haco, Dion. *Rob Cobb Kennedy, The Incendiary Spy*. New York: Hurst and Co., 1866.

Hartley, Cecil B. *The Gentlemen's Book of Etiquette*. Boston: DeWolfe Fiske, 1873.

Higginson, Thomas Wentworth. *Army Life in a Black Regiment*. Boston: Fields, Osgood and Company, 1870.

———. *The Complete Civil War Journal and Selected Letters of Thomas Wentworth Higginson*. Edited by Christopher Looby. Chicago: University of Chicago Press, 1999.

Holland, John. *A Treatise on the Progressive Improvement and Present State of the Manufactures in Metal*. Vol. 3. London: Longman, Rees, Orme, Brown, Green & Longman, 1834.

Hopkins, Alphonso A. *The Life of Clinton Bowen Fisk*. New York: Funk and Wagnalls, 1890.

Hopley, Catherine C. *Life in the South from the Commencement of the War*. Vol. 1. London: Chapman and Hall, 1863.

Howe, S. G. (Samuel Gridley). *An Essay on Separate and Congregate Systems of Prison*. Boston, 1846.

Hunter, Alexander. *Johnny Reb and Billy Yank*. New York and Washington, DC: Neale Publishing Company, 1905.

The Illustrated Exhibitor and Magazine of Art. Vol. 2. London: John Cassell, La Belle Sauvage Yard, Ludgate Hill, 1852.

Index of Reports of Committees of the House of Representatives for the Second Session of the Forty-First Congress, 1869–1870, vol. 265. Washington, DC: Government Printing Office, 1870.

Kelley, William D. *Remarks of William Kelley, of Pennsylvania*. Washington, DC: L. Towers, 1864.

Kirkland, Frazier. *Pictorial Book of Anecdotes and Incidents of the War of the Rebellion*. Hartford, CT: Hartford Publishing Co., 1866.

The Ladies' Companion. London: Rogerson and Tuxford, 1855.

Lewis, Richard. *Camp Life of a Confederate Boy of Bratton's Brigade, Longstreet's Corps, C.S.A.* Charleston, SC: News and Courier Book Presses, 1883.

Lieber, Francis. "General Order No. 100: Instructions for the Government of the Armies of the United States in the Field." 1863. Reprint, Washington, DC: Government Printing Office, 1898.

Love, Thomas. *The Art of Cleaning, Dyeing, Scouring and Finishing, Etc.* London: Longman, Brown, Green, and Longmans, 1854.

Matthews, James M., ed. *The Statutes at Large of the Provisional Government of the Confederate States of America from the Institution of the Government.* Richmond, VA: R. M. Smith, 1864.

McKim, J. Miller. *The Freedmen of South Carolina: Address Delivered by J. Miller M'Kim.* Philadelphia: Willis P. Hazard, 1862.

Moore, Frank. *Women of the War: Their Heroism and Self-Sacrifice.* Hartford, CT: S. S. Scranton and Company, 1867.

Moore, George H. *Historical Notes on the Employment of Negroes in the American Army of the Revolution.* New York: Charles T. Evans, 1862.

Napier, James. *Chemistry Applied to Dyeing.* Philadelphia: Henry Carey Byrd, 1853.

———. *A Manual of the Art of Dyeing.* Glasgow: Richard Griffin and Co., 1853.

National Freedman's Relief Association. "Appeal to the Women of the United States in Behalf of the Freedwomen and Children." New York, March 1862.

A Naval Encyclopaedia. Philadelphia: L. R. Hamersley, 1881.

New York Association for Colored Volunteers. *First Organization of Colored Troops in the State of New York.* New York, 1864.

Nicolay, John George, and John Hay. *Abraham Lincoln: A History.* Vol. 6. 1886. Reprint, New York: Century Company, 1914.

Nordhoff, Charles. *The Freedmen of South Carolina.* New York: Charles T. Evans, 1863.

Parnell, Edward Andrew. *Dyeing and Calico-Printing.* London: Taylor, Walton, and Maberly, 1849.

Penny, Virginia. *The Employments of Women: A Cyclopaedia of Women's Work.* Boston: Walker, Wise, and Company, 1863.

Pollard, Edward A. *The Lost Cause: A New Southern History of the War of the Confederates.* New York: E. B. Treat and Co., 1866.

Preston, Walter. *Report of the Committee on Quartermaster and Commissary Departments, CSA.* Richmond, VA: 1864.

Prichard, Sarah J. *Kate Morgan and Her Soldiers.* Philadelphia: American Sunday School Union, 1862.

Refugee Relief Commission of Ohio. *First Semi-Annual Report of the Refugee Relief Commission of Ohio.* Cincinnati, OH: Times Steam Book and Job Printing Establishment, 1864.

Regulations of the Army of the Confederate States, 1862. Richmond, VA: J. W. Randolph, 1862.

Report of the Commissioner of Patents for the Year 1863. Washington, DC: Government Printing Office, 1866.

Report to the Executive Committee of New England Yearly Meeting of Friends upon the Condition and Needs of the Freed People of Color in Washington and Virginia. New Bedford, MA: E. Anthony & Sons, 1864.

Report of the General Superintendent of Freedmen, Department of the Tennessee and State of Arkansas for 1864. Memphis, TN, 1865.

Report of the Proceedings of a Meeting Held at Concert Hall, Philadelphia. Philadelphia: Merrihew and Thompson, 1863.

Report of the Secretary of the Navy, December 1862. Washington, DC, 1863.

Reports of the [Boston] Soldiers' Memorial Society. Boston, 1867.

Revised United States Army Regulations of 1861: With an Appendix Containing the Changes and Laws Affecting Army Regulations and Articles of War to June 25, 1863. Washington, DC: Government Printing Office, 1863.

Rice, Allen Thorndike, ed. *Reminiscences of Abraham Lincoln by Distinguished Men of His Time*. New York: Harper & Brothers, 1909.

Rollin, Frank A. *Life and Public Services of Martin R. Delany*. Boston: Lee and Shepard, 1883.

Saguezs, Aaron F. *The Tailor's Master-piece*. New York: Lomax and Vinten, 1834.

Scott, Genio C. *The Cutter's Guide: Being a Series of Systems for Cutting Every Kind of Modern Garment*. New York, 1859.

Shankland, John R. *Parris' System of Garment Draughting*. Philadelphia: John H. Gihon, 1847.

Sigourney, Lydia Howard. *Letters to Mothers*. New York: Harper and Brothers, 1845.

Stacy, Thomas H. *Otis Robinson Bacheler: Fifty-Three Years a Missionary to India*. Boston: Morning Star, 1904.

The Tailor's Manual; Or Twenty Years a New England Tailor. Worcester, MA: Chas. Hamilton, 1856.

The Town of Wayland in the Civil War of 1861–1865. Boston: Rand, Avery and Frye, 1871.

Trowbridge, John T. *The South: A Tour of Its Battlefields and Ruined Cities*. Hartford, CT: L. Stebbins, 1866.

United States Army. *The Freedmen of Louisiana: Final Report of the Bureau of Free Labor, Dept. of the Gulf, to Major General E. R. S. Canby*. New Orleans, LA: New Orleans Times Book and Job Office, 1865.

United States Sanitary Commission. *Sanitary Commission*. New York, 1862.

United States War Department. *The War of the Rebellion: A Compilation of the Official Records of the Union and Confederate Armies*, Ser. I–IV. Washington, DC: Government Printing Office, 1880–1901.

Walker, William Carey. *History of the Eighteenth Regiment, Conn. Volunteers*. Norwich, CT, 1885.

Walsh, John Henry. *The Economical Housekeeper*. London: Routledge and Company, 1857.

Ward, Asahel F. *The Philadelphia Fashions & Tailors' Archetypes for Spring and Summer, 1864*. Philadelphia: Asahel F. Ward, 1864.

Warren, Horatio N. *Two Reunions of the 142nd Regiment, PA*. Buffalo, NY: Courier Co., 1890.

Washington and Jackson on Negro Soldiers. Philadelphia: H. C. Baird, 1863.

Woman's Work for the Lowly: As Illustrated in the Work of the American Missionary Association among the Freedmen. Boston: South Boston Inquirer Press, 1874.

Women's Patriotic Association for Diminishing the Use of Imported Luxuries. New York: Sanford, Harroun & Co., 1864.

The Workwoman's Guide. London: Simpkin and Marshall, 1838.

Works Progress Administration. *Slave Narratives: A Folk History of Slavery in the United States from Interviews with Former Slaves*. 17 vols. Washington, DC, 1941.

Wright, Caleb Earl. *Two Years behind the Plough; or, The Experience of a Pennsylvania Farm-Boy*. Philadelphia: Claxton, Remsen & Haffelfinger, 1878.

Published Diaries, Memoirs, and Letter Collections

Abbott, Lemuel Abijah. *Personal Recollections and Civil War Diary, 1864*. Burlington, VA: Free Press Print Co., 1908.

Andrews, Eliza Frances. *The Wartime Journal of a Georgia Girl*. Edited by Jean V. Berlin. Lincoln: University of Nebraska Press, 1997.

Ashby, Thomas A. *The Valley Campaigns: Being Reminiscences of a Non-Combatant While Between the Lines in the Shenandoah Valley during the War of the States*. New York: Neale Publishing Company, 1914.

Bailey, George. *A Private Chapter of the War (1861–1865)*. St. Louis: G. I. Jones and Company, 1880.

Bartol, Cyrus A. *The Nation's Hour: A Tribute to Major Sidney Willard, Delivered in the West Church*. Boston: Walker, Wise and Company, 1862.

Berlin, Ira, Barbara J. Fields, Thavolia Glymph, Joseph P. Reidy, and Leslie S. Rowland, eds. *Freedom: A Documentary History of Emancipation, 1861–1867*. Ser. I, Vol. 1, *The Destruction of Slavery*. Cambridge, UK: Cambridge University Press, 1985.

Billings, John Davis. *Hardtack and Coffee; or, The Unwritten Story of Army Life*. Boston: George M. Smith and Company, 1887.

Blackford, Susan Lee, and Charles Minor Blackford. *Letters from Lee's Army*. Edited by Charles Minor Blackford III. Lincoln: University of Nebraska Press, 1998.

Blease, Cole L. *Destruction of Property in Columbia S.C. by Sherman's Army, Speech of Hon. Cole L. Blease, a Senator of the State of South Carolina*. 71st Cong., 2d. Sess, Senate Doc. 149. Washington, DC: Government Printing Office, 1930.

Bokum, Herman. *The Testimony of a Refugee from East Tennessee*. Philadelphia, 1863.

Botume, Elizabeth Hyde. *First Days among the Contrabands*. Boston: Lee and Shepard, 1893.

Boyce, Charles William. *A Brief History of the Twenty-Eighth Regiment, New York State Volunteers*. Buffalo, NY: Matthews-Northrup, 1896.

Boyd, Cyrus F. *The Civil War Diary of Cyrus F. Boyd, Fifteenth Iowa Infantry, 1861–1863*. Edited by Mildred Throne. Baton Rouge: Louisiana State University Press, 1998.

Bradbury, William H. *While Father Is Away: The Civil War Letters of William H. Bradbury*. Edited by Jennifer Cain Bohrnstedt. Louisville: University Press of Kentucky, 2003.

Brockett, L. P., and Mary C. Vaughan. *Woman's Work in the Civil War: A Record of Heroism, Patriotism, and Patience*. Philadelphia: Zeigler and McCurdy, 1867.

Burge, Dolly Lunt. *The Diary of Dolly Lunt Burge, 1848–1879*. Edited by Christine Jacobson Carter. Athens: University of Georgia Press, 1997.

Butler, Benjamin F. *Private and Official Correspondence of Gen. Benjamin F. Butler, during the Period of the Civil War*. Vol. 2. Springfield, MA: Plimpton Press, 1917.

Cheney, John C. *Illinois Artillery Officer's Civil War: The Diary and Letters of John Cheney*. Edited by Gordon Armstrong. College Station, TX: Virtualbookworm.com Publishing Inc., 2005.

Chesnut, Mary Boykin. *A Diary from Dixie*. Edited by Ben Ames Williams. 1962. Reprint, Cambridge, MA: Harvard University Press, 2002.

Clarke, Caroline Cowles Richards. *Village Life in America, 1852–1872, Including the Period of the American Civil War as Told in the Diary of a School-Girl*. New York: Henry Holt & Co., 1913.

Clayton, Sarah Conley. *Requiem for a Lost City: A Memoir of Civil War Atlanta and the Old South*. Edited by Robert S. Davis Jr. Macon, GA: Mercer University Press, 1999.

Conyngham, David P. *Sherman's March through the South*. New York: Sheldon and Company, 1865.

Corby, William. *Memoirs of Chaplain Life*. Chicago: La Monte, O'Donnell and Co., 1893.

Cumming, Kate. *A Journal of Hospital Life in the Confederate Army of the Tennessee*. Louisville, KY: John P. Morton and Co., 1866.

———. *Kate: The Journal of a Confederate Nurse*. Edited by Richard Barksdale Harwell. Baton Rouge: Louisiana State University Press, 1998.

———. *A Northern Daughter and a Southern Wife: The Civil War Reminiscences and Letters of Katharine H. Cumming, 1860–1865*. Edited by Kirk Wood. Augusta, GA: Richmond County Historical Society, 1976.

Daly, Maria Lydig. *Diary of a Union Lady, 1861–1865*. Edited by Harold Earl Hammond. 1962. Reprint, Lincoln: University of Nebraska Press, 2000.

Davis, William C., Brian Pohanka, and Don Troiani, eds. *Civil War Journal: The Legacies*. New York: Harper Collins, 1998.

Day, David L. *My Diary of Rambles with the 25th Massachusetts Volunteer Infantry*. Milford, MA: King and Billings, 1884.

Demos, John, ed. *Remarkable Providences: Readings on Early American History*. 1972. Reprint, Boston: Northeastern University Press, 1991.

De Velling, Charles. *History of the Seventeenth Regiment: First Brigade, Third Division, Fourteenth Corps, Army of the Cumberland*. Zanesville, OH: E. R. Sullivan, 1889.

Douglas, Henry Kyd. *I Rode with Stonewall: The War Experiences of the Youngest Member of Jackson's Staff*. 1940. Reprint, Chapel Hill: University of North Carolina Press, 1968.

Edmonston, Catherine Ann Devereux. *Journal of a Secesh Lady: The Diary of Catherine Ann Devereux Edmonston, 1860–1866*. Edited by Beth G. Crabtree and James W. Patton. 1979. Reprint, Raleigh, NC: Division of Archives and History, Department of Cultural Resources, 1995.

Eppes, Susan Bradford. *The Negro of the Old South: A Bit of Period History*. Chicago: Joseph P. Branch Publishing Company, 1925.

———. *Through Some Eventful Years*. Macon, GA: J. W. Burke, 1926.

Favill, Josiah Marshall. *The Diary of a Young Officer Serving with the Armies of the United States during the War of the Rebellion*. Chicago: R. R. Donnelly and Sons, 1909.

Fisk, Wilbur. *Hard Marching Every Day: The Civil War Letters of Private Wilbur Fisk, 1861–1865*. Edited by Emil Rosenblatt and Ruth Rosenblatt. Lawrence: University of Kansas Press, 1992.

Ford, Jennifer W., ed. *The Hour of Our Nation's Agony: The Civil War Letters of Lt. William Cowper Nelson of Mississippi*. Knoxville: University of Tennessee Press, 2007.

Galloway, T. H., ed. *Dear Old Roswell: The Civil War Letters of the King Family, of Roswell, Georgia*. Macon, GA: Mercer University Press, 2003.

Hague, Parthenia Antoinette. *A Blockaded Family: Life in Southern Alabama during the Civil War*. Boston: Houghton Mifflin, 1888.

Higginson, Henry Lee. *Life and Letters of Henry Lee Higginson*. Edited by Bliss Perry. Boston: Atlantic Monthly Press, 1921.

Hitchcock, Henry. *Marching with Sherman: Passages from the Letters and Campaign Diaries of Henry Hitchcock, Major and Assistant Adjutant General of Volunteers, November 1864–May 1865*. Edited by M. A. DeWolfe Howe. New Haven, CT: Yale University Press, 1927.

Holt, Daniel M. *A Surgeon's Civil War: The Letters and Diary of Daniel M. Holt, M.D.* Edited by James M. Greiner, Janet L. Coryell, and James R. Smither. Kent, OH: Kent State University Press, 1994.

Hunt, James. *The Negro's Place in Nature: A Paper Read before the London Anthropological Society*. New York, 1864.

Jackson, Oscar Lawrence. *The Colonel's Diary: Journals Kept before and during the Civil War by the Late Colonel Oscar L. Jackson*. Sharon, PA, 1922.

Jacobs, Harriet. *Incidents in the Life of a Slave Girl*. Boston: L. Maria Child, 1860.

Johns, Henry T. *Life with the Forty-Ninth Massachusetts Volunteers*. Pittsfield, MA, 1864.

Johnson, Charles F. *The Civil War Letters of Colonel Charles F. Johnson, Invalid Corps*. Edited by Fred Pelka. Amherst: University of Massachusetts Press, 2004.

Jones, James P., ed. *Tennessee in the Civil War: Selected Contemporary Accounts of Military and Other Events, Month by Month*. Jefferson, NC: McFarland, 2011.

Jones, John Beauchamp. *A Rebel War Clerk's Diary at the Confederate States Capital*. Philadelphia: J. B. Lippincott & Co., 1866.

Kemble, Frances Anne. *Journal of a Residence on a Georgian Plantation in 1838–1839*. New York: Harper & Brothers, 1864.

Lee, Laura, and Julia Chase. *Winchester Divided: The Civil War Diaries of Julia Chase & Laura Lee*. Edited by Michael G. Mahon. Mechanicsburg, PA: Stackpole Books, 2002.

Livermore, Mary A. *My Story of the War: A Woman's Narrative of Four Years Personal Experience*. Hartford, CT: A. D. Worthington and Company, 1890.

Lucas, Daniel R. *History of the 99th Indiana Infantry*. Lafayette, IN, 1865.

Marshall, Albert O. *Army Life of a Soldier's Journal: Incidents, Sketches, and Record of a Union Soldier's Army Life in Camp and Field, 1861–1864*. Joliet, IL, 1884.

McDonald, Cornelia Peake. *A Woman's Civil War: A Diary with Reminiscences of the War from March 1862*. Edited by Minrose C. Gwin. Madison: University of Wisconsin Press, 1992.

McGuire, Judith. *Diary of a Southern Refugee during the War*. Richmond, VA: J. W. Randolph & English, 1889.

Mellon, James, ed. *Bullwhip Days: The Slaves Remember, An Oral History*. New York: Grove/Atlantic, 1988.

Miller, Edwin Haviland, ed. *Selected Letters of Walt Whitman*. Iowa City: University of Iowa Press, 1990.

Moore, Frank. *The Rebellion Record: A Diary of American Events*. New York: G. P. Putnam, 1862.

Morgan, Thomas Jefferson. *Reminiscences of Service with Colored Troops*. Providence: Soldiers' and Sailors' Historical Society of Rhode Island, 1885.

Morgan Dawson, Sarah. *A Confederate Girl's Diary*. Boston: Houghton Mifflin, 1913.

Northup, Solomon. *Twelve Years a Slave: Narrative of Solomon Northup*. New York: Miller, Orton, and Mulligan, 1855.

Olmsted, Frederick Law. *A Journey in the Seaboard Slave States*. New York: Dix and Edwards, 1856.

Osborn, Thomas Ward. *The Fiery Trail: A Union Officer's Account of Sherman's Last Campaigns*. Edited by Richard Harwell and Philip N. Racine. Knoxville: University of Tennessee Press, 1986.

Our Women in the War: The Lives They Lived; The Deaths They Died. Charleston, SC: News and Courier Book Presses, 1885.

Patrick, Jeffrey L., ed. *Three Years with Wallace's Zouaves: The Civil War Memoirs of Thomas Wise Durham*. Macon, GA: Mercer University Press, 2003.

Phinney, Mary. *Adventures of an Army Nurse in Two Wars*. Edited by James Phinney Munroe. Boston: Little, Brown, and Company, 1904.

Putnam, Sallie Brock. *Richmond during the War; Four Years of Personal Observation*. New York: G. W. Carleton & Co, Hay, 1866.

———. *Richmond during the War: Four Years of Personal Observation*. Edited by Virginia Scharff. Lincoln: University of Nebraska Press, 1996.

Rhodes, Robert Hunt, ed. *All for the Union: The Civil War Diary and Letters of Elisha Hunt Rhodes*. New York: Vintage Books, 1992.

Rogers, Seth. *Letters of Major Seth Rogers*. Edited by Thomas Wentworth Higginson. Boston: John Wilson and Son, 1910.

Saxon, Elizabeth Lyle. *A Southern Woman's War Time Reminiscences*. Memphis, TN: Pilcher Printing Co, 1905.

Small, Abner R. *The Road to Richmond: The Civil War Memoirs of Major Abner R. Small of the Sixteenth Maine Volunteers*. 1939. Reprint, New York: Fordham University Press, 2000.

Stevenson, William G. *Thirteen Months in the Rebel Army*. New York: A. S. Barnes & Company, 1862.

Stone, Kate. *Brokenburn: The Journal of Kate Stone, 1861–1868*. Edited by John Q. Anderson. 1955. Reprint, Baton Rouge: Louisiana State University Press, 1995.

Taylor, Mrs. Thomas, Mrs. Smythe, Mrs. August Kohn, Miss Poppenheim, and Miss Martha B. Washington, eds. *South Carolina Women in the Confederacy*. Vol. 1. Columbia, SC: State Company, 1903.

Venet, Wendy Hamand. *Sam Richards's Civil War Diary: A Chronicle of the Atlanta Home Front*. Athens: University of Georgia Press, 2009.

Waitz, Julia LeGrand. *The Journal of Julia LeGrand, New Orleans, 1862–1863*. Edited by Kate Mason Rowland and Agnes E. Croxall. Richmond, VA: Everett Waddey Co., 1911.

Watson, William. *Letters of a Civil War Surgeon*. Edited by Paul Fatout. 1961; West Lafayette, IN: Purdue University Press, 1996.

Wightman, Edward King. *From Antietam to Fort Fisher: The Civil War Letters of Edward King Wightman, 1862–1865*. Edited by Edward G. Longacre. Madison, NJ: Fairleigh Dickenson University Press, 1985.

Wilder, Burt G. *Practicing Medicine in a Black Regiment: The Civil War Diary of Burt G. Wilder, 55th Massachusetts*. Edited by Richard M. Reid. Amherst: University of Massachusetts Press, 2010.

Wilson, Joseph T. *The Black Phalanx: A History of the Negro Soldiers of the United States in the War of 1775–1812, 1861–1865*. Hartford, CT: American Publishing Company, 1888.

Worsham, John. *One of Jackson's Foot Cavalry*. New York: Neal Publishing Company, 1912.

Wright, Charles. *A Corporal's Story: Experiences in the Ranks of the Company C, 81st Ohio Vol. Infantry*. Philadelphia: James Beale, 1887.

Wyeth, John Allan. *With Sabre and Scalpel: The Autobiography of a Soldier and Surgeon.* New York: Harper & Brothers, 1914.

Yellin, Jean Fagan, ed. *The Harriet Jacobs Family Papers.* Chapel Hill: University of North Carolina Press, 2008.

Secondary Sources

Abruzzo, Margaret. *Polemical Pain: Slavery, Cruelty, and the Rise of Humanitarianism.* Baltimore: Johns Hopkins University Press, 2011.

———. "The Sins of Slaves and the Slaves of Sin: Toward a History of Moral Agency." In *The Worlds of Intellectual History*, edited by Joel Isaac, James T. Kloppenberg, Michael O'Brien, and Jennifer Ratner-Rosenhagen. Oxford, UK: Oxford University Press, 2017.

Adams, Michael C. C. *Living Hell: The Dark Side of the Civil War.* Baltimore: Johns Hopkins University Press, 2014.

Adolphus, Frederick R. *Imported Confederate Uniforms of Peter Tait & Co., Limerick, Ireland.* Frederick R. Adolphus, 2010.

Andreas, Peter. *Smuggler Nation: How Illicit Trade Made America.* New York: Oxford, 2013.

Ash, Juliet. *Dress behind Bars: Prison Clothing as Criminality.* London: I. B. Tauris, 2009.

Ash, Stephen V. *Middle Tennessee Society Transformed, 1860–1870: War and Peace in the Upper South.* 1988; Knoxville: University of Tennessee Press, 2006.

———. *When the Yankees Came: Conflict and Chaos in the Occupied South, 1861–1865.* Chapel Hill: University of North Carolina Press, 1995.

Attie, Jeannie. *Patriotic Toil: Northern Women and the American Civil War.* Ithaca, NY: Cornell University Press, 1998.

Auslander, Leora. "Beyond Words." *American Historical Review* 110, no. 4 (October 2005): 1015–45.

———. *Cultural Revolutions: Everyday Life and Politics in Britain, North America, and France.* Berkeley: University of California Press, 2008.

———. *Taste and Power: Furnishing Modern France.* Berkeley: University of California Press, 1996.

Auslander, Leora, and Tara Zahra, eds. *Objects of War: The Material Culture of Conflict and Displacement.* Ithaca, NY: Cornell University Press, 2018.

Bailey, Anne J. *War and Ruin: William T. Sherman and the Savannah Campaign.* Wilmington, DE: Scholarly Resources, 2003.

Balleisen, Edward J. *Navigating Failure: Bankruptcy and Commercial Society in Antebellum America.* Chapel Hill: University of North Carolina Press, 2001.

Balogh, Brian. *A Government Out of Sight: The Mystery of National Authority in Nineteenth-Century America.* Cambridge, UK: Cambridge University Press, 2009.

Barnett, Teresa. *Sacred Relics: Pieces of the Past in Nineteenth-Century America.* Chicago: University of Chicago Press, 2013.

Barthes, Roland. *Mythologies.* 1957. Reprint, New York: Hill and Wang, 2013.

Baumgarten, Linda. *What Clothes Reveal: The Language of Clothing in Colonial and Federal America.* New Haven, CT: Yale University Press, 2002.

Beatty, Bess. *Alamance: The Holt Family and Industrialization in a North Carolina County, 1837–1900.* Baton Rouge: Louisiana State University Press, 1999.

Beckert, Sven. *Empire of Cotton: A Global History*. New York: Vintage Books, 2014.

Bederman, Gail. *Manliness and Civilization: A Cultural History of Gender and Race in the United States, 1880–1917*. 1996. Reprint, Chicago and London: University of Chicago Press, 2008.

Beilein, Joseph M., Jr. *Bushwhackers: Guerrilla Warfare, Manhood and the Household in Civil War Missouri*. Kent, OH: Kent State University Press, 2016.

———. "The Guerrilla Shirt: A Labor of Love and the Style of Rebellion in Civil War Missouri." *Civil War History* 58, no. 2 (June 2012): 151–79.

Belz, Herman. *Reconstructing the Union: Theory and Policy during the Civil War*. Ithaca, NY: Cornell University Press, 1969.

Benedict, Michael Les. *A Compromise of Principle: Congressional Republicans and Reconstruction, 1863–1869*. New York: Norton, 1974.

Bensel, Richard. *Yankee Leviathan: The Origins of Central State Authority in America, 1859–1877*. Cambridge, UK: University of Cambridge Press, 1990.

Benson, Elaine, and John Esten. *A Brief History of Underwear: Unmentionables*. New York: Simon & Schuster, 1996.

Bercaw, Nancy. *Gendered Freedoms: Race, Rights, and the Politics of Household in the Delta, 1861–1875*. Gainesville: University Press of Florida, 2003.

Beringer, Richard E., Herman Hattaway, Archer Jones, and William N. Still Jr. *Why the South Lost the Civil War*. Athens: University of Georgia Press, 1986.

Berman, Marshall. *All That Is Solid Melts into Air: The Experience of Modernity*. London: Verso, 1983.

Berry, Stephen William, ed. *Weirding the War: Stories from the Civil War's Ragged Edges*. Athens: University of Georgia Press, 2011.

Berry, Stephen William. *All That Makes a Man: Love and Ambition in the Civil War South*. New York: Oxford University Press, 2003.

Biddle, Daniel R., and Murray Dubin. *Tasting Freedom: Octavius Catto and the Battle for Equality in Civil War America*. Philadelphia: Temple University Press, 2010.

Black, J. Anderson, and Madge Garland. *A History of Fashion*. New York: William Morrow and Company, 1980.

Blair, William A. *Cities of the Dead: Contesting the Memory of the Civil War in the South, 1865–1914*. Chapel Hill: University of North Carolina Press, 2004.

Bledstein, Burton J., and Robert D. Johnston, eds. *The Middling Sorts: Explorations in the History of the American Middle Class*. New York: Routledge, 2001.

Blight, David. *Beyond the Battlefield: Race, Memory, and the American Civil War*. Amherst: University of Massachusetts Press, 2002.

———. *Race and Reunion: The Civil War in American History*. Cambridge, MA: Harvard University Press, 2001.

Bohannon, Keith S. "Dirty, Ragged, and Ill-Provided For: Confederate Logistical Problems in the 1862 Maryland Campaign and Their Solutions." In *The Antietam Campaign*, edited by Gary W. Gallagher. Chapel Hill: University of North Carolina Press, 1999.

Boydston, Jeanne. *Home and Work: Housework, Wages, and the Ideology of Labor in the Early Republic*. New York: Oxford University Press, 1990.

Bradley, Mark L. *Bluecoats and Tar Heels: Soldiers and Civilians in Reconstruction North Carolina*. Lexington: University Press of Kentucky, 2009.

Brady, Lisa. *War upon the Land: Military Strategy and the Transformation of Southern Landscapes during the American Civil War*. Athens and London: University of Georgia Press, 2012.

Breakwell, Amy. "A Nation in Extremity: Sewing Machines and the American Civil War." *Textile History* 41, supp. 1 (2010): 98–107.

Breen, T. H. *The Marketplace of Revolution: How Consumer Politics Shaped American Independence*. New York: Oxford University Press, 2004.

Breward, Christopher. *The Culture of Fashion: A New History of Fashionable Dress*. Manchester, UK: Manchester University Press, 1995.

———. *The Hidden Consumer: Masculinities, Fashion and City Life, 1860–1914*. Manchester, UK: Manchester University Press, 1999.

———. "The Politics of Fashion: The Politics of Fashion Studies." *Journal of Contemporary History* 42, no. 4 (2007): 673–81.

Broomall, James. *Private Confederacies: The Emotional Worlds of Southern Men as Citizens and Soldiers*. Chapel Hill: University of North Carolina Press, 2019.

Brown, Elsa Barkley. "Negotiating and Transforming the Public Sphere: African American Political Life in the Transition from Slavery to Freedom." *Public Culture* 7, no. 1 (Fall 1994): 107–46.

Brown, Kathleen. *Foul Bodies: Cleanliness in Early America*. New Haven, CT: Yale University Press, 2009.

Brown, Thomas J. *Reconstructions: New Perspectives on the Postbellum United States*. New York: Oxford University Press, 2008.

Bruckridge, Steve O. *The Language of Dress: Resistance and Accommodation in Jamaica, 1760–1890*. Kingston, Jamaica: University of the West Indies Press, 2004.

Brundage, W. Fitzhugh. *The Southern Past: A Clash of Race and Memory*. Cambridge, MA: Harvard University Press, 2005.

Burman, Barbara, ed. *The Culture of Sewing: Gender, Consumption and Home Dressmaking*. Oxford, UK: Berg, 1999.

Bushman, Richard L. *The Refinement of America: People, Houses, Cities*. New York: Vintage Books, 1993.

Butchart, Ronald E. *Schooling the Freedpeople: Teaching, Learning and the Struggle for Black Freedom, 1861–1876*. Chapel Hill: University of North Carolina Press, 2011.

Butler, Scott, et al. *Archaeological Data Recovery at Mitchelville (38BU2301) Hilton Head Island Airport Improvements Study*. Beaufort County, SC, December 2013.

Brundage, W. Fitzhugh, ed. *Where These Memories Grow: History, Memory, and Southern Identity*. Chapel Hill: University of North Carolina Press, 2000.

Bynum, Victoria. *Unruly Women: The Politics of Social and Sexual Control in the Old South*. Chapel Hill: University of North Carolina Press, 1992.

Byrd, Dana. "Loot, Occupy, and Re-envision: Material Culture of the South Carolina Plantation." In *The Civil War and the Material Culture of Texas, the Lower South, and the Southwest*: The David B. Warren Symposum, Vol. 3. Houston: Bayou Bend, Museum of Fine Arts, Houston, 2012.

———. "Northern Vision, Southern Land." In *The Civil War in Art and Memory*, edited by Kirk Savage. New Haven, CT: Yale University Press, 2015.

Camp, Stephanie M. H. *Closer to Freedom: Enslaved Women and Everyday Resistance in the Plantation South*. Chapel Hill: University of North Carolina Press, 2004.

Campbell, Edward D. C., Jr., and Kym S. Rice, eds. *A Woman's War: Southern Women, Civil War and the Confederate Legacy*. Charlottesville: University Press of Virginia, 1996.

Campbell, Jacqueline Glass. *When Sherman Marched North from the Sea: Resistance on the Confederate Home Front*. Chapel Hill: University of North Carolina Press, 2003.

Carmichael, Peter S. "The Trophies of Victory and the Relics of Defeat: Returning Home in the Spring of 1865." In *War Matters: Material Culture in the Civil War Era*, edited by Joan E. Cashin. Chapel Hill: University of North Carolina Press, 2018.

———. *War for the Common Soldier: How Men Thought, Fought, and Survived in Civil War Armies*. Chapel Hill: University of North Carolina Press, 2018.

Cashin, Joan E. "Into the Trackless Wilderness: The Refugee Experience in the Civil War." In *A Woman's War: Southern Women, Civil War and the Confederate Legacy*, edited by Edward D. C. Campbell Jr. and Kym S. Rice. Charlottesville: University Press of Virginia, 1996.

———. "Torn Bonnets and Stolen Silks: Fashion, Gender, Race, and Danger in the Wartime South." *Civil War History* 61, no. 4 (December 2015): 338–61.

———. "Trophies of War: Material Culture in the Civil War Era." *Journal of the Civil War Era* 1, no. 3 (September 2011): 339–67.

———, ed. *War Matters: Material Culture in the Civil War Era*. Chapel Hill: University of North Carolina Press, 2018.

———. *War Stuff: The Struggle for Human and Environmental Resources in the American Civil War*. Cambridge, UK: Cambridge University Press, 2018.

———, ed. *The War Was You and Me: Civilians in the American Civil War*. Princeton, NJ: Princeton University Press, 2002.

Cavallaro, Dani, and Alexandra Warwick. *Fashioning the Frame: Boundaries, Dress and Body*. New York: Berg, 1998.

Cimbala, Paul A. *The Freedmen's Bureau: Reconstructing the American South after the Civil War*. Malabar, FL: Krieger, 2005.

Cimbala, Paul A., and Randall M. Miller, eds. *The Freedmen's Bureau and Reconstruction: Reconsiderations*. New York: Fordham University Press, 1999.

———, eds. *An Uncommon Time: The Civil War and the Northern Home Front*. New York: Fordham University Press, 2002.

———, eds. *Union Soldiers and the Northern Home Front: Wartime Experiences, Postwar Adjustments*. New York: Fordham University Press, 2002.

Clarke, Frances. *War Stories: Suffering and Sacrifice in the Civil War North*. Chicago: University of Chicago Press, 2011.

Clavin, Michael J. *Toussaint Louverture and the American Civil War: The Promise and Peril of a Second Haitian Revolution*. Philadelphia: University of Pennsylvania Press, 2009.

Clinton, Catherine, ed. *Southern Families at War: Loyalty and Conflict in the Civil War South*. Oxford, UK: Oxford University Press, 2000.

———, ed. *Tara Revisited: Women, War and the Plantation Legend*. New York: Abbeville Press, 1995.

Clinton, Catherine, and Nina Silber, eds. *Battle Scars: Gender and Sexuality in the American Civil War*. New York: Oxford University Press, 2004.

———, eds. *Divided Houses: Gender and the Civil War*. New York: Oxford University Press, 1992.

Coddington, Ronald S. *African American Faces of the Civil War: An Album*. Baltimore: Johns Hopkins University Press, 2012.

Coffin, Judith G. *The Politics of Women's Work: The Paris Garment Trades, 1750–1915*. Princeton, NJ: Princeton University Press, 1996.

Cohen, Joanna. *Luxurious Citizens: The Politics of Consumption in Nineteenth-Century America*. Philadelphia: University of Pennsylvania Press, 2017.

———. "Reckoning with the Riots: Property, Belongings, and the Challenge to Value in Civil War America." *Journal of American History* 109, no. 1 (June 2022): 68–89.

Cole, David. "Survey of U.S. Army Uniforms, Weapons, and Accoutrements." US Army, 2007.

Coleman, Peter J. *Debtors and Creditors in America: Insolvency, Imprisonment for Debt, and Bankruptcy, 1607–1900*. Washington, DC: Beard Books, 1999.

Collins, Herbert Ridgeway. *Threads of History: Americana Recorded on Cloth, 1775 to the Present*. Washington, DC: Smithsonian Institution Press, 1979.

Conn, Steven. *Museum and American Intellectual Life, 1876–1926*. Chicago: University of Chicago Press, 1998.

Connor, Holly Pyne, ed. *Off the Pedestal: New Women in the Art of Homer, Chase, and Sargent*. New Brunswick, NJ: Newark Museum and Rutgers University Press, 2006.

Cooper, Grace Rogers. *The Sewing Machine: Its Invention and Development*. Washington, DC: Smithsonian Institution Press, 1976.

Corrales-Diaz, Erin R. "Remembering the Veteran: Disability, Trauma and the American Civil War, 1861–1915." PhD diss., University of North Carolina at Chapel Hill, 2016.

Cowan, Ruth Schwartz. *More Work for Mother: The Ironies of Household Technology from the Open Hearth to the Microwave*. New York: Basic Books, 1983.

Cox, Karen L. *Dixie's Daughters: The United Daughters of the Confederacy and the Preservation of Confederate Culture*. Gainesville: University Press of Florida, 2003.

Cox, Shae Smith. *The Fabric of Civil War Society: Uniforms, Badges, and Flags, 1859–1939*. Baton Rouge: Louisiana State University Press, 2024.

Craik, Jennifer. *The Face of Fashion: Cultural Studies in Fashion*. New York: Routledge, 1994.

Creighton, Margaret. "Gettysburg Out of Bounds: Women and Soldiers in the Embattled Borough, 1863." In *Occupied Women: Gender, Military Occupation, and the American Civil War*, edited by Lee Ann Whites and Alecia P. Long. New Orleans: Louisiana State University Press, 2009.

Cronon, William. *Nature's Metropolis: Chicago and the Great West*. New York: W. W. Norton, 1991.

Crowston, Clare. *Fabricating Women: The Seamstresses of Old Regime France, 1675–1791*. Durham, NC: Duke University Press, 2001.

Cunliffe, Marcus. *Soldiers and Civilians: The Martial Spirit in America, 1775–1965*. Boston: Little, Brown, and Company, 1968.

Davis, Robert Scott, Jr. "A Soldier's Story: The Records of Hubbard Pryor, Forty-Fourth United States Colored Troops." *Prologue* 31, no. 4 (Winter 1999): 266–72.

Dean, Bashford. *Helmets and Body Armor in Modern Warfare*. New Haven, CT: Yale University Press, 1920.

Dean, Eric T. *Shook Over Hell: Post-Traumatic Stress, Vietnam, and the Civil War*. Cambridge, MA: Harvard University Press, 1997.

DeCredico, Mary A. *Mary Boykin Chesnut: A Confederate Woman's Life*. 1998. Reprint, Lanham, MD: Rowman & Littlefield, 2002.

———. *Patriotism for Profit: Georgia's Urban Entrepreneurs and the Confederate War Effort*. Chapel Hill: University of North Carolina Press, 1990.

De la Haye, Amy, and Elizabeth Wilson, eds. *Defining Dress: Dress as Object, Meaning and Identity*. New York: Manchester University Press, 1999.

Delfino, Susanna, and Michele Gillespie, eds. *Neither Lady Nor Slave: Women of the Old South*. Chapel Hill: University of North Carolina Press, 2002.

———, eds. *Technology, Innovation, and Southern Industrialization: From the Antebellum Era to the Computer Age*. Columbia: University of Missouri Press, 2008.

Deyle, Steven. *Carry Me Back: The Domestic Slave Trade in American Life*. New York: Oxford University Press, 2006.

Dobak, William. *Freedom by the Sword: The U.S. Colored Troops, 1862–1867*. Washington, DC: Government Printing Office, 2011.

Doering, Mary, ed. *Pre-colonial Times through the American Revolution*. Vol. 1. of *Clothing and Fashion: American Fashion from Head to Toe*, edited by José Blanco. Santa Barbara, CA: ABC-CLIO, 2016.

Downs, Gregory P. *After Appomattox: Military Occupation and the Ends of War*. Cambridge, MA: Harvard University Press, 2015.

Downs, Jim. *Sick from Freedom: African-American Illness and Suffering during the Civil War*. New York: Oxford University Press, 2012.

Dublin, Thomas. *Women at Work: The Transformation of Work and Community in Lowell,Massachusetts, 1826–1860*. 1979. Reprint, New York: Columbia University Press, 1993.

Dunaway, Wilma A. *The First American Frontier: Transition to Capitalism in Southern Appalachia, 1700–1860*. Chapel Hill: University of North Carolina Press, 1996.

Duncan, Richard R. *Beleaguered Winchester: A Virginia Community at War, 1861–1865*. Baton Rouge: Louisiana State University Press, 2007.

Dunkelman, Mark H. *Brothers One and All: Esprit de Corps in a Civil War Regiment*. Baton Rouge: Louisiana State University Press, 2004.

———. *War's Relentless Hand: Twelve Tales of Civil War Soldiers*. Baton Rouge: Louisiana State University Press, 2006.

Dyer, Thomas G. *Secret Yankees: The Union Circle in Confederate Atlanta*. Baltimore: Johns Hopkins University Press, 1999.

Earle, Alice Morse. *Two Centuries of Costume in America*. New York: Macmillan, 1903.

Eaton, Aurore. *The Amoskeag Manufacturing Company: A History of Enterprise on the Merrimack River*. Charleston, SC: History Press, 2015.

Edling, Max M. *A Hercules in the Cradle: War, Money, and the American State, 1783–1867*. Chicago: University of Chicago, 2014.

Edwards, Laura F. *Gendered Strife and Confusion: The Political Culture of Reconstruction*. Urbana: University Press of Illinois, 1997.

———. *Only the Clothes on Her Back: Clothing and the Hidden History of Power in the Nineteenth-Century United States*. Oxford, UK: Oxford University Press, 2022.

———. *Scarlett Doesn't Live Here Anymore: Southern Women in the Civil War Era*. Urbana: University of Illinois Press, 2000.

Eggleston, Larry C. *Women in the Civil War: Extraordinary Stories of Soldiers, Spies, Nurses, Doctors, Crusaders, and Others*. Jefferson, NC: McFarland, 2003.

Elahi, Babak. *The Fabric of American Literary Realism: Ready-Made Clothing, Social Mobility and Assimilation*. Jefferson, NC: McFarland Press, 2009.

Emerson, William K. *Encyclopedia of United States Army Insignia and Uniforms*. Norman and London: University of Oklahoma Press, 1996.

Escott, Paul D. *After Secession: Jefferson Davis and the Failure of Confederate Nationalism*. Baton Rouge: Louisiana State University Press, 1992.

Evans, Curtis J. *The Conquest of Labor: Daniel Pratt and Southern Industrialization*. Baton Rouge: Louisiana State University Press, 2001.

Fahs, Alice. *The Imagined Civil War: Popular Literature of the North and South, 1861–1865*. Chapel Hill: University of North Carolina Press, 2001.

Farmer-Kaiser, Mary. *Freedwomen and the Freedmen's Bureau: Race, Gender, and Public Policy in the Age of Emancipation*. New York: Fordham University Press, 2010.

Faulkner, Carol. "The Root of Evil: Free Produce and Radical Antislavery, 1820–1860." *Journal of the Early Republic* 27 (2007): 377–405.

Faust, Drew Gilpin. "Civil War Home Front." In *Rally on the High Ground: The National Park Service Symposium on the Civil War*. Fort Washington, PA: Eastern National, 2001.

———. *The Creation of Confederate Nationalism: Ideology and Identity in the Civil War South*. Baton Rouge: Louisiana State University Press, 1988.

———. *Mothers of Invention: Women of the Slaveholding South in the American Civil War*. Chapel Hill: University of North Carolina Press, 1996.

———. *This Republic of Suffering: Death and the American Civil War*. New York: Alfred A. Knopf, 2008.

Fellman, Michael. *Inside War: The Guerrilla Conflict in Missouri during the American Civil War*. New York: Oxford University Press, 1990.

Fillin-Yeh, Susan, ed. *Dandies: Fashion and Finesse in Art and Culture*. New York: New York University Press, 2001.

Fine, Ben. *The World of Consumption: The Material and Cultural Revisited*. London: Routledge, 2002.

Fischer, Gayle. *Pantaloons and Power: A Nineteenth-Century Dress Reform in the United States*. Kent, OH: Kent State University Press, 2001.

Fisher, Noel C. *War at Every Door: Partisan Politics and Guerrilla Violence in East Tennessee, 1860–1869*. Chapel Hill: University of North Carolina Press, 1997.

Foner, Eric. *Reconstruction: America's Unfinished Revolution, 1863–1877*. New York: Harper & Row, 1988.

Foner, Philip S. *Women and the American Labor Movement: From the First Trade Unions to the Present*. New York: Free Press, 1982.

Foote, Lorien. *Gentlemen and the Roughs: Manhood, Honor, and Violence in the Union Army*. New York and London: New York University Press, 2010.

Ford, Lacy K., ed. *A Companion to the Civil War and Reconstruction*. Malden, MA: Blackwell Publishers, 2005.

Foster, Gaines M. *Ghosts of the Confederacy: Defeat, the Lost Cause, and the Emergence of the New South, 1865–1913*. New York: Oxford University Press, 1997.

Foster, Helen Bradley. *"New Raiments of Self": African American Clothing in the Antebellum South*. Oxford, UK: Berg, 1997.

Fox-Amato, Matthew. *Exposing Slavery: Photography, Human Bondage, and the Birth of Modern Visual Politics in America*. Oxford, UK: Oxford University Press, 2019.

Fox-Genovese, Elizabeth. *Within the Plantation Household: Black and White Women of the South*. Chapel Hill: University of North Carolina Press, 1988.

Frank, Lisa Tendrich. "Bedrooms as Battlefields: The Role of Gender Politics in Sherman's March." In *Occupied Women: Gender, Military Occupation, and the American Civil War*, edited by Lee Ann Whites and Alecia P. Long. New Orleans: Louisiana State University Press, 2009.

———. *The Civilian War: Confederate Women and Union Soldiers during Sherman's March*. New Orleans: Louisiana State University Press, 2015.

———, ed. *Women in the American Civil War*. 2 vols. Santa Barbara, CA: ABC-CLIO, 2008.

Freehling, William W. *The South vs. the South: How Anti-Confederate Southerners Shaped the Course of the Civil War*. New York: Oxford University Press, 2001.

Friend, Craig Thompson, and Lori Glover. *Southern Manhood: Perspectives on Masculinity in the Old South*. Athens: University of Georgia Press, 2004.

Frost, J. William. "From Plainness to Simplicity: Changin Quaker Ideals for Material Culture." In *Reflections on a Quaker Ethic in American Design and Consumption*, edited by Emma Jones Lapansky and Anne A. Verplanck. Philadelphia: University of Pennsylvania Press, 2003.

Gallagher, Gary W., ed. *The Antietam Campaign*. Chapel Hill: University of North Carolina Press, 1999.

———. *The Confederate War*. Cambridge, MA: Harvard University Press, 1997.

———, ed. *The Fredericksburg Campaign: Decision on the Rappahannock*. Chapel Hill: University of North Carolina Press, 1995.

———. *The Union War*. Cambridge, MA: Harvard University Press, 2011.

Gallagher, Gary W., and Alan T. Nolan, eds. *The Myth of the Lost Cause and Civil War History*. Bloomington: Indiana University Press, 2000.

Gallman, J. Matthew. *Northerners at War: Reflections on the Civil War Home Front*. Kent, OH: Kent State University Press, 2010.

Gamber, Wendy. *The Female Economy: The Millinery and Dressmaking Trades, 1860–1930*. Champaign: University of Illinois Press, 1997.

Gansler, Laura Leedy. *The Mysterious Private Thompson: The Double Life of Sara Emma Edmonds, Civil War Soldier*. New York: Free Press, 2005.

Garber, Marjorie. *Vested Interests: Cross-Dressing & Cultural Anxiety*. New York: Routledge, 1992.

Garfinkel, Susan. "Quakers and High Chests: The Plainness Problem Reconsidered." In *Reflections on a Quaker Ethic in American Design and Consumption*, edited by Emma Jones Lapansky and Anne A. Verplanck. Philadelphia: University of Pennsylvania Press, 2003.

Geier, Clarence R., David G. Orr, and Matthew B. Reeves, eds. *Huts and History: The Historical Archaeology of Military Encampment during the American Civil War*. Gainesville: University Press of Florida, 2006.

Geier, Clarence R., and Stephen R. Potter, eds. *Archaeological Perspectives on the American Civil War*. Gainesville: University Press of Florida, 2003.

Giesberg, Judith. *Army at Home: Women and the Civil War on the Northern Home Front*. Chapel Hill: University of North Carolina Press, 2009.

———. *Civil War Sisterhood: The U.S. Sanitary Commission and Women's Politics in Transition*. Boston: Northeastern University Press, 2000.

Gilchrist, David T., and W. David Lewis, eds. *Economic Change in the Civil War Era*. Greenville, DE: Eleutherian-Mills-Hagley Foundation, 1965.

Glass, Brent D. *The Textile Industry in North Carolina: A History*. Raleigh: Division of Archives and History, North Carolina Department of Cultural Resources, 1992.

Glatthaar, Joseph T. *Forged in Battle: The Civil War Alliance of Black Soldiers and White Officers*. Baton Rouge: Louisiana State University Press, 2000.

———. *General Lee's Army: From Victory to Collapse*. New York: Free Press, 2009.

———. *The March to the Sea and Beyond: Sherman's Troops in the Savannah and Carolinas Campaigns*. New York: New York University Press, 1985.

Glickman, Lawrence B. *Buying Power: A History of Consumer Activism in America*. Chicago: University of Chicago Press, 2009.

———. "'Through the Medium of Their Pockets': Sabbatarianism, Free Produce, Non Intercourse and the Significance of 'Early Modern' Consumer Activism." In *The Expert Consumer: Associations and Professionals in Consumer Society*, edited by Alain Chatriot, Marie-Emmanuelle Chessel, and Matthew Hilton. London: Routledge, 2006.

Glymph, Thavolia. *Out of the House of Bondage: The Transformation of the Plantation Household*. Cambridge, UK: Cambridge University Press, 2008.

———. *The Women's Fight: The Civil War's Battles for Home, Freedom, and Nation*. Chapel Hill: University of North Carolina Press, 2019.

Goff, Richard D. *Confederate Supply*. Durham, NC: Duke University Press, 1969.

Golay, Michael. *A Ruined Land: The End of the Civil War*. New York: Wiley, 1999.

Gordon, Beverly. *Bazaars and Fair Ladies: The History of the American Fundraising Fair*. Knoxville: University of Tennessee Press, 1998.

———. "Meanings in Mid-Nineteenth Century Dress: Images from New England Women's Writings." *Clothing and Textile Research Journal* 10, no. 3 (Spring 1992): 44–53.

———. "Textiles and Clothing in the Civil War." *Clothing and Textile Research Journal* 5, no. 3 (Spring 1987): 41–47.

Gordon, Lesley J., and John C. Inscoe, eds. *Inside the Confederate Nation: Essays in Honor of Emory M. Thomas*. Baton Rouge: Louisiana State University Press, 2005.

Greenberg, Amy S. *Manifest Manhood and the Antebellum American Empire*. Cambridge and New York: Cambridge University Press, 2005.

Grier, Katherine C. *Culture and Comfort: Parlor Making and Middle-Class Identity, 1850–1930*. Washington, DC: Smithsonian Institution Press, 1988.

Griffiths, Antony. *Prints and Printmaking: An Introduction to the History and Techniques*. Berkeley and Los Angeles: University of California Press, 1996.

Grimsley, Mark. *The Hard Hand of War: Union Military Policy toward Southern Civilians, 1861–1865*. Cambridge, UK: Cambridge University Press, 1995.

Gross, Ariela J. *What Blood Won't Tell: A History of Race on Trial in America*. Cambridge, MA: Harvard University Press, 2008.

Hacker, Barton C., and Margaret Vining. "Cutting a New Pattern: Uniforms and Women's Mobilization for War, 1854–1919." *Textile History and Meaning* 41, no. 1 (May 2010): 108–43.

Halbwachs, Maurice. *On Collective Memory*. Chicago: University of Chicago Press, 1992.

Hale, Grace Elizabeth. *Making Whiteness: The Culture of Segregation in the South, 1890–1940*. New York: Pantheon Books, 1998.

Haltunnen, Karen. *Confidence Men and Painted Women: A Study of Middle-Class Culture in America, 1830–1870*. New Haven, CT: Yale University Press, 1982.

Hamilton, Daniel W. *The Limits of Sovereignty: Property Confiscation in the Union and the Confederacy during the Civil War*. Chicago: University of Chicago Press, 2007.

Hargrove, Hondon B. *Black Union Soldiers in the Civil War*. Jefferson, NC: McFarland and Company, 1998.

Harris, Neil. *Building Lives: Constructing Rights and Passages*. New Haven, CT: Yale University Press, 1999.

Harrison, Carol E., and Thomas J. Brown. *Zouave Theaters: Transnational Military Fashion and Performance*. Baton Rouge: Louisiana State University Press, 2024.

Harte, N. B., ed. *Fabrics and Fashions: Studies in the Economic and Social History of Dress*. London: Parsold Research Fund, 1991.

Harvey, Eleanor Jones. *The Civil War in American Art*. New Haven, CT: Yale University Press, 2012.

Haulman, Kate. *The Politics of Fashion in Eighteenth-Century America*. Chapel Hill: University of North Carolina Press, 2011.

Hearden, Patrick J. *Independence and Empire: The New South's Cotton Mill Campaign, 1865–1901*. DeKalb: Northern Illinois University Press, 1982.

Heineman, Kenneth J. *Civil War Dynasty: The Ewing Family of Ohio*. New York: New York University Press, 2012.

Hess, Earl. *Liberty, Virtue and Progress: Northerners and their War for the Union*. New York: New York University Press, 1988.

———. *The Rifle Musket in Civil War Combat: Reality and Myth*. Lawrence: University Press of Kansas, 2008.

Hicks, Leonie. *Religious Life in Normandy, 1050–1330: Space, Gender, and Social Pressure*. Woodbridge, UK: Boydell Press, 2007.

Hillyer, Reiko. "Relics of Reconciliation: The Confederate Museum and Civil War Memory in the New South." *Public Historian* 33, no. 4 (November 2011): 35–62.

Hitt, Michael D. *Charged with Treason: Ordeal of 400 Mill Workers during Military Operations in Roswell, Georgia, 1864–1865*. Monroe, NY: Library Research Associates, 1992.

Hodes, Martha. *White Women, Black Men: Illicit Sex in the Nineteenth-Century South*. New Haven, CT: Yale University Press, 1998.

Holcomb, Julie L. *Moral Commerce: Quakers and the Transatlantic Boycott of the Slave Labor Economy*. Ithaca, NY: Cornell University Press, 2016.

Hollander, Anne. *Seeing through Clothes*. New York: Avon Books, 1978.

———. *Sex and Suits: The Evolution of Modern Dress*. New York: Alfred A. Knopf, 1994.

Holt, Thomas C. *Children of Fire: A History of African Americans*. New York: Hill and Wang, 2010.

———. *The Problem of Freedom: Race, Labor and Politics in Jamaica and Britain, 1832–1938*. Baltimore, MD: Johns Hopkins University Press, 1992.

Holzer, Harold, and the New-York Historical Society. *The Civil War in 50 Objects*. New York: Penguin, 2013.

Holzer, Harold, and Sara Vaughn Gabbard, eds. *Lincoln and Freedom: Slavery, Emancipation, and the Thirteenth Amendment*. Carbondale: Southern Illinois University, 2007.

Holzer, Harold, Edna Greene Medford, and Frank J. Williams, eds. *The Emancipation Proclamation: Three Views*. Baton Rouge: Louisiana State University Press, 2006.

Horwitz, Tony. *Confederates in the Attic: Dispatches from the Unfinished Civil War*. New York: Pantheon Books, 1998.

Hoy, Suellen. *Chasing Dirt: The American Pursuit of Cleanliness*. Oxford, UK: Oxford University Press, 1995.

Hunter, Tera. *To 'Joy My Freedom: Southern Black Women's Lives and Labors after the Civil War*. Cambridge, MA: Harvard University Press, 1997.

Hyman, Harold M. *A More Perfect Union: The Impact of the Civil War and Reconstruction on the Constitution*. New York: Knopf, 1973.

Inscoe, John C., and Robert C. Kenzer. *Enemies of the Country: New Perspectives on Unionists in the Civil War South*. Athens: University of Georgia Press, 2004.

Irwin, Douglas A. *Clashing over Commerce: A History of US Trade Policy*. Chicago: University of Chicago Press, 2017.

Jackson, Cassandra. *Violence, Visual Culture, and the Black Male Body*. New York: Routledge, 2011.

Janney, Caroline E. *Burying the Dead but Not the Past: Ladies' Memorial Associations and the Lost Cause*. Chapel Hill: University of North Carolina Press, 2008.

———. *Ends of War: The Unfinished Fight of Lee's Army after Appomattox*. Chapel Hill: University of North Carolina Press, 2021.

———. *Remembering the Civil War: Reunion and the Limits of Reconciliation*. Chapel Hill: University of North Carolina Press, 2016.

Jenkins, Earnestine, and Darlene Clark Hine, eds. *A Question of Manhood: A Reader in U.S. Black Men's History and Masculinity*. 2 vols. Bloomington: Indiana University Press, 1999–2001.

Jimerson, Randall. *The Private Civil War: Popular Thought during the Sectional Conflict*. Baton Rouge: Louisiana State University Press, 1988.

Johnson, Walter. *Soul by Soul: Life Inside the Antebellum Slave Market*. Cambridge, MA: Harvard University Press, 1999.

Jones, Ann, and Peter Stallybrass. *Renaissance Clothing and the Materials of Memory*. Cambridge, UK: Cambridge University Press, 2000.

Jones, Gordon L. *Confederate Odyssey: The George W. Wray Jr. Civil War Collection at the Atlanta History Center*. Athens: University of Georgia Press, 2014.

Jones, Jacqueline. *Labor of Love, Labor of Sorrow: Black Women, Work, and the Family from Slavery to the Present*. 1985. Reprint, New York: Basic Books, 2010.

———. *Saving Savannah: The City and the Civil War*. New York: Alfred A. Knopf, 2008.

Jones, Jennifer. *Sexing La Mode: Gender, Fashion and Commercial Culture in Old Regime France*. Oxford, UK: Berg, 2004.

Jones, Katharine, ed. *When Sherman Came: Southern Women and the "Great March."* Indianapolis, IN: Bobbs-Merrill, Inc., 1964.

Jones, Sarah Leigh. "'A Grand and Ceaseless Thoroughfare': The Social and Cultural Experience of Shopping on Chestnut Street, Philadelphia, 1820–1860." Master's thesis, University of Delaware, 2008.

Jones-Rogers, Stephanie. *They Were Her Property: White Women as Slave Owners in the American South*. New Haven, CT: Yale University Press, 2019.

Joseph, Nathan. *Uniforms and Nonuniforms: Communication through Clothing*. New York: Greenwood Press, 1986.

Kagan, Neil, and Stephen G. Hyslop, eds. *Smithsonian Civil War: Inside the National Collection*. Washington, DC: Smithsonian Books, 2013.

Kamphoefner, Walter D., and Wolfgang Johannes Helbich, eds. *Germans in the Civil War: The Letters They Wrote Home*. Chapel Hill: University of North Carolina Press, 2006.

Kennett, Lee. *Marching through Georgia: The Story of Soldiers and Civilians during Sherman's Campaign*. New York: Harper Collins, 1995.

Kerber, Linda. *Women of the Republic: Intellect and Ideology in Revolutionary America*. Chapel Hill: University of North Carolina Press, 1980.

Kidwell, Claudia Brush, and Valerie Steele, eds. *Men & Women: Dressing the Part*. Washington, DC: Smithsonian Institution Press, 1989.

Klingberg, Frank W. *The Southern Claims Commission*. Berkeley: University of California Press, 1955.

Knötel, Herbert, Jr., and Herbert Sieg, eds. *Uniforms of the World: A Compendium of Army, Navy, and Air Force Uniforms, 1700–1937*. Translated by Ronald G. Ball. New York: Charles Scribner's Sons, 1980.

Knowles, Katie. "Fashioning Slavery: Slaves and Clothing in the U.S. South, 1830–1865." PhD diss., Rice University, 2014.

Kopytoff, Igor. "The Cultural Biography of Things: Commoditization of Process." In *The Social Life of Things: Commodities in Cultural Perspective*, edited by Arjun Appadurai. Cambridge, UK: Cambridge University Press, 1989.

Kreiser, Lawrence A., Jr. *Marketing the Blue and Gray: Newspaper Advertising and the American Civil War*. Baton Rouge: Louisiana State University Press, 2019.

Küchler, Suzanne, and Daniel Miller. *Clothing as Material Culture*. Oxford, UK: Berg, 2005.

Kuchta, David. "The Making of the Self-Made Man: Class, Clothing and English Masculinity, 1688–1832." In *The Sex of Things: Gender and Consumption in Historical Perspective*, edited by Victoria de Grazia and Ellen Furlough. Berkeley: University of California Press, 1996.

———. *The Three-Piece Suit and Modern Masculinity: England, 1550–1850*. Berkeley: University of California Press, 2002.

Lander, Ernest McPherson, Jr. *The Textile Industry in Antebellum South Carolina*. Baton Rouge: Louisiana State University Press, 1969.

Langley, Harold D. "From the Collection: Warren Opie's Sailor's Uniform at Winterthur." *Winterthur Portfolio* 38, nos. 2/3 (Summer–Autumn 2003): 131–42.

Latour, Bruno. *Reassembling the Social: An Introduction to Actor-Network-Theory*. Oxford, UK: Oxford University Press, 2005.

Lauer, Jeanette C., and Robert H. Lauer. *Fashion Power: The Meaning of Fashion in American Society*. Englewood Cliffs, NJ: Prentice-Hall, 1981.

Laver, Harry S. *Citizens More than Soldiers: Kentucky Militia and Society in the Early Republic*. Lincoln: University of Nebraska Press, 2007.

Lee, Susanna Michele. *Claiming the Union: Citizenship in the Post–Civil War South*. Cambridge, UK: Cambridge University Press, 2014.

Lennard, Katherine. "Uniform Threat: Manufacturing the Ku Klux Klan's Visible Empire, 1866–1931." PhD diss., University of Michigan, 2017.

Leonard, Elizabeth. *Yankee Women: Gender Battles in the Civil War*. New York: W. W. Norton, 1994.

Levine, Robert S. *Martin Delany, Frederick Douglass: The Politics of Representative Identity*. Chapel Hill: University of North Carolina Press, 1997.

Linderman, Gerald. *Embattled Courage: The Experience of Combat in the American Civil War*. New York: Free Press, 1987.

Litwack, Leon. *Been in the Storm So Long: The Aftermath of Slavery*. 1979. Reprint, New York: Vintage Books, 1980.

Long, J. Grahame. *Stolen Charleston: The Spoils of War*. Charleston, SC: History Press, 2014.

Long, Lisa A. *Rehabilitating Bodies: Health, History, and the American Civil War*. Philadelphia: University of Pennsylvania Press, 2004.

Lookingbill, Brad D. *War Dance at Fort Marion: Plains Indian War Prisoners*. Norman: University of Oklahoma Press, 2006.

Lord, Francis A. *Civil War Sutlers and Their Wares*. New York: T. Yoseloff, 1969.

Lurie, Alison. *The Language of Clothes*. New York: Random House, 1981.

Luskey, Brian, and Jason Phillips, eds. "Material Culture." Special issue, *Civil War History* 63 (June 2017).

Mackey, Robert R. *The Uncivil War: Irregular Warfare in the Upper South, 1861–1865*. Norman: University of Oklahoma Press, 2004.

Malone, Patrick M. *Waterpower in Lowell: Engineering and Industry in Nineteenth-Century America*. Baltimore: Johns Hopkins University Press, 2009.

Mann, Bruce H. *Republic of Debtors: Bankruptcy in the Age of American Independence*. Cambridge, MA: Harvard University Press, 2002.

Marten, James. *Sing Not War: The Lives of Union and Confederate Veterans in Gilded Age America*. Chapel Hill: University of North Carolina Press, 2011.

Marten, James, and Caroline E. Janney, eds. *Buying and Selling Civil War Memory in Gilded Age America*. Athens: University of Georgia Press, 2021.

Martin, Paul. *European Military Uniforms: A Short History*. London: Spring Books, 1967.

Martinez, Katharine, and Kenneth L. Ames. *The Material Culture of Gender, the Gender of Material Culture*. Winterthur, DE: Henry Francis DuPont Winterthur Museum, 1997.

Massey, Mary Elizabeth. *Bonnet Brigades: American Women and the Civil War*. New York: Alfred Knopf, 1966.

Mather, Mary Denis. *To Bind Up the Wounds: Catholic Sister Nurses in the U.S. Civil War*. Westport, CT: Greenwood Press, 1989.

Matlock, Jann. "Masquerading Women, Pathologized Men: Cross-Dressing, Fetishism, and the Theory of Perversion, 1882–1935." In *Fetishism as Cultural Discourse*, edited by Emily Apter and William Pietz. Ithaca, NY: Cornell University Press, 1993.

Matson, Cathy. *The Economy of Early America: Historical Perspectives and New Directions*. University Park: Pennsylvania State University Press, 2006.

Matthews, Richard E. *The 149th Pennsylvania Volunteer Infantry Unit in the Civil War*. Jefferson, NC: McFarland, 1994.

Mattingly, Carol. *Appropiate(ing) Dress: Women's Rhetorical Style in Nineteenth Century America*. Carbondale: Southern Illinois Press, 2002.

Mauro, Hayes Peter. *The Art of Americanization at the Carlisle Indian School*. Albuquerque: University of New Mexico Press, 2011.

McClellan, Elizabeth. *History of American Costume, 1607–1870*. New York: Tudor Publishing, 1937.

McCracken, Grant. *Culture and Consumption: New Approaches to the Symbolic Character of Consumer Goods and Activities*. Bloomington and Indianapolis: Indiana University Press, 1988.

McCurry, Stephanie. *Confederate Reckoning: The Political Transformation of the Civil War South*. Cambridge, MA: Harvard University Press, 2010.

———. *Women's War: Fighting and Surviving the American Civil War*. Cambridge, MA: Harvard University Press, 2019.

McDonnell, Lawrence T. *Performing Disunion: The Coming of the Civil War in Charleston, South Carolina*. Cambridge, UK: Cambridge University Press, 2018.

McInnis, Maurie D. *Slaves Waiting for Sale: Abolitionist Art and the American Slave Trade*. Chicago: University of Chicago Press, 2011.

McPherson, James M. "American Victory; American Defeat." In *Why the Confederacy Lost*, edited by Gabor S. Boritt. New York: Oxford University Press, 1992.

———. *Battle Cry of Freedom: The Civil War Era*. New York: Oxford University Press, 1988.

———. *The Negro's Civil War: How American Blacks Felt and Acted during the War for the Union*. New York: Knopf, 1991.

McPherson, James M., and William J. Cooper, eds. *Writing the Civil War: The Quest to Understand*. Columbia: University of South Carolina Press, 1998.

Meneely, A. Howard. *The War Department, 1861: A Study in Mobilization and Industrialization*. New York: Columbia University Press, 1928.

Mendelsohn, Adam D. *The Rag Race: How Jews Sewed Their Way to Success in America and the British Empire*. New York: New York University Press, 2014.

Michel, Sonya, and Robyn Muncy, eds. *Engendering America: A Documentary History, 1865 to the Present*. Boston: McGraw-Hill College, 1999.

Mitchell, Mary Niall. *Raising Freedom's Child: Black Children and Visions of the Future after Slavery*. New York: New York University Press, 2008.

Mitchell, Reid. *The Vacant Chair: The Northern Soldier Leaves Home*. New York: Oxford University Press, 1993.

Mobley, Joe A. *Weary of War: Life on the Confederate Home Front*. Westport, CT: Praeger, 2008.

Mollo, John. *Military Fashion: An Interpretive History of the Uniforms of the Great Armies from the 17th Century to the First World War*. New York: G. P. Putnam's Sons, 1972.

Monnickendam, Andrew. *Dressing Up for War: Transformations of Gender and Genre in the Discourse and Literature of War*. New York: Rodopi, 2001.

Montgomery, David. "Wage Labor, Bondage and Citizenship in Nineteenth-Century America." *International Labor and Working-Class History* 48 (1995): 6–27.

Montgomery, Florence. *Textiles in America: 1650–1870*. New York: W. W. Norton, 2007.

Neely, Mark. "Was the Civil War a Total War?" *Civil War History* 50, no. 4 (2004): 434–58.

Nelson, Megan Kate. *Ruin Nation: Destruction and the American Civil War*. Athens: University of Georgia Press, 2012.

Nelson, William E. *The Fourteenth Amendment: From Political Principle to Judicial Doctrine*. Cambridge, MA: Harvard University Press, 1988.

Newell, Clayton R. *The Regular Army before the Civil War, 1845–1860*. Washington, DC: Center of Military History, 2014.

Newell, Clayton R., and Charles R. Shrader. *Of Duty Well and Faithfully Done: A History of the Regular Army in the Civil War*. Lincoln: University of Nebraska Press, 2011.

Noe, Kenneth W. *Perryville: This Grand Havoc of Battle*. Lexington: University Press of Kentucky, 2001.

Norton, Mary Beth. *Liberty's Daughters: The Revolutionary Experience of American Women, 1750–1800*. Boston: Little and Brown, 1980.

Oakes, James. *Freedom National: The Destruction of Slavery in the United States*. New York: W. W. Norton, 2013.

Ofele, Martin. *German-Speaking Officers in the U.S. Colored Troops, 1863–1867*. Gainesville: University Press of Florida, 2004.

Ott, Victoria. *Confederate Daughters: Coming of Age during the Civil War*. Carbondale: Southern Illinois University Press, 2008.

Paludan, Philip S. *A Covenant with Death: The Constitution, Law and Equality in the Civil War Era*. Urbana: University of Illinois Press, 1975.

Parkinson, Scott. "Edgar County, Illinois in the Civil War, 1861–1865." Master's thesis, Eastern Illinois University, 1988.

Parsons, Elaine Frantz. *Ku Klux: The Birth of the Klan during Reconstruction*. Chapel Hill: University of North Carolina Press, 2015.

———. *Manhood Lost: Fallen Drunkards and Redeeming Women in the Nineteenth-Century United States*. Baltimore, MD: Johns Hopkins University Press, 2003.

Penningroth, Dylan. *The Claims of Kinfolk: African American Property and Community in the Nineteenth-Century South*. Chapel Hill: University of North Carolina Press, 2003.

Petite, Mary Deborah. *"The Women Will Howl": The Union Army Capture of Roswell and New Manchester, Georgia, and the Forced Relocation of Mill Workers*. Jefferson, NC: McFarland and Company, 2008.

Phillips, Jason. *Looming Civil War: How Nineteenth-Century Americans Imagined the Future*. Oxford, UK: Oxford University Press, 2018.

Prown, Jules David. "Mind in Matter: An Introduction to Material Culture Theory Method." *Winterthur Portfolio* 17, no. 1 (Spring 1982): 1–19.

Putzi, Jennifer. *Identifying Marks: Race, Gender, and the Marked Body in Nineteenth-Century America*. Athens: University of Georgia Press, 2006.

———. "'The Skin of an American Slave': African American Manhood and the Marked Body in Nineteenth-Century Abolitionist Literature." *Studies in American Fiction* 30, no. 2 (Autumn 2002): 181–206.

Rable, George C. *Civil Wars: Women and the Crisis of Southern Nationalism*. Urbana: University of Illinois Press, 1989.

———. *Fredericksburg! Fredericksburg!* Chapel Hill: University of North Carolina Press, 2002.

Ramold, Steven J. *Baring the Iron Hand: Discipline in the Union Army*. DeKalb: Northern Illinois University Press, 2009.

———. *Slaves, Sailors, Citizens: African Americans in the Union Navy*. DeKalb: Northern Illinois University Press, 2002.

Ransom, Roger L. *Conflict and Compromise: The Political Economy of Slavery, Emancipation and the American Civil War*. Cambridge, UK: Cambridge University Press, 1989.

Rao, Gautham. *National Duties: Custom Houses and the Making of the American State*. Chicago: University of Chicago Press, 2016.

Revels, Tracy J. *Grander in Her Daughters: Florida's Women during the Civil War*. Columbia: University of South Carolina Press, 2004.

Rhea, Gordon C. *To the North Anna River: Grant and Lee, May 13–24, 1865*. Baton Rouge: Louisiana State University Press, 2000.

Richards, Eliza. "U.S. Civil War Print Culture and Popular Imagination." *American Literary History* 17, no. 2 (Summer 2005): 349–59.

Risch, Erna. *Quartermaster Support of the Army: A History of the Corps*. Washington, DC: Office of the Quartermaster General, 1962.

Rivard, Paul E. *A New Order of Things: How the Textile Industry Transformed New England*. Hanover, NH: University Press of New England, 2002.

Roach-Higgins, Mary Ellen, Joanne B. Eicher, and Kim K. P. Johnson. *Dress and Identity*. New York: Fairchild, 1995.

Roberts, Mary Louise. "Samson and Delilah Revisited: The Politics of Women's Fashions in 1920s France." *American Historical Review* 98, no. 3 (June 1993): 657–84.

Robertson, Stacey M. *Hearts Beating for Liberty: Women Abolitionists in the Old Northwest*. Chapel Hill: University of North Carolina Press, 2010.

Rockman, Seth. *Plantation Goods: A Material History of American Slavery*. Chicago: University of Chicago Press, 2024.

Rosenheim, Jeff L. *Photography and the American Civil War*. New Haven, CT: Yale University Press, 2013.

Rotundo, E. Anthony. *American Manhood: Transformations in Masculinity from the Revolution to the Modern Era*. New York: Basic Books, 1993.

Rowe, Mary Ellen. *Bulwark of the Republic: The American Militia in the Antebellum West*. Westport, CT: Praeger, 2003.

Royster, Charles. *The Destructive War: William Tecumseh Sherman, Stonewall Jackson and the Americans*. New York: Knopf, 1991.

Russel, Robert Royal. *Economic Aspects of Southern Sectionalism, 1840–1861*. Urbana: University of Illinois Press, 1924.

Samito, Christian G. *Becoming American under Fire: Irish Americans, African Americans, and the Politics of Citizenship during the Civil War Era*. Ithaca, NY: Cornell University Press, 2009.

Samuels, Shirley. *Facing America: Iconography and the Civil War*. New York: Oxford University Press, 2004.

Sandage, Scott. *Born Losers: A History of Failure in America*. Cambridge, MA: Harvard University Press, 2005.

Sarris, Jonathan Dean. *A Separate Civil War: Communities in Conflict in the Mountain South*. Charlottesville: University of Virginia Press, 2006.

Savage, Kirk. *Standing Soldiers, Kneeling Slaves: Race, War, and Monument in Nineteenth-Century America*. Princeton, NJ: Princeton University Press, 1997.

Saville, Julie. *The Work of Reconstruction: From Slave to Wage Laborer in South Carolina, 1860–1870*. Cambridge, UK: Cambridge University Press, 1994.

Schick, I. T., ed. *The Uniforms of the World's Great Armies, 1700 to the Present*. New York: Gallery Books, 1984.

Schoen, Brian. *The Fragile Fabric of Union: Cotton, Federal Politics and the Global Origins of the Civil War*. Baltimore: Johns Hopkins University Press, 2009.

Schultz, Jane E. *Woman at the Front: Hospital Workers in Civil War America*. Chapel Hill: University of North Carolina Press, 2004.

Schwalm, Leslie A. *A Hard Fight for We: Women's Transition from Slavery to Freedom in South Carolina*. Champaign: University of Illinois Press, 1997.

Scott, Anne Firor. *The Southern Lady: From Pedestal to Politics, 1830–1930*. Charlottesville: University Press of Virginia, 1970.

Scranton, Philip. *Proprietary Capitalism: The Textile Manufacture at Philadelphia, 1800–1885*. New York: Cambridge University Press, 2003.

Seed, David, Stephen C. Kenny, and Chris Williams, eds. *Life and Limb: Perspectives on the American Civil War*. Liverpool, UK: Liverpool University Press, 2015.

Severa, Joan. *Dressed for the Photographer: Ordinary Americans and Fashion, 1840–1900*. Kent, OH: Kent State University Press, 1995.

Shannon, Fred Albert. *The Organization and Administration of the Union Army*. Cleveland, OH: Arthur C. Clark, 1928.

Shaw, Madelyn, and Lynne Z. Bassett. *Homefront & Battlefield: Quilts and Context in the Civil War*. Lowell, MA: American Textile Museum, 2012.

Sheehan-Dean, Aaron. *The Calculus of Violence: How Americans Fought the Civil War*. Cambridge, MA: Harvard University Press, 2018.

———. "The Southern Home Front and the Problem of Synthesis: A Review Essay." *Georgia Historical Quarterly* 93, no. 1 (Spring 2009): 86–97.

Silber, Nina. *Daughters of the Union: Northern Women Fight the Civil War*. Cambridge, MA: Harvard University Press, 2005.

Skinner, Carolyn. *Women Physicians and Professional Ethos in Nineteenth-Century America*. Carbondale: Southern Illinois University Press, 2014.

Smith, Barbara Clark, and Kathy Peiss. *Men and Women: A History of Costume, Gender, and Power*. Washington, DC: National Museum of American History, 1989.

Smith, John David, ed. *Black Soldiers in Blue: African American Troops in the Civil War Era*. Chapel Hill: University of North Carolina Press, 2002.

Smith, Mark Michael. *Sensing the Past: Seeing, Hearing, Smelling, Tasting, and Touching in History*. Berkeley: University of California Press, 2007.

Spar, Ira. *New Haven's Civil War Hospital: A History of Knight U.S. General Hospital, 1862–1865*. Jefferson, NC: McFarland and Company Inc., 2014.

Spruill, Marjorie Julian, Valinda W. Littlefield, and Joan Marie Johnson, eds. *South Carolina Women: Their Lives and Times*. Vol. 2. Athens: University of Georgia Press, 2010.

Stamper, Anita, and Jill Condra. *Clothing through American History: The Civil War through the Gilded Age, 1861–1899*. Santa Barbara, CA: ABC-CLIO, 2011.

Stanley, Amy Dru. *From Bondage to Contract: Wage Labor, Marriage and the Market in the Age of Slave Emancipation*. Cambridge, UK: Cambridge University Press, 1998.

Stansell, Christine. "The Origins of the Sweatshop: Women and Early Industrialization in New York City." In *Working-Class America: Essays on Labor, Community, and American Society*, edited by Michael H. Frisch and Daniel J. Walkowitz, 78–103. Urbana: University of Illinois Press, 1983.

Starke, Barbara M., Lillian O. Holloman, and Barbara K. Nordquist. *African American Dress and Adornment: A Cultural Perspective*. Dubuque, IA: Kendall Hunt, 1990.

Stauffer, John. *The Black Hearts of Men: Radical Abolitionists and the Transformation of Race*. Cambridge, MA: Harvard University Press, 2001.

Stearns, Peter N. *Battleground of Desire: The Struggle for Self Control in Modern America*. New York: New York University Press, 1999.

Steele, Valerie. *The Corset: A Cultural History*. New Haven, CT: Yale University Press, 2001.

Sternhell, Yael. *Routes of War: The World of Movement in the Confederate South*. Cambridge, MA: Harvard University Press, 2012.

Stevenson, C. Ian. "Vacationing with the Civil War: Maine's Regimental Summer Cottages." *Civil War History* 63, no. 2 (2017): 151–80.

Stewart, James Brewer. *Holy Warriors: The Abolitionists and American Slavery*. 1976. Reprint, New York: Hill and Wang, 1997.

Stoker, Donald. *The Grand Design: Strategy and the U.S. Civil War*. New York: Oxford University Press, 2010.

Strasser, Susan. *Waste and Want: A Social History of Trash*. New York: Henry Holt and Company, 1999.

Styles, John. "Dress in History: Reflections on a Contested Terrain." *Fashion Theory* 2, no. 4 (1998): 383–90.

———. *The Dress of the People: Everyday Fashion in Eighteenth-Century England*. New Haven, CT: Yale University Press, 2007.

Sutherland, Daniel E., ed. *Guerrillas, Unionists, and Violence on the Confederate Home Front*. Fayetteville: University of Arkansas Press, 1999.

Tap, Bruce. *Over Lincoln's Shoulder: The Committee on the Conduct of the War*. Lawrence: University Press of Kansas, 1998.

Taylor, Amy Murrell. *Embattled Freedom: Journeys through the Civil War's Slave Refugee Camps*. Chapel Hill: University of North Carolina Press, 2018.

Taylor, Lou. *The Study of Dress History*. Manchester, UK: Manchester University Press, 2002.

Tebutt, Melanie. *Making Ends Meet: Pawnbroking and Working-Class Credit*. London: Methuen, 1984.

Thomas, Emory M. *The Confederate Nation: 1861–1865*. New York: Harper and Row, 1979.

Tomblin, Barbara Brooks. *Bluejackets and Contrabands: African Americans and the Union Navy*. Lexington: University Press of Kentucky, 2009.

Tomlins, Christopher. "Indentured Servitude in Perspective: European Migration into North America and the Composition of the Early American Labor Force, 1600–1775."

In *The Economy of Early America: Historical Perspectives and New Directions*, edited by Cathy Matson, 146–82. University Park: Pennsylvania State University Press, 2006.

Tortora, Phyllis G., and Ingrid Johnson. *The Fairchild Books Dictionary of Textiles*. 8th ed. New York: Bloomsbury, 2013.

Troiani, Don, Earl J. Coates, and Michael J. McAfee. *Don Troiani's Civil War Zouaves, Chasseurs, Special Branches and Officers*. 2002. Reprint, Mechanicsburg, PA: Stackpole Books, 2006.

Trudeau, Noah Andrew. *Voices of the 55th: Letters from the 55th Massachusetts Volunteers, 1861–1865*. Dayton, OH: Morningside House, Inc., 1998.

Tsesis, Alexander. *The Thirteenth Amendment and American Freedom: A Legal History*. New York: New York University Press, 2004.

Ulrich, Laurel Thatcher. *The Age of Homespun: Objects and Stories in the Creation of an American Myth*. New York: Knopf, 2001.

Upton, Dell. *Another City: Urban Life and Urban Spaces in the New American Republic*. New Haven, CT: Yale University Press, 2008.

Valente, A. J. *Rag Paper Manufacture in the United States, 1801–1900: A History, with Directories of Mills and Owners*. Jefferson, NC: McFarland and Company, 2010.

Varon, Elizabeth. *Southern Lady, Yankee Spy: The True Story of Elizabeth Van Lew, A Union Agent in the Heart of the Confederacy*. New York: Oxford University Press, 2003.

Vinovskis, Maris A. "Have Social Historians Lost the Civil War? Some Preliminary Demographic Speculations." *Journal of American History* 76, no. 1 (June 1989): 34–58.

———. *Toward a Social History of the American Civil War: Exploratory Essays*. New York: Cambridge University Press, 1990.

Vorenberg, Michael. *Final Freedom: The Civil War, the Abolition of Slavery, and the Thirteenth Amendment*. Cambridge, UK: Cambridge University Press, 2001.

Wagner, David. *The Poorhouse: America's Forgotten Institution*. Oxford, UK: Oxford University Press, 2005.

Walsh, Margaret. "The Democratization of Fashion: The Emergence of the Women's Dress Pattern Industry." *Journal of American History* 66, no. 2 (September 1979): 299–313.

Warren, Charles. *Bankruptcy in United States History*. Cambridge, MA: Harvard University Press, 1935.

Weeden, William B. *War Government: Federal and State in Massachusetts, New York, Pennsylvania, and Indiana*. Boston: Houghton Mifflin, 1906.

Weicksel, Sarah Jones. "Armor, Manhood and the Politics of Mortality." In *Astride Two Worlds: Technology and the American Civil War*, edited by Barton C. Hacker. Washington, DC: Smithsonian Institution Scholarly Press, 2016.

———. "Confederate Cultures of Military Clothing Production." In *Clothing and Fashion in Southern History*, edited by Ted M. Ownby and Becca Walton. Oxford: University of Mississippi Press, 2020.

———. "The Dress of the Enemy: Clothing and Disease in the Civil War Era." *Civil War History* 63, no. 2 (June 2017): 133–50.

———. "Fitted Up for Freedom: The Material Culture of Refugee Camps." In *Objects of War: Material Culture in the Civil War Era*, edited by Joan Cashin, 151–75. Chapel Hill: University of North Carolina Press, 2018.

———. "'Make Up a Box to Send Me:' Consumer Culture and Camp Life in the American Civil War." In *The Military and the Market*, edited by Mark Wilson and Jennifer Mittelstadt. Philadelphia: University of Pennsylvania Press, 2022.

———. "'Peeled' Bodies, Pillaged Homes: Looting and Material Culture in the American Civil War Era." In *The Things They Carried: War, Mobility, and Material Culture*, edited by Leora Auslander and Tara Zahra. Ithaca, NY: Cornell University Press, 2018.

———. "Quand l'uniforme fait l'homme libre: Les soldats noirs dans la Guerre civile américaine (1861–1865)" [To look like men of war: Visual transformation narratives of African American Union soldiers]. *Clio: Femmes, Genre, Histoire* 40, no. 2 (2014): 137–52.

Weigley, Russell F. *Quartermaster General of the Union Army: A Biography of M. C. Meigs*. New York: Columbia University Press, 1959.

Weiner, Annette B., and Jane Schneider, eds. *Cloth and the Human Experience*. Washington, DC: Smithsonian Institution Press, 1989.

White, Shane, and Graham White. *Stylin': African American Expressive Culture from Its Beginnings to the Zoot Suit*. Ithaca, NY: Cornell University Press, 1999.

Whites, LeeAnn. "Forty Shirts and a Wagonload of Wheat: Women, the Domestic Supply Line, and the Civil War on the Western Border." *Journal of the Civil War Era* 1, no. 1 (March 2011): 56–78.

———. *Gender Matters: Civil War, Reconstruction and the Making of the New South*. New York: Palgrave Macmillan, 2005.

Whites, LeeAnn, and Alecia P. Long, eds. *Occupied Women: Gender, Military Occupation, and the American Civil War*. Baton Rouge: Louisiana University Press, 2009.

Whitman, James Q. *Verdict of Battle: The Law of Victory and the Making of Modern War*. Cambridge, MA: Harvard University Press, 2012.

Wiley, Bell. *Confederate Women*. Westport, CT: Greenwood Press, 1975.

———. *The Life of Billy Yank: The Common Soldier of the Union*. Indianapolis, IN: Bobbs-Merrill, 1952.

———. *The Life of Johnny Reb: The Common Solider of the Confederacy*. Indianapolis, IN: Bobbs-Merrill, 1943.

Wilkie, Laurie A. *Creating Freedom: Material Culture and African American Identity at Oakley Plantation, Louisiana, 1850–1950*. Baton Rouge: Louisiana State University Press, 2000.

Williams, David. *Rich Man's War: Class, Caste, and Confederate Defeat in the Lower Chattahoochee Valley*. Athens: University of Georgia Press, 1998.

Willis, Deborah. *Envisioning Emancipation: Americans and the End of the Civil War*. Philadelphia: Temple University Press, 2013.

Wilson, Elizabeth. *Adorned in Dreams: Fashion and Modernity*. New York: I. B. Tauris, 1985; 2003.

Wilson, Harold. *Confederate Industry: Manufacturers and Quartermasters in the Civil War*. Jackson: University Press of Mississippi, 2002.

Wilson, Keith P. *Campfires of Freedom: The Camp Life of Black Soldiers during the Civil War*. Kent, OH: Kent State University Press, 2002.

Wilson, Mark. *The Business of Civil War: Military Mobilization and the State, 1861–1865*. Baltimore: Johns Hopkins University Press, 2006.

———. "The Extensive Side of Nineteenth-Century Military Economy: The Tent Industry in the Northern United States during the Civil War." *Enterprise and Society* 2 (June 2001): 297–337.

Wilson, Mark, and Jennifer Mittelstadt, eds. *The Military and the Market*. Philadelphia: University of Pennsylvania Press, 2022.

Winders, Richard Bruce. *Mr. Polk's Army: The American Military Experience in the Mexican War*. College Station: Texas A&M University Press, 1997.

Winkler, Gail Caskey. "Influence of Godey's 'Lady's Book' on the American Woman and Her Home: Contributions to a National Culture, 1830–1877." PhD diss., University of Wisconsin–Madison, 1988.

Witt, John Fabian. *Lincoln's Code: The Laws of War in American History*. New York: Simon and Schuster, 2013.

Woodward, Ian. *Understanding Material Culture*. Los Angeles: Sage Publications, 2007.

Woloson, Wendy A. *In Hock: Pawning in America from Independence through the Great Depression*. Chicago: University of Chicago Press, 2009.

Woshner, Mike. *India-Rubber and Gutta-Percha in the Civil War Era*. Alexandria, VA: O'Donnell Publications, 1999.

Wrigley, Richard. *The Politics of Appearances: Representations of Dress in Revolutionary France*. Oxford, UK: Berg, 2002.

Zakim, Michael. *Ready-Made Democracy: A History of Men's Dress in the American Republic, 1760–1860*. Chicago: University of Chicago Press, 2003.

Zeller, Bob. *The Blue and Gray in Black and White: A History of Civil War Photography*. Westport, CT: Praeger, 2005.

Zimring, Carl A. *Cash for Your Trash: Scrap Recycling in America*. New Brunswick, NJ: Rutgers University Press, 2005.

Index

Italic page numbers refer to illustrations.